Television Networks

Also by Dave Blevins

Halls of Fame: An International Directory
(McFarland, 2004)

UFO Directory International:
1,000+ Organizations and Publications in 40+ Countries
(McFarland, 2003)

Television Networks

More Than 750 American and Canadian Broadcasters and Cable Networks

DAVE BLEVINS

McFarland & Company, Inc., Publishers
Jefferson, North Carolina, and London

Library of Congress Cataloguing-in-Publication Data

Blevins, David.
Television networks : more than 750 American and
Canadian broadcasters and cable networks / Dave Blevins.
p. cm.
Includes bibliographical references and index.

ISBN 0-7864-2096-0 (illustrated case binding : 50# alkaline paper) ∞

1. Television broadcasting — United States— Directories.
2. Television broadcasting — Canada — Directories. I. Title.
HE8700.8.B547 2006 384.55029'73 — dc22 2005027080

British Library cataloguing data are available

Manufactured in the United States of America

McFarland & Company, Inc., Publishers
Box 611, Jefferson, North Carolina 28640
www.mcfarlandpub.com

Contents

Preface

Nothing has influenced and affected our lives more than television. Not radio. Not the movies. Not the automobile. Not space travel. Not computers. Nothing. Over the past 60 or so years, television has been a baby-sitter; informed us of world events; entertained us; and has been background noise to our everyday lives. It has let us feel the immediacy of breaking events anywhere in the world; allowed us to savor our favorite sports and sports heroes as the games unfolded; gave us a much-too-close look at politics and the politicians who govern our lives; made us laugh and cry; introduced us to the world of infomercials, showed us wars and armed conflicts from around the world; and made us question monumental social upheavals as they happened.

What television does not allow us to do is ignore it—can't be done. Want instant news? Turn on the TV. Want updated sports scores? Turn on the TV. Want to watch your favorite show or movie or latest music video? Turn on the TV. Want mindless drivel? Turn on the TV. Whatever you want, television can give it to you. Or so we have been conditioned to believe. Television permeates our surroundings so completely that its influence is barely noticed by those who it affects. This all-pervasive medium is now an integral part of our everyday lives, which is amazing when you realize that the impetus for the beginning of the television industry was no more noble than to convince consumers to buy more television sets!

This book, however, is not a discussion on the good and/or evils of television, nor of its negative/positive affect on our lives. That discussion is for another time and for another book. The focus of this work is to detail the hundreds of networks and channels available to viewers in the United States and Canada; the "content providers" who give us the reasons we need to turn the television on and who provide the endless hours of programming that television viewers demand. And in these days of cheaper, ever-changing technology, the number of networks and channels is expanding like never before in the history of our favorite medium.

In the early days of television, the distinctions between a network and a channel (as these terms were used by the general public) were very clear and mainly based on technology, economic scale, and broadcast reach. Early networks (such as NBC, CBS, ABC, and the short-lived DuMont) were national operations that created or purchased programs, converted the content for transmission, and broadcasted signals to their affiliated stations. The stations, called channels, were initially located primarily on the East Coast of the United States and would rebroadcast the network signals to their local viewing audience while filling the rest of their broadcast day with locally produced programming, usually live. Basically, and without delving into complex technological definitions, a network was national in scope while a channel was local. This format still exists today in the United States with the six national networks (NBC, CBS, ABC, Fox, UPN, and The WB) broadcasting programming fare to their affiliate stations throughout the country.

This basic broadcast structure dominated the television industry for nearly 40 years. However, the landscape changed dramatically in the mid–1980s with advances in cable and satellite technology used to transmit television signals. Advances in technology brought about lower costs, which meant that a broadcaster did not have to establish a national operation with affiliate stations in order to be competitive and profitable. This change allowed for the development of niche, or specialty, channels, which could be targeted to specific viewers. Home Box Office had started this trend as far back as 1976 when it became the first television network to broadcast its signal via satellite when it showed the "Thrilla From Manila" boxing match between Muhammad Ali and Joe Frazier. This new broadcasting model completely revolutionized the television industry to the point where, in today's market, the national networks now garner less than 50 percent of the viewing audience while cable, satellite, and niche channels attract the majority of viewers.

In addition to providing a much larger and richer programming choice, this industry change has also blurred the line between a network and a channel. Using the old model to label today's broadcasting entities no longer works. A network does not need affiliate stations to reach a national market while a channel can be transmitted on cable and/or satellite where its signal can be seen throughout the country. Today's broadcasters use the terms network and channel interchangeably (Arts & Entertainment Network, Biography Channel, Cable News Network, Cartoon Network, Courtroom Television Network, Discovery Channel, Disney Channel, Food Network, History Channel, Home Shopping Network, Independent Film Channel), while other entities don't use the terms at all (American Movie Classics, Animal Planet, Black Entertainment Television, Comedy Central, Home Box Office, Music Television). To simplify matters, this book does not attempt to define each listing as a channel or a network and simply uses the name the broadcaster has adopted.

We are not approaching the "500-channel" world, we have already surpassed it, as evidenced by the more than 750 networks and channels listed in this book, 500 or so in the United States alone. The proliferation of niche channels, while a fairly recent occurrence, is quickly becoming the standard as more and more channels begin operations each year. In today's vast world of television programming, viewers can watch one of the six national networks or tune into a plethora of programming genres with something for everyone, such as: news (Cable News Network, Cable-Satellite Public Affairs Network (C-SPAN), Fox News, MSNBC); sports (College Sports Television, Entertainment Sports Programming Network (ESPN), Fox Sports, Madison Square Garden Network); movies (American Movie Classics, B Movie Channel, Cinemax, Home Box Office (HBO), Independent Film Channel); music (Country Music Television, Gospel Music Television Network, Music Television (MTV), Video Hits One

(VH1); religion (Adventist Television Network, Catholic Cammunity Television Network, Christian Broadcasting Network, Church Channel, Cornerstone TeleVision, FamilyNet Television); shopping (America's Store, Home Shopping Network, ShopNBC, QVC); family and kids (ABC Family, Cartoon Network, Disney Channel, Kids and Teens Television, Nickelodeon); ethnic (Arabic Channel, Black Entertainment Television (BET), Black Family Channel, Filipino Channel, RAI International, Univision); or adult entertainment (Adam & Eve Channel, Hustler TV, Playboy TV Networks, Spice).

Five hundred channels ... and nothing's on? I don't think so!

The listings in this book are fairly straightforward. Each entry includes name, address, telephone and fax numbers, launch date, broadcast day, e-mail, Web site, and broadcast structure and history. For the most updated information about each listing, or for a current broadcasting schedule, it is suggested that you contact each entry directly. Broadcast entities listed in this book are limited to state-wide, regional, and national broadcasters and the book does not include local area channels or local public affairs cable outlets.

The information detailed in this book was primarily gathered from direct contact with the broadcaster or through the use of materials provided from their respective Web sites. Additional information was provided through several television-related books and Web sites. Please see the Bibliography for a complete listing of reference sources.

Introduction

While the development of the television industry was a natural evolution from radio in both the United States and Canada, the two countries took markedly different approaches to how the industry was allowed to develop. In the United States, as a general rule, the industry grew with relatively little government interference, especially when compared to other industries, such as automobiles, manufacturing, and banking. While the government, mainly through the Federal Communications Commission (FCC), did provide an oversight role and blocked early NBC monopolistic practices (with its NBC Blue and NBC Red networks), it basically adopted a hands-off attitude and let the industry develop through its own means. However, once technology became widely available and numerous broadcasting applications were being processed, the FCC was forced to assume a more active role and initiated steps to better regulate the industry and to provide some sense of order to a hodgepodge of networks and channels popping up around the country.

In the United States, as the four basic networks (NBC, CBS, ABC, and the short-lived DuMont) established their dominance, the government began to regulate the industry more to keep the status quo than to allow for growth. This regulatory stance ensured that the first four networks, later dwindled to the "big 3," would dominate broadcasting for almost 40 years, with little fear of competition. Some critics charged that the FCC acted more as a protector of the networks rather than as a regulator. There was some truth to this charge as evidenced by the fact that the FCC basically ruled on every television-related issue as the "big 3" networks wanted. The FCC's continued actions help explain why it took so long for the "big 3's" monopoly to be challenged. For years, the major networks fought long and hard to keep cable, and later, satellite technology at bay and unavailable to viewers.

However, this protective stance taken by the FCC began to change with the introduction of new technologies (primarily cable and satellite) until the government had no choice but to allow the virtual stranglehold the major networks had on viewers to be challenged by other broadcast entities. Slowly, cable providers began to make inroads in the marketplace and in 1975, when Home Box Office became a national service by using a communications satellite to distribute its signal, the floodgates opened and the broadcast landscape we know today was born.

The Canadian television industry, while also influenced by early pioneers and affected by technology, has always been more tightly controlled by the government, mainly through the Canadian Radio-Television and Telecommunications Commission (CRTC). This government oversight has been guided by two principles: (1) the desire to develop Canadian-owned networks, channels, and programming and (2) the need to hinder the penetration of American broadcast signals into the television lives of Canadian viewers.

The CRTC regulates these concerns by (1) limiting the amount of foreign ownership of any network or channel (currently at about 20 percent), (2) imposing a quota on the amount of Canadian programming that must be aired in prime time (currently at about 60 percent), and (3) dictating the amount of Canadian content that must be shown on networks or channels that are imported from the United States. This dual role of encouraging Canadian television development and controlling the influence of American programming has caused the Canadian television industry to grow at a slower pace than in the United States and to impose some unusual rules, such as dictating that no American signal can be seen by Canadian viewers if an equivalent Canadian service exists. For example, initially CNN was allowed on Canadian cable services, but not MTV, which competed directly with established Canadian channels. As technologies advanced and viewer demands were taken into account, these rules have been eased and viewers in Canada can now see many American-produced channels, even though they are required to carry a heavy dose of Canadian content.

The history of Canadian television began in 1952 with the launching of bilingual French-English broadcasts by the Canadian Broadcasting Corporation (CBC). The CBC had been given the responsibility of establishing a public service television system modeled on the British Broadcasting Corporation (BBC) format. This initial step was the beginning of television in Canada and the CBC is still a major player in the television industry, although it has recently begun losing viewers to the ever-growing list of specialty channels.

All specialty channels, as they are called in Canada, are strictly controlled and their renewable licenses must be approved by the CRTC. Applicants have to meet defined criteria, such as broadcast hours, Canadian-related content rules, and the quota use of English, French, and other languages in their programming. However, much like in America, these rules have not stopped the list of specialty channels from growing at a rapid rate. Just as in the United States, this rapid growth is caused by three factors: the easing of government regulations, the advent of new technologies, and viewer demands.

The biggest trend in both American and Canadian television is the explosion of cable (or specialty) channels, which are usually aimed at specific markets and provide niche programming. The lower cost of technology and the segmenting of viewers allows these niche channels to be financially viable. Although Home Box Office was an early competitor to the "big 3" and offered viewers then-unprecedented access to commercial-free movies, the best examples of early niche channels are Music Television (MTV) and Court TV. MTV basically created the concept of music videos and established a market where none existed before. Beginning with its first-ever video, *Video Killed The Radio Star* by The Buggles, MTV has set the pace for the industry and is now considered a leader in music television. The influence of MTV can be easily measured by the number of stars it helped create and by the number of copy-cat channels that have begun broadcasting. Court TV also had no predecessor and successfully introduced a program genre that had never been seen on television before. The channel had many doubters when it first aired in 1991 with the majority opinion being that no one wanted to watch live trials on television. Well, the critics were wrong and Court TV proved to be highly successful and very popular. The early trials of William Kennedy Smith for rape and football star O.J. Simpson for murder firmly established Court TV's presence.

It can be safely said that the success of MTV and Court TV proved the viability of non-network programming and led the way for the hundreds of channels that have followed, most of which are listed in this book. In a remarkably short time, 25 years or so, American and Canadian viewers have witnessed a rapid increase in the number of niche channels available, covering a wide range of interests, sometimes vying for the same viewers. Some of the more well-known specialty channels include A&E Network, American Movie Classics, Black Entertainment Channel, Cartoon Network, Christian Broadcasting Network, CNN, Court TV, C-SPAN, Disney Channel, ESPN, Fox News, Hallmark Channel, HBO, Home and Garden Television, Home Shopping Network, MSNBC, MTV, Nickelodeon, Playboy TV, QVC, Showtime, USA Network, and VH1.

In addition to the six major broadcast networks (ABC, CBS, NBC, Fox, UPN, and the WB), this book lists more than 750 niche and specialty channels in the United States and Canada. While most of the listings are well-known, some are regional or targeted to specific viewers. All are worth checking out. Each listing in this book includes contact information and a brief history of the channel.

Brief History of Television in the United States

NETWORKS

Although the definition has somewhat changed over the years due to the advances in delivery technologies, networks are generally defined as organizations that produce or acquire the rights to programs, distribute these programs using one or more delivery formats, and secure uniform broadcast times on affiliate channels. It was realized early in the development of radio and television programs that being a network was where maximum profits could be realized, since most production costs are fixed and revenues depend on exposure to as large an audience as possible. With the advent of cable and satellite technology, this standard definition of a network is somewhat outdated.

In the United States, the number of active networks and the number of entities trying to enter the broadcasting market have always depended on two factors: the cost of technology and the role of government regulation. High technology costs limit the financial availability of prospective networks to enter the market. Government regulation, either in enforcing anti-trust laws or preventing monopolistic activities, have also played a major role in the number of active networks, their size, and extraneous non-network activities.

Television broadcasting, which developed as a natural expansion from radio, had a tentative start in the late 1930s and early 1940s, but was basically suspended during World War II. In 1946, about a year after the war ended, stations became active on the East Coast and the television industry began in earnest. The history of television development began with radio in the 1920s, with radio stations and networks developing information and entertainment programs, mainly originating from live performances at local stations. Many of these stations were in the New York City area and their programs were transmitted in real time to local affiliates over telephone lines. These feeds were all live, including commercials. Strong local stations prospered in this early system, but the biggest profits, and visibility, were already being recognized by two major networks: the Columbia Broadcasting System (CBS) and the National Broadcasting Company (NBC), which was a division of the Radio Corporation of America (RCA), a major manufacturer of radio equipment. By this time RCA was operating two networks, NBC Red and NBC Blue.

From the industry's early beginnings, government regulations focused not on networks but on affiliate stations. The first major law dealing with radio broadcasting, the Radio Act of 1927, did not give the government power to regulate networks, but focused its enforcement authority on affiliate stations, called "chain broadcasting." Focusing on individual stations allowed the government to exercise control over those networks that already existed. Among other provisions, this law mandated that individual stations were to be allotted in a manner that fairly served the various states and localities. The law also withheld actual station ownership of broadcast channels in favor of renewable licenses for limited periods of time. Another section of the law dictated that an individual or entity previously convicted of unfair competition or monopolistic activities could not obtain a broadcast license. These primary provisions were continued through subsequent legislation and shaped the ongoing relationships between stations, networks, and the government.

Just prior to America entering World War II, the FCC, which had the power to investigate and regulate local stations, concluded its probe of "chain broadcasting" and decreed numerous prohibited practices, one of the primary being that a single entity could not own two networks. This dictate was aimed directly at RCA and its ownership of NBC Blue and NBC Red. In 1943 when the Supreme Court upheld the FCC's findings, RCA sold NBC Blue to Edward Noble, owner of Lifesaver, and the network's name was changed to the American Broadcasting Company.

The development of the television industry began in earnest after the end of the war and by the end of 1946, seven stations were broadcasting and approximately 5,000 household receivers were in use. Although there was no proven audience or any established technical standards, the FCC received so many applications for new stations that on September 30, 1948 it imposed a freeze on new applications. However, many applicants who had filed before the freeze continued to build broadcast facilities and when the freeze was lifted on April 13, 1952, more than 100 VHF stations had been activated in 63 markets, and the number of receivers in use had grown to almost 15 million. During the freeze, NBC had activated stations in top markets and CBS, which had started slowly, acquired its first stations by direct purchase. ABC and DuMont, a short-lived fourth network, participated actively in the FCC proceedings but did not initiate major station investment.

When the applications freeze was lifted in 1952, the FCC allotted television channels to specific communities throughout the United States, roughly in proportion to market size. Even though both VHF (channels 2 through 13) and UHF (channels 14 to 83) were authorized for use, virtually all sets of the day were capable of receiving only VHF signals. Industry leaders NBC and CBS each emerged with five owned-and-operated stations, and program offerings spun off from their popular radio shows were used to expand their affiliate base.

The rise in network dominance can be clearly seen by viewing the results of the first three Emmy Awards programs. The first Emmy Awards show (broadcast on January 25, 1949) was dominated by a local station, KTLA (in Los Angeles), which won for most popular program, *Pantomime Quiz Time*, most outstanding personality, Shirley Dinsdale and her puppet, Judy Splinters, and the station award. However, the impact of the networks was already showing after only two broadcast years. In the second Emmy Awards show, even though KTLA was still on top, NBC (with its New York affiliate KNBH) won best kinescope show, *Texaco Star Theatre*, and personality, Milton Berle. Additionally, a network spot for Lucky Strike cigarettes won best commercial. In the show's third year presentation, for the 1950 season, Alan Young and Gertrude Berg were best actor and actress, for CBS (in combination with Los Angeles independent station KTTV), and their co-produced *Alan Young Show* was recognized for best variety program. The outstanding personality was NBC/KNBH's Groucho Marx. The rise of the networks had begun and by the end of the FCC's freeze, CBS and NBC had established themselves as undisputed industry leaders. Throughout this early period of network development, ABC was barely operating, but began to grow when it merged with United Paramount Theaters.

As the networks consolidated their control over affiliates and station time during the 1950s, a significant shift occurred in their relationship with sponsors; a shift that would enhance the networks' power even more. Initially, most programs were live and produced by the sponsors or contracted for by the sponsors and delivered to the networks on expensive film or kinescope and virtually all production activities centered in New York City. With the introduction in 1956 of quadruplex videotape recording by Ampex, it became possible for programs to be produced and recorded anywhere. Immediately, new entertainment orders were removed from the sponsors' domain and shifted to the expertise of Hollywood studios. This shift in the production concept allowed the networks to create their own programs and to sell advertising time to numerous sponsors instead of relying on only one. Once the networks understood the financial rewards to be gained, the single-sponsor program basically disappeared. Another important programming innovation occurred in the mid–1950s with the networks' creation of prime-time and block programming, which included the situation comedy, cop shows, westerns, and regularly-scheduled newscasts.

The assassination of President John Kennedy in 1963 also solidified another growing television concept, the idea of the nightly news program. Although the networks had news programs on their schedules, their broadcasts were haphazard and their formats were constantly changing. From 1963 until the late 1970s, the three networks' newscasts were basically the same, presenting viewers with synopsis of the day's most important events. The news shows, and their formats, began to change only when competition arrived with the introduction of cable television and 24-hour news channels, such as CNN, Fox News, and MSNBC.

The dominance of the "big three" networks was ended by the very thing they had helped create: technology. The network viewing decline began with the introduction of cable television and then the advent of satellite broadcasts. Although the growth of cable had been effectively stymied for almost 10 years by the three networks' pressure on the FCC, eventually technology prevailed. The use of domestic communications satellites had been authorized in 1972 and by 1975 RCA and Western Union had launched working space satellites. The beginning of the end of network dominance came in 1975 when RCA sold time on its Satcom I satellite to Home Box Office (HBO), the first program service designed to bypass conventional delivery channels.

With the introduction of new technologies and a change in government attitude, the floodgates to broadcasting opened. The FCC began evaluating its heavy-handed treatment of cable and its bowing to network pressure to stymie cable growth. Ted Turner, operator of WGTB (later changed to WTBS) took advantage of this changing attitude and approached the FCC with a plan to offer his Channel 17 to a common carrier he had created, Southern Satellite Systems. The carrier would, in turn, deliver the station's signal by satellite to cable systems across the United States for five cents per household per month. This bold step created the first "super station" in 1980 and signaled the end of the "big three" network dominance. By 1981 the FCC began the process of cable deregulation and halted its efforts to stymie cable growth. The cable industry was born and the landscape of American television was forever changed. Not only has the dominance of the "big three" networks ended, three more broadcast networks have joined the fray (Fox, UPN, and The WB), and the big three, themselves, have been purchased: NBC by General Electric, CBS by Westinghouse (and now Viacom), and ABC by Walt Disney. To add insult to injury, the six major networks now account for less than 50 percent of the viewing audience, while cable, satellite, and specialty (niche) channels now play the dominant role in attracting viewers.

Educational Television

Broadcast television in the United States evolved as a commercial entity, with no government involvement except in a regulatory capacity. Within this established commercial system, efforts to use television for educational purposes have always been overwhelmed by the networks' needs for profits and their focus on entertainment programming. Television, after all, was designed to be a for-profit enterprise and, it can be argued, the industry's sole purpose was to make viewers active consumers ("to sell more soap" as old-timers say). Non-profit, or not-for-profit, educational television, left to its own devices, could not compete in this commercially-driven environment.

In the United States, educational television (ETV) mainly refers to programs that emphasize formal, classroom instruction, and enrichment programming. In 1967, educational television was officially renamed "public television" and, as specified by the Public Broadcasting Act, was meant to reflect new mandates of quality and diversity. Similar to broadcast television, public television initiatives constantly change due to technological progress and the introduction of new cable channels, many education related. The proliferation of cable and satellite networks has altered the traditional definition of educational television in the United States.

In 1953, the FCC allotted 242 channels for educational use and KUHT in Houston, Texas became the first non-commercial television licensee. Although a positive beginning, the development of educational television was a slow process, mainly because educators did not have the financial or technical capabilities to operate a television station. What was a problem for educators was an opportunity for commercial broadcasters.

Commercial broadcasters lobbied against the reservation of channels for educational use with the self-serving argument that they were opposed to the "waste" of unused spectrum space by licensees who were financially unable to air programming. This argument persuaded the FCC to allow the sale of numerous ETV frequencies to commercial broadcasters. Many universities, unable to provide programming content, garnered profits by selling their unused frequencies to commercial broadcasters.

From its beginnings, public television has constantly battled financial problems and has always had to rely on outside funding, primarily from the government. However, federal funding caused concerns due to the potential for programming bias or government pressure; but it became clear rather quickly that private financing could not completely fund educational broadcasting needs. The 1962 Educational Television Facilities Act addressed this funding problem by providing $32 million federal dollars for the creation of ETV stations only. Creating the Carnegie Commission in 1965 became an essential element in ensuring the survival of ETV. The findings and recommendations of this Commission prompted Congress to pass the 1967 Public Broadcasting Act, which created the Corporation for Public Television.

The evolution of ETV (which initially was a narrowly-defined broadcasting goal) into "public television" gave the issue a new public relations image, one that promised to educate the nation through formal instruction and enrichment programming emphasizing culture, geography, arts, science, foreign language, and public affairs. Additionally, public television was directed to provide programming for "underserved" audiences (those ignored by commercial broadcasters), such as minorities and children. While the ETV goals were laudable, it quickly became obvious that its broadcasting vision would never succeed within the frame-work of a commercial broadcasting system. The establishment of the Public Broadcasting System ensured the survival of public television and its success has allowed the non-profit genre to grow while providing unique programming to its dedicated viewers.

Cable Television

In its relatively short history, cable television has redefined the broadcasting landscape and has promoted narrow-niche programming. The service has significantly altered viewing habits and changed the way news, sports, and music programming are aired as well as introducing industry-altering channels, such as Cable News Network (CNN), Cable-Satellite Public Affairs Network (C-SPAN), Entertainment and Sports Programming Network (ESPN), Court TV, and Music Television (MTV).

With changing technology and constantly decreasing costs, cable television has spawned an ever-increasing variety of general-interest and niche (or specialty) programming services, that number over 750 as of this writing. Regardless of the quality of network television programming (which is always a topic of debate), the growth of cable television is the major factor for the loss of audience share from the broadcast networks, which has fallen from 100 percent in the early days of television to under 50 percent in today's market. Programming has expanded into numerous narrow-niches genres, including infomercials, 24-hour news and weather services, music videos, home shopping, arts, science and technology, travel, home decorating, movies, sports, comedy, cartoons, and more.

Although cable television is now seemingly everywhere, the service actually began in rural areas of North America where traditional broadcast signals could not be received by remote households. Initially called "community antenna television" (CATV), the service began when antenna towers or microwave repeater stations were erected to intercept over-the-air broadcast signals and redeliver them to households that could not receive them using VHF or UHF antennas.

Controversy arose when cable systems began importing signals from more distant stations using microwave links. Broadcasters complained that their programs were being delivered to an audience that had not paid for the service. The FCC, initially reluctant to act on these complaints because the services' technology did not use the airwaves, began regulating CATV in 1962 due to cable's impact on broadcasters. While the FCC had seemingly acted properly and within its designated mandate to regulate and promote broadcasting, its rulings later were overturned by the courts.

In 1965 and again in 1966 the FCC issued policy statements that required cable services to carry local broadcast signals under the so-called "must carry" rules. The FCC also dictated that cable companies must limit imported programming that duplicated anything on local broadcasts. Subsequent rulings further inhibited the growth of cable television by keeping the services out of urban areas; preventing the services from entering the top 100 television markets; mandating the creation of local public access channels; prohibiting cable operators from showing movies less than 10 years old; and not allowing cable services to show sporting events that had been on broadcast television within the previous five years.

Attempts to convince the FCC to ease its rules failed and cable operators lost all their legal challenges. These conditions limited the programming options of cable operators and severely hindered the pay-per-view channels' ability to show movies and sports. These strict rules were challenged in the late 1960s and early 1970s as the FCC began to feel pressure from the viewing audience, educators, community groups, and a growing number of cable operators.

Under pressure and after internal review, the FCC began revising its policies and the 1972 Cable Television Report and Order issued revised rules that softened some of the restrictions on cable television's expansion to new markets, but maintained numerous restrictions that still limited cable's growth, especially its ability to offer movies and sports programming. However, the television landscape shifted significantly in 1975 when HBO became a national service by using a communications satellite to distribute its signal. More significantly, a series of judicial decisions overturned some FCC rules and reinforced the cable industry's right to program as it pleased, to enter the top television markets, and to offer new services (including movies and sporting events).

With regulatory barriers to market entry eliminated, cable television exploded from the late 1970s to the mid–1980s and by 1985 more than 6,600 cable systems were serving nearly 40 million subscribers. Numerous, now-well-known channels came into existence, including superstation WTBS (later renamed TBS), the Christian Broadcast Network's CBN Cable (later called the Family Channel), Showtime, Nickelodeon, The Movie Channel, ESPN, and CNN, to name a few.

The Cable Communications Policy Act of 1984 addressed two issues that still hindered cable television's growth and profitability: rate regulation and franchise renewals. The Act's primary provisions created a standard procedure for renewing franchises and deregulated rates so that operators could charge what they wanted for different service tiers. The cable industry enjoyed another victory a year later when "must-carry" rules were overturned.

Brief History of Television in Canada

The history of Canadian television begins in 1952 with the launching of bilingual French-English broadcasts by the Canadian Broadcasting Corporation (CBC) in Montreal. The CBC had been given the responsibility of establishing a public service television system after a study conducted in 1951. The CBC, established in 1936 and using the British Broadcasting Corporation as its model, began developing the Canadian radio industry in the 1930s and 1940s. Radio developed under mixed ownership, with public and private stations co-existing in a single system, and competing for the same advertising revenues. This operating model would be emulated in the development of the Canadian television industry. While the CBC enjoyed a virtual monopoly for most of television's early years in Canada, private commercial television began to appear in 1960 and by 1961 CTV, a national network linking private television stations, was on the air and competing directly with the CBC.

The 1950s were critical in setting the tone for Canadian television. News and current affairs programming proved to be very popular with viewers and French-language broadcasts were having great success airing dramatic serials known as téléromans. *Hockey Night in Canada*, programmed in both official languages (French and English), became a national broadcast ritual which continues to this day.

The basic set of laws governing Canadian broadcasting were revised in 1958 following the election of a conservative government that proved to be more friendly to the interests of the private broadcasting industry. The Board of Broadcast Governors (BBG) was created, which was mandated station-licensing authority, previously controlled by the CBC. In 1959, the CBC faced two major political problems: (1) attempts by the government to interfere with English-language programming led to massive resignations among current affairs staff and (2) a coordinated strike by French-language Radio-Canada producers paralyzed the French television service for over two months. The Radio-Canada producers strike would later become an important symbolic reference point for the emerging Quebec nationalist movement.

During the 1960s, news and information programming continued to be a source of friction both within the CBC and with its relationship to the government. The highly-rated, but controversial, weekly program *This Hour Has Seven Days* provoked an internal management crisis that eventually toppled CBC's senior management and re-defined the style of Canadian television journalism. Simultaneously, French-language news programs angered the government by paying serious attention to Quebec separatist politicians and issues. In response to this perceived two-pronged broadcast attack, the government wrote laws requiring the CBC to contribute to national unity. These laws proved to be symbolic only, were completely ignored, and never enforced.

While the CBC continued to enjoy a virtual monopoly in Canadian programming, private television broadcasters were slowly gaining market share, mainly by airing popular American programs and by competing with the CBC for the broadcasting rights to Canadian sporting events, such as the Canadian Football League's Grey Cup. Private television market penetration continued to increase over the years and by the late 1980s the CBC's share of the Canadian television audience was down to 20 percent in English and 30 percent in French.

Since the industry's inception, regulators were concerned about the broadcast mix of Canadian and American programs. Beginning in 1960, rules were established that required Canadian television broadcasters to air at least 55 percent of their schedule with Canadian programming content. In 1970, the required percentage was increased to 60 percent for prime-time schedules. This content requirement has been a constant controversial issue in the Canadian television industry. Two primary points of contention dominate the issue: (1) the legitimacy of government intervention in audience choice and (2) the effectiveness of creating content quotas to force viewers to watch Canadian programs. Even though Canadian broadcasters are unhappy with government-dictated content rules, most within the industry have always conceded that without some content requirement, commercial broadcasters would have no incentive to produce expensive Canadian programs when they could acquire American shows at relatively little cost.

The 1968 Broadcasting Act replaced the BBG with the Canadian Radio-Television Commission (CRTC), which was renamed the Canadian Radio-Television and Telecommunications Commission in 1976. During the 1970s, the CRTC worked on developing a regulatory framework for the rapidly-expanding cable industry, which had emerged in the 1950s as community antenna television serving remote areas, similar to its developments in the United States at the same time. By re-transmitting signals picked up from U.S. border-town transmitters (for which they paid no license fees until 1989), the Canadian cable industry built a popular product for Canadian viewers, and enjoyed the best of both worlds, Canadian and American programs.

The growth of the cable industry, and its increasing reliance on American programming, forced the CRTC to pass regulations ensuring that cable broadcasters provided Canadian television to Canadians. Must-carry provisions ensured that every available Canadian over-the-air signal in any area was offered as a basic service, along with a local community channel. In exchange for abiding by these rules, cable companies were allowed to distribute the three primary American commercial networks (ABC, CBS, and NBC) as well as PBS. For many years, these rules dictated the basic cable package available to Canadian cable subscribers, and cable penetration grew to 76 percent of Canadian homes by 1992.

At the same time, the CRTC also established broadcasting ownership rules, such as limiting foreign ownership of Canadian broadcasting to 20 percent. This policy is directly responsible for the fact that current Canadian television is basically 100 percent Canadian-owned. While limiting foreign ownership, the rules did nothing to stop media conglomerates from forming. Much like the American broadcasting landscape, today's Canadian television industry faces the reality that a small number of media giants own most of the broadcasting outlets. Since the mid–1980s, the industry trend has been the taking over of private television broadcasters by cable companies, thus creating multimedia conglomerates that operate as virtual monopolies.

An important shift in Canadian television occurred in the 1970s when the CRTC began licensing secondary private stations in large metropolitan markets. Regional networks (such as Global (in southern Ontario) and Quatre Saisons (in Quebec)) grew out of this policy, which also saw the establishment of independent stations. The resulting audience fragmentation further contributed to the erosion of CBC's market share.

Although the CBC accepts advertising revenues, its basic funding is provided by an annual grant from Parliament, which by the late–1980s had grown to more than $1 billion Canadian dollars a year. Advertising revenues amount to about 20 percent of CBC's budget, enough to be an important consideration in programming decisions, but not enough to ease the public-support burden. Much like the Public Broadcasting System in America, the CBC's dilemma has always been two-fold: (1) how to maintain a distinctive television profile while competing commercially and (2) how to meet its broadcasting mandate in the face of government cutbacks.

Cable and Pay Television

Even private television began to feel the financial squeeze. After two lucrative decades in the 1960s and 1970s, the industry began experiencing financial problems caused by a weak market starting in the 1980s. As advertising revenues fell, many private television stations became takeover targets, mainly by cable companies. Broadcasters faced a further challenge with the introduction, in 1982, of pay-television and later, beginning in the late–1980s, the introduction of specialty channels. The CRTC had resisted increased pressure from the cable industry to allow the importation of new American–based services, such as Home Box Office, that came on the market in the mid–1970s. Instead, the Commission wanted to promote the development of Canadian services, similar to American offerings. As broadcasters began airing a mix of programming options (mainly movies, sports, and music videos), Canadian services approached the level of their American counterparts, but since they were Canadian-owned, they were subject to CRTC licensing.

The regulatory justification for creating Canadian pay-television in 1982 was to provide an additional outlet for Canadian feature films; however, the actual number of Canadian films broadcast has never been very high. Weak penetration of the cable market by film channels made them commercially unviable. When the CRTC decided to license new specialty channels in 1987, cable operators were allowed to provide the new range of services to all subscribers in their territory. Additionally, cable operators could still offer the available Canadian pay-television channels, which were being packaged to include authorized American services not considered to be competitors of established Canadian channels. Since 1987, Canadian cable subscribers in most markets have received a 24-hour CBC news channel (in English), channels featuring music videos, sports, weather, and children's programming (in either English or French), and the international French channel, TV5. Viewers can also subscribe to pay-television movie channels, specialized channels in the other official language, and a range of American channels, including the Cable News Network (but not, for example, Music Television (MTV), which was a direct competitor of the new Canadian music channel).

By the early 1990s, combined viewing of all of these services accounted for less than 20 percent of the overall audience share. Even with this low penetration rate, however, pressure to establish even more Canadian services mounted with the intention of competing in the upcoming "500-channel universe" and to stall viewer defection to direct broadcast satellites. By 1995 a cabled Canadian household (which had grown to 76 percent of the market) could receive additional services, such as a French-language CBC news channel; arts-and-entertainment channels in English or French (depending on the market); a science channel; a women's channel; a lifestyle channel; a Canadian country music channel; and a channel featuring older programs. Although Canadian viewers in general had more programming choices, specific offerings within each territory of the country varied depending on the leeway given to local cable operators by the CRTC. This complicated service-provider system was the focal point of consumer dissatisfaction as viewers discovered their channel availability was limited in their area and that they, as a group, had no say on what services could be provided to them.

In the mid–1990s, the Canadian television industry was having difficulty adjusting to new technologies and economies brought on by the expansion of the internet. The CRTC's regulatory powers were under review, the CBC faced increasing budget restrictions, and private broadcasters were competing for ever-decreasing advertising revenue. However, Canadian distribution activities, protected from U.S. dominance under the North American Free Trade Agreement, were well-positioned in the Canadian market and independent production entities were finding an audience. Additionally, Canadian television provided some unique programming services in the form of provincial government-supported educational broadcasters, community broadcasters, and autonomous activities operated by native broadcasters.

First Peoples Television Broadcasting in Canada

First Peoples of Canada are considered to have the most advanced Fourth World (indigenous peoples) broadcasting system. Their system is based on a 1991 legislative recognition of their collective communications and cultural rights as Peoples with a special status. In the Canadian context, "First Peoples" is an inclusive term referring to both the Inuit (known elsewhere as Eskimos) and the Amerindian populations, also known as First Nations. Aboriginal-initiated media in northern Canada (north of the 55th parallel) have had a relatively long history when compared with other so-called Fourth World/indigenous communities around the world. The First Peoples have worked and lobbied a very long time for the right to be included in Canada's policy decisions pertaining to broadcasting services offered to their communities.

Much like broadcasting history everywhere, it is difficult to understand the introduction of television into the North without recognizing the role of radio. First Peoples expected that television would have local and regional indigenous input, as had been the case with radio. Radio entered the North in the late 1920s and by the early 1930s, trading posts, the Royal Canadian Mounted Police centers, and religious missions were equipped with radios to maintain contact with their headquarters in the South. Native peoples did not have direct access to these early radio services, but that changed in 1958 when the CBC's Northern Service was established. In 1960, the first Inuit-language broadcasts occurred and by 1972, 17 percent of the CBC shortwave service was in Inuktitut (the language of the Inuits). Since the early 1970s, First Peoples have demanded access to radio in the North and provincial, territorial, and federal government authorities have provided funding to build radio services. As a consequence of proactive government actions, native-language radio programming has become an integral part of the Northern media infrastructure.

The Canadian government's subsidizing of native-produced media began in 1974 with the development of the Native Communications Program and by 1996, 117 First Peoples' community radio stations had become operational across Canada, including those below the Hamelin line (the line at latitude 55 that separates the North from the South). With the exception of the Inuit service in the Northwest Territories, all other Northern regions have both a network of local radio stations and one publicly-subsidized regional service. Citing budgetary concerns, the Native Communications Program was terminated in 1990 and funding for Native local radio has been sporadic ever since. Most Northern communities do not have a large enough advertising base to make private radio viable and therefore depend on either public subsidies or outside financing to maintain stable operations.

Both radio and television broadcasting evolved quickly with the launching of the Anik satellite in 1972. By 1973 the North was hooked up to the South through radio and television services and for the first time Inuit and First Nations viewers were able to have access to American and Canadian programming. The launching of Southern television programming into Northern communities through the CBC Northern Service spurred the indigenous communities to organize broadcasting services in their own languages and reflecting their own cultures, just as they had achieved in radio. The communities wanted participatory and language rights, as well as decision-making responsibilities about programming and Southern service expansion. By the mid–1970s, First Peoples had secured funding, established Native Communications Societies responsible for regulating broadcast activities, and begun operating local community television projects.

Beginning in 1976, the government provided grants to native organizations for technical experiments with the Hermes (1976) and Anik B satellites (1978–1981) and by 1981 five Northern television production studios had been established and hundreds of hours of programming had been broadcast. In 1981, having proved its capabilities, the CRTC licensed the Inuit Broadcasting Corporation as a Northern television service, with the function of providing Inuktitut-language services to the Northwest Territories, Northern Quebec, and Labrador. At the same time other Native Communications Societies across the North were at varying stages of radio and television development and were also preparing for the licensing process. In 1983 the government adopted the Northern Broadcasting Policy and the Northern Native Broadcast Access Program (NNBAP), both of which became the foundation for the Aboriginal Broadcasting Act in 1991. The Northern Broadcasting Policy established the principle of "fair access" by native Northerners to the production and distribution of programming in their territories. It further established the principle of consultation with First Peoples before Southern-based decisions were made about Northern telecommunications services. The NNBAP provided grants to regional Native Communication Societies to help them establish their own broadcasting facilities.

In 1988, the federal government provided $10 million to establish a dedicated Northern satellite transponder (channel) and by 1992 Television Northern Canada (TVNC) was on the air. Owned and programmed by 13 aboriginal broadcast groups, plus government and education organizations in the North, TVNC is a pan–Arctic satellite service that distributes 100 hours of programming to 94 Northern communities. In 1995, TVNC petitioned the CRTC to be placed on the list of eligible channels to be picked up by cable operators in the South and in November approval was granted, making it possible for TVNC to become available in a variety of Southern Canadian markets, should cable operators choose to carry the channel.

United States Networks

@Max, 1100 Avenue of the Americas, New York, NY 10036; *Telephone*: 212-512-1000; *Fax*: 212-512-1182; *Launch Date*: 2001; *Broadcast Day*: 24 hours; *Email*: Contact channel through its web site; *Web site*: http://www.cinemax.com

@Max is a multiplexed channel from Cinemax that broadcasts contemporary movies and movies with attitude aimed at the 18–30-year-old viewer market.

@Max Choice, 1100 Avenue of the Americas, New York, NY 10036; *Telephone*: 212-512-1000; *Fax*: 212-512-1182; *Launch Date*: 2001; *Broadcast Day*: 24 hours; *Email*: Contact channel through its web site; *Web site*: http://www.cinemax.com

@Max Choice is a multiplexed channel from Cinemax that broadcasts popular and award-winning classic movies aimed at all audiences.

3ABN Latino, 3391 Charlie Good Road, P.O. Box 220, West Frankfort, IL 62896; *Telephone*: 618-627-4651; *Fax*: 618-627-2726; *Launch Date*: 2003; *Broadcast Day*: 24 hours; *Email*: mail@ 3abn.org; *Web site*: http://www.3abn.org

3ABN Latino is a Spanish/Portuguese-language multiplexed channel from Three Angels Broadcasting Network that broadcasts religious-related music videos.

5StarMax, 1100 Avenue of the Americas, New York, NY 10036; *Telephone*: 212-512-1000; *Fax*: 212-512-1182; *Launch Date*: 2001; *Broadcast Day*: 24 hours; *Email*: Contact channel through its web site; *Web site*: http://www.cinemax.com

5StarMax is a multiplexed channel from Cinemax that broadcasts popular and award-winning modern classic movies aimed at all audiences.

5StarMax Choice, 1100 Avenue of the Americas, New York, NY 10036; *Telephone*: 212-512-1000; *Fax*: 212-512-1182; *Launch Date*: 2002; *Broadcast Day*: 24 hours; *Email*: Contact channel through its web site; *Web site*: http://www.cinemax.com

5StarMax Choice is a multiplexed channel from Cinemax that broadcasts specific movie genres each night to a targeted audience.

ABC Family Channel (http://www.abcfamily.com) *see* **American Broadcasting Company**

ABS-CBN International (The Filipino Channel), 859 Cowan Road, Lopez Building, Burlingame, CA 94010; *Telephone*: 800-345-2465, 650-697-3700; *Fax*: 650-697-3500; 1557 East Amar Road, Suite H, West Covina, CA 91792; *Telephone*: 866-832-2875; 636 Newark Avenue, Jersey City, NJ 07306; *Telephone*: 201-386-0802; *Fax*: 201-386-9799; *Launch Date*: 1994 (in the United States); *Broadcast Day*: 24 hours; *Email*: rencarnacion@abs-cbni.com, feedback@abs-cbn.com; *Web site*: http://www.abs-cbn.com

ABS-CBN International (also known as The Filipino Channel) airs a mix of news, children's programming, entertainment, documentaries, movies, and sports. The channel is a premium programming product of ABS-CBN, the Philippines' dominant broadcaster, program producer, and cable television operator. The Filipino Channel delivers programming to the North American Filipino market, as well as the Filipino population throughout the Pacific, Europe, and the Middle East. Filipinos became part of the global village through ABS-CBN's satellite broadcasts of the 1968 Mexico Olympics and the 1969 moon landing of Apollo 11, captured live on ABS-CBN's *Man on the Moon* telecast.

ABS-CBN time line (U.S. Only): *February 1992*— ABS-CBN International is incorporated in Daly City, California; *January 1993* — ABS-CBN International Productions ventures into the Filipino video market through the RNJ Corporation of Los Angeles, California; *April 1994*— ABS-CBN International signs a 10-year contract with the largest cable operator in United States, TCI Cablevision; The Filipino Channel, the first all–Filipino premium channel in the U.S., is launched in Daly City, Pacifica, Millbrae, Brisbane, Colma, and Broadmoor (all in California), providing eight hours of programming daily, carried by TCI Cablevision and Western Cable Systems; *September 1994*— The Filipino Channel begins broadcasting 24 hours a day; *November 1994*— The Filipino Channel begins broadcasting in Hawaii; *March 1995*— The Filipino Channel Direct!, a home satellite network, is launched in the United States; *October 1995*— ABS-CBN Telecom is launched in the continental United States.

AccentHealth, 5440 Beaumont Center Boulevard #400, Tampa, FL 33634; *Telephone*: 813-349-7127; *Fax*: 813-349-7227; 747 Third Avenue, 14th Floor, New York, NY 10017; *Telephone*: 212-763-5102; *Fax*: 212-763-5200; *Subscribers*: 11,000 (doctor's offices); *Email*: ehodkinson@accenthealth, dfournier@accenthealth.com; *Web site*: http://www. accenthealth.com, http://www. axolotl.com

Calling itself "America's #1 Health Television Network" AccentHealth, whose name has recently been changed to Axolotl Corporation, provides multimedia e-healthcare solutions and patient care management information. The network is delivered to 11,000 medical office waiting rooms nationwide and reaches approximately 19 million viewers each month. Its programming is produced by the Cable News Network and is designed specifically to engage, entertain, and educate patients while they wait to see the doctor. Popular programs include *Healthline* (issues in the news affecting consumer health); *Food for Thought* (practical tips for healthier eating); *Your Health* (devoted to helping viewers take control of their own health); *Healthy Variety* (wellness, travel, pets, and healthy lifestyle profiles); *Parenting Today* (information on preparing for and raising children from pregnancy through adolescence); *Informed Decisions* (a joint production between AccentHealth and the American Cancer Society that shows viewers how to make the right choices to help prevent and fight cancer); *On the Menu* (latest in nutrition and healthy food alternatives); *Baby & You* (focuses on the first year of a baby's life); *Fast Track* (fitness and exercise information to improve the mind and body); *Safety First* (shows viewers how to enjoy peace of mind at home, in the car, on the street, and at play); *Just for Kids* (focuses on topics of interest to the curious child and adult); *Living Well* (lifestyle issues that impact the quality of life); and *MindBenders/True or False* (airs health trivia and true/false questions designed to test viewers' knowledge of health-related issues).

ActionMax, 1100 Avenue of the Americas, New York, NY 10036; *Telephone*: 212-512-1000; *Fax*: 212-512-1182; *Launch Date*: August 1988; *Broadcast Day*: 24 hours; *Email*: Contact channel through its web site; *Web site*: http://www.cinemax.com

ActionMax is a multiplexed channel from Cinemax that broadcasts action-based blockbusters, westerns, war movies, and martial arts films.

Action Pay-Per-View, One BET Plaza,

1235 W Street Northeast, Washington, D.C. 20018; *Telephone*: 202-608-2000; *Fax*: 202-608-2519; *Broadcast Day*: 24 hours; *Email*: Contact channel through its web site; *Web site*: http://www.bet.com

Action Pay-Per-View is a multiplexed channel from Black Entertainment Television that targets its high-intensity, action-filled programming to the African-American audience.

Adam & Eve Channel, 2706 Media Center Drive, Los Angeles, CA 90065; *Telephone*: 323-276-4000; *Fax*: 323-276-4500; *Email*: info@playboy.com; *Web site*: http://www.playboytv.com, http://www.cyberspice.com.

The Adam & Eve Channel is a multiplexed pay-per-view channel from Playboy TV Networks that broadcasts adult entertainment programming.

Adult Swim, 1050 Techwood Drive NW, Atlanta, GA 30318; *Telephone*: 404-885-4205; *Fax*: 404-885-2355; *Email*: katie.morgan@turner.com; *Web site*: http://www. adult swim.com

Adult Swim is not a separate network or channel but a theme-specific program block from the Cartoon Network that airs late-night animated programming fare aimed at the 18–34 age group. On June 17, 2003 Adult Swim garnered, for the first time in the Comedy Network's history, a viewing audience of more than 1,000,000 adults with its broadcast of the prime-time animated series, *Family Guy*, which became the network's most popular program among young adults.

Adventist Television Network, 12501 Old Columbia Pike, Silver Spring, MD 20904; *Telephone*: 301-680-5100, 250-491-8285; *Fax*: 250-491-8287; *Launch Date*: 1995; *Broadcast Day*: 24 hours; *Subscribers*: 13,000 (global satellite links); *Email*: askATN@ adventist.tv, prayer@ adventist.tv, comments@adventist.tv; *Web site*: http://adventist.tv

Also known as the Hope Channel, the Adventist Television Network is a global satellite television service of the world church of Seventh-Day Adventists. As the satellite voice of the Adventist church, ATN broadcasts a mix of international, non-political features around the world in numerous languages. Current programming includes evangelistic series, major church organizational meetings, sermons, Sabbath School study, weekly church news, public health, education, family life, and special church events. The network broadcasts to North America, Africa, Asia, Europe, Central America, South America, and the Pacific Rim.

The Adventist Church currently has more than 13,000 worldwide satellite downlink sites, located mainly at local churches. Since 1995, the Adventist Global Communication Network has been the official broadcast organization of the Adventist Church. Eventually, ATN plans to produce between 60 to 150 minutes of original programming content every week and to distribute ATN to private homes around the world.

The Africa Channel (http://www.theafricachannel.com) (Planned for future operation)

African Independent Television, 8900 Liberty Circle, Englewood, CO 80122; *Telephone*: 303-712-5400; *Fax*: 303-268-5465; *Launch Date*: December 1996 (in the United States); *Broadcast Day*: 24 hours; *Email*: ininfo@i-channel.com; *Web site*: http://www.i-channel.com; http://www.aittv.com

African Independent Television, available in the United States through the International Channel, is an independent global satellite television station operating from Lagos, The Federal Republic of Nigeria, and is available in North America, Mexico, and the Caribbean. Even though the channel's main language is English, selected programs are aired in various African languages, such as Hausa, Igbo, Swahili, and Yoruba. Programming includes news reports, action sports, soap operas, cultural entertainment shows, musicals, and documentaries.

Africast Television Network, 182 Sound Beach Avenue, Old Greenwich, CT 06870; *Telephone*: 800-957-4406, 203-862-0210; *Broadcast Day*: 24 hours; *Email*: info@ africast.com; *Web site*: http://www.africast.com.

A planned future operation, the Africast Television Network will provide a range of pan-African educational, informational, and entertainment programming free of excessive violence, explicit sexual themes, and foul language. While primarily targeting African-Americans and African and Caribbean resident populations in America, the network hopes that its programming mix will also appeal to a wider, non-minority, U.S.-based cable audience interested in connecting with other cultures in the United States and around the world.

Air & Space Network *see* **NASA Television**

Airport Network, One CNN Center, P.O. Box 105366, Atlanta, GA 30348; *Telephone*: 404-827-1500; *Fax*: 404-827-3368; *Launch Date*: January 1992; *Broadcast Day*: 24 hours; *Email*: Contact network through its web site; *Web site*: http://www.cnn. com/airport/

The Airport Network (also called the CNN Airport Network) is the only satellite-delivered televison service available to national and international air travelers. Available at more than 1,800 gate areas at 39 U.S. airports, the network uses CNN, CNNfn and CNN Headline News anchors to provide 24-hour a day CNN-produced news and live breaking stories, business and financial reports, sports updates, weather, lifestyle and general interest segments, and entertainment and travel features.

Alegria *see* **Outstanding Latin Entertainment Channel**

Al Jazeera TV, Allied Media Corporation, 5252 Cherokee Avenue #105, Alexandria, VA 22312; *Telephone*: 703-333-2008; *Fax*: 703-783-8627; *Launch Date*: November 1996 (in the United States); *Broadcast Day*: 24 hours; *Email*: info@allied-media.com; *Web site*: http://www.allied-media.com

Based in Qatar and with 30 bureaus around the world, Al Jazeera TV is the only Arabic News Channel in the Middle East providing news coverage 24 hours a day from around the world with a focus on reporting from the hottest regions of conflict. Programming includes political talk shows, documentaries, business, culture, sports, and health. The network became widely known to the American audience after the U.S. military became involved with conflicts in Afghanistan and the invasion of Iraq in the early 21st Century.

Almavision Hispanic Network, 759 South Central Avenue, Los Angeles, CA 90021, P.O. Box 2434, La Puenta, CA 91746; *Telephone*: 213-627-8900, 213-627-8711; *Fax*: 213-627-8712; *Launch Date*: December 2002; *Broadcast Day*: 24 hours; *Subscribers*: 9,100,000; *Email*: info@ almavision.com; *Web site*: http://www.almavision.com

Using the tag line "Christian Television God's Way" (Television Cristiana a la Manera de Dios), the Almavision Hispanic Network's programming is aimed at the international Hispanic market. The network airs family-oriented programs, Christian music, and religious talk shows.

America Channel, 120 International Parkway #220, Heathrow, FL 32746; *Telephone*: 407-333-3031; *Fax*: 503-217-0605; *Launch Date*: June 2004; *Broadcast Day*: 24 hours; *Email*: info@americachannel.us; *Web site*: http://www.americachannel.us

The America Channel tells the stories of America, including its people and places, issues and passions, and struggles and dreams. The channel's programming focuses on how Americans face challenges, overcome obstacles, work, and play. Stories are mixed with lifestyle shows, news from around the country, games and competitions, issues commentary, culture, comedy and music, and coverage of live events.

Popular programs include *American*

Stories (profiles of ordinary Americans who have accomplished extraordinary things); *Road Trip* (focuses on adventurers who set off across the country exploring towns, people, and events off the beaten path); *America From Afar* (a look at what the media in other countries are saying about America); *Faces of America* (in-depth profiles of the diverse communities and social, ethnic, religious, and political groups that form American society); *Occupational Hazard* (a look at Americans with unusually dangerous or off-beat jobs); *Personal Quest* (follows a group of young Americans, week by week, as they strive to make their own American dream come true); and *Campus Report* (documents the trials, tribulations, and triumphs of college life).

America National Network, 1601 Cloverfield Boulevard, 2nd Floor, South Tower, Santa Monica, CA 90404; *Telephone*: 310-460-3526; *Fax*: 310-309-4702; *Launch Date*: October 2004; *Broadcast Day*: 24 hours; *Email*: Contact network through its web site; *Web site*: http://www. sentinel-america.com

The America National Network airs news, original and purchased made-for-television movies, dramatic series, sitcoms, and documentaries, all with the goal of reinforcing America's traditional patriotic values, standards, ethics, and ideals. The goal of ANN is to offer a patriotic, constructive view of America through positive entertainment programming with broad, general appeal aimed at a worldwide audience. The nature of each program (movie, news magazine, reality show, discussion panel, documentary, talk show, sitcom, and drama series) is to be constructive and positive while accentuating, re-affirming, and re-enforcing traditional American ideals and standards.

America One Television Network, VOTH Network, Inc., 6125 Airport Freeway #100, Fort Worth, TX 76117; *Telephone*: 682-432-0300; *Fax*: 682-432-0345; *Launch Date*: 1995; *Broadcast Day*: 24 hours; *Subscribers*: 20,000,000; *Email*: mail@ americaone.com; *Web site*: http://www.america com

Calling itself "The Voice of the Homeland," the America One Television Network is a national, family-values, general entertainment television network with a western flair that serves the ranch, farm, and equestrian communities. The network's programming includes news and information, equestrian sports, classic western movies, western television shows, vintage Hollywood films, lifestyle (music, cuisine, and home and gardening shows), American music and documentaries (western, country, bluegrass, jazz, and rock with live performances, music videos, biographies, and music variety shows), sports and outdoor adventure (rodeo, hunting, fishing, travel adventure, and motor sports), and kids and adults (entertainment for the entire family).

American Broadcasting Company, 77 West 66th Street, New York, NY 10023; 500 South Buena Vista Street, Burbank, CA 91521; *Telephone*: 818-460-7477; *Fax*: 212-456-1424; *Launch Date*: 1943; *Broadcast Day*: 24 hours; *Email*: Contact network through its web site; *Web site*: http://www.abc.com

Destined to become one of America's "Big 3" networks and now owned by the Walt Disney Company, the American Broadcasting Company began its life as an offshoot to a government monopoly probe. In 1940 the Federal Communications Commission (FCC) issued its *Report on Chain Broadcasting*, which proposed, in an effort to increase competition, the selling of either NBC Red or NBC Blue by the Radio Corporation of America (RCA). At the time, NBC Red was the dominant NBC radio network and the report said RCA used NBC Blue to suppress competition against NBC Red.

While the FCC had no authority to regulate networks directly, the Commission had been given the mandate to regulate individual stations. Using this power, the FCC ordered that no license would be issued to a standard broadcast station affiliated with a network which maintained more than one network (a rule aimed directly at RCA, which owned NBC). RCA/NBC appealed the decision and lost, thus forcing the sale of NBC Blue. On October 12, 1943 the FCC approved the sale of NBC Blue to Edward Noble (the owner of Lifesaver candy) for $8 million. The Blue Network Company Inc. was soon sold to American Broadcasting System Inc. and was renamed the American Broadcasting Company (ABC).

During television's infancy, ABC was in a poor competitive position because there were not enough local VHF stations in the country on which to put the three existing networks (CBS, DuMont, and NBC) on the air in most major cities, much less four when ABC joined the mix. Help for the network came when the movie theaters were divested from the studios in the early 1950s and cash-heavy United Paramount Theaters (UPT) bought ABC for $25 million, giving the fledgling network much-needed capital. However, there were potential FCC problems with the purchase since UPT already owned 10 stations and a piece of the DuMont Network. After negotiating with government officials, the merger was allowed because Paramount had divested itself fully of the theater group. In its early days, ABC routinely lagged behind the other more established networks in ratings and viewers and was always in need of a cash infusion.

With the UPT-ABC merger and its corresponding influx of capital, the network began making a major push to attract viewers. This effort escalated in 1954 when Walt and Roy Disney approached ABC with the idea of building a new theme park in California. The Disney brothers needed financing for their venture and ABC needed new programming, the classic definition of a "win-win" situation. ABC lent the brothers $15 million in return for 35 percent of Disneyland and the network also agreed to pay $35 million in license fees for seven years for the rights to a new Walt Disney TV series. The resulting television show, *Disneyland*, premiered in the fall of 1954 and was the network's first Nielsen Top Ten hit. ABC followed that success a year later when the network aired the show *Cheyenne*, the first prime-time series produced by a major studio (Warner Brothers).

The network's ratings and financial fortunes began to turn around as it focused its programming efforts on the emerging "Baby Boomer" television audience and shows were created specifically aimed at that growing market segment. Fortune smiled on the network as a significant television revolution occurred when a relatively unknown producer, Roone Arledge, completely changed how Americans viewed sports on television. In the process, he helped turn worldwide sports broadcasting into a multi-billion dollar industry, with ABC at the forefront of this movement. When ABC began broadcasting NCAA college football games, Arledge completely revised how the game was telecast by focusing not only on the contest itself, but on the crowd and by following story lines of the athletes.

Arledge also began using cameras and graphics in ways never seen on broadcasts before and his games became known for cutting-edge camera angles and graphics technology. He used these same techniques when ABC began, for the first time ever on any network, broadcasting National Football League games on Monday nights. His show, *Monday Night Football*, completely changed the way the professional game was shown on American television and helped make it the popular viewing sport it is today. These revolutionary sports broadcast strategies, along with the network's famous *Wide World of Sports* show, made ABC a powerhouse in sports broadcasting.

Even with its sports broadcasting success, ABC consistently ran number three behind CBS and NBC (the DuMont Network had ceased to exist years before) during most of the 1960s and had some moderate success in the 1970s. However, one of television's biggest programming mistakes, the refusal to air the classic television show *All in the Family*, haunted the network for years. After financing the development of two pilot episodes, the network (fearful that the edgy comedy would offend conservative affiliates) decided to turn down the Norman Lear show. Lear then took the show to CBS and, as the saying goes, the rest is history. To make matters worse for ABC's broadcasting ego, the show became a television legend and spawned two highly successful (and profitable) spin-offs (*Maude* and *The Jeffersons*) for CBS. This decision by ABC was a severe blow to the network's credibility and reputation.

The network's fortunes rebounded in the mid–1970s when it hired Fred Silverman away from CBS, who immediately began to refocus ABC's broadcast vision. Soon after his arrival at the network, two events pushed ABC to the top of the ratings: the Winter Olympics broadcast from Innsbruck (where ABC used its highly-regarded sports vision) and the twelve-hour mini-series, *Rich Man, Poor Man*, network television's first big miniseries. Also in the mid 1970s, the network's ratings soared when ABC aired the first, and most successful, of the so-called "jiggle" shows, *Charlie's Angels*. These types of shows became so successful, popular, and profitable for the network that they became the cornerstone of a new programming genre. As the network's ratings soared, so did its profits, from $29 million in 1975 to $165 million by 1977.

However, "jiggle" television was not the network's sole contribution (or even its most important) to the prime time schedule. In 1977 ABC aired the classic 12-hour miniseries, *Roots*, which attracted 130 million viewers, garnered the highest Nielsen ratings in television history, highlighted the role of the miniseries as a valuable programming genre, and garnered international praise for the network. This success triggered a sudden rise in the network's ratings and during the 1977-1978 season, ABC posted 12 programs in the Nielsen Top Twenty (including *The Six Million Dollar Man, Happy Days, Laverne and Shirley, Three's Company, Eight is Enough, Charlie's Angels, Baretta, Welcome Back, Kotter, Barney Miller*, and *The Love Boat*).

ABC's good fortune continued during the 1978-1979 season as the network placed 14 shows in the Top Twenty, including the top five spots. This season also made history when ABC became the first television network to generate more than $1 billion in revenue. However, after enjoying years of success, the network took a broadcasting blow when programming legend Fred Silverman left ABC and moved to NBC, where he would make it the "Must See" network by creating a powerful Thursday night lineup. ABC's programming superiority came to an end and the network was forced to re-focus its efforts.

In 1980, ABC made history again when it became the first network to hire a woman, Barbara Walters, as its evening news anchor. In 1976 the network had hired Walters from NBC with a contract for $1 million. Four years later she was elevated to co-anchor the *ABC Evening News with Harry Reasoner*. However, the pairing did not work and the ratings suffered. Walters moved on to host numerous and highly-rated interview programs and became a regular on the network's news magazine, *20/20*.

Sometimes, ratings success and critical acclaim came from unexpected sources and unplanned events. In 1979, the Iranian government stormed the American embassy in Tehran and took American hostages. In November, ABC News broadcast *The Iran Hostage Crisis: America Held Hostage*. The broadcast was a ratings success and ABC News President Roone Arledge announced that the network would air nightly late-night specials until the crisis was resolved and Ted Koppel joined the program as a substitute for its main anchor, Frank Reynolds. On March 24, 1980, day 142 of the hostage crisis, ABC premiered *Nightline* with Koppel as its permanent anchor. The program took advantage of advances in satellite technology and the ability to bring multiple guests "together" from around the world to develop an in-depth, interview-format news program that explored the top news stories of the day. The program continued after the hostage crises was over and became the gold standard for late-night news programming.

In the late 1970s, ABC jumped into the fray of the emerging specialized (or niche networks) by purchasing ESPN (Entertainment Sports Programming Network), with the hopes of gaining access to pay-per-view sports and the potential to bid on, and broadcast, big-time sporting events around the world. ESPN has since grown to become the recognized leader in sports broadcasting.

In the early 1980s, ABC focused on its non-prime-time schedule and realized tremendous financial success with its daytime soap operas (such as *General Hospital*, *All My Children*, and *Ryan's Hope)*, which generated 75 percent of the network's profits. However, as the 1980s progressed, the network again found itself in third place behind CBS and NBC, due to its rising expenses and sagging ratings.

In the mid–1980s another television revolution began, focused on the industry itself and not on programming. In 1986, Capital Cities Communication initiated the first television network takeover since ABC's earlier merger with United Paramount Theaters by purchasing ABC for $3.5 billion. This was the beginning of broadcast mergers that led to the purchase of all major networks by the end of the 1980s. In 1995 the Walt Disney Company acquired Capital Cities/ABC for $19 billion, the biggest media merger in history and the second-highest price ever paid for a U.S. company. This move triggered other so-called "super mergers" as Westinghouse merged with CBS and Time Warner merged with Ted Turner's cable network empire, including CNN, TBS, TNT, and Turner Classic Movies.

The 24-hour ABC Family Channel (http://www.abcfamily.com), launched in fall 2001, started its broadcast life on the Christian Broadcasting Network (CBN) and airs programming aimed at families, teens, and young children, including *The 700 Club*, which had originated on CBN. The channel features original and acquired series and movies, major theatrical releases, and related programming from the ABC Television Network.

American Christian TV System, 6350 West Freeway, Fort Worth, TX 76150; *Telephone*: 817-737-3241; *Fax*: 817-737-7853; *Email*: Contact channel through its web site; *Web site*: http://www.familynet.com

The American Christian TV System airs religious-based programming aimed at the entire family. See FamilyNet Television for more information.

American David, 825 West End Avenue #13C, New York, NY 10025; *Telephone*: 212-663-1037; *Fax*: 212-663-1051; *Broadcast Day*: 24 hours; *Email*: Contact channel through its web site; *Web site*: http://www.americandavid.com

Planned for future operations, American David will be an entertainment channel with a Jewish flavor and is dedicated to the advancement of art, science, knowledge, music, and culture. Through its programming, the channel will aim to connect the past, present, and future of Jewish civilization while attempting to attract viewers of all races, religions and creeds.

American Forces Network (a production facility of the **Armed Forces Radio and Television Service**)

American Legal Network (Planned for future operation)

American Movie Classics, 200 Jericho Quadrangle, 3rd Floor, Jericho, NY 11753; *Telephone*: 516-803-4300; *Fax*: 516-803-4354; *Launch Date*: October 1984; *Broadcast Day*: 24 hours; *Subscribers*: 85,000,000; *Email*: Contact channel through its web site; *Web site*: http://www. amctv.com

Owned and operated by Rainbow Media Holdings, Inc., American Movie Classics is cable's first 24-hour, all-classic movie-based network and offers a comprehensive mix of popular movies, original series, documentaries, and specials. Initially, AMC aired classic, uncut, black-and-white Hollywood films of the 1930s, 1940s, and 1950s, with no commercial interruptions. AMC began as a pay service but switched to cable's basic tier in 1987. It has since broadened its movie offerings, expanded it documentaries and specials, but no longer runs its movies without commercial interruption.

AMC's early popularity was due to its ability to find a niche market of movie lovers who had very few options for viewing classic movies. Over-the-air television (the major broadcast networks) had traditionally served as the venue for second-run Hollywood films from the mid–1950s into the 1970s, but the number of over-the-air TV stations in any one market limited the possible broadcast of many classic Hollywood films. While this gap was somewhat served by local independent stations, movie buffs did not like the fact that the films were cut to fit into prescribed time slots and were constantly interrupted with commercials. AMC entered this market by broadcasting uncut movies with no commercials. This broadcasting concept in its early years brought a loyal fan base to the network.

In addition to its regular movie fare, AMC also airs documentaries that focus on various parts of the movie business, such as a corporate profile of Republic Studios, *Stars & Stripes: Hollywood and World War II*, and *Knockout: Hollywood's Love Affair with Boxing*. In June 1988 AMC began producing a monthly magazine that features articles about the stars from the Golden Age of Hollywood, inside movie-related stories, and a listing of the month's broadcast lineup.

In addition to its broadcast function, AMC raises money for The Film Foundation, which funds film archives across the country, including the UCLA Film and Television Archive, the Museum of Modern Art, the Library of Congress, the International Museum of Photography at George Eastman House, the National Center for Film and Video Preservation at the American Film Institute, the Academy of Motion Picture Arts & Sciences Film Archive, and the National Film Preservation Foundation.

In 1993, the network launched its first annual film preservation festival and joined forces with The Film Foundation to raise awareness and funds needed to identify and restore films. The festival offered viewers films, historical shorts, newsreels, and featured testimonials by well-known film makers and actors including Martin Scorsese, Clint Eastwood, Jodie Foster, Ron Howard, Penny Marshall, Tom Cruise, Robert DeNiro, Dustin Hoffman, and Barry Levinson. The network's fund-raising efforts made the preservation of *My Darling Clementine* (1946) and *Stagecoach* (1939) possible.

Another of its film restoration projects occurred in 2003 when AMC and MGM teamed up (in partnership with Martin Scorsese's The Film Foundation) to restore Sergio Leone's masterpiece, *The Good, the Bad and the Ugly*. The newly restored film includes 14 minutes of missing footage and new voice work from Clint Eastwood and Eli Wallach. The restored movie made its world premiere at the Tribeca film festival on May 8th and its world television premiere on AMC on May 10th.

American Muslim Lifestyle Network *see* **Bridges TV**

American Sports Network (http://www.asntv.com) (Planned for future operation)

American West Network (Planned for future operation)

America's Collectibles Network (now called **Jewelry Television**)

America's Disability Network (begun in 1984 and changing its name to the Silent Network in 1990, America's Disability Network aired programs for the hearing impaired and used sign language to allow viewers to enjoy the broadcasts. The network was sold to Kaleidoscope Television in 1990 and soon after stopped broadcasting programs aimed at the hearing-impaired viewer audience).

America's High School Network *see* **Varsity Television**

America's Store, 1 HSN Drive, St. Petersburg, FL 33729; *Telephone*: 800-284-3400; *Broadcast Day*: 24 hours; *Email*: Contact channel through its web site; *Web site*: http://www.americasstore.com

Owned and operated by the Home Shopping Network, America's Store is a home shopping channel that focuses on selling jewelry, coins, electronics, fashion and accessories, beauty, health, and fitness, cooking, sports and collectibles, crafts, and sewing products.

Amigos *see* **Outstanding Latin Entertainment Channel**

AMP Television Network (http://www.amptvnet.com)—planned for future operation, the 24-hour AMP Television Network will focus on the 18–34 age group and will broadcast original extreme sports, music, and action programming.

Angel One, c/o Dominion Video Satellite, 3050 North Horseshoe Drive, Naples, FL 34101; *Telephone*: 941-403-9130; *Fax*: 941-403-9105; *Broadcast Day*: 24 hours; *Email*: skyangelpr@aol.com; *Web site*: http://www.skyangel.com

Angel One broadcasts on Sky Angel (http://www.skyangel.com) and carries programming from more than 150 ministries from across America and around the world. The network offers a mix of programs geared toward biblical teaching with an emphasis on evangelism, educational and learning programs, children's shows with a focus on educational learning, and Christian-oriented news programs.

Angel Two, c/o Dominion Video Satellite, 3050 North Horseshoe Drive, Naples, FL 34101; *Telephone*: 941-403-9130; *Fax*: 941-403-9105; *Broadcast Day*: 24 hours; *Email*: skyangelpr@aol.com; *Web site*: http://www.skyangel.com

Angel Two broadcasts on Sky Angel (http://www.skyangel.com) and airs religious-based events from conferences, seminars, debates, special prayer gatherings, celebrations, and concerts.

Animal Planet, One Discovery Place, Silver Spring, MD 20910; *Telephone*: 240-662-2000; *Launch Date*: October 1996; *Broadcast Day*: 24 hours; *Email*: Contact channel through its web site; *Web site*: http://www.animalplanet.com

Owned and operated by the Discovery Channel (Discovery Communications, Inc.), Animal Planet broadcasts shows dedicated to the connection between humans and animals. Programming includes original movies, adventure series, documentaries, animal videos, sports, reality shows, dramas, and sitcoms. Popular shows include *Animal Cops*, *Animal Precinct*, *The Crocodile Hunter*, *Emergency Vets*, *The Jeff Corwin Experience*, and *Pet Star*.

In addition to its broadcasting schedule, Animal Planet has teamed up with the American Humane Association to create the Animal Planet Rescue Vehicle, which helps rescue animals left behind after natural disasters, such as hurricanes, floods, tornadoes, and wildfires. The Animal Planet Expo is an extension of Animal Planet Rescue and is a tour that visits cities across the United States from April through August. The Expo is usually set up for two days in each city and features fun activities and interactive games for the entire family. There is an educational part of Expo events that helps to educate people on how to care for their pets and how to prepare themselves and their pets for natural disasters.

Animania HD, 200 Jericho Quadrangle, Jericho, NY 11753; *Telephone*: 516-803-6010; *Email*: Contact channel through its web site; *Web site*: http://www.voom.com

Animania HD is a multiplexed channel from Voom that shows a mix of high definition animation programming from around the world.

Anime Network, 10114 West Sam Houston Parkway South #200, Houston, TX 77009; *Telephone*: 818-382-2233; *Fax*: 818-382-2244; *Launch Date*: June 2004; *Broadcast Day*: 24 hours; *Email*: info@theanimenetwork.com; *Web site*: http://www.the animenetwork.com

Owned by ADV Films (http://www.advfilms.com), the Anime Network is the first television channel in North America dedicated to anime (Japanese animation). The network has gained a cult following in the United States through a program mix of aesthetic quality, complexity of characters, serialized stories, and satirical humor. The network targets the 18–35 male population with four distinct genres: martial arts, comedy, science fiction, and drama.

Annenberg / CPB Channel, c/o Harvard-Smithsonian Center for Astrophysics, 60 Garden Street, MS 82, Cambridge, MA 02138; *Telephone*: 800-228-8030; *Fax*: 617-496-7670; *Broadcast Day*: 24 hours; *Email*: channel@learner.org; *Web site*: http://www.learner.org/channel

The Annenberg / CPB Channel is a free satellite channel used by schools, colleges, libraries, public broadcasting stations, public access channels, and other community agencies that airs teacher-professional development and instructional programs funded by Annenberg / CPB in an effort to advance excellent teaching in American schools. The channel's resources help teachers increase expertise in their fields and assist in improving teaching methods. Many of the programs are also intended for students in the classroom and viewers at home.

Antenna Satellite, 645 Fifth Avenue #406, New York, NY 10022; *Telephone*: 212-688-5475; *Fax*: 212-688-8136; *Launch Date*: 1993; *Broadcast Day*: 24 hours; *Email*: antennasatellite@ antennasatellite.com, antennausa@aol.com, satellite@antenna.gr; *Web site*: http://www.satellite.antenna.gr

Antenna Satellite is the first Greek radio and television network in the United States and uses its programming to link Greece with all Greek citizens throughout the world. The channel offers Greek-related news, series, sports, economic news, music programs, movies, and documentaries.

Anti-Aging Network, Inc., P.O. Box 3485, Beverly Hills, CA 90212; *Telephone*: 805-379-2373; *Fax*: 805-373-6595; *Broadcast Day*: 24 hours; *Email*: antiagenet@adelphia.net; *Web site*: http://www.antiagenet.tv

The Anti-Aging Network airs programs designed to help viewers live better, longer, and more productive lives. Broadcast fare includes the latest national and global anti-aging breakthroughs, hormonal therapies, health issues, financial fitness, cosmetic and surgical procedures, medicine, the body and mind connection, beauty and body makeovers, the new retirement, alternative medicine, and therapies. The network addresses the growing needs of an aging America and focuses on the betterment and the extension of life.

Appadana Television, P.O. Box 2787, Saratoga, CA 95070; *Telephone*: 408-741-1500, 408-988-5555; *Fax*: 408-741-1590, 408-988-2727; *Launch Date*: 1981; *Broadcast Day*: 24 hours; *Email*: info@appadanatv.com; *Web site*: http://www.appadanatv.com

Appadana Television is a Persian broadcasting network that airs programs focusing on news of Iran and the world, local news, entertainment, music videos, commentaries, interviews, and documentaries. The network is available in all 50 states, Canada, Europe, the Middle East, and Iran.

Applause Networks, 7805 Sunset Boulevard #203, Los Angeles, CA 90046; *Telephone*: 323-850-5000; *Broadcast Day*: Daily, 6:00 A.M.—9:00 A.M., 2:00 P.M.—4:00 P.M.; *Email*: applausetv@aol.com

Applause Networks airs classic 1950's television shows, feature films, and children's programs drawn from over 10,000 episodes and more than 4,000 hours of wholly-owned entertainment. The network also acts as an alternative global showcase featuring experimental film and video, animation, performance art, cult and foreign films, and - festival-winning shorts; all of which have virtually no exposure on commercial television.

Arab Network of America (ANA Television Network), 1510 H Street Northwest #400, Washington, D.C. 20005; *Telephone*: 202-898-8222; *Fax*: 202-898-8088; *Launch Date*: December 1991; *Broadcast Day:* 24 hours; *Email*: Contact network through its web site; *Web site*: http://www.anatv.com

The Arab Network of America provides news, public affairs, educational, and entertainment programming in Arabic and English to Arab-Americans and Arab-Canadians. The ANA Television Network and its sister company, the Middle East Broadcasting Centre (MBC), have joined forces to entertain, inform, and promote the cultural and linguistic heritage of Arabs living throughout the world. ANA is the sole U.S. distributor for MBC news, the London-based broadcast that is the leading source of news for Arabic speaking audiences worldwide. ANA Television is the largest Arab-American network in the United States and broadcasts in both Arabic and English.

ANA's programming lineup includes movies, soap operas, cultural programs, news, public affairs, live coverage of local and national elections and community events, sports, science, children's shows, family entertainment, and how-to programs. ANA also showcases Arabic dramatic and cinematic productions as well as independently produced programs aimed at the special interests of the Arab-American audience.

The Middle East Broadcasting Centre (MBC) (http://www.mbc1.com) started its satellite transmissions in September 1991 from London and broadcasts throughout the Middle East, Europe, Africa, and North and South America, reaching an Arabic audience of over 300 million. MBC, currently headquartered in Dubai Media City, is the largest and most-watched Arabic language network available and is sometimes called "the CNN of the Arab world." With expansion, MBC has also launched two new channels offering 24-hour news and entertainment to the Arab world: MBC2 (an entertainment movie channel) and Al Arabiya (a news channel).

Arab Radio and Television, 8900 Liberty Circle, Englewood, CO 80122; *Telephone*: 303-712-5400; *Fax*: 303-268-5465; *Launch Date*: 1999 (in the United States); *Broadcast Day*: 24 hours; *Email*: ininfo@i-channel.com; *Web site*: http://www.i-channel.com; http://www.art-tv.net

Arab Radio and Television serves Arab-Americans by linking them to their homeland with programming in their own language from the largest general entertainment library in the Middle East. Programs are selected and produced to cater to Moslems and Arabs living in America. In an effort to give their viewers a touch of home, ART provides over 6,000 live and recorded Arabic and multi-language shows consisting primarily of mini-series, dramas, sports, movies, music videos, children's educational programs, and coverage of national events, festivals, and religious celebrations.

Arabic Channel, 366 86th Street, Brooklyn, NY 11209; *Telephone*: 718-238-2450; *Fax*: 718-238-2465; *Launch Date*: April 1991; *Broadcast Day*: 24 hours; *Subscribers*: 1,250,000; *Email*: gmt@ethnicnet.com; *Web site*: http://www.ethnicnet.com

The Arabic Channel is the first Arabic television station in the world that is not owned or controlled by a government or group in the Middle East. The channel offers Arabic-language programming, including children's shows, soccer matches, news, films (some subtitled in English), soap operas, specialty programming, and *Tarek El Nour*, a program that focuses on the Moslem religion.

Armed Forces Radio and Television Service, AFRTS Broadcast Center, 1363 Z

Street, Building 2730, March Air Force Base, CA 92518; *Telephone*: 909-413-2225; *Fax*: 909-413-2234; *Launch Date*: 1954 (as AFRTS); *Broadcast Day*: 24 hours; *Email*: affrel@dodmedia.ods.mil; *Web site*: http://www.afrts.osd.mil

The Armed Forces Radio and Television Service is part of the Department of Defense (DOD) and its mission is to communicate DOD policies, priorities, programs, goals, and initiatives. AFRTS provides stateside radio and television programming (a touch of home) to U.S. service men and women, DOD civilians, and their families serving outside the continental United States and on naval ships. AFRTS includes the Radio and Television Production Office, NewsCenter, Television-Audio Support Activity, and the Defense Media Center.

The AFRTS programming hub at March Air Force Base obtains programs from commercial networks and syndicators and sends them to more than 150 AFRTS broadcast centers worldwide through land-based outlets or Navy ships at sea. Some land-based outlets are organized as networks to serve specific geographical areas; most locations, however, consist of small, closed-circuit facilities that provide service to remote and isolated locations where normal over-the-air AFRTS signals are unavailable.

The primary television facility of AFRTS is the American Forces Network (AFN), a worldwide radio and television broadcast entity. Since World War II, AFN's programming has been supported and provided by all major broadcast networks, syndicates, public radio services, and individual stations and program producers throughout the United States. Their coverage of news, professional and collegiate sporting events, and other programs make it possible for AFN to keep America's overseas forces entertained and informed by providing a morale-boosting touch of home.

Entertainment and information programming is acquired and distributed by the AFRTS Broadcast Center based on its scheduling needs, the popularity of programs within the specific DOD audience demographics, and unique interests of military audiences. All religious programs are selected and approved by the Armed Forces Chaplains Board.

AFN News provides a full-time television news and information service. National and international news and information programs from ABC, CBS, CNN, FOX-News, MSNBC, and NBC dominate the schedule. AFN News is the primary means for the AFRTS audience to stay in touch with national and international events and general military information.

AFN Sports provides a full-time television sports and sports news service. Coverage is provided primarily by ABC, CBS, CNN, ESPN, FOX, and NBC. In addition to the most popular American sports (Major League Baseball, NBA Basketball, NFL Football, NFL Hockey, etc.) this service provides a variety of other sporting events based upon the interests of local AFRTS audiences.

AFN Spectrum is an alternate entertainment television channel for the AFRTS audience and represents diverse programming featuring movies, multiple channels (such as PBS, A&E, Discovery Channel, the History Channel, and more), classic series, and cartoons. Packaged as three identical eight-hour wheels, programming is designed to air in each major time zone during prime time.

AFRTS' history can be traced to several small radio stations established by servicemen in Panama, Alaska, and the Philippines near the start of World War II. Following the success and popularity of these small operations, the Armed Forces Radio Service (AFRS) was established by the War Department on May 26, 1942 with the expressed intent of improving troop morale by giving service members a touch of home. The military also used this service to provide a source of information to U.S. servicemen that would counter enemy propaganda (such as that found in the broadcasts of Axis Sally and Tokyo Rose), though the military denied the move was an attempt at counter-propaganda.

Programs during the war proved popular with the troops and were made financially possible through the contributions of radio and film stars who donated their time regularly without charge. Two of the more popular programs were *Command Performance* and *Mail Call*, which featured such stars as Bob Hope, Jack Benny, Clark Gable, Red Skelton, Bing Crosby, Dinah Shore, and the Andrews Sisters. Though major stars did unselfishly give of their time to contribute to the war effort, their careers definitely didn't suffer from the exposure of a somewhat captive audience. By the end of the war, there were about 300 AFRS radio stations operating worldwide (television was not yet available), though the number drastically decreased within four years to about 60. Since its inception, the number of AFRTS stations constantly increases and decreases, depending on the level of U.S. military commitments worldwide.

Even though television had a tremendous impact on American society, it came relatively late to AFRS. The first television broadcasts were aired solely to address morale problems within the Strategic Air Command. Armed Forces Television (AFT) got its start at Limestone Air Force Base in Maine in 1953 and its impact was obvious in helping to reduce AWOLs, court martials, and the divorce rate at this military installation. AFT joined forces with AFRS in 1954 and adopted its current name, AFRTS. In 1968 it was one of the first broadcasters to use satellites for live news and sporting events. AFRTS introduced color broadcasting in the early 1970s.

Although AFRTS insists that its programming is provided without censorship, propaganda, or manipulation, there have been times in its history when this claim has been challenged. During the Vietnam War period (1963–1967), AFRTS was instructed by Defense Secretary Robert McNamara to broadcast United States Information Agency (USIA)-produced news analysis programs, material that was widely recognized as propaganda. However, a more serious challenge to AFRTS's non-interference claims came from broadcast outlets and journalists in Vietnam itself. Though AFRTS and military policy makers maintained that censorship of programming was prohibited, numerous public and internal controversies arose over news, quotes, and specific words and phrases that were kept off the air due to AFRTS guidelines, including the editing of President Johnson's comments that the command believed were inaccurate. Justifications for such restrictions usually were based on troop morale, helping the enemy, or offending the host nation's sensitivities.

In addition to AFRTS, America's service members and DOD employees can watch the Pentagon Channel, presented by AFN (info@pentagonchannel.mil, http://pentagonchannel.mil). The channel features Department of Defense news briefings, military news, interviews with top Administration and Defense officials, and short stories about the work of the military, The Pentagon Channel provides viewers with timely access to military information and news 24 hours a day, 7 day a week. Programs include *Around the Services* (daily half-hour program featuring military news from top Defense officials and the Military Services from around the world); *Pentagon Channel Reports* (one-minute news updates airing at the top of each hour); *Why I Serve* (allows military members the opportunity to share their stories and motivation for serving in the military); *Target* (29-second public-service-announcement spots focusing on consumer information for the military audience); *America Supports You* (highlights corporate and volunteer support of military members and their families); *Pacific Report* (daily news and information from the military's U.S. Pacific Command); *Daily News Update* (daily news reports aired six times a day); *Korea Destinations* (monthly preview of great get away locations in and around the Korean peninsula); *Destinations* (monthly look at Europe's hottest attractions); *Navy Marine Corps News* (a weekly look at the men and women of today's sea service working around the world); *Your Corps* (monthly view of the men and women of the Marine Corps); *Army Newswatch* (bi-weekly report on the men and women of the Army); *Air Force Television News* (bi-weekly magazine show focusing on the men and women of the Air Force); *Studio Five* (weekly interviews of Defense Department leaders about today's top issues); *Army Healthwatch* (focuses on health issues concerning military personnel); *American Forces Network Europe Evening News* (daily news and information from the U.S. European Command); *Focus on the Force* (weekly program highlighting missions, operations, and people of the U.S. military); *On Assignment* (focuses on Air Force issues covering Europe, Southwest Asia, and Africa); *Air Force Prime Time* (a weekly news program covering Air Force events and people for all of Europe, Southwest Asia, and Africa); *AFN Chronicles* (a monthly magazine that focuses on a mix of command topics); and *Eye on Nellis* (a monthly news program focusing on Nellis Air Force Base in Nevada).

Arts & Entertainment Network, 235 East 4th Street, New York, NY 10017; *Telephone*: 212-210-1400; *Fax*: 212-692-9269; *Launch Date*: February 1984; *Broadcast Day*: 24 hours; *Subscribers*: 86,000,000; *Email*: Contact network through its web site; *Web site*: http://www.aande.com; http://www.aetv.com

A&E Television Networks (AETN), a joint venture of the Hearst Corporation, ABC, and NBC, is comprised of the A&E Network, the Biography Channel, the History Channel, History Channel International, and AETN Enterprises. Focusing on biographies, documentaries, and dramas, the A&E Network offers a mix of programming, including original series and movies, documentaries, dramatic specials, feature film presentations, and contemporary performances.

Through its international division (http://www.AETNinternational.com) and with offices in New York and London, AETN channels and programs are available in more than 120 countries to over 200 million TV households in more than 20 languages. Brand channels include the Biography Channel, History Channel, and History Channel International.

The Asia Channel, Inc., 4340 Cross Street, 2nd Floor, Downers Grove, IL 60515; *Telephone*: 630-719-9800; *Fax*: 888-448-9331; *Launch Date*: Fall 2004; *Broadcast Day*: 24 hours; *Email*: Contact channel through its web site; *Web site*: http://www.the asiachannel.com

The Asia Channel is an integrated media brand that combines cable television and the internet to present a modern, contemporary, and positive representation of today's issues to its Asian Pacific American viewing audience. The channel features music, talk shows, variety programs, news, movies, sports, and the arts and is the only American television network that focuses on the 18-45 year old, English speaking, upscale Asian-American viewer.

The Asia Network (http://www.tantv.com) (Planned for future operation)

Asian American Channel (Planned for future operation)

Asian Broadcasting Network (Planned for future operation)

Asianet USA, 9920 Rhode Island Avenue, College Park, MD 20740; *Telephone*: 888-898-0020; *Fax*: 301-345-8160; *Launch Date*: 2003 (in the United States); *Broadcast Day*: 24 hours; *Email*: info@asianetusa.tv; *Web site*: http://www.asianetusa.tv

Asianet USA, the first 24-hour Malaysian television channel in North America, broadcasts current affairs programs, family entertainment shows, news, and sport, all in Malaysian. In addition to North America, its parent company, Asianet, can be seen in the entire Indian sub-continent, Sri Lanka, China, South East Asia, the Persian Gulf, the United Kingdom, and Europe.

AssyriaSat, P.O. Box 4116, Modesto, CA 95352; *Telephone*: 209-538-4130, 209-537-0933; *Fax*: 209-538-2795; *Launch Date*: April 1996; *Broadcast Day*: 24 hours; *Email*: assyriasat@yahoo.com; *Web site*: http://www.bet-nahrain.org/assyriasat/assyriasat.htm

Operated by Bet-Nahrain, AssyriaSat (KBSV-TV 23) uses the tag line "Assyrians for Assyria" and is the first and only Assyrian television station in the world. Bet-Nahrain is an Assyrian educational and cultural organization dedicated to promoting the national aspirations and well being of the Assyrian people and is incorporated in California as a non-profit education and public benefit organization.

Auburn Sports Network, 197 East University Drive, Auburn, AL 36830; *Telephone*: 334-826-2929; *Fax*: 334-826-9151; *Email*: support@aunetwork.com; *Web site*: http://www.aunetwork. com

The Auburn Sports Network, a division of ISP Sports, delivers Auburn radio and television programming, as well as game publications, to thousands of listeners, viewers, and readers each week. The network coordinates and distributes football games, men's basketball and baseball radio broadcasts, a weekly call-in/talk radio show, and weekly television shows focusing on football and men's basketball. The network is also responsible for Auburn's pay-per-view television production, all Auburn home video projects, and is heavily involved in event marketing and licensing activities related to Auburn Athletics.

Auction HD, 200 Jericho Quadrangle, Jericho, NY 11753; *Telephone*: 516-803-6010; *Email*: Contact channel through its web site; *Web site*: http://www.voom.com

Auction HD, a Voom high definition multiplexed channel, broadcasts from the most famous auction houses around the world and showcases collectors and the art of collecting.

The Auto Channel, 332 West Broadway #1604, Louisville, KY 40202; *Telephone*: 502-992-0200; *Broadcast Day*: 24 hours; *Email*: Contact channel through its web site; *Web site*: http:// www.theautochannel.com

A planned service for future operation, The Auto Channel will be dedicated to the automobile, its history, consumer reports, and product evaluations. Programming will also include the business of motorsports, how-to shows, collector car features, and interactive use of the internet.

Automotive Satellite Television Network, 4101 International Parkway, Carrollton, TX 75007; *Telephone*: 800-223-2786, 972-309-4000; *Fax*: 972-309-5260; *Email*: Contact network through its web site; *Web site*: http://www.astn.com

The Automotive Satellite Television Network provides on-demand, over-the-air training to automotive dealerships nationwide that focuses on Sales Management, F & I, Reception, Motivation, Fixed Operations, and e-commerce, among other topics. ASTN delivers nationally- recognized sales trainers, management experts, and fixed operations specialists with the goal of providing dealer training above and beyond that offered solely at the factory or by the automotive manufacturer.

Automotive Television Network, 274 Great Road, Acton, MA 01720; *Telephone*: 800-538-0539, 978-264-9921; *Fax*: 978-264-9547; *Email*: jimbar@globaltelevision.com; *Web site*: http://www.wildaboutwheels.com

Wild About Wheels Media, which operates the Automotive Television Network, serves the Original Equipment Manufacturer and automotive aftermarket industries with automotive television and video productions. To date, the network's three most popular programs are *Wild About Wheels* (a top-rated prime-time series for three years on The Discovery Channel), *Motor Trend Television* (the highest rated show on the Speedvision Network), and *Wheels* (the PBS documentary series covering the history of the automobile).

Azadi TV (Iran), 21045 Superior Street, Chatsworth, CA 91311; *Telephone*: 818-700-0666; *Fax*: 818-700-0577; *Launch Date*: September 2001; *Email*: info@azaditv.com; *Web site*: http://www.azaditv.com

Azadi TV provides a broadcast platform for highlighting Iran's past, present, and future and has the ultimate goal of promoting individual freedoms and collective rights in the country. The network airs social, political and educational programing as well as news and special investigative reports. From an American point of view, this network (and others like it that originate outside the United States but broadcast within America) is unique in its goals of creating and promoting social and legal change within its home country.

Azteca America, 271 Madison Avenue #1000, New York, NY 10017; *Television*: 212-684-6750; *Launch Date*: August 2004; *Broadcast Day*: 24 hours; *Subscribers*: 1,000,000; *Email*: Contact channel through its web site; *Web site*: http://www. aztecaamerica.com

Azteca America's Spanish-language programming originates from TV Azteca in Mexico City and consists mainly of Mexican League Soccer (over 150 games per year), soap operas, boxing, wrestling, reality shows, talent competitions, and movies.

B Mania, 560 Village Boulevard #250, West Palm Beach, FL 33409; *Telephone*: 561-684-5657; *Launch Date*: November 2000; *Broadcast Day*: 24 hours; *Subscribers*: 500,000; *Email*: info@bmania.tv; *Web site*: http://www.bmania.tv

With a primarily male target market, the B Mania network showcases the best of B movies from cult classics to current B movies, Drive-In movie favorites, shorts, and independent B films. The network programs all genres, including horror and monster classics, action, science fiction, war, thrillers, and comedy. Viewers also watch B Mania to find the latest B Movie creations from independent film makers and various film festivals.

B Movie Channel, 10736 Jefferson Boulevard #512, Culver City, CA 90230; *Telephone*: 323-299-9851; *Fax*: 323-296-3635; *Email*: info@b-moviechannel.com; *Web site*: http://www.b-moviechannel.com

The B Movie Channel airs the best (or worst, depending on your point of view) from the rich history of B Movies made around the world. The channel reaches a devoted and somewhat niche audience that aspires to view the quirky, the unusual, or the plain campy.

The traditional definition of a B Movie is a film that was the low-budget backend of a double feature. However, just like A-List Hollywood movies, B Movies have evolved over the years. While there are no specific, mutually agreed upon definitions for what qualifies as a B Movie, a general list would include cult classics (such as *Rocky Horror Picture Show*, *Attack of the Killer Tomatoes*, and *The Toxic Avenger*), Spaghetti westerns, Drive-In movies, and direct-to-video films.

Started in the 1920s, B Movies were the non-feature or "backend" of a double feature (the "B" in B Movies). Functioning as fillers, these films were low budget and were usually a launching pad for aspiring actors and directors. The popularity of B Movies rose dramatically in the 1950s with the advent of the Drive-In theater. When the number of drive-ins reached the thousands, Hollywood produced an assembly line of movies to meet the rising demand, with science fiction and horror movies becoming the most popular. B Movies faded with the decline of the Drive-In but their popularity rebounded in the 1970s with the introduction of cable television, which allowed for a more diverse range of movie ideas to be made and broadcast. The 1990s introduced digital technologies which allowed film makers to produce higher quality films at lower costs.

Baby TV (Planned for future operation)

Bandamax, 5999 Center Drive, Los Angeles, CA 90045; *Telephone*: 310-348-3370; *Fax*:

310-348-3643; *Broadcast Day*: 24 hours; *Subscribers*: 750,000; *Email*: bandamax@televisanetworks.com; *Web site*: http://www.tutv.tv

Bandamax, a brand channel from TuTV, features Spanish-language country music videos from top Hispanic artists in the Grupero, Norteño, Banda, Tex-Mex and Mariachi genres. In addition to music videos, the channel also airs the popular magazine show *Furia Musical*.

BBC America, P.O. Box 6266, Florence, KY 41022; *Telephone*: 859-342-4070; *Broadcast Day*: 24 hours; *Email*: Contact channel through its web site; *Web site*: http://www.bbcamerica.com

Distributed through the Discovery Channel, BBC America broadcasts the best of British television to the United States and Canada, including classic and contemporary dramas, cutting-edge comedies (such as *Monty Python*, *Fawlty Towers*, and *Absolutely Fabulous*), documentaries, and the latest world news, all from a British point of view. The channel strives to bring a global perspective (in entertainment and news) to North American audiences. Brand channels include BBC News (an international news service that provides round-the-clock news from around the world and special features—all from a British perspective) and BBC Kids (educational and entertainment programs aimed at younger viewers).

Be-Well Television, 11 Stanwix Street #2, Lower Lobby, Pittsburgh, PA 15222; 12318 Mossycup Street, Houston, TX 77024; *Telephone*: 412-642-3561; *Fax*: 412-642-3562, 713-722-0972; *Email*: info@bewell-tv.com; *Web site*: http://www.bewell-tv.com

Be-Well Television broadcasts programs that helps its viewing audience live better and healthier lives, including *Why People Don't Heal and How They Can*; *Three Levels of Power and How to Use Them*; *Love, Medicine and Miracles*; *How to Live Between Office Visits*; *Recovering the Soul*; *A Passion for the Possible*; *Qigong for Health*; *The Fountain of Youth*; *Eating Well For Optimum Health*; *Overcoming the Fear of Death*; *Explorations into Consciousness*; *Faces of Hope: Women & Breast Cancer*; *Prostate Health—What Every Man Should Know*; *Women & Heart Disease*; and *HealthBeat* (short 30-second health tips).

Beach TV (Planned for future operation)

Beauty Channel, 814 South Wooster #201, Los Angeles, CA 90035; *Telephone*: 310-652-3812; *Broadcast Day*: 24 hours; *Email*: info@beautychannel.tv; *Web site*: http://www.beauty-channel.com

The Beauty Channel targets the female audience with original programs focusing on beauty tips and healthy living. Programming consists of beauty news, education, and entertainment. The channel also functions as a resource center where both men and women can call to get information on featured and advertised products; enrolling in national beauty schools, hairdressing academies, and other related associations around the country; and on beauty contests locations.

The channel is aimed at home audiences as well as the thousands of people who work in more than 200,000 salons in the United States. The Beauty Channel also addresses the needs of the African-American audience, which annually accounts for about one-third of the total beauty-related revenue in the United States. Belle-TV (http://www.beauty-channel.com/belletv.com) is a woman's beauty magazine on television and is a show designed to interact with the beauty-conscious viewer.

Bikini Television (http://www.bikinitv.com) (Planned for future operation)

Billiard Channel (Planned for future operation)

Bingo TV, Inc., 700 East Main Street #1622, Richmond, VA 23219; *Telephone*: 804-918-1846; *Fax*: 804-562-7503; *Launch Date*:

September 2004; *Broadcast Day*: 24 hours; *Email*: info@bingotv.com; *Web site*: http://www.bingotv.com

Bingo TV is an interactive channel that allows its audience to play in live games through their remote control and set top box. The channel is totally product sponsored. Each game revolves around one advertised product and the bingo pattern needed to win is related to that product (for example, the pattern "T" might relate to winning a Toyota). The channel's hosts physically demonstrate key features of the product, while spokes people and advertisers are given the opportunity to appear on camera with the Bingo TV hosts to discuss the product.

Biography Channel, 235 East 4th Street, New York, NY 10017; *Telephone*: 212-210-1400; *Fax*: 212-210-1340; *Launch Date*: 1998; *Broadcast Day*: 24 hours; *Email*: Contact channel through its web site; *Web site*: http://www.biography.com, http://www.biographychannel.com

A brand channel of the A&E Television Networks, the Biography Channel takes viewers into the world of exceptional people using documentaries, movies, and original short features. The channel was created due to the popularity of A&E's original program *Biography.*

Blab Television Network, 121 South Palafox Place, Pensacola, FL 32501; *Telephone*: 850-432-8982; *Fax*: 850-435-6821; *Broadcast Day*: 24 hours; *Subscribers*: 450,000; *Email*: Contact network through its web site; *Web site*: http://www.blabtv.com

The Blab Television Network produces and airs more than 40 hours of live local talk television programs each week. The remaining schedule consists of re-runs of those shows. Topics and guests vary and include law firms, physician groups, realtors, government groups, the Escambia County Sheriffs Department, the Santa Rosa County Sheriffs Department, the Pensacola City Police, restaurants, automobile dealers, auto repair shops, garden centers, and a diverse mix of local professional, business, civic, cultural, and sporting events.

Black Belt TV / The Martial Arts Network, 880 Calle Primavera, San Dimas, CA 91773; *Telephone*: 909-971-9300; *Fax*: 909-394-0791; *Launch Date*: October 2003; *Broadcast Day*: 24 hours; *Email*: Contact network through its web site; *Web site*: http://www.blackbelttv.com

Black Belt TV broadcasts to the growing number of martial arts fans throughout the United States and its programs include movies, martial arts training and self defense, self-improvement programs, demonstrations, and matches.

Black Education Network, 1165 Allgood Road #13, Marietta, GA 30062; *Telephone*: 770-971-2607; *Broadcast Day*: 24 hours; *Email*: Contact network through its web site; *Web site*: http://www.blackednetwork.com

Planned for future operation, the Black Education Network will provide family entertainment from an African-American perspective and will broadcast movies, documentaries, how-to programs, faith-based fare, talk shows, news, and informational programs. BEN will air some of its programs on the PAX-TV Network, has strong ties with numerous African-American churches and educational institutions, and helps fund educational goals.

Black Entertainment Television, One BET Plaza, 1235 W Street Northeast, Washington, D.C. 20018; *Telephone*: 202-608-2000; *Fax*: 202-608-2519; *Launch Date*: January 1980; *Broadcast Day*: 24 hours; *Subscribers*: 80,000,000; *Email*: michael.lewellen@bet.net; *Web site*: http://www.www.bet.com

Started with only $15,000 and making its initial broadcast one year before MTV began, Black Entertainment Television began by focusing its programming on music videos and brought numerous black artists and music forms to a wider audience. As the network grew and evolved, it de-emphasized music videos and began to expand its broadcast horizon. By 1990 the network had aired several original programs, such as *For the Record* (focusing on the Congressional Black Caucus), *Inside Studio A* (concerts and interviews taped before a live audience), *Personal Diary* (one-on-one interviews with prominent black citizens and leaders), *On Stage* (plays written and performed by black writers and performers), and *Our Voices* (a daily talk show).

Available in the United States, Canada, and the Caribbean, BET is the nation's leading television network providing quality entertainment, music, news, and public affairs programming to the African-American audience. Branded channels include Action Pay-PerView (a satellite-delivered action-genre, pay-per-view movie channel), BET Gospel, BET Hip Hop, BET Jazz, and BET Movies.

When its viewers tired of seemingly endless infomercials, the network responded by launching BET Gospel in 2002. Broadcasting 24 hours a day, this channel showcases the best in gospel talent and features notable and legendary gospel artists through music videos, exclusive in-depth interviews, and concert performances. Also launched in 2002 and broadcasting 24 hours a day, BET Hip Hop aims to be the ultimate source for hip-hop performances and presents popular artists, along with "old school" rap stars to give this channel its distinctive flavor.

BET Jazz: The Jazz Channel (http://www.bet.com/betjazz/) was launched in 1996 and reaches over 10,000,000 subscribers. Airing 24 hours a day, the channel was the nation's first programming service dedicated exclusively to jazz through in-studio performances, documentaries, concert coverage, and celebrity interviews. In addition to jazz, the channel's music genres also features blues, classical, Latin, world, and new age. BET Movies (http://www.betmoviechannel.com), also referred to as Black Starz!, was launched in 1997 and is the first and only movie channel created exclusively to meet the unique entertainment choices of African-American viewers. Broadcasting 24 hours a day, the channel features hosted movie segments, interviews, movie trivia between films, and original programming.

Black Family Channel, 800 Forrest Street Northwest, Atlanta, GA 30318; *Telephone*: 404-350-2509; *Fax*: 404-350-9894; *Launch Date*: Fall 1999; *Broadcast Day*: 24 hours; *Subscribers*: 30,000,000; *Email*: Contact channel through its web site; *Web site*: http://www.mbcnetwork.com

Originally called the Major Broadcasting Cable (MBC) Network, the Black Family Channel provides original, wholesome programming to African-American families and urban communities. Broadcast fare includes black college sports, entertainment, news, movies, information, children's programming, and ministry-based shows.

Black Home Shopping Network (Planned for future operation)

Black Starz! *see* **Black Entertainment Television**

Black Women's TV, 555 South Flower Street #4510, Los Angeles, CA 90071; *Telephone*: 213-920-6783; *Broadcast Day*: 24 hours; *Email*: Contact channel through its web site; *Web site*: http://www.blackwomenstv.com

Planned for future operation, Black Women's TV will target the female African-American viewer with news, fashion shows, and general entertainment programming.

Bloomberg Television, 499 Park Avenue, New York, NY 10022; *Telephone*: 212-893-3331; *Fax*: 202-522-2400; *Launch Date*: January 1995; *Broadcast Day*: 24 hours; *Subscribers*: 30,000,000; *Email*: Contact channel through its web site; *Web site*: http://www.bloomberg.com/media/tv

Bloomberg Television broadcasts up-to-the-minute coverage of international financial news and markets, as well as providing perspective and analysis of current monetary-related events. The channel broadcasts anchor-driven programs and its multi-screen format allows viewers to see current news and information as market conditions change. Throughout the broadcast day, the channel airs its Bloomberg Television Syndicated Reports, which are integrated into local newscasts that provide timely and brief updated market reports.

BlueHighways TV, 111 Shivel Drive, Hendersonville, TN 37075; *Telephone*: 615-264-3292; *Fax*: 615-264-3308; *Launch Date*: 2004; *Broadcast Day*: 16 hours; *Subscribers*: 1,000,000; *Email*: info@bluehighwaystv.com; *Web site*: http://www.bluehighwaystv.com

BlueHighways TV focuses on the people, stories, traditions, and cultures of America and airs a mix of entertainment, folklore, and information programming for audiences interested in all aspects of American life and heritage. The network offers a window into the experiences, music, neighborhoods, art, festivals, and celebrations that define America's culture and character. The name BlueHighways describes the backroads of America when years ago map makers marked the main roads in black and the secondary roads in blue. Well-seasoned travelers know that the main roads are used for speed, but to truly see and experience America, the "blue highways" are the way to go.

Network shows include *Across America* (spotlights the character, beauty, and music of America); *American Journeys* (documentary series on artist communities around the country, life in rural America, community festivals, and historic locations); *An Inside Look* (focuses on the character of a particular community); *BHTV Backroads* (travels the backroads meeting the regular folk of America and showcasing America's roots through special events, festivals and concerts); *BlueHighways in Concert* (broadcasts from intimate concert venues across the country); *Due West* (explores the mystique of the American west); *Forgotten Treasures* (focuses on historic and unique locations); *Great Rivers of America*, *Heart to Heart* (interview and storytelling series featuring the best in classic country music); *Old Country Church* (features the best from traditional, country, and bluegrass gospel music performed live from a 150-year-old church outside Springfield, Missouri); *Smoky Mountain Memories* (variety and music program broadcast live from the heart of the Smoky Mountains in Pigeon Forge, Tennessee from the Classic Country Theater); *Stewards of the Land* (features unique, historical, and famous ranches across the country); *Storytellers Theater* (features the best storytellers from around the country); *The Melting Pot* (focuses on the unique lifestyle, food, music, and language of the various cultures that make up the melting pot of America); *The Red Road* (explores the lives, history, and culture of the American Indian); and *The Sampler* (highlights the root music of America, such as blues, jazz, country, classic country, gospel, and bluegrass, through original performances and music videos).

Boating Channel, 60 Bay Street, Sag Harbor, NY 11963; *Telephone*: 631-725-4440; *Fax*: 631-725-0748; *Launch Date*: November 1998; *Broadcast Day*: 24 hours; *Email*: Contact channel through its web site; *Web site*: http://www.boatingchannel.com

The Boating Channel airs nautical-related programming, including marine news, boating sports, entertainment, information, and educational programs for the recreational and professional boater and cruise vacationer.

Bob Jones Help Network, Center for Educational Technology, Bob Jones University, Greenville, SC 29614; *Telephone*: 800-739-8199, 864-242-5100; *Fax*: 864-271-2775, 870-933-0956; *Email*: info@homesat.com; *Web site*: http://www.homesat.com

The Bob Jones Help Network provides instructional programming aimed at the home-schooling audience and airs educational and teaching programs, Christian living seminars, and cultural shows. The network's programs feature specific topics and are presented in modular formats, which allow those teaching in the home-school environment to pick and choose the subjects to be taught to their children.

Bollywood 4U Movies, 1099 Wall Street West #355, Lyndhurst, NJ 07071; *Telephone*: 201-964-1000; *Fax*: 201-964-1182; *Launch Date*: 1999; *Email*: b4uusa@b4uworld.com; *Web site*: http://www.b4utv.com/movies/

Bollywood 4U originated in the United Kingdom and quickly expanded its operation to the United States. Today the channel is available in more than 100 countries and broadcasts the best of movies made in India.

Boomerang, 1050 Techwood Drive Northwest Atlanta, GA 30318; *Telephone:* 404-885-4205, 404-885-2263; *Fax:* 404-885-2355, 404-885-4312; *Launch Date*: October 1992; *Broadcast Day:* 24 hours; *Email:* Contact the network through its web site; *Web site:* http://www.cartoonnetwork.com.boomerang

Boomerang is the Cartoon Network's first all-cartoon digital network devoted exclusively to classic cartoons and is available to more than 20 million subscribers, in both English and Spanish.

Bosnian-American TV, P.O. Box 6278, Long Island City, NY 11106; *Telephone*: 718-956-8423, 718-392-2632; *Fax*: 718-956-8423; *Launch Date*: May 1999; *Email*: batvny@aol.com; *Web site*: http://www.batv.tv

Bosnian-American TV is the only channel in the United States broadcasting programs aimed at the Bosnian-American television audience. Originally focused at the Bosnian audience in the five boroughs of New York City, the channel now broadcasts throughout the United States and Canada. Programming fare includes entertainment, news, sports, and informational shows.

Boston Catholic Television, 55 Chapel Street, Newtonville, MA 02460; *Telephone*: 617-965-0050; *Email*: bctv@catholictv.org; *Web site*: http://www.catholictv.org

Boston Catholic Television brings the religious message of the Roman Catholic Church to its audience and presents its viewers worship, education, and the church's response to social issues of the day. Programs include *Conversations with Archbishop Sean*; *This is the Day* (a live talk-show); *Caritas Christi Healthlink* (provides updated health information); *Woman to Woman* (spirituality, self-help, and counseling series); *Buena Nueva* (aims its message to the local Spanish-speaking audience); *Remarkable True Stories*; *Exploring Faith*; *The Heart of Prayer*; and *Online* (a youth series that discusses topics relevant to Catholic adolescents).

Box TV — The Boxing Channel, 814 Fourth Street, Secaucus, NJ 07094; *Telephone*: 201-330-9535; *Fax*: 806-209-4330; *Broadcast Day*: 24 hours

Planned for future operation, BoxTV — The Boxing Channel will be the first cable network focused solely on the sport of boxing and will feature daily news, talk shows, original programs, and on-the-scene reporting that will highlight the biggest events in boxing. The channel also plans to broadcast previously un-televised boxing events from the United States and around the world.

Bravo, 30 Rockefeller Plaza, 14th Floor East, New York, NY 10012; 3000 West Alameda Avenue, Burbank, CA 91523; *Telephone*: 212-664-4444; *Fax*: 646-202-4036; *Launch Date*: December 1980; an NBC cable network since 2002; *Subscribers*: 75,000,000; *Broadcast Day*: 24 hours; *Email*: Contact network through its web site; *Web site*: http://www.bravotv.com

Bravo was the first round-the-clock network dedicated to film and the performing arts. Evolving over time, the network now shows arts and entertainment programming, original series, independent and mainstream feature films, theater, dance, music, and documentaries. The channel's popular original series include *Inside the Actors Studio*, *Bravo Profiles*, *Cirque du Soeil Fire Within*, and *Page to Screen*. Bravo has also launched a high-definition network called Bravo HD+. This network is not an HDTV simulcast, but rather has its own schedule and programming.

Bridges TV, 5378 Big Tree Road, Orchard Park, NY 14127; *Telephone*: 716-578-1317; *Fax*: 707-885-0004; *Email*: info@bridgestv.com; *Web site*: http://www.bridges.tv

Planned for future operation, Bridges TV (sometimes called the American Muslim Lifestyle Network) will be the first nationwide American Muslim television network in the United States. Programs are shown in English or with English sub-titles and the network will attempt to introduce Islamic values to American audiences through family-oriented programs, including talk shows, documentaries, short films, children's programming, comedy shows, and movies.

Brief Original Broadcasts, 10901 West Toller Drive, Littleton, CO 80127; *Telephone*: 303-904-7110; *Fax*: 303-904-7115; *Broadcast Day*: 24 hours; *Email*: Contact channel through its web site; *Web site*: http://www.watchbob.com

Targeting its programming primarily to an 18-34 age group American audience with short attention spans, Brief Original Broadcasts airs short-form content programs between one and eight minutes in length and showcases comedy, drama, action, and animation, all commercial-free.

Brigham Young University TV, 2000 Ironton Boulevard, Brigham Young University, Provo, UT 84602; *Telephone*: 866-662-9888, 801-378-8450; *Fax*: 801-378-8478; *Email*: byutv@byu.edu; *Web site*: http://www.byutv.org

Brigham Young University TV offers Church of Jesus Christ of Latter-day Saints programming to an international audience. Most program content derives primarily from the campuses of BYU and the Church of Jesus Christ of Latter-Day Saints, while additional content is provided by independent producers. Programs includes BYU devotionals and forums, Church firesides, General Conference broadcasts and rebroadcasts, BYU Education Week and Women's Conferences, BYU sporting events, BYU musical performances, *Music and the Spoken Word*, *Center Street and Family Times*, BYU documentaries, and BYU discussions and symposia.

Buzztime Entertainment, Inc., 5966 La Place Court #100, Carlsbad, CA 92008; *Telephone*: 760-476-1976; *Fax*: 760-438-3505; *Launch Date*: 1984; *Broadcast Day*: 24 hours; *Email*: Contact channel through its web site; *Web site*: http://www.buzztime.com

Buzztime Entertainment, Inc., a subsidiary of NTN Communications, Inc., is a leading developer and distributor of realtime interactive television entertainment programming. Buzztime is the only 24-hour interactive entertainment broadcast created exclusively for television audiences and features play-along trivia games for players of all interests and ability levels with real-time competition and rankings among households.

C3D Television (Planned for future operation)

Cable Health Network *see* **Lifetime Television**

Cable News Network, One CNN Center, P.O. Box 105366, Atlanta, GA 30348; *Telephone*: 404-827-1500; *Fax*: 404-827-3368; *Launch Date*: June 1980; *Broadcast Day*: 24 hours; *Subscribers*: 90,000,000; *Email*: cnn@cnn.com; *Web site*: http:// www.cnn.com

Founded by Ted Turner and now owned by Time Warner, the Cable News Network was the world's first international cable news network that immediately challenged the "big 3" (ABC, CBS, NBC) and is noted for introducing the concept of 24 hour news coverage. The network is available to more than 90 million U.S. households and over 900,000 U.S. hotel and motel rooms. At the insistence of Ted Turner, the network's anchors, field reporters, and analysts never use the word "foreign," replacing it with "international." This gave the network a feel that all news was important and relevant, regardless from where it originated. The network's reach extends to 16 cable and satellite networks, 12 web sites, two radio networks, and CNN Newsource, the world's most extensively syndicated news service. CNN's combined branded networks and services are available to more than 1 billion people in over 212 countries and territories.

CNN's global reputation was greatly enhanced in 1991 during the Gulf War, when its saturated coverage was carried around the world. However, there was a down-side to the praise. The network obtained much of that coverage through close cooperation with the U.S. government, which led to accusations that it did not attempt to get accurate coverage and was serving as a propaganda outlet. CNN has also been criticized by political and social conservatives for having a liberal bias, and has recently lost market share to the more conservative Fox News Channel. One constant criticism of CNN has been its perceived coverage of international news events from a U.S.-only perspective. As an answer to this complaint, CNN provides several editions of its news service, in response to international demand for news and a desire for less U.S.-centric news.

Regardless of its perceived problems and critics, CNN ranks as one of the most important innovations in cable television during the final quarter of the 20th century. In 1984 CNN first began to earn wide-spread recognition and praise for its nearly round-the-clock coverage of the Democratic and Republican conventions. By 1990 Ted Turner's creation had become the major source for breaking news.

However, the network's rise to respectability and profitability has not come without problems. Initially mocked as the "Chicken Noodle Network" when first launched by then-tiny Turner Broadcasting, the network started its life by losing almost $2 million a month. However, Turner was able to continue his news network by transferring money from his profitable SuperStation (WTBS). As the network grew, CNN established bureaus across the United States, and then around the world, beginning with Rome and London. As a statement of dedication to being a major player in the "news game," Turner created Headline News (a 24-hour-a-day headline news service) in January 1982. At this point CNN took off. By 1985 the network claimed its first profit and had added news bureaus in Bonn, Moscow, Cairo, and Tel Aviv. In the years before the creation of Court TV, CNN televised celebrated trials, such as the Claus von Bulow murder case.

By 1989 CNN was available in 65 countries and aired specialized segments such as a daily entertainment report (*Show Biz Today*) and a nightly evening newscast (*The World Today*). Larry King had also moved his interview show to CNN and became famous for attracting ambitious politicians and infamous celebrities. In 1991, as the only television network in the world operating live from the very beginning of Operation Desert Storm, CNN reported everything the military permitted, from the first bombing of Baghdad to the tank blitz that ended the conflict. The network's coverage was so extensive that political and military leaders admitted that they were getting much of their war information from CNN.

Branded channels include CNN Headline News, CNNfn, Airport Network, AccentHealth, and CNN International. CNN Headline News (http://www.headlinenews.com), a 24-hour international news service, was launched in 1982 and provides updated news every 30 minutes. Each half-hour covers top national and international stories and consumer, sports, and entertainment news, as well as extended weather forecasts. CNNfn (5 Penn Plaza, New York, NY 10001; http://www.money.cnn.com; http://www.money.com) was launched in 1995 and delivered updated, comprehensive business news and personal finance programming each weekday from Wall Street and throughout the world. The channel also offered viewers in-depth personal finance programming, interview shows, and call-in programs. CNNfn was the first network to broadcast business programming throughout prime time. However, the channel was discontinued by CNN in late 2004 due to continuous low ratings.

Launched in January 1992 the Airport Network (also called the CNN Airport Nctwork, (http://www.cnn.com/airport) is the only satellite-delivered television service available to national and international air travelers. Available at more than 1,800 gate areas at 39 airports, the network provides 24-hour a day CNN-produced news and live breaking stories, business and financial reports, sports updates, weather, lifestyle and general interest segments, and entertainment and travel features. Launched in October 1995, CNN is the exclusive programming supplier for AccentHealth (http://www.accent health.com), which delivers preventive health-care information to doctors' waiting rooms. Reaching more than 17 million patients in 11,000 doctors' waiting rooms, the network airs preventive health-care information, sports medicine, parenting tips, and nutrition and safety information.

Launched in 1985, CNN International (http://www.cnn.com/cnni) airs global news and information, 24 hours a day. The channel provides live, breaking world news coverage in addition to global business, sports, features, and weather. CNN International can be seen in more than 165 million television households in more than 200 countries. The network serves seven separate regions: Europe/Middle East/Africa (September 1985), Asia Pacific (August 1989), South Asia (2000), CNNj (Japan) (2003), Latin America (1991), USA/fn (2000), and North America (2000). International broadcast entities also include CNN en Español (1997), CNN en Español — Mexico (1999), CNN+ (1999), n-tv (1992), CNN Deutschland (1997), and CNN Türk (1999).

Cable-Satellite Public Affairs Network, 400 North Capitol Street NW #650, Washington, D.C. 20001; *Telephone*: 202-737-3220; *Launch Date*: March 1979; Broadcast Day: *24 hours*; *Subscribers*: 90,000,000; *Email*: viewer@c-span.org; *Web site*: http://www.c-span.org

The Cable-Satellite Public Affairs Network was created by the cable television industry to provide gavel-to-gavel coverage of the U.S. House of Representatives. As the network grew and evolved, its coverage expanded to include the U.S. Senate and other public events from Washington, D.C., across the country, and around the world. C-SPAN provides live unedited coverage of events as they unfold, with no editing, commentary, or analysis. Its round-the-clock programming consists of live coverage of congressional hearings, news conferences, public policy and author events, viewer call-in programs, speeches, international governmental activities, publishing industry events, and public affairs activities. These broadcasts also provide government officials and others who influence public policy a direct conduit to the audience without having their views filtered, analyzed, or "spun." The network's telephone call-in programs allow audience viewers direct access to elected officials, other decision makers, and journalists.

C-SPAN is a private, nonprofit public affairs network whose funding is derived directly by the fees paid by America's cable and satellite television companies to carry its signal. No tax dollars are used to finance the network's operation. C-SPAN's various web sites offer live video coverage of congressional proceedings, public affairs events, and call-in programs. Their web sites also provide updated programming schedules, reporter analysis of legislation, searchable archives of public affairs events, C-SPAN in the Classroom Online, and public affairs linked to related web sites.

As its coverage expanded, the network created C-SPAN2 and C-SPAN3 to cover specific events not handled by C-SPAN. C-SPAN2, launched in June 1986, was created to cablecast live sessions of the U.S. Senate in its entirety. The network's round-the-clock programming complements the original C-SPAN network by offering more viewing alternatives to cable TV audiences interested in public affairs programming. In 1998 the network launched *Book TV*, a 48-hour weekend programming block devoted to nonfiction books, libraries, book fairs, and the publishing industry. C-SPAN3, launched in January 2001, expands the basic C-SPAN coverage even further and provides live broadcasts of national events on weekdays and long-form history programming overnight and on weekends.

Milestone dates in C-SPAN's history include: October 7, 1980 (live call-in programs begin airing that allow viewers direct access to public policy makers); September 13, 1982 (24-hour-a-day programming begins); July/August 1984 (live, uninterrupted coverage of the Democratic and Republican National Conventions are broadcast for the first time); November 1985 (coverage expands to include the Canadian House of Commons); November 9, 1988 (the United States Information Agency transmits C-SPAN to 90 countries via WORLDNET, creating the first global satellite television network); November 21, 1989 (regular coverage of the British House of Commons begins); November 1, 1993 (the C-SPAN School Bus (a moving exhibit) is launched in Washington, D.C. and quickly becomes a favorite to school children); June 1997 (the C-SPAN School Bus travels to Hawaii, marking the 50th state the bus visited since its launch in 1993); and December 19, 1998 (live coverage of the House impeachment vote of President Clinton is aired).

Cable Science Network (CSN)— Planned for future operation and using the Cable-Satellite Public Affairs Network as a model of operation, the Cable Science Network will be a 24/7 channel devoted exclusively to science. The network will broadcast science-related programming, including interviews, debates, educational programs, scientific meetings and organizations, news, documentaries, classroom teachings, Congressional hearings, archived footage, and lectures.

California Channel, 1121 L Street #110, Sacramento, CA 95814; *Telephone*: 916-444-9792; *Fax*: 916-444-9812; *Launch Date*: February 1991; *Broadcast Day*: 33.5 hours per week; *Subscribers*: 5,800,000; *Email*: Contact channel through its web site; *Web site*: http://www.calchannel.com

The California Channel is an independent, non-profit public affairs cable network governed by California's cable television industry, and modeled after the national Cable-Satellite Public Affairs Network service. The channel's primary mission is to provide Californians direct access to gavel-to-gavel proceedings of the California Assembly and Senate, and other forums where public policy is discussed, debated, and decided, all without editing, commentary, or analysis and with a balanced presentation of viewpoints.

Additionally, the channel strives to: provide an electronic bridge between Californians and their elected officials; educate civic leaders and citizens about the functions and activities of state government; provide elected and appointed officials and others who influence public policy a direct conduit to Californians without filtering or otherwise distorting their points of view; and provide Californians, through interactivity, direct access to elected officials, and other decision makers on a frequent and open basis.

California Community College Satellite Network, 365 South Rancho Santa Fe Road #203, San Marcos, CA 92078; *Telephone*: 760-744-1150; *Fax*: 760-510-8340; *Email*: Contact network through its web site; *Web site*: http://www.cccsat.org

The California Community College Satellite Network (CCCSAT) is an educational distribution network dedicated to assisting California Community Colleges in providing access to academic and vocational instruction as well as relevant information and entertainment. The network serves over 2,500,000 students, 85,000 faculty and staff, and delivers digital broadcasts to affiliate locations including every California Community College, college district office, and the CCC Chancellor's Office. CCCSAT is a statewide, grant-funded initiative established by the California Community College Chancellor's Office in 1997 to advance distance learning and support the mission of the California Community College system.

California POST Television Network, 1601 Alhambra Boulevard, Sacramento, CA 95816; *Telephone*: 916-227-3913; *Fax*: 916-227-4011; *Email*: cptn@post.ca.gov; *Web site*: http://www.post.ca.gov/training/cptn/default.asp

The California POST Television Network delivers in-service training videos to law enforcement agencies in the California POST program, including *Case Law Today*, a monthly law and legal training series. The network also features an assortment of short training and information videos.

The Commission on Peace Officer Standards and Training (POST) was established by the Legislature in 1959 to set minimum selection and training standards for California law enforcement. POST funding comes from the Peace Officers' Training Fund, which receives monies from the State Penalty Assessment Fund, which in turn receives monies from penalty assessments on criminal and traffic fines. Thus, the POST program is funded primarily by persons who violate the laws that peace officers are trained to enforce. No tax dollars are used to fund the POST program.

Canal 24 Horas, 1100 Ponce de Leon Boulevard, Coral Gables, FL 33134; *Telephone*: 305-444-4402; *Launch Date*: June 1999; *Broadcast Day*: 24 hours; *Email*: Contact channel through its web site; *Web site*: http://www.rtve.es

Canal 24 Horas is a news network modeled after Cable News Network's Headline News, with 30-minute broadcast blocks that are updated continuously. Each half hour presents national and international breaking news, economy, sports, and weather.

Career Entertainment Television, 10573 West Pico Boulevard #168, Los Angeles, CA 90064; *Telephone*: 310-277-2388; *Fax*: 310-277-1037; *Broadcast Day*: 24 hours; *Email*: info@ce.tv; *Web site*: http://www.ce.tv

Career Entertainment Television focuses its programming on work and work-related topics, all with a goal of educating and entertaining its viewers. Popular programs include *Destination Dream Job* (advises viewers how to identify the jobs they really want and how to get them); *Dressed for Success* (each episode shows a complete makeover for two viewers, to include an image consultant, a make-up artist, a stylist, a job recruiter, and a career coach); *For This I Went to College?* (follows those coming out of college and entering the job market); *I Get Paid for This* (stories about some of the coolest and most unusual jobs in the world); *Get a Job!* (a game show where the winner's prize is an actual job); and *Dipping the Pen* (the ins and outs of office romances). In addition to original programming, the network also broadcasts interviews, 15-second "hire me" videos throughout the day, movies, news, infotainment, and documentaries.

Caribbean Visions Television, 572 Lawton Street #1300, Atlanta, GA 30310; *Telephone*: 404-753-6626; *Launch Date*: September 2004; *Broadcast Day*: 2 hours a day, 7 days a week; *Email*: Contact channel through its web site; *Web site*: http:// www.caribbeanvisions.com

Caribbean Visions Television provides coverage of events taking place in Caribbean communities, including news, sports, entertainment, travel, and other variety programming features.

Cartoon Network, 1050 Techwood Drive NW, Atlanta, GA 30318; *Telephone*: 404-885-4205, 404-885-2263; *Fax*: 404-885-2355,

404-885-4312; *Launch Date*: October 1992; *Broadcast Day*: 24 hours; *Subscribers*: 86,000,000; *Email*: Contact the network through its web site; *Web site*: http://www.cartoonnetwork.com

Originally created by Ted Turner's TBS and now owned by the Time Warner Company, the Cartoon Network offers more cartoons and more characters (over 2,000) than any other network and draws its shows from the world's largest cartoon library (including more than 14,000 Warner Bros., MGM, Hanna-Barbera titles) and its own original series and shorts. The network is available in over 15 languages in 140 countries to more than 150 million households throughout the world, including more than 85 million in the United States.

Opened in 2000, the network owns the 45,000-square-foot Cartoon Network Studios in Burbank, California that is used to produce original animated programming. Its web site is the top-rated kid's entertainment site in the world. The Cartoon Network is the exclusive television home to DC Comics characters Batman and Superman and airs such popular action series as *Justice League*, *Batman: The Animated Series*, *The Adventures of Batman & Robin*, *The New Batman/Superman Adventures*, and *Superman*.

Adult Swim (http://www.adultswim.com) is the Cartoon Network's late-night fare for adult-oriented animation. The popularity of this broadcasting block has substantially increased the Cartoon Network's viewing adult audience in the 18-34 age group. On June 17, 2003 Adult Swim garnered, for the first time in the network's history, an audience of more than one million viewers with its broadcast of the prime-time animated series, *Family Guy*, which became the network's most popular program among young adults. Boomerang (http://www.cartoonnetwork.com/boomerang) is the first all-cartoon digital network devoted exclusively to classic cartoons and is available to more than 20 million subscribers in both English and Spanish.

Casa Club TV (House Club TV), Two Alhambra Plaza, 2800 Ponce de Leon Boulevard #1320, Coral Gables, FL 33134; *Telephone*: 305-445-4350; *Fax*: 305-445-2058; *Launch Date*: July 1997; *Broadcast Day*: 24 hours; *Subscribers*: 3,250,000; *Email*: webmaster@ casaclubtv.com; *Web site*: http://www.casaclubtv.com

Casa Club TV's programming focuses on home improvement, renovation tips, cooking, gardening, and lifestyle topics.

Casino & Gaming Television, 3969 Howard Hughes Parkway #500, Las Vegas, NV 89109; *Telephone*: 702-990-3913; *Broadcast Day*: 24 hours; *Email*: Contact channel through its web site; *Web site*: http://www.cgtv.com

Planned for future operation, Casino & Gaming Television (CGTV) will be the first and only 24-hour entertainment and information cable network devoted to celebrating the gaming industry and lifestyle. CGTV covers international casino and gaming action, from the epicenter of Las Vegas casinos to the elite poker tables of the French Riviera. The channel's programs focus on the world of sports betting, casino management, VIP gamblers and whales, gaming tables, slots, restaurants, shows, nightclubs, and nightlife.

Programs on CGTV will include *CGTV SportsBook* (a preview of the upcoming weekend's gaming action from the world of sports); *CGTV University* (airs all the channel's instructional shows that are aimed at increasing viewer understanding of various gambling games); *CGTV Showcase* (features current and vintage entertainment from the showrooms of Las Vegas, Reno, Atlantic City, and other gaming resorts around the world); *CGTV Gaming Central* (informational program covering topics that are relevant to the sports bettor); *CGTV Night Life* (on-location show featuring the hottest nightclubs in gaming casinos around the world); and *Great Casinos of the World* (a travelogue program that visits the world's great casinos and resorts).

Catholic Community Television Network, St. Paul's Church, 1330 Sunshine Avenue, Leesburg, FL 34748; *Telephone*: 352-787-6354; *Email*: Contact network through its web site; *Web site*: http://www.cctn.org

Using television and internet technologies, the Catholic Community Television Network's mission is to proclaim the Good News of Jesus Christ to the world; promote, educate, and celebrate the practices in the Roman Catholic Church; highlight what various Roman Catholic Church Communities are doing to spread the message of Christ; encourage understanding and tolerance from its viewers concerning the teachings of the Roman Catholic Church; provide open awareness of other Christian and Non-Christian beliefs; and show its viewers the teachings of the Roman Catholic Church.

Channel One, 6203 B. Variel Avenue, Woodland Hills, CA 91367; *Telephone*: 800-805-5131, 818-226-6200; *Fax*: 818-347-4757; *Launch Date*: January 1989 (initial phase); *Email*: info@channelonetv.com; *Web site*: http://www.channelone.com

Channel One is a twelve-minute television news program targeted to teenagers and distributed via satellite to over 12,000 middle and high schools across the United States each school day. Reaching an audience of over eight million students, from its inception the channel has been a controversial educational program tool, primarily because two minutes of each program are devoted to advertising.

Originally produced by Whittle Communications, Inc. in Knoxville, Tennessee, Channel One began its pilot phase in January 1989; however, in 1995, Whittle Communications, Inc. ceased operations and sold the channel to K-III Communications Corporation, a large diversified communications company focused on education, information, and magazine publishing.

In order for a school to receive Channel One, it must sign a three-year agreement to carry the program in its entirety each school day, and to make the telecast available to at least 90 percent of the student body. In return, each school receives a satellite dish (TVRO), two videocassette recorders, one 19-inch television set per classroom, and all of the necessary cabling. No money is exchanged.

The channel's news content is geared to teenagers and delivered by anchors and reporters typically in their early to mid–20s. Program content includes the latest news as well as week-long series for more in-depth topics such as jobs, drug abuse, science, technology, and international politics. The channel's five educational goals are to enhance cultural literacy; promote critical thinking; provide a common language and shared experience; provide relevance and motivation; and strengthen character and build a sense of responsibility. In addition to the daily Channel One news program, schools are also provided with approximately 250 hours per school year of non-commercial educational programming that is designed to serve as a supplemental teaching tool to support existing curricula.

Channel One Russia Worldwide Network, 4100 East Dry Creek Road, Suite A300, Centennial, CO 80122, 8900 Liberty Circle, Englewood, CO 80122; *Telephone*: 310-826-4777, 303-712-5400, 720-853-2933; *Fax*: 310-447-7906, 303-268-5465; *Broadcast Day*: 24 hours; *Email*: ininfo@i-channel.com; *Web site*: http://www.i-channel.com

The Channel One Russia Worldwide Network, available in the United States through the International Channel, is a Russian-language channel specially tailored for Russian communities throughout the United States. The channel originates from Moscow and airs dramas, movies, news, children's programming, sports, talk shows, family entertainment, science, and nature programs.

China Central Television, 4100 East Dry Creek Road, Suite A300, Centennial, CO 80122, 8900 Liberty Circle, Englewood, CO 80122; *Telephone*: 310-826-4777, 303-712-

5400, 720-853-2933; *Fax*: 310-447-7906, 303-268-5465; *Email*: ininfo@i-channel.com; *Web site*: http://www.i-channel.com

China Central Television, available in the United States through the International Channel, reaches more than 240 million households in its homeland and is the country's only national broadcasting network. CCTV-4, a service of CCTV, was created to keep the 50 million Chinese living outside of China informed of news from their homeland.

The Chinese Channel, 230 North Washington Street #408, Rockville, MD 20850; *Telephone*: 301-468-9392; *Fax*: 301-881-3838; *Broadcast Day*: 24 hours; *Email*: info@wcl.net; *Web site*: http://www.wcl.net

Owned by the World Chinese League and planned for future operation, The Chinese Channel will air Chinese-language programming.

Chop TV (Planned for future operation)

Christian Broadcasting Network, 977 Centerville Turnpike, Virginia Beach, VA 23463; *Telephone*: 804-579-7000; *Launch Date*: January 1960; *Broadcast Day*: 24 hours; *Email*: Contact network through its web site; *Web site*: http://www.cbn.org

The Christian Broadcasting Network (CBN) grew from the vision of one man, Pat Robertson, who started in 1960 with a UHF station in Portsmouth, Virginia that he bought for only $37,000. While many religious broadcasters of the time relied on sermons to convey their message, Robertson developed a talk show approach on his station, in which interviews, music, teaching, prayer, and healing were all provided in a program format. CBN's first telethon to raise funds in the fall of 1963 was named The 700 Club because Robertson asked for 700 people to pledge $10 a month to support the new station and keep it on the air. The name stuck and became the title of his religious talk show, which is still being broadcast.

Three innovations adopted by CBN helped the fledgling network grow rapidly to become one of the biggest religious broadcasting networks in the world: the use of the telephone to provide ongoing interactive contact with viewers, which has since grown to more than sixty counseling centers across the nation to respond to calls 24 hours a day; following the lead of Home Box Office and Cable News Network, the network built its own satellite operation instead of relying on network affiliate stations; and providing 24-hour religious programming to the nation's growing network of cable stations, which became the impetus for the network's rapid growth.

In 1980, *The 700 Club* changed its format from an all religious show to a contemporary talk program with news and current events, getting its feeds from news bureaus in Virginia Beach, Washington DC, and later in Jerusalem. One of its programs, *Another Life*, was a daily soap opera that followed the adventures of a Christian family and ran for 800 episodes from 1981 to 1984 and still airs in many countries around the world. The network's most successful productions at the time were two animated bible story series, *Superbook* and *Flying House*. These series were syndicated worldwide and when broadcast in Russia and the Ukraine in 1991 produced more than eleven million requests for gospel literature.

Current program content on *The 700 Club* stresses a biblical world view, based on the belief that there exists a set of moral absolutes revealed in scripture that should be the foundation of society's institutions, laws, and public policy. During the 1980s, the growth of religious television and the resurgence of the New Religious Right in American politics went hand in hand and eventually led Robertson to launch an unsuccessful bid for the Republican presidential nomination in 1986, in which he was defeated by George Bush.

Christian Television Network Detroit, 15565 Northland Drive #900W, Southfield, MI, 48075; *Telephone*: 248-559-4200; *Email*:

info@ctnusa.org; *Web site*: http://www. ctnusa.org

Broadcasting on Sky Angel (http://www.skyangel.com), Christian Television Network Detroit originates from the heart of "Motor City" and is a cross-denominational Christian urban network with a focus on the African American Christian family. The network features teaching and ministry, call-in talk shows, family and children's programs, gospel films, classic movies, and gospel music. The mission of the network is to communicate the Gospel of Jesus Christ by producing inspirational engaging interactive Christian programming and wholesome family-oriented entertainment.

Chronicle DTV, 53 West 36th Street #203, New York, NY 10018; *Telephone*: 212-337-9700; *Launch Date*: September 2002; *Broadcast Day*: 24 hours; *Subscribers*: 1,000,000; *Email*: Contact channel through its web site; *Web site*: http://www. chronicledtv.com

Chronicle DTV, Inc. is a digital television programming network that broadcasts a mix of feature-length non-fiction and documentary programs. Although many networks offer documentary programming, Chronicle DTV tries to separate itself from the others by focusing only on real life stories, as opposed to history, travel, health, science, courtroom forensics, and contemporary political issues.

Church Channel, 2823 West Irving Boulevard, Irving, TX 75061; *Telephone*: 800-735-5542; *Launch Date*: January 2002; *Broadcast Day*: 24 hours; *Subscribers*: 11,000,000; *Email*: Contact network through its web site; *Web site*: http://www.churchchannel.tv, http://www.tbnnetworks.com

A digital network owned and operated by Trinity Broadcasting Network, the Church Channel features round-the-clock (live and tape-delayed) church service programs from Protestant, Catholic, and Jewish faith groups.

Cinemax, 1100 Avenue of the Americas, New York, NY 10036; *Telephone*: 212-512-1000; *Fax*: 212-512-1182; *Launch Date*: August 1980; *Broadcast Day*: 24 hours; *Subscribers*: 40,000,000; *Email*: Contact network through its web site; *Web site*: http://www.cinemax.com

Cinemax was launched by Home Box Office as an alternative choice and has developed into a premium service that broadcasts movies, documentaries, specials, and sporting events (especially boxing). As it grew and expanded, Cinemax developed several multiplexed channels, all showing specific program genres aimed at targeted audiences. These channels include @Max, @ Max Choice, 5StarMax, 5StarMax Choice, ActionMax, MartialMax, MoreMax, MoreMax Choice, MoreMax Vanguard, OuterMax, ThrillerMax, WMax, and WMax Choice.

Classic Arts Showcase, The Lloyd E. Rigler — Lawrence E. Deutsch Foundation, P.O. Box 828, Burbank, CA 91503; *Telephone*: 323-878-0283; *Fax*: 323-878-0329; *Launch Date*: May 1994; *Broadcast Day*: 24 hours; *Subscribers*: 60,000,000; *Email*: casmail@earthlink.net; *Web site*: http://www.classicartsshowcase.org

Classic Arts Showcase is a free cable television channel designed to bring the classic arts experience to the largest audience possible by providing video clips of the arts in hopes that these samples tempt the viewer to support the arts in their community. Broadcast fare includes video samplings of animation, architectural art, ballet, chamber and choral music, dance, folk art, museum art, musical theater, opera, orchestral, recital, solo instrumental, solo vocal, and theatrical performances, as well as classic films and archival documentaries. CAS is commercial-free, broadcasts to most of North and South America, and is available free of charge to cable companies and broadcasters.

Since CAS is a non-commercial service, many broadcast networks and cable companies do not provide its programming. If not already available on cable or through local broadcast outlets (the network's web site displays all areas of coverage and provides times of broadcast), viewers can find the network's programming in a variety of ways, including local community channels (such as local public, educational and government community access channels), PBS, local satellite providers, closed circuit systems (hotels, libraries, schools, hospitals), satellite dish (able to receive C-Band satellite signals), Direct-TV, or through local arts organizations (since CAS was created solely to help increase local ticket sales).

CAS is completely funded by the Lloyd E. Rigler — Lawrence E. Deutsch Foundation, a major arts supporter that created CAS to inspire viewers to go out and see live performances in their own communities and to help build a future audience for the arts. The network does not produce original material, but edits a new eight-hour show (broken down into one-hour blocks) every week that features about 150 clips. Since the mission of CAS is to present a wide range of arts each hour, the network's clips are kept short (normally not more than five minutes in length) and does not show entire concerts or full-length films. The show is then sent out three times a day via satellite to North and South America, the Bahamas, and Hawaii. Most of the clips come from record companies, but other sources include public and private archives, the Lincoln Center for the Performing Arts, the National Gallery of Art, and the Library of Congress.

Classic Sports Network (now called **ESPN Classic**) *see* **Entertainment Sports Programming Network**

Classics HD, 200 Jericho Quadrangle, Jericho, NY 11753; *Telephone*: 516-803-6010; *Email*: Contact channel through its web site; *Web site*: http://www.voom.com

Classics HD is a high definition multiplexed channel from Voom that broadcasts all-classic-movies, all the time.

Classified Channel TV, 1000 Universal Studios Plaza, Building 22-A, Orlando, FL 32819; *Telephone*: 407-224-6847; *Email*: info@classifiedchannel.tv; *Web site*: http://www.classifiedchannel.tv/

Planned for future operation, Classified Channel TV is a photo-classified cable channel that enables local businesses to reach a very targeted television and web audience. The channel serves the local-area small-to-medium sized business owner.

CN8 — The Comcast Network, 1500 Market Street, 28th Floor, West Tower, Philadelphia, PA 19102; *Telephone*: 215-981-7750, 215-981-7782; *Fax*: 215-981-8420; *Launch Date*: October 1997; *Broadcast Day*: 24 hours; *Subscribers*: 6,500,000; *Email*: Contact network through its web site; *Web site*: http://www.cn8.com

Created by Comcast Cable Communications, CN8 — The Comcast Network is a news, talk, sports, and entertainment cable network that provides locally-produced programming in four main areas: live, interactive television; regional news; entertainment; and coverage of high school, college and professional sports.

Collecting Channel, 4 Brussels Street, Worcester, MA 01610; *Telephone*: 508-791-6710; *Email*: Contact channel through its web site; *Web site*: http://www. collectingchannel.com

Owned by Sales Online Direct, the Collecting Channel is a broadcast and online entertainment and information entity that focuses on the international collecting market. The channel produces *Treasures in Your Home: The World of Collecting*, which was the first nightly prime-time access television series.

Collectors Channel, 67 River Street, Box 702, Hudson, MA 01749; *Telephone*: 508-864-4498; 508-788-5474; *Email*: Contact channel through its web site; *Web site*: http://www.allcollectors.com

The Collectors Channel offers educational and shopping programming for collectors and vendors of eclectic and investment-quality collectible merchandise. Shopping categories include antiques and vintage collectibles, primary and secondary markets of modern collectibles, collector's books and supplies, news, auctions, and events.

College Entertainment Network (now called **Ruckus Network**)

College Sports Television, Chelsea Piers, Pier 62 #316, New York, NY 10011; *Telephone*: 212-342-8700; *Fax*: 212-342-8899; *Launch Date*: April 2003; *Broadcast Day:* 24 hours; *Subscribers*: 15,000,000; *Email*: fans@cstv.com; *Web site*: http:// www.cstv.com; http:// www.collegesports.com

College Sports Television is the first 24-hour college sports network and since its inception has televised more than 2,500 hours of original programming, including men's and women's basketball, baseball, hockey, soccer, lacrosse, and volleyball. The channel's game broadcasts, studio shows, and original programs have highlighted more than 1,000 colleges and universities across all NCAA divisions and the NAIA. The network televises regular season and championship event coverage from every major collegiate athletic conference and televises nine NCAA Championships.

College Television Network, 1515 Broadway, 23rd Floor, New York, NY 10036; *Telephone*: 212-258-8000, 212-846-4629; *Fax*: 212-846-1893; *Broadcast Day*: 24 hours; *Email*: Contact network through its web site; *Web site*: http://www.mtvu.com

Owned and operated by Music Television (MTV), the College Television Network airs music and programs from today's college stations throughout the United States.

Colours TV, 5929 East 38 Avenue, Denver, CO 80207; *Telephone*: 303-331-0339; *Fax*: 303-370-2032; *Email*: info@ colourstv.com; *Web site*: http://www.colourstv.com

A production of Black Star Communications, an African-American owned non-profit corporation formed for civic, charitable, and educational purposes, Colours TV is a multi-cultural television network that airs original series, movies, short films, documentaries, and sports, all bringing a positive image of people of color. Sample programs include *SwitchplayTV* (an hour-long video and sketch comedy show that features the latest hip/hop, R&B, and pop music videos); *Black Life in Japan* (reports on how urban American culture is making an impact on Japan and how well African-American entrepreneurs fare in the world's second largest economy); and *Treasures from Colours* (displays collections of art, decorative objects, and collectibles by artists of color).

Columbia Broadcasting System, 51 West 52nd Street, New York, NY 10019; *Telephone*: 212-975-4321; *Fax*: 212-975-4516; *Launch Date*: September 1927 (as the Columbia Phonograph Broadcasting Company), January 1929 (under its current name); *Broadcast Day*: 24 hours; *Email*: Contact network through its web site; *Web site*: http://www.cbs.com

The Columbia Broadcasting System (CBS), traditionally referred to as the "Tiffany Network," began its broadcasting life because of a snub. In 1927 David Sarnoff was assembling a roster of stars for the new NBC radio network and, for a variety of reasons, did not use any talent represented by agent Arthur Judson. Infuriated at the perceived insult, Judson created his own network and called it United Independent Broadcasters (UIB), which very quickly merged with the Columbia Phonograph Company. The new network went on the air September 18, 1927 as the Columbia Phonograph Broadcasting Company and broadcast to 47 radio stations. Within a year, heavy monetary losses forced the sale of the radio network to Jerome Louchheim and Ike and Leon Levy, who was engaged to William Paley's sister. Paley purchased the fledgling network, which by this time had only 22 affiliates, for $400,000 on January 18, 1929 and renamed it the Columbia Broadcasting System.

Although a relative newcomer to the broadcasting game, Paley soon showed himself up to the challenge. One of his first steps that eventually would ensure the success of the network was to offer affiliates free programming in exchange for an option on advertising time. In an effort to grab a higher profile, the radio network soon signed well-known singers such as Bing Crosby, Kate Smith, and Morton Downey. Paley's plan to sign major talent soon unraveled, however, when NBC began luring the stars away from CBS, after they had gained recognition and a following.

Paley had better luck retaining talent in his news division. Initially, he was so desperate for programming that he allowed CBS to be used by several demagogues, such as Father Charles Coughlin. However, by 1931 he had terminated Coughlin's broadcasts and began building a first-rate news division, under the supervision of former New York Times editor Edward Klauber and ex-United Press reporter Paul White. The network struck gold when Klauber assigned a young Edward R. Murrow to London as director of European talks in 1937. The reporting of these events in Europe became the forerunner of *The CBS World News Roundup*. During World War II, Murrow assembled a team of reporters who would later go on to successful broadcast careers of their own. Known as "Murrow's Boys," this team included Eric Sevareid, Charles Collingwood, Howard K. Smith, Winston Burdett, Richard K. Hottelet, and Larry LeSueur.

With the news division on solid ground and garnering the network unprecedented credibility, Paley again focused on talent and raided rival NBC by signing such stars as Jack Benny, Red Skelton, and Burns and Allen. He also upstaged NBC in what it thought was its domain, technology, when his CBS Research Center developed the Long Playing phonograph recording technique and color television.

Surprisingly, with all his radio success, Paley was hesitant to enter broadcast television. Under pressure from Dr. Frank Stanton (who Paley had appointed CBS president in 1946) and the obvious growing popularity of television, Paley began increasing CBS investment in the new medium. His strategy worked as the network dominated audience ratings for almost 20 years due to several factors: the talent the network had raided from NBC was extremely popular; CBS had spent years cultivating its own in-house talent; and the network aired what would later be considered classic programs, such as *I Love Lucy*, *The Ed Sullivan Show*, *The Arthur Godfrey Show*, and *Gunsmoke*.

However, amidst the successes were some troubling signs. CBS found itself dubbed the "Communist Broadcasting System" by political and social conservatives during the McCarthy era. Bowing to this pressure, the network caved and embarrassed itself by requiring loyalty oaths of its staff and by hiring a former FBI agent as head of a loyalty clearance office. Murrow, considered a paragon of integrity and professionalism, to his ever-lasting shame, tolerated (and some would say, supported) the loyalty oaths.

However, perception (and reality) quickly changed and CBS regained some much-needed credibility with Murrow's famous March 9, 1954 *See It Now* broadcast which investigated Senator McCarthy and, combined with other political and social forces, basically put an end to his political career. While considered a high point in the network's history, many CBS executives tired of Murrow's power and his penchant for controversy. In 1961, he resigned (some would say forced out) and went on to run the United States Information Agency.

Even though the news division had proved its worth and considered itself the crown jewel of the network, it soon became obvious that it was subordinate to the ever-demanding entertainment values of the company, a trend highlighted at the end of the 1950s by the quiz show scandals. This entertainment priority originated at the top as Paley became more and more interested in profits and began to view the news division as a financial drain (it is said that he once dictated that the sole purpose of a network existing at all was to "sell more soap"). One undeniably clear sign of the changing trend occurred when the network aired reruns of *I Love Lucy* instead of the 1966 Senate hearings on the Vietnam War. This incident forced Fred Friendly (a close friend of Murrow and the CBS News division president) to resign.

This entertainment trend continued into the 1960s when, despite receiving almost universal criticism and bad reviews, *The Beverly Hillbillies*, *Green Acres*, and *Petticoat Junction* were CBS's biggest hits. The 1970s, however, saw a dramatic shift away from seemingly mindless programs when the network aired a series of controversial but very popular sitcoms, such as *All in the Family*, *The Mary Tyler Moore Show*, and *M*A*S*H*. Even though the level of entertainment had been elevated, it is important to understand that the change came about primarily because the network needed to appeal to a younger audience with disposable income and not because of any corporate disdain for its earlier shows. The change in programming strategy worked and audiences responded. During the early 1970s, profits rapidly increased and by 1974 the network changed its name to CBS, Inc. Its holdings now consisted of radio and TV networks, a publishing division (Holt, Reinhart and Winston), a magazine division (*Woman's Day*), a recording division (Columbia Records), and the New York Yankees (1964-1973).

As the network entered the mid 1970s, a question loomed over its operation: who would succeed the legendary William Paley, who refused to retire. Corporate intrigue raised its ugly head as he forced the retirement in 1973 of his logical successor, Frank Stanton. Paley then appointed and quickly forced the resignations of a series of network presidents and CEOs, and the turmoil took a toil on the success of the network and the morale of its employees. The unease left the network vulnerable to a takeover, primarily from media mogul Ted Turner. To defend itself against a corporate takeover, CBS turned to Lawrence Tisch. He soon owned a 25 percent share in the company and became president and CEO of CBS in 1986.

The Tisch era began with him immediately cutting expenses and selling assets, such as the recording, magazine, and publishing divisions. These drastic moves further lowered morale and caused Dan Rather (who had succeeded Walter Cronkite as the *CBS Evening News* anchor) to write a scathing editorial in the *New York Times* titled "From Murrow to Mediocrity." Paley died in 1990 and that same year the *CBS Evening News*, which had dominated the ratings for over 20 years, fell to number three.

The network enjoyed a brief ratings surge due to the success of the 1992 Winter Olympics and the 1993 programming coup of convincing late-night host David Letterman to leave NBC. However, CBS was outbid for the rights to NFL football by the upstart Fox network and watched as twelve top affiliates defected to Fox. Despite repeated denials that the company was for sale, in November 1995 CBS was sold to the Westinghouse Corporation for $5.4 billion, effectively ending CBS's independent history. Today the network is owned by Viacom.

Comcast/Charter Sports (CCS) Southeast, 2995 Courtyards Drive, Norcross, GA 30071; *Telephone*: 770-559-7800; *Fax*: 770-559-2418; *Launch Date*: September 1999; *Broadcast Day*: 24 hours; *Subscribers*: 4,000,000; *Email*: css@cable.comcast.com; *Web site*: http://www.css-sports.com

Comcast Sports Southeast/Charter Sports Southeast (CSS) is a partnership between Comcast Corporation and Charter Communications and is a regional sports network. Currently, CSS has approximately four million subscribers across 11 southeastern states and offers a mix of live sports programming, sports news, and in-depth sports analysis. Programming includes NCAA football games, SEC football games, NCAA basketball games, NCAA baseball, softball, soccer, volleyball and gymnastics, minor league baseball and hockey, weekly coach's and preview shows, outdoor shows, auto racing, and ESPNews

Comcast SportsNet, First Union Center, 3601 Broad Street, Philadelphia, PA 19148; *Telephone*: 215-952-5990; *Fax*: 215-952-5996; *Launch Date*: October 1997; *Broadcast Day*: 24 hours; *Subscribers*: 3,000,000; *Email*: Contact channel through its web site; *Web site*: http://www.comcastsportsnet.com

Comcast SportsNet is a basic cable sports network that offers regional fans coverage of local professional teams, local sports news, and sports talk shows. The channel televises over 300 live professional events each year, including the Philadelphia Flyers, Philadelphia 76ers, and the Philadelphia Phillies, as well as local college football and basketball, and professional boxing.

Comcast SportsNet (Mid Atlantic), 7700 Wisconsin Avenue #200, Bethesda, MD 20814; *Telephone*: 301-718-3200; *Fax*: 301-718-3300; *Launch Date*: April 1984; *Broadcast Day*: 24 hours; *Subscribers*: 4,400,000; *Email*: viewermail@comcast sportsnet.com; *Web site*: http://www.midatlantic.comcast-sportsnet.com

Comcast SportsNet (Mid Atlantic) is a regional sports network serving the Mid-Atlantic region and features Baltimore Orioles baseball, Washington Capitals hockey, Washington Wizards basketball, WNBA Mystics basketball, DC United soccer, collegiate events, sports-related events of regional and national interest, and Fox Sports Net Programming.

Comedy Central, 1775 Broadway, 10th Floor, New York, NY 10019; *Telephone*: 212-767-8600; *Fax*: 212-767-8592; *Launch Date*: April 1991; *Broadcast Day*: 24 hours; *Subscribers*: 84,800,000; *Email*: Contact network through its web site; *Web site*: http://www.comedycentral.com

Owned and operated by Music Television, Comedy Central is an all-comedy network that features 60 percent original programming and the biggest comedy stars from the past and present as well as current hottest newcomers. The network's schedule is a mix of original programming, stand-up and sketch comedy, classic television shows, and movies. The channel began on April Fool's Day in 1991 after Home Box Office merged its Comedy Channel with Music Television's Ha! Comedy Network. The new network initially drew a relatively small viewing audience until it aired the program *South Park*, which became one of its biggest hits and was the impetus for the network's popularity and growth.

Comedy Central's most popular programs include *The Daily Show with Jon Stewart*, *South Park*, *Reno 911!*, *Chappelle's Show*, *Tough Crowd with Colin Quinn*, *The Man Show*, *Crank Yankers*, *Insomniac with Dave Attell*, *I'm with Busey*, *Primetime Glick*, *Trigger Happy TV*, and *Kid Notorious*.

Comedy Channel *see* **Comedy Central**

Computer Television Network (Planned for future operation)

Consumer News & Business Channel, 900 Sylvan Avenue, One CNBC Plaza, Engelwood Cliffs, NJ 07632; *Telephone*: 201-735-2622; *Fax*: 201-735-3592; *Launch Date*: April 1989; *Broadcast Day*: 24 hours; *Subscribers*: 86,000,000; *Email*: Contact network through its web site; *Web site*: http://www.cnbc.com

The Consumer News & Business Channel (CNBC) is a joint venture between NBC and Dow Jones (publisher of the *Wall Street Journal*) that provides real-time international financial market coverage and business information to more than 175 million homes worldwide. During prime time broadcasts, the network airs news reports, talk shows, interviews, and entertainment programming. CNBC World (http://www.nbccable info.com) is a 24-hour network that provides global financial market information in real-time, live, worldwide. The channel combines the resources of CNBC business news facilities from the United States, Asia, and Europe.

Cornerstone TeleVision, 1 Signal Hill Drive, Wall, PA 15148; *Telephone*: 412-824-3930; *Fax*: 412-824-5442; *Launch Date*: April 1979; *Broadcast Day*: 24 hours; *Subscribers*: 50,000,000; *Email*: cornerstone@donation-net.net; *Web site*: http://www.ctvn.org

Cornerstone TeleVision broadcasts on Sky Angel (http://www.skyangel.com) and is a viewer-supported ministry with over 100 programs committed to using television as a way of dispensing its religious message. The network broadcasts the Gospel and strives to bring a fresh, positive, Christ-centered outlook to its audience. The non-profit Cornerstone TeleVision ministers salvation, encouragement, and healing through two full-power television stations, over 100 affiliate stations, in-house production of 16 innovative original programs, and a nationwide satellite outreach through Sky Angel. The network is also committed to one-on-one ministry through 24-hour-a-day phone prayer lines, outreach to prisoners and their families, and support for missions.

Country Music Television, 2806 Opryland Drive, Nashville, TN 37214; 330 Commerce Street, Nashville, TN 37201; *Telephone*: 615-916-1000, 615-335-8400; *Fax*: 615-335-8615; *Launch Date*: March 1983; *Broadcast Day*: 24 hours; *Subscribers*: 74,000,000; *Email*: questions@country.com; *Web site*: http://www.cmt.com

Country Music Television is a video channel that airs original country music programming, live concerts and events, and music videos by established and cutting-edge artists. The channel premiered in 1983 with only about 20 videos and a very small audience. Initially, many in the country music industry did not take the channel seriously because there were concerns about the image already created by Music Television (MTV), an image decidedly at odds with that created by the country music establishment in Nashville.

After years of struggle, the network was purchased by Gaylord Communications and Group W Satellite Communications in 1991, which coincides with its rise in popularity and profitability. In 1992, the channel was launched in Europe, went on the air in the Asia-Pacific region in 1994, and began broadcasting in Latin America in 1995. The success of CMT has also become a major influence in the success of country music artists and the marketing of their records.

The channel airs such popular programs as *CMT Most Wanted Live*; the *Grand Ole Opry Live*; *CMT Flameworthy* (allows fans to pick their favorite videos and country stars); the *CMT Music Video Awards*; *CMT Crossroads* (explores the common country music roots of artists from diverse backgrounds); *CMT Inside Fame* (a behind-the-scenes look at the lives of country music's stars); *CMT Ultimate Country Home* (showcases the home design skills of various country artists); *CMT Got Me in the Band* (allows viewers to go behind-the-scenes at video shoots, live concerts, and recording sessions and to hear the stories of country music from the artists themselves); and *Controversy* (examines the inside stories on how some of country music's most famous names found themselves in trouble when they dared to take a stand on controversial subjects).

Courtroom Television Network (Court TV), 600 Third Avenue, 2nd Floor, New York, NY 10016; *Telephone*: 212-973-2800; *Launch Date*: July 1991; *Broadcast Day*: 24 hours; *Subscribers*: 80,000,000; *Email*: Contact network through its web site; *Web site*: http://www.courtv.com

Owned by Time Warner and Liberty Media Corporation and using the tag line "Seriously Entertaining," Court TV is the leader in the investigative genre of television. In addition to its main fare of broadcasting live court trials, the network also airs documentaries, original movies, popular network shows (such as *NYPD Blue* and *Cops*), and other related investigation-focused series and specials. Some of the network's more popular shows include *Forensic Files*; *The System*; *Dominick Dunne's Power, Privilege and Justice*; *I, Detective*; and *Body of Evidence: From the Case Files of Dayle Hinman*. Newer shows on the schedule include *Masterminds*, *Smoking Gun TV* (based on the network's popular and award-winning website (http://www.the smokinggun.com), and *Hollywood at Large*.

Court TV's daytime schedule focuses on live trial coverage, the cornerstone of the network's existence. It is the only network that regularly shows high-profile and drama-charged trials live and unedited. While it has shown trials that did not draw national attention, its fame comes from broadcasting sensational trials, such as the William Kennedy Smith rape trial, the O.J. Simpson murder trial, the Robert Blake preliminary hearing, CA v. Knoller and Noel (San Francisco dog mauling trial), TX v. Yates (mother convicted of drowning her five children), and North Carolina v. Carruth (murder trial of Carolina Panthers running back Rae Carruth, who was convicted of plotting the murder of his girlfriend). The first-ever trial on Court TV was that of Florida v. Robert Scott Hill, who eventually was acquitted of charges of murdering his stepmother-in-law more than 20 years earlier.

Court TV operates three distinct web sites: CourtTV.com (provides news and features, information on major trials, special reports, video archives, educational resources and public affairs events, the Court TV store, and a book store), CrimeLibrary.com (a vast collection of fiction and non-fiction stories on criminal justice), and the award-winning TheSmokingGun.com (offers an irreverent look at the law, justice, and celebrities that uses public documents to expose activities of those in the news).

The timing of Court TV's founding coincided with the merging of two divergent forces. Since the 1930s, there had been an ongoing debate within the legal community about the affect of having media cameras in the courtroom on the defendant's right to a fair trial as guaranteed under the 6th Amendment of the U.S. Constitution. Over the years, with stringent court-ordered rules and procedures to follow, the media began having more and more access to public trials. By the late 1980s camera presence in the courtroom was becoming a common scene.

Also in the late 1980s there was a rapid proliferation of cable channels which were all vying for the same viewers and quickly learned, in order to survive, they had to mutate into specialty niche channels focusing on such subjects as music, sports, and movies. It was this combination of loosening court rules about cameras in the court room and the proliferation of cable channels that allowed the Courtroom Television Network (later shortened to Court TV) to step in and create a niche no other network had addressed. While Court TV had a bumpy and uneven start (there was a question as to how many people would actually want to watch live court trials every day), it grew quickly and gained a vast and loyal audience.

In its inception, the format of the network was very simple and straightforward. It programmed its day emphasizing two or three courtroom trials from around the country. During evening prime time, its schedule provided a summary of the day's court cases, along with various original material. During the weekend, trial highlights from the preceding week were paired with special programming oriented specifically for lawyers. Criticized early on by some observers for its "play-by-play"-like commentary by the channel's legal experts during trial coverage, Court TV has developed a reputation for aggressive trial reporting while fulfilling its mission of demystifying the national court system for the general public.

Cox Sports Television, 800 West Commerce Road, 4th Floor, Harahan, LA 70123; *Telephone*: 504-304-7345, 504-304-8004; *Fax*: 504-304-2243; *Launch Date*: October 2002; *Broadcast Day*: 24 hours; *Subscribers*: 900,000; *Email*: Contact channel through its web site; *Web site*: http://www.coxsportstv.com

Cox Sports Television is a regional sports network that broadcasts professional and amateur men and women's collegiate sporting events, hunting, fishing and other outdoor programs, as well as Louisiana-area high school championships to cable households in Louisiana, southern Mississippi, western Alabama and the Florida panhandle.

CTI Zhong Tian Channel, 1255 Corporate Center Drive #212, Monterey Park, CA 91754; *Telephone*: 720-853-2913; *Fax*: 720-853-2901; *Launch Date*: 1995; *Broadcast Day*: 24 hours; *Email*: Contact the channel through its web site; *Web site*: http:// www.ctitv.tw

The CTI Zhong Tian Channel provides programming derived from Chinese Television International's Zhong Tian news, entertainment, and information channel. Headquartered in Taiwan, CTI ZTC provides viewers with the latest news, sports, dramas, variety, and entertainment television programming.

CVN Shopping Channel (Purchased by **QVC, Inc.** in October 1989)

Dallas Cowboys Channel, 2951 Kinwest Parkway, Irving, TX 75063; *Telephone*: 972-830-3800; *Launch Date*: September 2004; *Broadcast Day*: 24 hours

The Dallas Cowboys Channel is a round-the-clock Comcast Sports Network dedicated to the National Football League's Dallas Cowboys. With daily live programming and full access to the team's organization, the channel aims to be the ultimate destination for information and entertainment for Cowboys fans. Programming includes daily live updates and highlight shows, daily live internet simulcasts, live press conferences, and other programming related to the Cowboys and the Dallas Cowboys Cheerleaders.

Dance Competition Network, 11 Park Avenue #3X, Mount Vernon, NY 10550; *Telephone*: 866-850-2533; *Fax*: 720-853-2901; *Broadcast Day*: 2 hours; *Email*: Contact network through its web site; *Web site*: http://www.dc-network.com

Planned for future operation, the Dance Competition Network will air two-hour weekly segments covering international dance competitions on various dance types in the arts and entertainment industry. The network will also provide the location of upcoming dance auditions around the world for its viewers who are trained dancers or want to make dance a career.

Daystar Television Network, 4201 Pool Road, Colleyville, TX 76034; P.O. Box 612066, Dallas, TX 75261; *Telephone*: 817-571-1229; *Fax*: 817-571-7458; *Launch Date*: December 1998; *Broadcast Day*: 24 hours; *Email*: comments@daystar.com; *Web site*: http://www.daystar.com, http://www.daystar.tv

The Daystar Television Network broadcasts on Sky Angel (http://www.skyangel.com) and features a contemporary, interdenominational, multi-cultural blend of Christian ministry and programming, music, and live Christian events from around the country. The network's flagship programs are *Celebration!* (hosted by Daystar founders Marcus and Joni Lamb and featuring active Christian leaders, authors, and performers) and *Joni* (a program for women combining talk, news, entertainment, and expert guests that discuss such topics as health and nutrition, divorce, coping with the death of a child, surviving cancer, and other relevant topics).

De Película, 5999 Center Drive, Los Angeles, CA 90045; *Telephone*: 310-348-3370; *Fax*: 310-348-3643; *Launch Date*: 2002; *Broadcast Day*: 24 hours; *Subscribers*: 750,000; *Email*: depelicula@televisanetworks.tv; *Web site*: http://www.tutv.tv

De Pelicula is a TuTV channel (http://www.tutv.com) that features films from the world's largest library of Spanish-language movies, including contemporary and classic films from all eras, presented without commercial interruption. The channel offers something for every member of the Hispanic household, including drama, romance, action, westerns, comedies, horror, mystery, musical and children's movies. De Película is distributed in Mexico, Latin America and the United States. De Película Clasico (depeliculaclasico@televisanetworks.tv) is a classic movie channel that features the best films from the 1930s, 1940s and 1950s, known as Mexico's "Golden Era" of film making. The channel segments its programming day for its audience by genre, featuring films with particular appeal to women and families during the day, titles for the whole household during the afternoon and in prime-time, and populating the evening hours with the more typically masculine westerns, wrestling, and action-oriented movies. De Película Clásico is distributed in Mexico and the United States.

Destiny Channel, 140 Broadway, New York, NY 10005; *Telephone*: 212-208-1438; *Broadcast Day*: 24 hours; *Email*: Contact channel through its web site; *Web site*: http://www.destinychannel.com

Planned for future operation, the Destiny Channel aims to become the leading round-the-clock digital cable and satellite channel dedicated to ethics and value-based contemporary content.

Direct 2 U Network (http://www.d2utv.com) (Planned for future operation)

Discovery Channel, One Discovery Place, Silver Spring, MD 20910; *Telephone*: 240-662-2000; *Fax*: 240-662-1854; *Launch Date*: June 1985; *Broadcast Day*: 24 hours; *Subscribers*: 88,300,000; *Email*: Contact channel through its web site; *Web site*: http://www.discovery.com

The Discovery Channel broadcasts a wide mix of general-interest programs, such as natural history, lifestyle and how-to shows, science and technology, exploration, adventure, history and in-depth, behind the scenes glimpses of the people, places and organizations that shape and share our world. Brand channels include Animal Planet, BBC America, Discovery Civilization Channel, Discovery en Español, Discovery HD Theatre, Discovery Health Channel, Discovery Home & Leisure Channel, Discovery Kids Channel, Discovery School, Discovery Science (The Science Channel), Discovery Times Channel, Discovery Wings Channel, FitTV, The Learning Channel, and the Travel Channel.

The Discovery Civilization Channel was launched in 1996 and broadcasts history, current and epic events; great leaders, changing world cultures, and geographic-based programs. The 24-hour Discovery en Español, launched in October 1998, offers Spanish-speaking audiences programs about nature, science and technology, history and world exploration, cooking and how-to, and children's programming. The 24-hour Discovery HD Theatre, launched in June 2002, offers high definition programming about nature, science and technology, and world culture. The 24-hour Discovery Health Channel (http://www.discoveryhealth.com), launched in July 1998, takes almost 50 million viewers inside the world of health, medicine, and wellness through medical breakthroughs and inspiring real life stories of individual and medical triumphs. The 24-hour Discovery Home & Leisure Channel, launched in October 1996, reaches almost 30 million viewers and airs programs that provide a how-to guide on improving the home and enriching lifestyles. Programs include *Designer Guys* (two designers who can never agree on all the details), *Roundabout* (allows viewers the opportunity to see locally-produced travel and leisure programming from around the country), and *Wine TV* (a look at the history and evolution of wine, as well as the cultures and cuisine of wine-producing regions around the world).

The 24-hour Discovery Kids Channel (http://www.discoverykids.com), launched in October 1996, airs programs for kids that explore the adult world, from space stations to shark-infested waters. The Discovery

School Channel (http://school.discovery.com) airs programs that provide innovative teaching materials for teachers, useful and enjoyable resources for students, and smart advice for parents about how to help their kids enjoy learning and excel in school. Discovery Science (The Science Channel) (http://www. science.discovery.com), launched in October 1996, uncovers the clues to the questions that have eluded mankind for centuries and reveals life's greatest mysteries and smallest wonders. Discovery Times Channel, launched in March 2003, is a joint venture network between Discovery Communications, Inc. and The New York Times Company, that offers viewers documentary series and specials that tell the stories behind the events and ideas shaping today's world. The 24-hour Discovery Wings Channel, launched in July 1998, is the destination-of-choice for flight enthusiasts and explores airplanes, helicopters, gliders, rockets, satellites, shuttles, and space stations.

Disney Channel, 3800 West Alameda Avenue, Burbank, CA 91505; *Telephone*: 818-569-7500; *Launch Date*: April 1983; *Broadcast Day*: 24 hours; *Subscribers*: 84,000,000; *Email*: Contact channel through its web site; *Web site*: http://www.disneychannel.com

Part of the ABC Cable Networks Group (a Division of the Walt Disney Company), the Disney Channel is a general entertainment network that aims its programming to kids and families through original series, selected and targeted acquired shows, specials, and movies. Although not completely absent, surprisingly most of the programming on this channel does not revolve around the classic Disney characters, such as Mickey Mouse, Donald Duck, and Goofy. Initially, vintage Disney shows and movies were the programming staple of this network but, over the years, their prominence has faded as new, updated fare has been added. Popular shows currently aired on the network include *Lizzie McGuire*, *Boy Meets World*, *The Proud Family*, *Sister, Sister*, *The Famous Jett Jackson*, *Even Stevens*, and *Kim Possible*.

The only actual spinoff of the original Disney Channel is Toon Disney (http://www.toondisney.com), launched in April 1998, which airs Disney animation (cartoons either created or distributed by Disney) and is aimed at children ages 2 to 11. The ABC Family Channel, originally created by the Christian Broadcasting Network, is now owned by Disney and features programming similar to the Disney Channel.

Distance Learning Network, 111 West Main Street, Boalsburg, PA 16827; *Telephone*: 800-326-9166, 814-466-7808; *Fax*: 814-466-7509; *Launch Date*: 1996; *Email*: dlnstaff@dl-network.com; *Web site*: http://dln.good-sam.com

Through the use of various media formats, the Distance Learning Network is dedicated to meeting the medical education and communications needs of physicians and medical health providers. As an educational resource with 450 available hours of continuing medical education, more than 150,000 physicians, nurses, and pharmacists turn to DLN each year for their medical education. In 2002 DLN began using digital satellite technology to expand its healthcare education network.

Divine HD, 200 Jericho Quadrangle, Jericho, NY 11753; *Telephone*: 516-803-6010; *Email*: Contact channel through its web site; *Web site*: http://www.voom.com

Divine HD is a high definition multiplexed channel from Voom that airs a mix of movies and programming of interest to the gay and lesbian audience.

DMX Music, 11400 West Olympic Boulevard #1100, Los Angeles, CA 90064; *Telephone*: 310-444-1744; *Fax*: 310-575-3936; *Launch Date*: September 1991; *Broadcast Day*: 24 hours; *Subscribers*: 10,500,000; *Email*: Contact channel through its web site; *Web site*: http://www.dmxmusic.com

DMX Music is a digital music service that delivers over 400 styles to homes, businesses, and airlines around the world. Using the world's largest music library, DMX Music provides cable and satellite operators up to 45 music programs in digital, stereo sound, including rock, jazz, rap, classical, country, and dance. All programs are delivered commercial-free with song, artist, and album information available on demand.

Do It Yourself Network, 9721 Sherrill Boulevard, Knoxville, TN 37932; *Telephone*: 865-694-2700; *Launch Date*: December 1994; *Broadcast Day*: 24 hours; *Subscribers*: 26,000,000; *Email*: Contact network through its web site; *Web site*: http://www. diynet. com

Operated by the Scripps Networks, the Do It Yourself Network focuses its programming on the do-it-yourself enthusiast, providing in-depth demonstrations and tips on home improvement and home building, tools and products, gardening and landscaping, automotive and boating, decorating and design, arts and crafts, cooking and entertaining, and recreation and hobbies. The network provides in-depth project instructions, easy to understand demonstrations, and product tips for home and hobby enthusiasts. Each program takes the viewer through an entire project from start to finish, with more detail available on its web site. The DIY web site contains more than 10,000 projects, with complete step-by-step instructions, resources, and related links.

Documentary Channel, 200 42nd Avenue North, Nashville, TN 37209; *Telephone*: 615-297-4410; *Fax*: 615-298-4420; *Launch Date*: December 2003; *Broadcast Day:* 24 hours; *Email*: Contact channel through its web site; *Web site*: http://www. documentarychannel. com

The Documentary Channel showcases the work of independent documentary film makers from around the world and features documentaries of all kinds and descriptions, of all lengths, and covering all categories and genres. The channel does not edit, censure, or otherwise alter a show, but allows the audience to determine the program's worth. The channel's programming is guided by a group of experts in the documentary and non-fiction field who serve on the channel's Advisory Board.

Dragon TV, P.O. Box 4328, Santa Clara, CA 95054; *Telephone*: 877-372-4668; *Launch Date*: October 2003; *Broadcast Day:* 24 hours; *Email*: support@dragontv.net; *Web site*: http://www.dragontv.net

Operated by VideoJump, Dragon TV is a multichannel service that targets its programming to Chinese and Taiwanese audiences by broadcasting programs from various popular Asian channels (from China, Taiwan, and Hong Kong). VideoJump's eventual broadcast strategy is to bring the best and the most Chinese channels to cable subscribers in different markets in America.

Dragon TV offers: SET International Schedule (a 24/7 channel that broadcasts in both Mandarin and Taiwanese; the channel focuses on modern Taiwanese society, culture and lifestyle and airs news, documentaries, dramas/series, variety, music, cooking, and game shows); ET- News Schedule (a 24/7 Mandarin channel, similar in format to CNN's *Headline News*, that airs breaking news and current affairs. While the channel focuses on news from China, Taiwan, and Hong Kong, it also airs daily Chinese-American community news produced in the United States); ET-Drama Schedule (a 24/7 channel that features first-run dramas and classic series, classic movies form 1940 to the present, and live stage productions in the Mandarin language); ET- Global Schedule (a 24/7 channel that airs a mix of news content, news magazines, dramas, movies, documentaries, comedies, game shows, and other general entertainment programming in the Mandarin language); ET-China Schedule (a 24/7 Mandarin channel that airs variety programs from Mainland China, a mix of news content, dramas, movies, comedy, mini series, game shows, and other general entertainment programming); ET-YOYO Schedule (a 24/7 Mandarin channel that features programming content for children up to age ten and focuses on Chinese educational programs, cartoons, interactive parent/child programming, and shows on parenting concerns); and CCTV Schedule (the national television station of the People's Republic of China that features 11 channels with a daily broadcasting schedule of more than 200 hours; CCTV-4 specializes in news reports and introduces various aspects of China (politics, economy, society, culture, science, education, and history) to the world.

The Dream Network, 9300 Georgia Avenue #206, Silver Spring, MD 20910; *Telephone*: 301-587-0000; *Launch Date*: December 1994; *Broadcast Day:* 24 hours; *Subscribers*: 46,000,000; *Email*: Contact network through its web site; *Web site*: http://www.thedreamnetwork.com

The Dream Network targets its programming to the urban family audience and broadcasts news, talk shows, sports, and gospel music videos.

DuMont Television Network (Defunct)

The DuMont Television Network was the first licensed American television network, predating CBS, NBC, and ABC and is sometimes called the Original Fourth Network. The network operated from 1946 to 1956 and was jointly owned by Allen B. DuMont, an inventor and television set manufacturer, and the Paramount Pictures movie studio, which became involved with the inventor when he sold them a stake in his network so he could raise funding for research. This single joint venture on his part would eventually prove to be the major cause of the network's demise. Eager to hinder the development of television, which was perceived as a serious threat to the motion picture industry, Paramount Pictures repeatedly blocked DuMont's expansion plans and even owned and operated its own stations that competed directly with DuMont's affiliates.

At the time of the merger, DuMont also owned three independent stations and had sought to own five, the maximum allowed under then-current FCC rules. However, the network's expansion plans were stopped when the FCC ruled that two stations owned by Paramount Studios counted as also being owned by the DuMont Network, even though these two stations did not broadcast any DuMont programs. This ruling basically put a stop to DuMont's network growth. Eventually, one of the network's three independent stations was sold and the other two would be the nucleus of what became MetroMedia, now known as the Fox Television Network.

The DuMont station in New York (WABD, named after Allen B. DuMont) became most famous for producing the classic television show, *The Honeymooners*, starring Jackie Gleason. Another of the network's ground-breaking programs was *DuMont's Cavalcade of Stars*, where Gleason got his start. In the late 1940s and early 1950s, DuMont was America's fourth television network, long before Fox, and competed directly with CBS, NBC and ABC. Two primary forces combined to put DuMont at a competitive disadvantage: the lack of a strong affiliate network base and being forced to use UHF affiliates in an era when UHF was not competitive. Unable to compete with the "big 3," DuMont eventually ceased operations in 1956.

In addition to operating a major network, DuMont also manufactured electronic equipment, broadcast equipment for the television industry, and television sets. One primary reason for entering the network business was to sell more DuMont-brand television sets. The DuMont Network evolved from the research efforts of DuMont Laboratories, whose inventions included the first long-lasting cathode ray tube, the basis of electronic television. The company was first to offer a home television receiver to the public and exhibited television sets at the 1939 New York World's Fair. For these and other important contributions to the early development of the industry, Dr. DuMont is often referred to as "The Father of Television."

Within the industry, it is generally agreed that the first network telecast occurred on August 9, 1945, when DuMont's New York and Washington television stations were linked via coaxial cable for an announcement concerning the dropping of the second atomic bomb on Nagasaki, Japan. Earlier, in 1943, NBC had linked a station in New York City and one in Schenectady, New York via direct over-the-air reception for a program called *War Bride*. However, since DuMont was first to be officially licensed as a television network, it generally gets the credit for airing the first network telecast.

The first scheduled DuMont Network series was *Serving Through Science*, which premiered on August 15, 1946. In 1947 DuMont's major network efforts began and the name DuMont Television Network was adopted. Television historians agree that the network probably would never have survived at all if not for its complete domination in Pittsburgh, Pennsylvania, which at the time was a Top 10 television market area. Except for DuMont, there were no other commercial VHF stations in the city until the late 1950s. There were several UHF stations but their signals could only reach a very small population of the television viewing audience.

Although small and in constant need of capital, the network became known for its creativity and low-budget productions, such as *Monodrama Theater* (which featured a single actor performing a monologue or play in front of a curtain), *Night Editor* (about the night editor of a newspaper who acted out some of the stories he described), and *The Plainclothesman* (which depicted the action from the point of view of the main character, who was never seen). The network was also credited with reviving professional wrestling, which had lost much of its appeal throughout most of the country until DuMont began airing regularly-scheduled matches.

Unfortunately, most of the network's shows were live and not taped, and thus have not been preserved for future generations. Unlike other shows from the 1940s and 1950s from the "big 3," it is very rare that a DuMont Network show of that era can be found today. Although short-lived, the network created some major programs that had immediate and long-lasting impact on the television industry. In addition to the *Cavalcade of Stars*, DuMont also aired *Life is Worth Living* (with Archbishop Fulton J. Sheen, the only show ever to achieve any success against the extremely popular Milton Berle show on NBC) and *Captain Video* (a children's space opera that is probably one of the most popular shows ever on the network). However, as time progressed the network could not compete with CBS and NBC and began losing its stars (such as Jackie Gleason and Ted Mack of the *Original Amateur Hour*) to the other networks.

In addition to a declining viewing audience, the network began suffering further financial losses when the sale of DuMont television sets, which had been the primary impetus for the network's creation, began to decline. In the early stage of the television industry, DuMont produced high-priced sets for a luxury market, since only a select few could afford to have their own televisions. However, with the growing popularity of television, other manufacturers (such as GE, RCA, and Westinghouse) began producing high-volume, low-cost sets and the DuMont product (considered the Cadillac of the industry) basically priced itself out of the market.

Even with a declining audience and financial losses, the DuMont Network may possibly have survived as the nation's number three network if the fortunes of ABC (which was fourth and having even more problems than DuMont) had not changed so quickly. In 1953 ABC merged with the United Paramount Theaters and used the resulting inflow of capital to revive itself and establish the network as a solid number three behind NBC and CBS. Already losing ground to CBS and NBC, the resurgence of ABC proved to be the deciding blow to DuMont. In a final attempt at survival, DuMont made an agreement to merge with ABC, but the plan was ultimately vetoed by Paramount.

In 1955 Paramount took complete control of the DuMont Network, ending its independence, and immediately began dismantling its operations. In April most of the network's shows were dropped and by May only eight programs remained on the network's schedule. A panel show called *What's the Story?* was its last regularly-scheduled non-sports program, with its final airing in September. Thereafter, the network only aired occasional live sporting events, with its last program of any kind, *Boxing from St. Nicholas Arena*, aired on August 6, 1956.

DuMont's demise marked the beginning of the dominance of the "big 3" networks in the United States for over 30 years. The network's television stations were formed into a new company called the DuMont Broadcasting Corporation. To distance itself from the perceived failure of the DuMont Network, the company's name was changed to Metropolitan Broadcasting, which after being acquired, changed its name to MetroMedia in 1960.

Some of the more well-known and ground-breaking shows that aired on the DuMont Network included *The Adventures of Ellery Queen*, *The Arthur Murray Show (Party)*, *Captain Video and His Video Rangers (The Secret Files of Captain Video)*, *Cavalcade of Stars*, *The Drew Pearson Show*, *Famous Fights from Madison Square Garden*, *Famous Jury Trials*, *The Hazel Scott Show* (the first network television series to be hosted by an African-American woman), *Major Del Conway of the Flying Tigers*, *The Morey Amsterdam Show*, *Night Editor*, *The Original Amateur Hour*, *Russ Hodges' Scoreboard*, *Serving Through Science* (the first DuMont Network series), *Tom Corbett, Space Cadet*, and *What's the Story?* (the last regularly scheduled non-sports program on the DuMont Network).

E! Entertainment Television, 5750 Wilshire Boulevard, Los Angeles, CA 90036; *Telephone*: 323-954-2400; *Fax*: 323-954-2662; *Launch Date*: June 1990 (launched in July 1987 as Movietime); *Broadcast Day*: 24 hours; *Subscribers*: 84,000,000; *Email*: Contact channel through its web site; *Web site*: http://www.eentertainment.com, http://www.eonline.com

E! provides pop culture coverage of popular entertainment, celebrity interviews, news, behind the scenes features, contemporary films, television and music, and entertainment awards shows. The E! Networks includes E! Entertainment Television, the Style Network (a separate cable channel dedicated to the fashion industry), and E! Online. The network is a joint venture between Comcast Communications Corporation and American Broadcasting Company, with AT&T also having a smaller stake in the cable channel. Popular programs include *E! True Hollywood Story*, *The Anna Nicole Show*, *Celebrities Uncensored*, *Talk Soup*, *It's Good to Be*, and rebroadcasts of taped Howard Stern radio shows.

Ecology Channel, 9171 Victoria Drive, Ellicott City, MD 21042; *Telephone*: 410-465-0480; *Fax*: 410-461-5152; *Launch Date*: November 1994; *Subscribers*: 10,000,000; *Email*: Contact channel through its web site; *Web site*: http://www.ecology.com

Primarily aimed at the 18-49 adult viewing market, the Ecology Channel focus its programming on ecology and the environment. Through cooperation with scientists, universities, and related educational facilities, the channel also offers its programming to middle and high school students and teachers.

Ecumenical Television Channel (Catholic Television Network of Youngstown), P.O. Box 430, 9531 Akron-Canfield Road, Canfield, OH 44406; *Telephone and Fax*: 330-533-2243; *Launch Date*: 1983; *Broadcast Day*: 24 hours; *Subscribers*: 300,000; *Email*: Contact network through its web site: *Web site*: http://www.doy.org

The Ecumenical Television Channel offers local and national religious and inspirational programming that represents all denominations and faiths. During the 1950s and 1960s, Catholic radio and television programs flourished through the Catholic Television Network of Youngstown (CTNY) and in 1954 its Sunday Mass was broadcasted on radio with the help of a local AM station. In the early 1960s, *TV Mass for Shut-Ins* was first broadcast and continues through CTNY today. The Catholic Telecommunications Network of Youngstown was begun in 1980 by the Diocese in order to expand the production and delivery of its radio and television programs. In the 1990s CTNY continued to expand it's programming to reach national audiences. CTNY also serves as the production and network facility for the Ecumenical Television Channel.

The Ecumenical Television Channel (ETC) serves Northeastern Ohio and Western Pennsylvania and is a collaboration of Christian denominations and the Jewish Community. The channel's primary purpose "is to communicate the word of God who calls, nurtures, and unites." This collaboration works in cooperation with the Catholic Telecommunications Network of the Diocese of Youngstown. ETC began broadcasting one hour a day in 1983 and in 1986 expanded to 24 hour a day, seven days a week of religious and inspirational programming, thus becoming the first Ecumenical Television Channel in the nation. National programs on ETC are provided by the Eternal Word Television Network, Boston Catholic Television, The Jewish Network, Cornerstone TeleVision, and the Inspirational Network.

EdgeTV, 100 North Crescent #323, Beverly Hills, CA 90210; *Telephone*: 310-385-4350; *Fax*: 310-385-4334; *Broadcast Day*: 24 hours; *Email*: Contact channel through its web site; *Web site*: http://www.theedgetv.com

Planned for future operation, EdgeTV will be the first round-the-clock television network devoted to games of skill, strategy, and chance. Appealing to all levels of game enthusiasts, the channel's programming will feature the most popular games and will encourage viewers to not only watch, but to play along.

Election Channel, 1000 Universal Studios Plaza, Building 22-A, Orlando, FL 32819; *Telephone*: 407-224-6848; *Launch Date*: July 2004; *Broadcast Day*: 24 hours; *Email*: info@electionchannel.com; *Web site*: http://www.electionchannel.com

The Election Channel delivers customized video-on-demand content that enables any local city, county, state, and/or federal election candidate to broadcast their election platform and ideas to any person on any internet-enabled device anywhere in the world, anytime.

Empire Sports Network, 795 Indian Church Road, West Seneca, NY 14224; *Telephone*: 716-558-8444; *Fax*: 716-558-8430; *Launch Date*: December 1990; *Broadcast Day*: 24 hours; *Subscribers*: 7,000,000; *Email*: Contact network through its web site; *Web site*: http://www.empiresports.com

The Empire Sports Network broadcasts local sporting events, such as Buffalo Sabers hockey, Triple A baseball, American Hockey League, men and women's Syracuse University sports, *FAN TV*, *Empire Sports Report*, *Buffalo Bills Postgame Report*, and *Inside the Orange*.

The Employment & Career Channel, 253 West 51st Street, 3rd Floor, New York, NY 10019; *Telephone*: 212-445-0754; *Fax*: 212-445-0760; *Launch Date*: July 2004; *Broadcast Day*: 24 hours; *Email*: info@employ.com; *Web site*: http://www.employ.com

The Employment & Career Channel creates and distributes employment and career development content in a digital video format for television and the internet. The video content focuses on all topics relating to obtaining or retaining a job, career development, training, workplace lifestyles, news, and other issues that impact a person's employment and career. The channel aims its broadcasts to all classes of workers, from first-time job seekers to high-income professionals and executives.

Encore, 8900 Liberty Circle, Englewood,

CO 80112; *Telephone*: 720-852-7700; *Fax*: 720-852-8555; *Launch Date*: April 1991; *Broadcast Day*: 24 hours; *Subscribers*: 21,000,000; *Email*: Contact channel through its web site; *Web site*: http://www. starz.com

Encore is a multiplexed channel from Starz! that was re-launched in May 1999. Using the tag line "A Great Movie Every Night. Guaranteed!" Encore airs first-run, recent big hit, and classic movies, all uncut and commercial-free. The channel features hosted movie segments, interviews, movie trivia between films, and Encore Originals, such as *The Directors*. The network focuses on high-quality movies that receive box office success or critical acclaim, and include notable stars and/or directors.

Enrichment Channel, 1116 Northwest 81st Terrace, Fort Lauderdale, FL 33322; *Telephone*: 954-423-4414; *Fax*: 954-423-2161; *Email*: moschwager@aol.com; *Web site*: http://www.enrichment.com

Planned for future operation, the Enrichment Channel will broadcast programs dedicated to lifting the human spirit and focuses on improving the lives of individuals and families in a positive manner. The channel will broadcast in three basic areas: human potential, self-help, personal growth and fulfillment; shows that build bridges between races, sexes, cultures and ideas; and breakthrough inspirational news dealing with hopeful human enterprises and discoveries.

Entertainment Sports Programming Network, ESPN Plaza, Bristol, CT 06010; *Telephone*: 860-766-2000; *Fax*: 860-766-2400; *Launch Date*: September 1979; *Broadcast Day*: 24 hours; *Subscribers*: 89,000,000; *Email*: Contact network through its web site; *Web site*: http://www.espn.com

Known simply by its acronym, ESPN was the first all-sports network, is the most-watched sports-related network in the world, and was the first network to televise all four major professional sports (National Football League, National Basketball Association, National Hockey League, and Major League Baseball). In addition to broadcasting the four major professional sports, each year the network airs more than 5,000 hours of live and/or original sports programming that feature more than 60 additional sports including the Women's National Basketball Association, college football, men's and women's college basketball, every game of the Women's Basketball Tournament, the X Games, and the Great Outdoor Games. The network has also developed original programming and movies.

Currently co-owned by ABC, Inc. (80 percent) and the Hearst Corporation (20 percent), ESPN began in 1978 as The ESP Network (The Entertainment & Sports Programming Network) but changed its name to ESPN prior to its launch on September 7, 1979. Calling itself the "Worldwide Leader in Sports" and initially started as a single-entity, cable sports network, ESPN has grown to become a multinational, multimedia sports entertainment conglomerate.

The network creates or acquires sporting events that it owns, markets, and televises in an effort to increase its value to advertisers, affiliates, and viewers. Program examples include the *X Games*, the *Winter X Games*, *X Games Global Championships*, the *Action Sports and Music Awards*, *ESPN Outdoors* (featuring the *Bassmasters Classic* and *Great Outdoor Games*), the *Skin Games*, *Jimmy V Classic* (men and women basketball), the Fort Worth, Hawaii, and Las Vegas Bowls, and the College Football Awards.

As the network has grown, ESPN has created several theme-based channels to focus on specific interests and target audiences. Launched in March 2003, ESPN HD is a 24-hour high-definition television service that features live telecasts including games from the National Hockey League, Major League Baseball, National Football League, and the NCAA Women's Basketball Championship. Launched in October 1993, ESPN2 has grown to becomes the nation's second largest sports network, behind the original ESPN. The 24-hour network airs almost 5,000 hours of live and/or original sports programming, including Major League Baseball, the National Basketball Association, the National Hockey League, college football and basketball, and sports-specific news and highlights shows.

Launched in May 1995 and initially called the Classic Sports Network, the channel changed its name to ESPN Classic when purchased by ESPN in 1997. ESPN Classic is a 24-hour, all-sports network that airs the greatest games, stories, heroes, and memories in the history of sports, while adding a current perspective to the events and moments. The network presents programming from the NFL, MLB, NBA, NHL, NASCAR, boxing, tennis, golf, and college football and basketball. One of its original programs, *SportsCentury*, has won both Peabody and Emmy awards.

ESPN Deportes first aired in September 2003 and is a 24-hour channel that broadcasts a variety of domestic and international sports programming, such as MLB, the NBA, European soccer, and other sports from around the world with a focus on Latin America, including Pacific League Baseball, ONEFA college football from Mexico, and coverage of Copa America Volleyball, the premier volleyball tournament in the Americas. The channel also provides Spanish-language sports news and information shows, including *SportsCenter*, *Gol ESPN: Fuera de Juego* (a round table discussion of the world of soccer), and *ESPN's Perfiles* (a 30-minute interview show that focuses on prominent Latin American sports stars).

The 24-hour ESPNews channel first aired in November 1996 and is the nation's only television sports news service. The channel provides its viewers access to news makers with live coverage of significant press conferences and breaking news stories. The channel was created to be an extension of ESPN's *SportsCenter* and to offer more in-depth coverage than can be provided by any single program. In an effort to combine ESPN's on-air and on-line entities, ESPNews re-launched in September 2001 with new updates, including enhanced interactive features, graphics, and sports highlights combined with box scores and shot charts.

In May 1994 ESPN acquired Creative Sports and re-named it ESPN Regional Television, which is a television and radio sports marketing, syndication, and production company. ESPN Regional Television produces events for the ESPN networks, ABC Sports, and other national, regional, and local outlets. Events include college football and basketball, *RPM 2Night*, the *Skins Games*, the Fort Worth, Hawaii, and Las Vegas Bowls, the College Football Awards, and more than 740 college TV programs (including games and coaches shows).

Launched in September 1999, ESPN Now is a full-time video and text television channel featuring live sports news, headlines and scores from ESPN.com., and updated sports television listings. First aired in June 2001, ESPN Today is the first interactive sports-only channel that provides viewers with text and graphics of sports-related information, including top news stories, scores, statistics, standings, and schedules. Launched in June 2003, ESPN Pay-Per-View features NCAA Baseball Championship games, martial arts programs, fantasy league specials, sports-related movies, *ESPN GamePlan*, and *ESPN Full Court*. ESPN-U (scheduled to being broadcasting in 2005) will focus entirely on college sports.

Formed in January 1988, ESPN International helps give the ESPN networks a global presence on all seven continents, reaching more than 120 million households. ESPN International currently consists of more than 20 networks reaching 145 countries and territories, in 11 languages including: ESPN (Latin America), ESPN Brazil, ESPN+, ESPN Dos (Mexico), TSN, RDS, ESPN Classic Canada, WTSN, NHL Network (Canada), ESPN Asia, ESPN India, ESPN Taiwan, Star Sports Asia, Star Sports India, Star Sports South East Asia, MBA-ESPN Sports (Korea), Sports-i ESPN (Japan), ESPN (Australia), ESPN (Pacific Rim), ESPN (New Zealand), Orbit ESPN Sports, ESPN

(Africa), ESPN (Israel), ESPN Classic Sport (France), and ESPN Classic Sport (Italy). Channel programming includes soccer, CART auto racing, Grand Prix Badminton, Indian and U.K. Cricket, the PGA Championship, the U.S. Open, Augusta Masters, ATP Tennis Masters Series, the Australian Open, Major League Baseball, the National Basketball Association, the National Football League, the National Hockey League, and the X Games.

Non-television entities from ESPN include ESPN Radio (launched in January 1992), its internet site, ESPN.com, launched in April 1995, ESPN The Magazine (launched in March 1988), SportsTicker (the leading supplier of real-time sports news and information), ESPN Enterprises, ESPN Zone (a sports-themed restaurant), ESPN Broadband (launched in August 2001 and is a PC-based service), ESPN Outdoors (created in 2001 and coordinates ESPN-wide multimedia efforts), BASS (acquired in April 2001 and is the world's largest fishing organization), ESPN Wireless (serves the sports fan any time, anywhere, and via any device), Team ESPN (a corporate outreach effort that uses the power of sports to make a difference in the lives of fans and their communities), and The V Foundation for Cancer Research (established at the inaugural ESPYs in 1993 by ESPN with the late Jim Valvano to raise funds for cancer research).

Broadcast milestones for ESPN include: April 1982 (ESPN becomes the first network to televise every round of a PGA Tour event, the USF&G from New Orleans), July 1982 (the network provides complete coverage of the John McEnroe-Mats Wilander Davis Cup match that lasted 9 hours and 30 minutes, the longest live sports telecast in television history), March 1983 (ESPN televises the first live professional football game on cable, the USFL's Birmingham against Michigan), February 1986 (ESPN becomes the first American network to produce the NHL All-Star Game), March 1987 (the network is awarded the National Football League's first cable contract), July 1987 (ESPN becomes the first cable network to achieve 50 percent penetration in the American television market, reaching 43.7 million homes), December 1988 (the network airs its 10,000th episode of *SportsCenter*, the most televised cable program in history), March 1993 (ESPN hosts the first ESPY Awards in New York), and Fall 1998 (ESPN introduces "1st & Ten," a computer-generated first-down line (usually appears yellow on tv screens) and uses it on NFL broadcasts.

Epics HD, 200 Jericho Quadrangle, Jericho, NY 11753; *Telephone*: 516-803-6010; *Email*: Contact channel through its web site; *Web site*: http://www.voom.com

Epics HD is a high definition multiplexed channel from Voom that airs classic movies.

Equator HD, 200 Jericho Quadrangle, Jericho, NY 11753; *Telephone*: 516-803-6010; *Email*: Contact channel through its web site; *Web site*: http://www.voom.com

Equator HD is a high definition multiplexed channel from Voom and is the first and only channel that broadcasts the amazing sights and sounds that capture the world's most unique people and places. The channel features documentaries, films, and original productions.

The Erotic Network, 7007 Winchester Circle, Boulder, CO 80301; *Telephone*: 303-786-8700; *Launch Date*: September 1998; *Broadcast Day*: 24 hours; *Subscribers*: 14,000,000; *Email*: Contact network through its web site; *Web site*: http://www.noof.com

Owned and operated by New Frontier Media, The Erotic Network is an adult pay-per-view service that uses the un-inhibited editing standard for its programming. The network's content is also available on Video-On-Demand platforms and the internet. TEN On Demand, launched in March 1999, offers a variety of adult programming from premiere features, clips, and network compilations and is available in three editing standards, from traditionally edited to completely edited. TENBlox, launched in January

2003, uses the same clip format as the popular TENClips; these 90-minute blocks take material from urban, ethnic, and amateur adult features and uses a less edited format. TENBlue, launched in January 2003, is a premiere-based service with over 20 exclusive features every month and focuses on content for adults seeking more urban, ethnic, and amateur fare. TENBlueplus, launched in January 2003, is an unedited adult channel that focuses on urban, ethnic, and amateur fare. TENClips launched in May 2000, is a "best of" compilation service that employs clips from the most popular feature films; programming is edited to a near revealing standard and the channel shows more than 45 unique titles every month. TENMax, launched in October 2002, is an adult clips service that focuses on delivering the best of the adult world in 90-minute thematic blocks, totally unedited. TENXtsy, launched in February 1998, is a premier feature that airs over 20 new films each month, all completely unedited. Another brand channel from TEN is the 24-hour Pleasure, which was launched in September 1998. It is an adult pay-per-view network that uses a soft edit standard and focuses on feature-length premieres from top stars and studios.

Esperanza TV *see* **Hope Channel**

Eternal Word Television Network, 5817 Old Leeds Road, Birmingham, AL 35210; *Telephone*: 205-271-2900; *Launch Date*: August 1981; *Broadcast Day*: 24 hours; *Subscribers*: 53,000,000; *Email*: Contact network through its web site; *Web site*: http://www.ewtn.com

Founded by Mother Angelica, a Franciscan nun, the Eternal Word Television Network is a religious cable broadcaster that airs commercial-free, family-oriented programming from a Catholic point of view, in both English and Spanish. EWTN features documentaries, music, dramas, live talk shows, animated children's programs, and special church events from around the world.

Popular programs include *The Journey Home* (a call-in show that examines why people are being drawn home to the Catholic Church), *Mother Angelica Classics* (one-hour focusing on Mother Angelica's insights), *EWTN Live* (an interview program with guests seeking to teach and prepare viewers for evangelism), *Life on the Rock* (a live call-in and interview show), *The World Over* (includes international news from a Catholic perspective, interviews, investigative reports, live coverage of special events, and cultural reporting), *Daily Mass* (live church service with two re-broadcasts during the day), and *Holy Rosary* (aired three times per day).

EuroCinema, 387 Park Avenue South, 3rd Floor, New York, NY 10016; *Telephone*: 212-763-5533; *Email*: contactus@eurocinema.com; *Web site*: http://www.eurocinema com

EuroCinema is an alternative movie channel that features award-winning films from the world's top film festivals and directors. The movies are offered as On Demand and Premium programming accompanied by commentary on directors, actors, producers, the time period, and other points of interest. The channel also airs documentaries, celebrity interviews, and coverage of major international film festivals and events.

Faith Television Network, 2607 Success Drive, Odessa, FL 33556; *Telephone*: 727-375-8200; *Email*: jim@faithtelevisionnetwork.com; *Web site*: http://www.faithtv.com, http://www.faithtelevisionnetwork.com

The Faith Television Network, more often referred to as Faith TV, broadcasts on Sky Angel (http://www.skyangel.com) and is a Christian movie, documentary, and biography channel featuring dramas, comedies, action, educational programs, music videos, and feature films.

Family Channel (now called **ABC Family Channel**)

FamilyLand Television Network, 3375 County Road 36, Bloomingdale, OH 43910;

Telephone: 800-773-2645, 740-765-5500; *Launch Date*: November 1999; *Broadcast Day*: 24 hours; *Subscribers*: 1,000,000; *Email*: Contact network through its web site; *Web site*: http://www.familyland.tv, http://www.familyland.org

The Familyland Television Network broadcasts on Sky Angel (http://www.skyangel.com) and airs family-oriented programming that has been edited to exclude foul language, immodesty, excessive violence, and disrespect for authority. The network airs spiritual talk shows, movie classics with spiritual commentaries, devotional programs, children's favorites, practical home shows, Christian music, family situation comedies, sports commentaries, and original Christian productions.

FamilyNet Television, 6350 West Freeway, Fort Worth, TX 76116; *Telephone*: 800-832-6638, 817-737-4011; *Fax*: 817-298-3388, 817-737-8209; *Launch Date*: April 1988; *Broadcast Day*: 24 hours; *Subscribers*: 34,000,000; *Email*: Contact network through its web site; *Web site*: http://www.familynettv.com

Owned and operated by the North American Mission Board of the Southern Baptist Convention, FamilyNet Television is an entertainment and information network that airs more than 50 hours of original, family-oriented programming each week, including *Mary Lou's Flip Flop Shop* (starring Olympic champion Mary Lou Retton), *Straight Talk, Just the Facts, This Generation, Gary McSpadden's Gospel Jubilee*, and *Healthy, Wealthy and Wise.*

Other popular programs include *Tonya's Creative Cooking*; *At Home Live* (enriches family life by presenting expert advice, and interviews with Christian authors, artists, and musicians); *The Call* (highlights true stories of people who have experienced the calling of God in their lives); *Family Showcase* (features the brightest stars in Christian entertainment, including live concerts, stand-up comedy, and special events); the *Family Enrichment Series* (a monthly program that addresses specific topics dealing with a variety of issues for the family); *Country Crossroads* (features music videos, interviews, and uplifting messages from top country music artists); and *Swan's Place* (caters to fans of southern gospel, country music, and laughter).

FamilyStar Learning Network (FSLN) (Planned for future operation)

Fanfare — The Classical Music Channel (Planned for future operation)

Fashion and Design Television, 14 Johnson Avenue, Englewood Cliffs, New Jersey 07632; *Telephone*: 201-503-0664; *Fax*: 201-586-0249; *Launch Date*: 2004; *Broadcast Day*: 24 hours; *Email*: Contact network through its web site; *Web site*: http://www. fadnetworks.com

Fashion and Design Television targets the Generation X audience with a focus on fashion, design, and pop culture. Related programming includes international travel, music, home shopping, entertainment, and reports on the latest cutting-edge trends.

FE TV, 4501 West Expressway 83 #220, Harlingen, TX 78552, P.O. Box 530760, Harlingen, TX 78553; *Telephone*: 956-412-5600; *Email*: Contact channel through its web site; *Web site*: http://www.fe-tv.com

FE TV broadcasts on Sky Angel (http://www.skyangel.com) from the Faith Pleases God Church (http://www.faithpleasesgod.com) and is a Spanish-speaking, Christian television network that brings together the largest Spanish-speaking ministries in North and South America. Network programming originates from Yiyi Avila's Miracle Network (Cadena De Milagros) and from the top Spanish-speaking churches in North America. FE-TV also broadcasts concerts, sitcoms, soap operas, talk shows, outdoor sports, movies, and blocks of programming aimed at children and teens.

Fifth Avenue Channel (Planned for future operation)

The Filipino Channel *see* **ABS-CBN International**

Film Festival Channel, 837 Traction Avenue #307, Los Angeles, CA 90013, P.O. Box 39349, Los Angeles, CA 90039; *Telephone*: 213-625-1242; *Launch Date*: September 2004; *Broadcast Day*: 24 hours; *Email*: info@filmfestivalchannel.com; *Web site*: http://www.filmfestivalchannel.com

The Film Festival Channel celebrates quality films and film makers and gives artists exposure to a wider audience. These films highlight the best and upcoming talent seen on the festival circuit, including writers, directors, and actors. Through original specials and interviews, the channel informs viewers of the latest film making techniques. The channel's programming mix includes drama, horror, comedy, feature-length films, shorts, and documentaries. The channel also hosts a broadcast film festival where viewers vote on the winners. Any genre is accepted and entrants pay a fee, the amount of which is based on the length of the submission. If accepted, the work is aired and viewers vote on their favorites via the internet, phone, or mail.

Fine Living Network, 5757 Wilshire Boulevard #220, Los Angeles, CA 90036; *Telephone*: 310-228-4500; *Launch Date*: March 2002; *Broadcast Day*: 24 hours; *Subscribers*: 20,000,000; *Email*: Contact the network through its web site; *Web site*: http://www.fineliving.com

Part of the Scripps Networks, the Fine Living Network broadcasts programming aimed at an audience that wants to enjoy the good life. The network's programs shows viewers how to save money and how to get the best bargains for their fine-living dollar. The network airs only original programming, produced from all over the world, that focuses on five lifestyle categories: adventure, personal space, favorite things, transport, and fine living every day.

Fire and Emergency Training Network; 4101 International Parkway, Carrollton, TX 75007; *Telephone*: 800-845-2443, 972-309-4000; *Fax*: 972-309-5452; *Email*: Contact network through its web site; *Web site*: http://www.fetn.com

The Fire and Emergency Training Network develops and delivers fire fighting and emergency-related training that helps emergency personnel react safely, swiftly, and capably to local and life-threatening emergencies. Reaching more than 250,000 viewers a month, FETN provides fire, emergency medical services, and technical rescue personnel access to consistent, quality training. FETN provides trainees access to the nation's top specialists and training that is compliant with the National Fire Protection Association, the Department of Transportation, International Standards Organization, the Occupational Safety and Health Administration, the Continuing Education Coordinating Board for Emergency Medical Services, and other standards. This training enables emergency response workers to learn about important regulations and satisfy certification requirements at a fraction of the cost needed to attend specialized workshops and seminars.

Fish TV (Planned for future operation)

FiT TV, One Discovery Place, Silver Spring, MD 20910; *Telephone*: 240-662-2000; *Launch Date*: January 2004; *Broadcast Day*: 24 hours; *Subscribers*: 30,000,000; *Email*: Contact the network through its web site; *Web site*: http://www.fittv.com, http://www. healthnetwork.com

FiT TV is a brand channel of the Discovery Channel and provides health and fitness information through programs and specials about exercise, wellness, nutrition, sports, and other health-related topics.

FLIX, 1633 Broadway, New York, NY 10019; *Telephone*: 212-708-1590; *Fax*: 212-708-1212; *Launch Date*: August 1992; *Broadcast Day*: 24 hours; *Subscribers*: 35,000,000; *Email*: Contact the network through its web site; *Web site*: http://www.sho.com

Flix is a multiplexed channel from Showtime that broadcasts movies from the 1970s, 1980s, and the 1990s. The channel airs about 55 titles per month, none of which are duplicated on other Showtime Networks.

Florida Channel, 1000 Universal Studios Plaza, Building 22-A, Orlando, FL 32819; *Telephone*: 407-224-6830; *Launch Date*: August 2004; *Broadcast Day*: 24 hours; *Email*: Contact channel through its web site; *Web site*: http://floridachannel.com

The Florida Channel is a regional governmental and public affairs cable network that airs Florida Assembly and Senate floor sessions and committee meetings, capitol press conferences, proceedings of regulatory boards and state commissions, and local county government proceeding and events.

Florida Education Channel, 753 West Boulevard, Chipley, FL 32428; *Telephone*: 877-873-7232, 850-638-6131; *Email*: Contact channel through its web site; *Web site*: http://www.fec.tv

The Florida Education Channel is a national direct satellite broadcast project originally funded in 2000 by the Florida Legislature and uses distance learning technology to reach every school in Florida. Popular programs include *A Biography of America, Air Force Television News, Conversations in Literature, Giant Pandas: The Science of Finding Food, Helping Schools Prepare for Possible Terrorism, Juvenile Justice, NASA, Project Oceanography, Social Studies in Action, Stress: Laughter is the Best Therapy, Teaching Foreign Languages, Veterans' Day: Honoring our Heritage*, and *Youth Crime Watch*.

Florida's News Channel, 3992 Bobbin Brook Circle, Tallahassee, FL 32317; *Telephone*: 850-222-6397; *Launch Date*: September 1998; *Broadcast Day*: 24 hours; *Email*: Contact channel through its web site; *Web site*: http://www.flnews.com

Florida's News Channel is a regional news broadcaster with a ground-breaking twist — the station uses state-of-the art "virtual set" technology that allows it to look like it is being broadcast from the area in which it is being watched. With this technology, what the viewer sees on the television set at home is not what a visitor would see in the studio. Virtual reality sets use chroma-key (blue-screen, green-screen, or whatever color is elected) to create a superimposed image on a television broadcast where none appears in real life. In this way, computer-generated desks or tables appear in front of anchors, charts and graphs appear in three dimensions and exist only in digital form, and advertisements can be electronically overlaid on the grass or artificial turf during broadcasts of sporting events.

Using this technology, what a viewer sees in Fort Myers looks like a local Fort Myers channel, with Fort Myers scenes in the background and Fort Myers news is generally at the top of the newscast. In Orlando, the anchors have Orlando's skyline behind them. In Palm Beach, the set looks like Palm Beach. Jacksonville looks like a local Jacksonville station set. And in Tallahassee, it looks like Tallahassee. The use of this technology extends beyond the news room. On the daily women's issue-oriented talk show, *The Florida Room*, the host and guests appear to be sitting in a Miami condo overlooking Biscayne Bay, but in reality they are sitting in Tallahassee.

Originally, the channel was envisioned as a statewide service, modeled after CNN *Headline News*, but covering only Florida. The station asked local NBC affiliates to invest in the channel as a network that they would co-own. Before this could happen, however, NBC announced its partnership with Microsoft to launch MSNBC, and the local affiliates lost interest in the Florida News Channel, although they still provide news content to the channel.

Food Network, 1180 Avenue of the Americas, 11th Floor, New York, NY 10036; *Telephone*: 212-398-8836; *Fax*: 212-736-7716; *Launch Date*: 1993; *Broadcast Day*: 24 hours; *Subscribers*: 84,000,000; *Email*: Contact the network through its web site; *Web site*: http://www.foodnetwork.com

The Food Network is part of the Scripps Networks and is the only round-the-clock cable television network and website devoted exclusively to all things related to food, cooking, travel, pop culture, and entertainment. Some of the network's popular shows include *30 Minute Meals*, *Boy Meets Grill*, *Calorie Commando*, *Emeril Live*, *Food 911*, *Recipe for Success*, *Sweet Dreams*, and *Wolfgang Puck's Cooking Class*.

The Football Network, Inc., One Touchdown Plaza, Baton Rouge, LA 70806; *Telephone*: 225-612-8000; *Fax*: 225-612-8001; *Broadcast Day*: 24 hours; *Email*: tfn-info@footballnetwork.com; *Web site*: http://www.footballnetwork.com

Planned for future operation, The Football Network will broadcast game highlights, news, features, profiles, movies, instruction, and educational programming, all dedicated to football.

Fox Broadcasting Company, 10201 West Pico Boulevard, Los Angeles, CA 90035; P.O. Box 900, Beverly Hills, CA 90213; *Telephone*: 310-369-1000; *Fax*: 310-369-1049; *Launch Date*: October 1986; *Broadcast Day*: 24 hours; *Email*: Contact network through its web site; *Web site*: http://www.fox.com

The Fox Broadcasting Company was originally created to be a national broadcast programming service for independent television stations, which would then become the network's affiliates. The growth of Fox would then allow its affiliates to compete with established affiliates of broadcast networks (ABC, CBS, and NBC) in prime time, late night, weekday afternoons, and Saturday mornings. The creation of Fox in the mid 1980s was considered risky because most television industry observers did not think the marketplace would support a fourth major broadcast network. This general industry view did not deter News Corporation Chairman and Chief Executive Officer Rupert Murdoch and his colleague Barry Diller, Chairman and Chief Executive Officer of Fox Inc. In 1986 they announced the formation of the FOX Broadcasting Company and revealed that Joan Rivers would be the host of the network's first series, *The Late Show Starring Joan Rivers*, which debuted on October 9 on 96 stations, reaching about 76 percent of the country.

On April 6, 1987 Fox launched its first night of prime time programming (Sunday) with an affiliate base of 106 stations, representing 80 percent of the country. The network's first Sunday night broadcast featured two half-hour comedies: *Married ... with Children* (a show that subverted the traditional family sitcom and became a surprise hit, putting the network on the map) and *The Tracey Ullman Show*, which would later spawn one of the network's biggest hits, *The Simpsons*. The network followed this start by airing *21 Jump Street*, which immediately attracted a large teenage following.

In July 1987 Fox launched its Saturday prime time schedule and then added Monday prime time programming, initially used for broadcasting movies and specials once or twice a month. Thursday programming was added in August 1990, Friday in September 1990, Wednesday in July 1992, and Tuesday in January 1993. Fox became a full seven-night-a-week network in June 1993 with its regularly-scheduled weekly Monday telecasts of *Fox Night at the Movies*, a mix of theatrical films, made-for-television movies, and original mini-series.

From its inception, the network strived to set itself apart from the "big 3" by adopting an irreverent program attitude and creating a youth-oriented brand identity with such programs as *The Simpsons* (the first prime time animated hit in decades), *America's Most Wanted*, *Cops* (generally identified at the originator of the reality television genre), *Beverly Hills 90210*, *Melrose Place*, *In Living Color* (which rejuvenated sketch comedy and launched the careers of Jim Carrey and Damon Wayans, among others), and the hugely successful *X-Files*.

Fox followed its growing entertainment

successes by moving into the realm of professional sports and became a major player very quickly. In December 1993, the National Football League signed an agreement that allowed the network to broadcast NFC games and the rights to Super Bowl XXXI in January 1997. In 1995 Fox signed a broadcast deal with Major League Baseball that revived the traditional game-of-the-week format and included live coverage of the 1996, 1998, and 2000 World Series, in addition to the 1997 and 1999 All-Star Games.

This period marked a rapid growth for Fox and major changes within the organization. The network aggressively pursued affiliate growth, especially with New World Communication Group Inc., that in February 1994 led to the largest affiliation switch in broadcast television history (a large part of this affiliate growth was due to the network's gaining rights to broadcast NFL games). Many of the markets that had been broadcasting Fox on a UHF signal now could broadcast on the much stronger VHF platform, allowing for better channel position and larger audience reach. This single agreement enabled Fox to establish a dominant position in many major television markets. News Corporation used its Fox Television Stations, Inc. to buy out New World Communications Group and became the largest owned and operated group of television stations in the United States. Success continued in the 1998-1999 television season when Fox proved to be the most popular network among adults 18-34 and teenagers for the first time. More importantly, the network also finished a close second among its ultimate target audience, adults 18-49.

As the Fox Broadcasting Network grew, it created brand channels to air specific programming genres aimed at targeted audiences. Launched in June 2001, the 24-hour Fox College Sports Network (http://www.foxcable.com) consists of three networks (FCS Pacific, FCS Central, and FCS Atlantic) that feature men's and women's college sporting events from across the country in all conferences. The Fox Kids Network (http://www.foxkids.com) airs programs and cartoons for younger viewers. Launched in November 1994, the Fox Movie Channel was Hollywood's first and only studio-based movie network and featured only 20th Century Fox films. As part of the 20th Century Fox Film Studio, the Fox Movie Channel has behind-the-scenes access to the stars and film makers currently making 20th Century Fox films, as well as the archives from over 75 years of movie making.

Launched in October 1996, the 24-hour Fox News Channel (http://www.foxnews.com) is a general news service that competes directly with CNN and MSNBC. Owned by News Corp. and using the tag line "Fair and Balanced" the Fox News Channel has attracted a devoted audience but has garnered intense criticism for its perceived conservative views and ties to right-wing Republican politics. The channel airs international and breaking news, talk shows, sports, entertainment, and business news. Fox Pay-Per-View (http://www.foxppv.com) provides pay-service movies, sporting events, and special broadcasts. In 2005, the network plans to launch the Fox Reality Channel that will be devoted entirely to reality television and will feature both original series and recycled programs that once aired on Fox.

Launched in June 2001, Fox Sports Digital Nets (http://www.foxcable.com) is made up of three regional broadcasts (Atlantic, Central, and Pacific) that enable digital cable subscribers living in one part of the country to see local coverage and hometown team news for their favorite teams from another part of the nation. Drawing from Fox's owned and affiliated regional networks, the three-channel multiplex offers NCAA Division I coverage, including 135 college football games, 100 college hockey games, and nearly 500 college basketball games from the top conferences.

Fox Sports en Español (http://www.fse.terra.com), first aired in February 1999, is the nation's first and largest Spanish-language sports network and delivers year-round coverage of global sporting events and programs tailored to the U.S.-based, Spanish-speaking audience. Sports coverage includes Latin American soccer, post-season Major League Baseball, auto racing, and championship boxing. Launched in 1996, Fox Sports Latin America (http://www.foxsportsla. com) is operated by Fox Pan American Sports, an international sports programming and production entity.

Launched in November 1996, Fox Sports Net (http://www.foxsports.com) is the only cable network that provides national, regional, and local sports programming. FSN serves as the cable television home to 65 of the 80 Major League Baseball, National Hockey League, and National Basketball Association teams based in the United States and produces more than 4,700 hours of live events each year. Its regional broadcasts are conducted through geographically-positioned outlets that provide local coverage of sporting news and events. Fox Sports Net (FSN) (West), based in Los Angeles, California and launched in October 1985, focuses on Southern California, Nevada, and Hawaii. Programming includes the Los Angeles Lakers, Los Angeles Kings, Anaheim Angels, Sunday Night Fights, Pac 10 and Pac 12 sports broadcasts, ACC basketball, *The Best Damn Sports Show Period*, and *The Southern California Sports Report*. Fox Sports Net (FSN) West 2 (also based in Los Angeles) programming includes the Los Angeles Dodgers, Clippers and Galaxy; the Mighty Ducks of Anaheim, USC and UCLA athletic events, live horse racing, live high school sports, *The Best Damn Sports Show Period*, and *The Southern California Sports Report*.

Fox Sports Net (FSN) Arizona, based in Phoenix and launched in September 1996, programming includes the National Hockey League's Phoenix Coyotes, Major League Baseball's Arizona Diamondbacks, Pac-10 football and basketball, University of Arizona, Arizona State University, Big 12 football, Fox Sport's Net's *Arizona Report*, and *The Best Damn Sports Show Period*. Fox Sports Net (FSN) Bay Area, located in San Francisco, California and launched in April 1990, broadcasts more than 300 live events each year, including San Francisco Giants and Oakland A's baseball, Golden State Warriors basketball, San Jose Sharks hockey, San Jose Earthquakes soccer, and Bay Area Cyber Rays, local college teams, NASCAR coverage, the *Best Damn Sports Show Period*, and the NFL Show, *Beyond the Glory*.

Fox Sports Net (FSN) Chicago (http://www.fsnchicago.com) was launched in January 1984 and its programming includes Chicago White Sox and Cubs baseball, Chicago Bulls basketball, Chicago Fire, Chicago Blackhawks hockey, and college football and basketball. FSN Chicago also airs the *Best Damn Sports Show Period*, the NFL Show, *Beyond the Glory*, and NASCAR coverage. Fox Sports Net (FSN) Detroit, launched in September 1997, programming includes Detroit Red Wings hockey, Pistons basketball, Tigers baseball, and local college sporting events.

Fox Sports Net (FSN) Florida, launched in December 1986, programming includes the Florida Marlins, Tampa Bay Devil Rays, Florida Panthers, and college football, basketball, and baseball games from the University of Miami Hurricanes, the University of South Florida Bulls, Big Ten, Big 12, and Pac-10 conferences. FSN Florida also airs the *Best Damn Sports Show Period*, the NFL Show, *Beyond the Glory*, and NASCAR coverage. Fox Sports Net (FSN) Midwest, located in St. Louis, Missouri and launched in November 1996, programming includes St. Louis Cardinals baseball, St. Louis Blues hockey, Indiana Pacers basketball, Indiana Fever basketball, Kansas City Royals baseball, Big 12 football, Big 12 Women's basketball, Big 12 Showcase, University of Missouri athletics, Kansas State University athletics, Missouri Valley Conference basketball and championship events, Gateway Conference football, Mid-Continent Conference basketball, Horizon League basketball, collegiate coaches shows, and local high school sports. FSN Midwest also features the *Midwest Sports Report*, the only nightly 30-minute show covering sports in the Midwest.

Fox Sports Net (FSN) New England (http://www.fsnnewengland.com), located in Woburn, Massachusetts and launched in November 1981, programming includes Boston Celtics basketball, Boston University hockey, New England Revolution, *New England Sports Tonight*, *The Best Damn Sports Show Period*, NASCAR coverage, and local college football and basketball. Fox Sports Net (FSN) North, located in Minneapolis, Minnesota and launched in March 1989, programming includes the NBA's Minnesota Timberwolves and Milwaukee Bucks, MLB's Milwaukee Brewers, the NHL's Minnesota Wild, the WNBA's Minnesota Lynx, University of Wisconsin, and University of Minnesota athletic events. Fox Sports Net (FSN) Northwest, located in Bellevue, Washington and launched in November 1988, programming includes the Seattle Mariners, Portland Train Blazers, Seattle Supersonics, Seattle Seahawks, PAC 10 sporting events, *Northwest Sports Report*, and national programming. Fox Sports Net (FSN) Ohio (http://www.fsnohio.com), located in Broadview Heights and launched in February 1989, programming includes the Cleveland Indians, Cincinnati Reds, Columbus Blue Jackets, Cleveland Cavaliers, and major college football and basketball sporting events.

Fox Sports Net (FSN) Pittsburgh (Pennsylvania), launched in April 1986, programming includes the Pittsburgh Penguins, Pittsburgh Pirates, the Big East, Big 10, Atlantic 10, the *Pittsburgh Regional Report*, and national Sports Net programming. Fox Sports Net (FSN) Rocky Mountain, located in Denver, Colorado and launched in November 1988, programming includes the Denver Nuggets, Utah Jazz, Colorado Rockies, Colorado Rapid, Colorado Avalanche, Utah Grizzlies, Big 12 and the University of Denver, Pac-10 Football & Basketball, ACC Basketball, and national Sports Net broadcasting.

Fox Sports Net (FSN) South, located in Atlanta, Georgia and launched in August 1990, programming includes Atlanta Braves and Baltimore Orioles baseball, Atlanta Hawks and Memphis Grizzlies basketball, Carolina Hurricanes and Nashville Predators hockey, college football, basketball, baseball, volleyball, soccer, and national Fox Sports Net shows. Fox Sports Net (FSN) Southwest, located in Irving, Texas and launched in January 1983, programming includes the Dallas Mavericks, San Antonio Spurs, Memphis Grizzlies, Texas Rangers, Houston Astros, the Dallas Stars, the Dallas Burn, Dallas Cowboys, high school sports, Big 12, ACC, SEC, WAC, Pac 10, Southland Conference, *Southwest Sports Report*, NFL Europe League, NASCAR and Formula One auto racing, PGA tour events, ATP tour events, regional outdoor shows, and national Fox Sports Net shows. Fox Sports World (http://www.foxsportsworld.com), located in Los Angeles, California and launched in November 1997, is America's soccer channel and provides year-round soccer coverage. The network airs championship rugby and nightly round-the-clock international sports news.

Free Speech TV, P.O. Box 6060, Boulder, CO 80306; *Telephone*: 888-550-3788, 303-442-8445; *Fax*: 303-442-6472; *Launch Date*: June 1995; *Broadcast Day*: 24 hours; *Subscribers*: 9,000,000; *Email*: comments@freespeech.org; *Web site*: http://www.freespeech.org

Free Speech TV uses its programs to reflect the diversity of American society and the channel tries to provide perspectives it feels are under-represented or ignored by the mainstream media. FSTV's programming focuses on citizens who are working for social change and is available on community access stations in 28 states. Free Speech TV is a public-supported, independent, non-profit television channel that is a project of Public Communicators, Inc., a non-profit organization.

The channel broadcasts independently-produced documentaries dealing with social, political, cultural, and environmental issues. The channel aims to: empower global citizens by exposing abuse of power in all forms and by highlighting efforts of resistance; build partnerships with social justice organizations and directing viewers to their work; work with, and support, the growth of independent media; and celebrate creativity and artistic expression.

Fuel TV, 1440 South Sepulveda Boulevard #1900, Los Angeles, CA 90025; *Telephone*: 310-286-3881; *Fax*: 310-286-6334; *Launch Date*: July 2003; *Broadcast Day*: 24 hours; *Subscribers*: 5,000,000; *Email*: hookup@fuel.tv; *Web site*: http://www.fuel.tv

Fuel TV is an extreme sports network that airs snowboarding, wakeboarding, surfing, BMX, motorcross, and skateboarding events.

Furia *see* **Outstanding Latin Entertainment Channel**

Fuse TV, 11 Penn Plaza, 15th Floor, New York, NY 10001; *Telephone*: 212-324-3400; *Fax*: 212-324-3469; *Launch Date*: May 2003; *Broadcast Day*: 24 hours; *Subscribers*: 35,000,000; *Email*: Contact network through its web site; *Web site*: http://www.fuse.tv

Fuse TV is America's only all-music, viewer-influenced television network and airs music videos, artist interviews, live concerts, and music-related specials. The channel targets the 12-34 audience age group and coordinates their viewing through television, internet content, and interactive games. Much of the network's on-air programming and on-site content are decided by viewer votes and input.

fX (Fox Basic Cable), 10000 Santa Monica Boulevard, Los Angeles, CA 90067, P.O. Box 990, Beverly Hills, CA 90213; *Telephone:* 310-286-3800; Fax: 310-286-6334; *Launch Date:* June 1994; *Broadcast Day:* 19 hours; *Subscribers:* 85,000,000; *Email:* Contact network through its web site; *Web site:* http://www.fxnetworks.com

Programming for the 18-49 age group, fX is a flagship general entertainment basic cable network from Fox that airs a mix of original series and movies, acquired hit television shows, box-office movie hits from 20th Century Fox, and sporting events, such as NASCAR (National Association for Stock Car Auto Racing). Popular programs include *Buffy the Vampire Slayer, COPs, Extreme Dating, Fear Factor, King of the Hill, Married ... with Children, the X-Files, Nip/Tuck*, and *The Shield* (whose star, Michael Chiklis, won basic cable's first prime time EMMY Award). Starting its broadcast life as a minor channel showing popular FOX television shows such as the *X-Files* and *Married ... with Children*, the network's reputation has been enhanced in recent years as it has emerged as a major force in original cable programming, gaining both acclaim and audience ratings for daring, edgy dramas.

G-Spot *see* **Outstanding Latin Entertainment Channel**

G4TechTV, 12312 West Olympic Boulevard, Los Angeles, CA 90064; *Telephone*: 310-979-5000; *Fax*: 310-979-5100; *Launch Date*: May 2004; *Broadcast Day*: 24 hours; *Subscribers*: 50,000,000; *Email*: info@g4media.com; *Web site*: http://www.g4techtv.com

Owned by Comcast Corporation (http://www.comcast.com), G4TechTV is dedicated to creating a lifestyle brand that is the source of entertainment, news, and information about the interactive entertainment industry, including videos, computers, online activities, and wireless games. The network (which itself is not an interactive game channel) broadcasts all original programming that currently consists of 13 weekly series and various annual specials.

Galavision, 605 Third Avenue, 12th Floor, New York, NY 10158, 9405 Northwest 41st Street, Miami, FL 33178; *Telephone*: 212-455-5300 (New York), 305-471-3900 (Miami); *Fax*: 212-455-5327 (New York), 305-471-4065 (Miami); *Launch Date*: October 1979; *Broadcast Day*: 24 hours; *Subscribers*: 40,000,000; *Email*: comments@galavision.

com; *Web site*: http://www.galavision.com, http://www.univisionnetworks.com

Owned and operated by Univision Communications, Inc. and available to 85 percent of all Hispanic cable households, Galavision is the leading Spanish-language cable network in the United States with round-the-clock programming aimed at the young Hispanic market. The network's programming includes sports (featuring coverage of the very popular Futbol Liga Mexicana), music, bi-cultural shows, educational children's programming, all Spanish-language news, novellas, variety, movies, and monthly specials.

Univision Communications Inc. is the premier Spanish-language media company in the United States. Its operations include Univision Network; TeleFutura Network (a general-interest Spanish-language broadcast television network, which was launched in 2002 and now reaches 80 percent of U.S. Hispanic Households); Univision Television Group (owns and operates 24 Univision Network television stations and one non-Univision television station); TeleFutura Television Group (owns and operates 31 TeleFutura Network television stations); Galavision; Univision Radio (leading Spanish-language radio group which owns and/or operates 68 radio stations in 17 of the top 25 U.S. Hispanic markets and four stations in Puerto Rico); Univision Music Group (includes Univision Records, Fonovisa Records, and a 50 percent interest in Mexico-based Disa Records labels as well as Fonomusic and America Musical Publishing companies); and Univision Online (http://www.univision.com, premier Spanish-language Internet destination in the United States). Univision Communications also has a 50 percent interest in TuTv, a joint venture formed to broadcast Televisa's pay television channels in the United States, and a non-voting 27 percent interest in Entravision Communications Corporation, a public Spanish-language media company.

Gallery HD, 200 Jericho Quadrangle, Jericho, NY 11753; *Telephone*: 516-803-6010; *Email*: Contact channel through its web site; *Web site*: http://www.voom.com

Gallery HD is a high definition multiplexed channel from Voom that showcases stunning artwork in visual detail and provides viewers a behind-the-scenes look at the art world.

Game Bank, 2300 Star Bank Center, Cincinnati, OH 45202; *Telephone*: 513-381-0777; *Launch Date*: November 1995; *Broadcast Day*: 8 hours; *Email*: Contact channel through its web site; *Web site*: http://www.lottery.com

Game Bank provides entertainment and informational programs focusing on state-sponsored lotteries.

Game Show Network, 2150 Colorado Avenue #100, Santa Monica, CA 90404; *Telephone*: 310-255-6800; *Fax*: 310-255-6975; *Launch Date*: December 1994; *Broadcast Day*: 24 hours; *Subscribers*: 54,000,000; *Email*: Contact network through its web site; *Web site*: http://www. gameshownetwork.com, http://www.gsn.com

Jointly owned by Sony Pictures Entertainment and Liberty Media Corporation, the Game Show Network (often referred to as GSN: The Network for Games) is the only American network dedicated to game-related programming and interactive game playing. The network features game shows, reality series, documentaries, video game programs, and casino games. GSN's interactive programming allows viewers a chance to win prizes by playing along with the network's televised games through its web site.

Gem Shopping Network, 3414 Howell Street, Duluth, GA 30096; *Telephone*: 888-791-8805, 770-814-0773; *Launch Date*: May 1997; *Email*: info@gemshopping.com; *Web site*: http://www.gemshopping.com

The Gem Shopping Network, in its current form, began operations in 1997; however, Gemologist Frank Circelli was the host of the first, and original, gemstone show on television in 1981. That show was seen only on weekends and reached a limited market. GSN now reaches a national market and offers a large variety of quality jewelry from around the world.

German TV, P.O. Box 573, Great Falls, VA 22066; *Telephone*: 703-759-9696; *Launch Date*: April 2002; *Broadcast Day*: 24 hours; *Email*: Contact channel through its web site; *Web site*: http://www.german.tv

German TV is a joint collaboration of ARD, ZDF, and Deutsche Welle that airs German publicly-supported television. An international premium service, the network presents a diverse selection of programming in German to American audiences, such as news, entertainment programs, children's shows, and soccer.

GETv Program Network, P.O. Box 38306, Pittsburgh, PA 15238; *Telephone*: 412-782-2921; *Fax*: 412-782-4242; *Broadcast Day*: 24 hours

Planned for future operation, the GETv Program Network will broadcast live entertainment, interactive games, tournaments, live simulcast races, shopping, business, news, and specials focusing on the international gaming entertainment industry.

Global Village Network, P.O. Box 6218, Honolulu, HI 96818; *Telephone*: 808-348-4028; *Fax*: 808-423-0565; *Broadcast Day*: 24 hours

Planned for future operation, the Global Village Network will broadcast international business and world culture programs.

Globalvision, 575 8th Avenue #2200, New York, NY 10018; *Telephone*: 212-246-0202; *Fax*: 212-246-2677; *Email*: Contact network through its web site; *Web site*: http://www.global vision.org

Globalvision is a full-service, independent, international media company specializing in information, entertainment, and educational programming. With a list of customers including CBS News, Time Warner, Disney, Nippon Television, Universal Pictures, The Gates Foundation, the Open Society, Greenpeace, Sierra Club, Amnesty International, UNICEF, the United Auto Workers, The Body Shop, Coca-Cola Company, Reebok International, and others, the network produces news magazines, nationally televised specials, documentary films, and public service campaigns.

God's Learning Channel, 3719 South County Road 1305, Odessa, TX 79765, P.O. Box 61000, Midland, TX 79711; *Telephone*: 800-707-0420, 432-563-0420; *Fax*: 432-563-1736; *Email*: Contact channel through its web site; *Web site*: http://www. godslearning channel.com

God's Learning Channel is a religious satellite network dedicated to broadcasting the Word Of God.

Gol TV, 1560 J. F. Kennedy Causeway, North Bay Village, FL 33141; *Telephone*: 305-864-9799; *Fax*: 305-554-6776; *Launch Date*: March 2003; *Broadcast Day*: 24 hours; *Email*: Contact channel through its web site; *Web site*: http://www.goltv.tv

Operated by Uruguayan company Tenfield, Gol TV airs more than 800 soccer games per year, many of them live, and focuses on teams from Mexico, Central and South America, Spain, and Italy. This is the first and only channel dedicated to broadcasting soccer to audiences in the United States and Canada.

Golden Eagle Broadcasting, 7777 South Lewis Avenue, Tulsa, OK 74171; *Telephone*: 800-255-4407, 918-495-7288; *Fax*: 918-495-7388; *Launch Date*: November 1998; *Broadcast Day*: 24 hours; *Subscribers*: 250,000; *Email*: golden-eagle@oru.edu; *Web site*: http://www.golden-eagle-tv.com

Golden Eagle Broadcasting airs on Sky Angel (http://www.skyangel.com) and originates from the campus of Oral Roberts University in Tulsa, Oklahoma. GEB aims to provide an alternative programming option to mainstream television and its fare includes after-school shows for kids, worship, healing and teaching programs, original shows, movies, musicals, and special presentations.

The Golf Channel, 7580 Commerce Center Drive, Orlando, FL 32819; *Telephone*: 407-355-4653; *Fax*: 407-363-7976; *Launch Date*: January 1995; *Broadcast Day*: 24 hours; *Subscribers*: 59,000,000; *Email*: Contact channel through its web site; *Web site*: http://www.thegolfchannel.com

Launched by entrepreneur Joseph Gibbs and golf legend Arnold Palmer, the Golf Channel features a programming schedule that includes more live golf coverage than any other network as well as news, instruction, and original specials. The Golf Channel's first live televised tournament was the Dubai Desert Classic, which aired January 19-22, 1995. The network airs a variety of tournaments, including the Nationwide Tour, the European Tour, the Champions Tour, the Ladies Professional Golf Association Tour, the United States Golf Association Tour, the Professional Golf Association Tour, the PGA Champions Tour of Australasia, and the Sunshine Tour of Southern Africa.

Original programs on the channel include *Golf Central*, a nightly golf news show; *Golf Talk*, a talk show featuring some of the game's biggest names; *Academy Live*, a weekly call-in show that offers viewers an opportunity to improve their game by consulting with top professional teachers; *The Golf Channel Academy*, a series of half-hour instructional programs; *Playing Lessons From the Pros*, a series that provides instruction from Tour players during their off-day practice rounds; *Peter Jacobsen Plugged In*, a series featuring Jacobsen's views on the world of golf; *The Golf Channel Pre- and Post-Game Show*, a twice-weekly tournament show featuring news, statistics, interviews, and analysis on the week's tournaments; *College Central*, a weekly news show covering men's and women's collegiate golf competition; *Inside the Nationwide Tour*, an in-depth look at the competition and life of the players on the Nationwide Tour; *Golf with Style*, a look at the lifestyle of golf, from travel to apparel to club living; and *What's in the Bag?*, a series focusing on golf equipment and accessories. Other programs focus on celebrity interviews, video tours of the world's great golf courses, classic and historical golf tournaments and moments in the sport, and golf-related documentaries.

The Golf Channel's 50,000-square-foot facility houses the network's corporate offices and studio operations. The highlight of the facility is a 6,000-square-foot, state-of-the-art television studio that includes four broadcast sets and an area for golf instruction. Important dates in the time line of The Golf Channel include January 20-22, 1995 (the network televises its first domestic tournament, the LPGA HealthSouth Disney Classic at Lake Buena Vista, Florida); July 20-23, 1995 (the network televises its first PGA Tour event, the Deposit Guaranty Classic at Madison, Mississippi); May 31-June 2, 1996 (The Golf Channel televises its first Senior PGA Tour event, the Bruno's Memorial Classic at Birmingham, Alabama); October 1, 1996 (broadcasting in Japan begins); October 17, 1997 (broadcasting begins in Canada); October 28, 1998 (the channel airs its first original documentary, *Arnold Palmer: Golf's Heart and Soul*, that explores the life of golf legend Arnold Palmer); and February 2001 (in an effort to bring viewers closer to the game, The Golf Channel begins fitting Canadian Tour players with microphones during competition).

GoodLife Television Network, 650 Massachusetts Avenue Northwest, Washington, D.C. 20001; *Telephone*: 202-289-6633; *Fax*: 202-289-6632; *Launch Date*: February 1985; *Broadcast Day*: 24 hours; *Subscribers*: 12,000,000; *Email*: Contact channel through its web site; *Web site*: http://www.goodtv.com

Part of the Nostalgia Network, the GoodLife Television Network is the nation's only full-time cable channel dedicated to improving the quality of American life through information and entertainment programs which reflect the attitudes and traditional values important to its primary audience, baby boomers and older viewers.

Gospel & Christian Music Television Network (Planned for future operation)

Gospel Music Channel (Planned for future operation)

Gospel Music Television Network, 3119 North River Road, Pigeon Forge, TN 37863; P.O. Box 606, Pigeon Forge, TN 37868; *Telephone*: 865-453-4683; *Broadcast Day*: 24 hours; *Email*: Contact network through its web site; *Web site*: http://www.gmtn.com

The non-profit Gospel Music Television Network broadcasts on Sky Angel (http://www.sky angel.com) and features popular southern gospel music artists such as The Gaithers, The Cathedrals, Kirk Tally, The Hoppers, J.D. Sumner, and The Isaacs. Programs include *Hill Country Gospel*, *Texas Gospel*, *Black Gospel*, and special events such as the Quartet Convention and the three-day Gospel World Premier (in August of each year). The network operates a Gospel Record Club through which viewers can order the latest videos, CD's, and audio cassettes of their favorite gospel recording artists.

Government Channel, 1000 Universal Studios Plaza, Building 22-A, Orlando, FL 32819; *Telephone*: 407-224-6830; *Launch Date*: August 2003; *Broadcast Day*: 24 hours; *Email*: Contact channel through its web site; *Web site*: http://www. governmentchannel.tv

The Government Channel is a national public affairs cable television network that broadcasts all local city, county, and state legislatures, assemblies, floor sessions and committee meetings, press conferences, and proceedings of regulatory boards.

Grandes Documentales, 1100 Ponce de Leon Boulevard, Coral Gables, FL 33134; *Telephone*: 305-444-4402; *Fax*: 305-554-6776; *Launch Date*: Fall 1996; *Email*: Contact channel through its web site; *Web site*: http://www.rtve.es

Grandes Documentales is a commercial-free educational documentary channel that features biographies; travel series; documentaries on nature, science, and adventure from all over the hemisphere; and stories and adventures from Patagonia to Baja, California. All programs are aired with no dubbing or subtitles.

Great American Country, 9697 East Mineral Avenue, Englewood, CO 80112; *Telephone*: 303-792-3111; *Launch Date*: December 1995; *Broadcast Day*: 24 hours; *Subscribers*: 27,000,000; *Email*: Contact network through its web site; *Web site*: http://www.gactv.com

Owned by Jones Media Networks, Great American Country is a country-music video network that targets its programs to the 25-54 year-old audience. The channel airs music videos, celebrity interviews, concerts, and exclusive performances.

GSN: The Network for Games *see* **Game Show Network**

Guardian Television Network, 3948 Townsfair Way, Columbus, OH 43219; *Telephone*: 614-416-6080; *Fax*: 614-416-6345; *Email*: comments@gtn.tv; *Web site*: http://www. gtn.tv

The Guardian Television Network airs on Sky Angel (http://www.skyangel.com) and is a Christian family channel that features popular Christian ministries and programs, entertainment shows (such as *Lassie*, *Miracle Pets*, *Green Acres*, *Mr. Ed*, and *America's Funniest Home Videos*), family dramas, game shows, and major sporting events. The network also airs family-oriented movies that are edited for language and content.

Gunslingers HD, 200 Jericho Quadrangle, Jericho, NY 11753; *Telephone*: 516-803-6010; *Email*: Contact channel through its web site; *Web site*: http://www.voom.com

Gunslingers HD is a high definition multiplexed channel from Voom that shows classic western movies.

Gwinnett News & Entertainment Television, 166 Buford Avenue, P.O. Box 603, Lawrenceville, GA 30046; *Telephone*: 770-963-9205; *Fax*: 770-339-5858; *Launch Date*: May 1997; *Broadcast Day*: 24 hours; *Subscribers*: 92,000

Operated by Gray Communications and located in suburban Atlanta, Gwinnett News & Entertainment Television offers a mix of news and community-focused programming. The channel provides exposure for the *Gwinnett Daily Post*, the Gray-owned newspaper, giving it a high local profile in its head-to-head competition with the *Atlanta Journal-Constitution*. The channel produces and airs daily sports, health, and public affairs programs and its schedule rotates throughout the day in a "Headline News" format.

Ha! Comedy Network *see* **Comedy Central**

Hallmark Channel, 17200 Ventura Boulevard #200, Studio City, CA 91604; *Telephone*: 818-755-2400; *Launch Date*: September 1988; *Broadcast Day*: 24 hours; *Subscribers*: 65,000,000; *Email*: Contact channel through its web site; *Web site*: http://www. hallmarkchannel.com

Owned by Crown Media Holdings, Inc, the Hallmark Channel broadcasts a diverse mix of programs and has developed original programming well-known for focusing on holidays. Its affiliate, the Hallmark Movie Channel, airs round-the-clock general entertainment movies. The combined channels are distributed to more than 120 countries and can be seen in over 120 million households around the world. Hallmark Channel programming includes movies, miniseries, and popular television shows (such as *Hawaii Five-O*, *Bonanza*, *JAG*, *Walker, Texas Ranger*, *Diagnosis Murder*, *M*A*S*H*, *Little House on the Prairie*, *Matlock*, *Magnum P.I.*, and *The Waltons*). The 24-hour Hallmark Movie Channel, launched in January 2004, is a digital network that features top-rated movies and miniseries from the 4,000 hours of programming in the Hallmark Channel library.

HD Cinema, 200 Jericho Quadrangle, Jericho, NY 11753; *Telephone*: 516-803-6010; *Email*: Contact channel through its web site; *Web site*: http://www.voom.com

HD Cinema is a series of high definition multiplexed channels from Voom that broadcast specialized genre movies targeted at specific audiences.

HDNet, 2400 North Ulster Street, Denver, CO 80238; *Telephone*: 303-388-8500; *Launch Date*: September 2001; *Broadcast Day*: 24 hours; *Email*: Contact channel through its web site; *Web site*: http://www.hd.net

HDNet features a variety of high definition television programming that includes live sporting events (such as Major League Soccer, National Hockey League, college and professional football and basketball, boxing, and horse racing), sitcoms, dramas, action series, documentaries, travel programs, music concerts, and news. HDNet also airs classic and recent television series from Paramount Domestic Television and Sony Pictures Television (such as *Hogan's Heroes*, *Charlie's Angels*, and *Square Pegs*). HDNet Movies, launched in January 2003, broadcasts full-length feature films converted from 35mm to high-definition format and airs a mix of theatrical releases, made-for-television movies, independent films, and shorts.

HD News, 200 Jericho Quadrangle, Jericho, NY 11753; *Telephone*: 516-803-6010; *Email*: Contact channel through its web site; *Web site*: http://www.voom.com

HD News is a high definition multiplexed channel from Voom and is the only national round-the-clock high definition source for news. The channel broadcasts late-breaking news, current headlines, long-form features, national and regional weather, and sports news and highlights.

HD World Cinema, 200 Jericho Quadrangle, Jericho, NY 11753; *Telephone*: 516-803-6010; *Email*: Contact channel through its web site; *Web site*: http://www.voom.com

HD World Cinema is a high definition multiplexed channel from Voom that features foreign films.

Headline News *see* **Cable News Network**

Healing and Health TV (Planned for future operation)

Health & Sciences Television Network, 4101 International Parkway, Carrollton, TX 75007; *Telephone*: 800-942-4786, 972-309-4000; *Fax*: 972-309-5105; *Email*: Contact network through its web site; *Web site*: http://www.hstn.com

Operated by PRIMEDIA Healthcare, the Health & Sciences Television Network educates and trains healthcare professionals with video-on-demand classes, instructional programs, and other distance learning technologies. The network partners with employers to create and sustain staff development programs that promote lifelong learning and ensure continued, updated certification-based curriculum.

Health Broadcasting Network *see* **Health TV Channel, Inc.**

Health Network, 7700 Wisconsin Avenue, Bethesda, MD 20814; *Telephone*: 301-986-0444; *Launch Date*: December 1993; *Broadcast Day*: 24 hours; *Subscribers*: 30,000,000; *Email*: info@healthnetwork.com; *Web site*: http://www.healthnetwork.com

The Health Network features doctors and health experts broadcasting from studios and discussing well-being and nutrition-related topics for both men and women. Programming includes *Aerobic Conditioning*, *Gilad's Bodies in Motion*, and *Food for Life*.

Health TV Channel, Inc., 3820 Lake Otis Parkway, Anchorage, AK 99508; *Telephone*: 907-770-6200; *Fax*: 907-336-6205; *Email*: info@ healthtvchannel.org, info@ healthbroadcastingnetwork.com; *Web site*: http://www.healthtvchannel.org, http://www.healthbroadcastingnetwork.com

The Health TV Channel, Inc. is a non-profit organization that provides health education and training with a focus on partnering with providers and originators of health information to create a multi-media resource for consumers and health professionals. The channel has also launched the World Health Digital Network, which is an educational television project aimed at medical and health professionals. Broadcast in the United States, Asia, Latin America, Europe, the Middle East, and Africa, the channel features medical and health training in 24 languages and dialects. Its educational content originates from universities, Ministries of Health, international development organizations, and medical and public health experts. The programs are aimed at health practitioners, policy decision-makers at local and national levels, elected officials, and hospital workers. The ultimate goal of the project is to increase the level of international medical and public health training in the hopes of saving lives and fighting global diseases, such as HIV/AIDS.

here! TV, 10990 Wilshire Boulevard, Penthouse, Los Angeles, CA 90024; *Telephone*: 310-806-4298; *Fax*: 310-806-4268; *Launch Date*: August 2003; *Broadcast Day*: 24 hours; *Subscribers*: 25,000,000; *Email*: Contact channel through its web site; *Web site*: http://www.heretv.com

here! TV broadcasts programs aimed at the gay and lesbian audience, including movies, original series, and documentaries.

High School TV Network (Planned for future operation)

Hip Hop Network, 541 One Center Boulevard #108, Altamonte Springs, FL 32701;

Telephone: 407-463-6122; *Launch Date*: January 1997; *Broadcast Day*: 24 hours

Planned for future operation, the Hip-Hop Network will be the official music video film channel for the hip-hop music genre.

Hispanic Information and Telecommunications Network, 449 Broadway, 3rd Floor, New York, NY 10013; *Telephone*: 212-966-5660; *Fax*: 212-966-5725; *Launch Date*: 1987; *Subscribers*: 10,000,000; *Email*: info@hitn.org; *Web site*: http://www.hitn.org; http://www.hitn.tv

The Hispanic Information and Telecommunications Network was the first Hispanic public television network in the United States and is the most distributed Spanish-language cable channel in America. HITN was initially formed as a private non-profit organization to create a network of non-commercial telecommunications facilities to advance the educational, social, cultural, and economic aspirations of Hispanics. Network programming includes *Corriente Cultural* (an original series that focuses on the cultural accomplishments and contribution of the Hispanic community to the United States culture), *Noticultura* (a ten-minute news segment on current events, art, theater, music and dance), *TeleAprende* (provides television-based lessons in Spanish), *La Hora de Bellas Artes* (*The Hour of Fine Arts*— a series focusing on performing and visual arts, opera, dance and ballet, and theater), documentaries, children's and family programs, immigration news, personal finance, health, and sports.

Hispanic TV Network (Planned for future operation)

History Channel, 235 East 4th Street, New York, NY 10017; *Telephone*: 212-210-1400; *Fax*: 212-692-9269; *Launch Date*: 1995; *Broadcast Day*: 24 hours; *Subscribers*: 86,000,000; *Email*: Contact channel through its web site; *Web site*: http://www. historychannel.com

A brand channel of the A&E Television Networks, the History Channel features historical documentaries, weekly series, miniseries, movie presentations, and specials that focus on the history of the world, including events and people. With the tag line "Where History Comes Alive," the channel uses its programming to help viewers experience history on a personal level and to show how events of the past affect their lives in today's world. Launched in June 2004, the 24-hour History Channel en Español (http://www. historychannel.com/espanol) broadcasts world and Latin America history programming to the Spanish-speaking audience in the United States. Launched in November 1998, the 24-hour History Channel International (http://www. historyinternational. com) provides viewers with a non-American perspective on international historical events and people, Viewers are offered a mix of historical documentaries, original short features, interviews with historians, and interaction with the network's web site.

Hollywood.com Television *see* **Totally Hollywood TV**

Home & Garden Television, 9721 Sherrill Boulevard, Knoxville, TN 37932; *Telephone*: 865-694-2700; *Fax*: 865-531-8933; *Launch Date*: 1994; *Broadcast Day*: 24 hours; *Subscribers*: 86,000,000; *Email*: Contact channel through its web site; *Web site*: http://www. hgtv.com

Home & Garden Television is part of the Scripps Networks, presents some of America's best home builders, decorators, gardeners, and craft experts, and offers practical information and creative ideas to help people make the most of their lives at home. The channel uses its web site as an interactive companion to its television broadcast and provides instructions for thousands of home and garden projects, video tips, an interactive Program Guide, and episode finder. HGTV owns 33 percent of HGTV Canada and provides much of the Canadian network's daily programming.

Home Box Office, 1100 Avenue of the

Americas, New York, NY 10036; *Telephone*: 212-512-1000; *Fax*: 212-512-1182; *Launch Date*: November 1972; *Broadcast Day*: 24 hours; *Subscribers*: 40,000,000; *Email*: Contact network through its web site; *Web site*: http://www.hbo.com

A division of Time Warner, Home Box Office is the oldest and most well-known of the original pay-for-service networks. HBO airs more than 1,600 movie titles a year in addition to comedy specials, documentaries, original series, music concerts, family programming, sports specials, and world championship boxing. HBO's multiplexed channels (HBO, HBO2, HBO Signature (formerly HBO3), HBO Family, HBO Comedy, HBO Zone, and HBO Latino) are known collectively as HBO The Works. Each channel airs its own programming and appeals to selected targeted markets.

In 1976, HBO became the first television network to broadcast its signal via satellite when it showed the "Thrilla From Manila" boxing match between Muhammad Ali and Joe Frazier. In 1981 the network aired the first made-for-pay-television movie, *The Terry Fox Story*, and in 1986, HBO became the first satellite network to encrypt its signal from unauthorized viewing.

HBO expanded its reach into broadcast television in 1990 with the formation of HBO Independent Productions, which develops and produces series television. Its first show was *Roc*, which aired on the Fox Network. HBO has since provided program content to CBS, ABC, TNT, and USA Lifetime, among others. Recognizing a change in viewer trend toward pre-recorded videocassettes, HBO further diversified in 1984 and formed (with Thorn EMI Entertainment) EMI/HBO Home Video (now known as HBO Home Video), which acquires and distributes home video programs in the United States and Canada.

In addition to its brand channels, HBO's affiliate channels include Cinemax, @Max, @MAX Choice, 5StarMax, 5StarMAX Choice, ActionMax, MartialMax, MoreMax, MoreMAX Choice, MoreMAX Vanguard, OuterMax, ThrillerMAX, Wmax, and WMax Choice.

HBO2, launched in October 1988, is a 24-hour pay channel that offers viewers movies, specials, original series, sports programming, and repeats of HBO broadcasts. The channel is designed to counter-program fare available on HBO. Launched in May 1999, HBO Comedy is a 24-hour comedy channel designed to appeal to a broad audience with a variety of comedic tastes. The channel shows Hollywood films, HBO original series, and stand-up specials—all uncut and uncensored.

The 24-hour HBO Family Channel, launched in October 1998, provides entertainment aimed at the entire family, including original productions, after-school specials, and movies. Launched in November 2000, HBO Latino broadcasts programs that reflect the diversity of Latino culture in the United States. The 24-hour channel features Spanish-language films, new and original on-air programming filmed around the country, live boxing commentary in Spanish, Hollywood movies, and original programming from HBO.

HBO on Demand allows viewers to choose from over 100 HBO offerings, including original programming, Hollywood movies, specials, and kids programming. HBO On Demand offers the best of what's currently on HBO, plus episodes of programming from past seasons. Launched in October 1998, HBO Signature is a 24-hour channel that offers programming that appeals to women, including contemporary documentaries, HBO original series, HBO original movies, and theatrical movies—all with a feminine perspective. The 24-hour HBO Zone channel, launched in May 1999, is aimed at young viewers and airs documentaries, original television series, and exclusive music videos.

Home Collector Network (Planned for future operation)

Home Improvement Channel, 1000 Universal Studios Plaza, Building 22-A,

Orlando, FL 32819; *Telephone*: 407-224-6830; *Launch Date*: December 2003; *Broadcast Day*: 24 hours; *Email*: Contact channel through its web site; *Web site*: http://www.homeimprovementchannel.com

Part of the Real Estate Channel, the Home Improvement Channel focuses on education, information, and electronic retailing for the home and garden market.

Home Shopping Network, P.O. Box 9090, Clearwater, FL 34618, One HSN Drive, St. Petersburg, FL 33729; *Telephone*: 727-872-1000; *Fax*: 727-872-6924; *Launch Date*: July 1985; *Broadcast Day*: 24 hours; *Subscribers*: 81,000,000; *Email*: Contact network through its web site; *Web site*: http://www.hsn.com

A subsidiary of IAC/InterActiveCorp and operating out of a 500,000-square-foot facility, the Home Shopping Network started the electronic retailing industry, as we know it today, in 1977. The initial idea materialized on a small AM radio station in Florida and has since grown into a global multichannel retailer with worldwide sales of more than $2 billion and a customer base of over five million. Its customer service center fields over 70 million calls a year. To ensure timely delivery of merchandise, HSN has established fulfillment centers in Salem and Roanoke, Virginia, Waterloo, Iowa, and Fontana, California, as well as in Germany, Japan, and China. HSN ships 90,000 to 130,000 packages per day; for a total of 44 million packages per year.

The network offers approximately 22,000 unique products in such categories as home and entertainment, health and beauty, fashion and jewelry, and electronics. Well-known celebrities have appeared on the network selling their own product lines, including actress Rita Wilson (jewelry), actress Raquel Welch (jewelry), singer Patti Labelle (fashion apparel), celebrity chef Wolfgang Puck (book about cooking), actress/model Lauren Hutton (makeup), actress Susan Lucci (fashion), and actress Suzanne Somers (fitness and fashion). Launched in September 1986, America's Store (http://www.americasstore.com) is a live, 24-hour retailing channel.

Home Team Sports (Planned for future operation)

Hope Channel *see* **Adventist Television Network**

Hope Channel (Esperanza TV), P.O. Box 4000, Silver Spring, MD 20914; *Telephone*: 301-680-6689; *Fax*: 301-680-6624; *Launch Date*: October 2003 (Esperanza TV launched in 2004); *Broadcast Day*: 24 hours; *Email*: info@hopetv.org; *Web site*: http://www.hopetv.org

The Hope Channel is a global satellite Christian television network that broadcasts programs aimed to inspire people with hope, faith, and enthusiasm for life. The channel's programs address real-life issues, while striving to entertain, and include documentaries, reality television, health, women's issues, and travel. The network broadcasts five channels in English, Spanish, and Portuguese, with over 40 production centers around the world.

Horror Channel, 161 Avenue of the Americas, 11th Floor, New York, NY 10013; *Telephone*: 212-337-0536; *Launch Date*: October 2004; *Broadcast Day*: 24 hours; *Email*: Contact channel through its web site; *Web site*: http://www.horrorchannel.com

Operated by Terrorvision Television, the Horror Channel will be the first and only round-the-clock channel dedicated to broadcasting the horror, terror, and suspense-movie genre and will air classic and contemporary movies, specials, and original series.

HorseRacing TV, 499 Racetrack Road, Meadow Lands, PA 15347; *Telephone*: 866-733-4788; *Launch Date*: January 2003; *Broadcast Day*: 24 hours (up to 15 hours are broadcast live each day); *Subscribers*: 1,500,000; *Email*: customerservice@hr.tv; *Web site*: http://www.horseracingtv.com

Operated by Magna Entertainment Corporation, HorseRacing TV provides wire-to-wire coverage of live horse racing action from more than 70 thoroughbred, harness, and quarter horse racetracks in the United States and Canada. MEC is also a leader in interactive wagering and owns a variety of racetracks, including Santa Anita Park near Los Angeles, Gulfstream Park near Miami, Lone Star Park at Grand Prairie near Dallas, and Pimlico Race Course in Baltimore, home of The Preakness Stakes. HRTV programming includes post parades, odds and results, and live racing and replays from up to three tracks at a time. A live host guides viewers, from track to track, and offers handicapping commentary between races.

HorseTV, 9434 Old Katy Road #380, Houston, TX 77055; *Telephone*: 713-468-2014; *Fax*: 713-468-2111; *Launch Date*: December 2000; *Broadcast Day*: 24 hours; *Email*: geninfo@horse-tv.com; *Web site*: http://www.-horse-tv.com

HorseTV was launched as part of the equestrian programming block on Rural Farm TV (RFD-TV) (see separate entry) and in August 2001 the channel moved its programming distribution to the America One Television Network (see separate entry). Since then, HorseTV has been providing up to 20+ hours of equestrian programming nationwide through local television stations, select cable systems, and satellite providers. HorseTV launched the HorseTV i-Channel on the internet, which provides access to its programming for viewers who are unable to watch the channel through traditional television methods. Programming includes documentaries, competitions and events from around the world, and educational, instructional, and veterinary shows.

Hot Choice, 909 Third Avenue, New York, NY 10022; *Telephone*: 212-486-6600; *Fax*: 212-688-9497; *Email*: Contact channel through its web site; *Web site*: http://www.ppv.com

Hot Choice is an adult pay-per-view channel available through a variety of cable and satellite television providers.

Hot Networks, 2706 Media Center Drive, Los Angeles, CA 90065; *Telephone*: 323-276-4000; *Launch Date*: March 1999; *Broadcast Day*: 24 hours; *Email*: Contact network through its web site; *Web site*: http://www.playboytv.com

Available through the Playboy TV Networks, the Hot Networks (Hot Net, Hot Zone, and Vivid TV), offer adult-oriented pay-per-view programming.

HTV (Hispanic TV), 404 Washington Avenue, Penthouse, Miami, FL 33139; *Telephone*: 305-894-3500; *Launch Date*: August 1995; *Broadcast Day*: 24 hours; *Subscribers*: 7,000,000; *Email*: Contact channel through its web site; *Web site*: http://www.htv.com

Available only in Spanish and programmed by customer requests, HTV is an all-Latin, all-music channel that has artists introduce each video, instead of Video Jockeys (VJs). The channel plays a variety of music genres, including salsa, meringue, bachata, cumbia, ballads, pop, Latin-rock, tropical, reggae, flamenco, and samba.

Hustler TV, 8484 Wilshire Boulevard #900, Beverly Hills, CA 90211; *Telephone*: 323-651-5400; *Launch Date*: October 2004; *Broadcast Day*: 24 hours; *Email*: Contact channel through its web site; *Web site*: http://hustlertv.com

Similar to Playboy TV, Hustler TV offers adult pay-per-view entertainment from Hustler Video, VCA Pictures, and original programs. The channel also offers Hustler TV Video-On-Demand.

The Ice Channel, 74-830 Velie Way, Suite A, Palm Desert, CA 92260; *Telephone*: 760-776-5500; *Fax*: 760-776-5575; *Broadcast Day*: 24 hours; *Email*: Contact channel through its web site; *Web site*: http://www.theicechannel.com

Planned for future operation, The Ice Channel broadcasts figure skating shows, live competitions, archival programs of past performances, reality shows, musicals on ice, coaches instructional shows, talent searches, cartoons, movies, and soap operas.

Idea Channel, 9006 Main Street, McKean, PA 16426; *Telephone*: 800-388-0662, 814-464-9068; *Fax*: 814-464-9068; *Email*: info@ideachannel.com; *Web site*: http://www.ideachannel.com

The Idea Channel airs videotaped conversations between some of the world's greatest thinkers, including numerous Nobel Prize Winners.

ImaginAsian TV, 450 Seventh Avenue #706, New York, NY 10123; *Telephone*: 212-239-4048; *Launch Date*: August 2004; *Broadcast Day*: 24 hours; *Email*: Contact channel through its web site; *Web site*: http://www.imaginasiantv.com

ImaginAsian TV is the first round-the-clock Asian-American network that provides Pan-Asian programming featuring box office hits, popular dramatic series, art house films, classics, anime, news, variety and game shows, sports, martial arts, children's programs, documentaries, and cult favorites.

Impulse TV, 8437 Warner Drive, Culver City, CA 90232; *Telephone*: 310-838-8327; *Fax*: 310-838-8394; *Launch Date*: 2004; *Email*: contactus@impulsedigital.com; *Web site*: http://www.impulsedigital.com

A division of the Impulse Digital TV Group, Impulse TV is an adult network with a unique twist — it was created by women for women. The network wants to expand adult broadcast fare to include women viewers and to provide an additional, previously untapped, source of revenue to cable and satellite providers.

Independent Film Channel, 200 Jericho Quadrangle, Jericho, NY 11753; *Telephone*: 516-803-3000; *Launch Date*: September 1994; *Broadcast Day*: 24 hours; *Subscribers*: 29,000,000; *Email*: Contact channel through its web site; *Web site*: http://www.ifctv.com

Owned and operated by the Bravo Networks (an NBC channel), the Independent Film Channel broadcasts independent films, uncut and commercial-free. The channel also airs original series and live events, including the Independent Spirit Awards and the Cannes Film Festival.

Independent Music Network, 20 Old Stagecoach Road, Redding, CT 06896, 675 Third Avenue, 12th Floor, New York, NY 10017; *Telephone*: 212-557-5557 (New York); *Fax*: 212-557-7416; *Launch Date*: June 2000; *Broadcast Day*: 24 hours; *Email*: info@imntv.com; *Web site*: http://www.imntv.com

A division of the Falcon Entertainment Corporation, the Independent Music Network broadcasts music videos by independent and unsigned musicians in an effort to give the artists a wider audience and, possibly, a shot at fame. All unknown musicians are welcome and the chance of getting their video aired on this network is almost 100 percent; the network states it will "play anything and everything."

Infinito, 1550 Biscayne Boulevard, Miami, FL 33132; *Telephone*: 305-894-3500; *Fax*: 305-554-6776; *Email*: Contact channel through its web site; *Web site*: http://www.infinito.com

Infinito airs original programming that focuses on unexplained phenomena, religion, spiritualism, the unknown, and the obscure.

Infomerical TV (planned for future operation)

Inspiration Network, 7910 Crescent Executive Drive, Fifth Floor, Charlotte, NC 28217, P.O. Box 7750, Charlotte, NC 28241; *Telephone*: 704-525-9800; *Fax*: 704-525-9899, 704-561-7960; *Launch Date*: 1990; *Broadcast Day*: 24 hours; *Subscribers*: 22,000,000; *Email*: info@insp.com; *Web site*: http://www.insp.org, http://www.insp.com; http://www. inspnets.com

The Inspiration Network broadcasts on

Sky Angel (http://www.skyangel.com) and provides more than 200 weekly programs produced by more than 75 ministries, representing 20 denominations. INSP features music shows, dramas, concerts, periodic specials, a talent-search program for Christians, and a variety of ministry programming. Launched in June 1998, its 24-hour sister channel, Inspirational Life Television (i-LifeTV) (http://www.ilifetv.com), broadcasts to six million viewers and is a digital lifestyles network featuring programming that aims for a stronger marriage and family, sound finances, and other life-enriching programs.

Interactive Channel *see* **TechTV**

International Channel, 8900 Liberty Circle, Englewood, CO 80122; *Telephone*: 720-853-2933; *Launch Date*: July 1990; *Broadcast Day*: 24 hours; *Subscribers*: 13,000,000; *Email*: ininfo@i-channel.com; *Web site*: http://www.i-channel.com

The International Channel is the only nationwide cable outlet serving multiple ethnic audiences with programming in more than 20 Asian, European, and Middle Eastern languages. Each channel focuses its programming to a specific audience and is independent of all other channels.

Broadcast channels include African Independent Television (AIT), Arab Radio & Television (ART), China Central Television (CCTV), Channel One Russia Worldwide Network, MunHwa Broadcasting Corporation (MBC), RAI International, RAI USA, Russian Television Network, Russian Television Network of America, Saigon Broadcasting Television Network (SBTN), TV5, TV Asia, TV Japan, TV Polonia, TV Polonia USA, Zee TV, Zee TV USA, and Zhong Tian Channel (ZTC).

International Programming Network, 21020 Superior Street, Chatsworth, CA 91311; *Telephone*: 818-709-6838; *Fax*: 818-709-8351; *Launch Date*: October 2002; *Broadcast Day*: 24 hours; *Subscribers*: 11,000,000; *Email*: info@ipntv.com; *Web site*: http:// www.ipntv.com

The International Programming Network Inc. is a multimedia company that owns and operates IPN TV, a round-the-clock global ethnic programming network aimed primarily at 200 million Persian and Arabic viewers worldwide, including five million in the United States. Programming consists of news, comedy shows, music, talk shows, game shows, movies, and documentaries from around the world.

International Television Broadcasting, Inc., P.O. Box 286, East Elmhurst, NY 11369; *Telephone*: 718-429-0900; *Launch Date*: April 1986; *Broadcast Day*: 24 hours; *Subscribers*: 500,000

International Television Broadcasting, Inc. airs programs targeted to American viewers from the Indian subcontinent (India, Pakistan, etc.).

Investigation Channel *see* **Court TV**

Investment TV, 555 South Flower Street, 45th Floor, Los Angeles, CA 90071; *Telephone*: 323-299-3471; *Broadcast Day*: 24 hours

Planned for future operation, Investment TV will offer investment and business news programming.

Jade East Channel (Jade Channel East), TVB USA, Inc., 15411 Blackburn Avenue, Norwalk, CA 90650; *Telephone*: 877-893-8888, 562-802-0220; *Fax*: 562-802-5096; *Launch Date*: 1984; *Broadcast Day*: 12 hours; *Subscribers*: 50,000; *Email*: Contact channel through its web site; *Web site*: http://www.tvbusa.com/

TVB USA, Inc., provides basic Chinese cable service through the Jade Channel in Southern California and airs serial dramas, daily satellite news from Hong Kong and Taiwan, music videos, sports, business programs, and variety shows. In 1991, the Jade Channel extended its coverage to the San Francisco Bay area. Launched in December

1994, the Jade Channel Satellite Service provides round-the-clock Chinese programming to nationwide subscribers. Brand channels include Jade West Channel (Jade Channel West) and Jade World Movie Channel.

Japan Network Group (TV Japan), 100 Broadway, 15th Floor, New York, NY 10005; *Telephone*: 212-262-3377; *Fax*: 212-262-5577; *Launch Date*: April 1, 1991; *Broadcast Day*: 24 hours; *Email*: tvjapan@tvjapan.net; *Web site*: http://www.tvjapan.net/

Japan Network Group, a joint venture of NHK group and Itochu Group in conjunction with 28 Japanese and American companies, operates TV Japan, a premium Japanese pay-television service available in the United States and Canada. JNG receives select programming from NHK, the largest and only public broadcaster in Japan, via international satellite every day, including live news, documentaries, dramas, sports, variety shows, and children's programming. Selected programs are edited and scheduled to a round-the-clock format to meet the needs of North American viewers in different time zones.

Jewelry Television, 10001 Kingston Pike #57, Knoxville, TN 37922; *Telephone*: 865-692-6000; *Fax*: 865-218-5049; *Launch Date*: October 1993; *Broadcast Day*: 24 hours; *Subscribers*: 65,000,000; *Email*: customerservice@acntv.com; *Web site*: http:// www.acntv.com

Originally called America's Collectibles Network, Jewelry Television is a shop-at-home network that sells jewelry and gemstones, primarily to a female audience. The network's primary programming mix is focused 70 percent on jewelry shows and 30 percent on gemstone shows, while also broadcasting special-event programs throughout the year. Under its original programming format, the network featured coins, knives, sports cards, quilts, jewelry, gemstones, and other collectible items. Realizing what products were of the most interest to its audience, in 2000 the channel refocused its sales efforts and now concentrates on jewelry and gemstone products. The network re-launched as Jewelry Television in early 2004.

Kids and Teens Television, P.O. Box 7609, Naples, FL 34101; *Telephone*: 888-759-2643; *Broadcast Day*: 24 hours; *Email*: Contact channel through its web site; *Web site*: http://www.ktvzone.com

Kids and Teens Television broadcasts on Sky Angel (http://www.skyangle.com) and is a religious-based network that broadcasts programming fare for younger viewers in an attempt to teach the Word of God. Offering Christ-centered and family-oriented fare, programs include animated shows, talk shows, cooking shows, music videos, dramas, musicals, shows centered on creation science and social issues, health, fitness, sitcoms, youth ministry services, and special events. The channel's broadcast day is divided into two segments: the 7:00 A.M. to 9:00 P.M. slot is aimed at young children while the 9:00 P.M. to 7:00 A.M. program block is aimed at the age 12-and-over audience.

La Familia Television Network *see* FE-TV

Law Enforcement Training Network, 4101 International Parkway, Carrollton, TX 75007; *Telephone*: 800-535-5386, 972-309-4000; *Fax*: 972-309-5105; *Email*: Contact network through its web site; *Web site*: http:// www.letn.com

The Law Enforcement Training Network (with its newly-adopted tag line, "The Homeland Security and Policing Solution") provides a variety of training programs to the nation's law enforcement community. The LETN has updated and modernized its training content to meet the new security needs demanded from the war against terrorist and terrorism. The LETN Academy broadcasts training segments, tests law enforcement personnel on their understanding of the material, and provides quarterly reports to its clients around the country detailing who in their department has been trained and on what subjects.

Since the terrorist attacks on New York City in 2001, the LETN updated its program and provides training designed to prepare law enforcement personnel for their role in the prevention and interdiction of terrorist activity within the United States, while continuing to provide training modules that focus on officer safety, tactical patrol, crime scene investigations, and forensics. LETN broadcasts its programs via satellite to law enforcement clients throughout the United States; airs a constant feed of Law Enforcement and Homeland Security news and information; and re-directs any important news feed from a monitor of the Homeland Threat Level.

The Learning Channel, One Discovery Place, Silver Spring, MD 20910; *Telephone*: 240-662-2000; *Fax*: 240-662-1574; *Launch Date*: November 1980; *Broadcast Day*: 24 hours; *Subscribers*: 90,000,000; *Email*: Contact channel through its web site; *Web site*: http://www.tlc.discovery.com

A brand broadcasting entity from the Discovery Channel, The Learning Channel, launched in November 1980, connects viewers to the human experience through its "life unscripted" approach to broadcasting. The network features nonfiction programming about science, history, real-life adventure, human behavior, lifestyle, and how-to shows.

Lesea Broadcasting Network, 61300 South Ironwood Road, South Bend, IN 46614, P.O. Box 12, South Bend, IN 46624; *Telephone*: 574-291-8200; *Fax*: 574-291-9043; *Subscribers*: 70,000,000; *Email*: Contact network through its web site; *Web site*: http://www.lesea.com

The Lesea (Lester Sumrall Evangelistic Association) Broadcasting Network owns and operates seven television stations in the United States, five shortwave radio stations covering six continents, two satellite television stations, and a television station broadcasting to the Middle East, all focused on ministry broadcasting. Lesea Broadcasting also operates the World Harvest Television Network (harvest@lesea.com) which broadcasts on Sky Angel (http:// www.skyangel.com) and airs a mix of Christian programming, sports, family shows, and University of Notre Dame sports.

The Liberty Channel, P.O. Box 10352, Lynchburg, VA 24506, *Telephone*: 800-332-1883, 434-582-2722; *Launch Date*: September 2001; *Broadcast Day*: 24 hours; *Subscribers*: 650,000; *Email*: info@thelibertychannel.org; *Web site*: http://www. thelibertychannel.org

The Liberty Channel broadcasts on Sky Angel (http://www.skyangel.com) and features traditional teaching and ministry programs, classic sitcoms, gospel films, children's and family-oriented shows, news, dramas, music videos, variety shows, traditional evangelical programming, political programs, and sports—all from a Christian perspective. A large portion of the channel's programming originates from the campus of Liberty University, in Lynchburg.

Lifetime Television, Worldwide Plaza, 309 West 49th Street, New York, NY 10019; *Telephone*: 212-424-7000; *Fax*: 212-957-4264; *Launch Date*: February 1984; *Broadcast Day*: 24 hours; *Subscribers*: 90,000,000; *Email*: Contact network through its web site; *Web site*: http://www.lifetimetv.com

A joint venture between the Hearst Corporation and the Walt Disney Company, Lifetime Television (which uses the tag line "Television for Women") broadcasts programs (including original productions) and specials aimed primarily at the female viewer market with content affecting women and their families. Lifetime was created by the merger of Daytime (created in March 1982 by Hearst/ABC Video Services featuring alternative programming for women) and Cable Health Network (CHN) (created in

June 1982 by Viacom as a 24-hour channel focusing on personal and family health, fitness, science, and medicine). CHN became Lifetime Medical Television (LMT) from November 1983 to July 1993.

The 24-hour Lifetime Movie Network, launched in July 1998, airs contemporary made-for-television movies, theatrical films, and miniseries from the Lifetime Television movie library. Movie genres include drama, suspense, family, romance, issue-oriented films, comedy, and mystery. LMN offers 200 different titles each month, including exclusive film and cable premieres. The 24-hour Lifetime Real Women (http://www.lifetimetv. com/lrw) network, created in August 2001, features real stories for and about women, including original series and fact-based movies.

Link TV, P.O. Box 2008, San Francisco, CA 94126; *Telephone*: 800-565-7495; *Launch Date*: December 1999; *Subscribers*: 23,000,000; *Email*: contact@linktv.org; *Web site*: http://www.linktv.com, http://www.linktv.org

Owned and operated by the non-profit Link Media, Inc., Link TV offers a global perspective on news, current events, and culture and airs viewpoints seldom covered by the American "mainstream" media. Broadcast fare includes documentaries on global issues, current affairs series, international news, classic foreign feature films, and world music. Ninety percent of the network's programs have never been shown in the United States before.

Locomotion Channel, 404 Washington Avenue, Penthouse, Miami Beach, FL 33139; *Telephone*: 305-894-3500; *Fax*: 305-894-3600; *Email*: email@locomotion.com; *Web site*: http://www.locomotion.com

The Locomotion Channel airs programs targeted to young adults and features international productions created specifically for audiences between 18 to 35 years old. The channel broadcasts adult satire in all forms, animation programming, electronic music, and digital culture fare.

LOGO, 1515 Broadway, 23rd Floor, New York, NY 10036; *Telephone*: 212-258-8000, 212-846-4629; *Fax*: 212-846-1893; *Broadcast Day*: 24 hours; *Email*: Contact network through its web site; *Web site*: http://www.mtv.com

An affiliate channel of Music Television (MTV) and slated for future operations, LOGO will target its programming directly to the gay and lesbian audience.

Long Term Care Network, 4101 International Parkway, Carrollton, TX 75007; *Telephone*: 800-777-5826, 972-309-4000; *Fax*: 972-309-5227; *Email*: Contact network through its web site; *Web site*: http://www.ltcn.com

Operated by Primedia Healthcare, the Long Term Care Network provides remote education and training to physicians, nurses, and health professionals throughout the United States. In addition to other fare, the LTCN broadcasts more than 17 hours of new continuing education programs per month via satellite, which reaches more than two million healthcare professionals. Monthly programming includes such subjects as acute care, long term care, Centers for Disease Control Public Health shows, psychiatric care, Joint Commission Accreditation shows, and Food and Drug Administration Patient Safety Watch.

Lottery Channel, 425 Walnut Street, 23rd Floor, Cincinnati, OH 45202; *Telephone*: 513-721-3900; *Email*: support@lottery.com; *Web site*: http://www.lottery.com

Planned for future television operation, the channel's current activities revolve solely around its web site, which provides current and past winning numbers for all government-sponsored lotteries within the United States and Canada.

Love Stories, 8900 Liberty Circle, Englewood, CO 80112; *Telephone*: 720-852-7700; *Launch Date*: 1994; *Broadcast Day*: 24 hours; *Email*: Contact network through its web site; *Web site*: http://www.starz.com

Love Stories is a multiplexed channel from Starz! that airs nothing but romance movies targeted mainly to the female audience. All movies focus on dramatic love stories, relationships, and passion and include heartthrobs, big stars, and exotic locations.

Luxury Television Network (http://www.ltvntv.com) (Planned for future operation)

Madison Square Garden Network, Two Pennsylvania Plaza, New York, NY 10021; *Telephone*: 212-465-6000; *Fax*: 212-465-6024; *Launch Date*: October 1969; *Broadcast Day*: 40+ hours per week; *Subscribers*: 9,000,000; *Email*: msgnetpr@msgnetwork.com; *Web site*: http://www.msgnetwork.com

The Madison Square Garden Network broadcasts live sporting events of local professional and college sports teams, special events from the Garden, studio and interview shows, a Saturday morning *KidsBlock* lineup for children, and *MSG SportsDesk*, a nightly sports wrap-up show.

Major Broadcasting Cable Network *see* **Black Family Channel**

Martial Arts Action Network, 1000 Universal Studios Plaza, Building 22A, Orlando, FL 32819; *Telephone*: 407-370-4460; *Fax*: 407-370-0857; *Launch Date*: Fall 2003; *Broadcast Day*: 24 hours; *Email*: Contact network through its web site; *Web site*: http://www.martial-arts-network.com

Aimed primarily at the 18-34 male viewer, the Martial Arts Action Network airs action-packed programming, including movies; weekly series; kickboxing and martial arts competitions; original programming; extreme sports; self-help and how-to clinics; and unique interactive contests linking the viewer to the network's web site.

Martial Arts Network *see* **Black Belt TV/The Martial Arts Network**

Martial Arts Television, *Telephone*: 310-824-0914, 925-200-4462; *Broadcast Day*: 24 hours; *Email*: martialartstv@mac.com; *Web site*: http://www.martialartstelevision.com

Planned for future operation, Martial Arts Television will broadcast international martial arts activities, including original programs, martial arts-related specials, features, mini-series, and tournaments.

MartialMax, 1100 Avenue of the Americas, New York, NY 10036; *Telephone*: 212-512-1000; *Fax*: 212-512-1182; *Launch Date*: 2001; *Broadcast Day*: 24 hours; *Email*: Contact channel through its web site; *Web site*: http://www.cinemax.com

MartialMax is a multiplexed channel from Cinemax that broadcasts martial arts movies.

Mav'rick Entertainment Network, 44 Inverness Drive East, Building D, Englewood, CO 80112; *Telephone*: 303-925-1340; *Launch Date*: October 2004; *Broadcast Day*: 24 hours; *Email*: Contact channel through its web site; *Web site*: http://www.mavtv.net

The Mav'rick Entertainment Network targets its programming to the 18-54 male viewer and focuses on topics of interest to men, such as sports, fitness, money, gadgets, and sex.

MBA-ESPN Sports (Korea) *see* **Entertainment Sports Television Network**

Meadows Racing Network *see* **HorseRacing TV**

Medical Channel (Planned for future operation)

MHz Networks, 8101A Lee Highway, Falls Church, VA 22042; *Telephone*: 703-770-7100; *Fax*: 703-770-7112; *Launch Date*: 1983 (as MHZ); *Email*: Contact network through its web site; *Web site*: http://www.mhznetworks.org

The MHz Networks is comprised of MHz, MHz2, and MHz Learn (formerly Instructional Television). Together, these three channels broadcast local, national, and international shows which cater to the diverse interests of its viewing audience. Launched in 1983, MHz has specialized in international programming since 1993 and includes newscasts from more than 25 countries, international films, sports, documentaries, and dramas. Launched in 1972, MHz2 showcases local music and entertainment, and national and international music and technology shows. MHz Learn is part of the weekday MHz2 lineup and broadcasts instructional series designed to serve students and teachers. Commissioned in 1974 by the state of Virginia to offer educational programs to Northern Virginia schools, MHz Learn airs each weekday from 9:00 A.M. to 3:30 P.M. to 320,000 students, 25,000 teachers, and 12 school districts in Northern Virginia.

Michigan Government Television, 111 South Capitol Avenue, 4th Floor, Lansing, MI 48909; *Telephone*: 517-373-4250; *Fax*: 517-335-7342; *Launch Date*: July 1996; *Broadcast Day*: 4 hours per day; *Subscribers*: 2,000,000; *Email*: mgtv@mgtv.org; *Web site*: http://www.mgtv.org

Operating similar in format established by the national C-SPAN network, Michigan Government Television is a public affairs initiative of Michigan's cable industry that broadcasts all branches of Michigan's state government, Senate sessions, Supreme Court oral arguments, and more, all live and without editing its content.

Middle East Broadcasting Centre *see* **Arab Network of America**

Mizlou Network, 8807 Citrus Village Drive #108, Tampa, FL 33626; *Telephone and Fax*: 813-792-8028; *Email*: office@mizlou.com; *Web site*: http://www.mizlou.com

With over 40 years of broadcasting history, Mizlou is an "occasional" or "independent" television network that produces television programs and events, and then sells these packages to local, regional, and/or national broadcast networks. Typically, a Mizlou network line-up consists of a combination of stations affiliated with major networks, in addition to selected non-affiliated, or independent, stations.

All Mizlou nationally-televised events guarantee advertisers 70 percent to 90 percent coverage of U.S. television homes, depending on the nature of the program (whether it is a regional or national broadcast). Using this broadcasting mode, Mizlou usually achieves parity with comparable program categories on the major networks and basically functions as a major network, but on a limited or occasional basis.

MLB Extra Innings, Major League Baseball, 245 Park Avenue, 31st Floor, New York, NY 10167; *Telephone*: 212-931-7800; *Email*: Contact service through its web site; *Web site*: http://mlb.com

MLB Extra Innings is a pay-per-view service from Major League Baseball that is available through a variety of cable and satellite television providers. The service provides up to 60 regular season, out-of-market games a week and are available in addition to those games seen on FOX, the ESPN networks, regional sports networks, and team television station affiliates.

MLS Direct Kick, Major League Soccer, 110 East 42nd Street, 10th Floor, New York, NY 10017; *Telephone*: 212-450-1200; *Fax*: 212-450-1300; *Email*: feedback@mlsnet.com; *Web site*: http://mlsnet.com

MLS Direct Kick is a pay-per-view channel from Major League Soccer that is available through a variety of cable and satellite television providers. The service provides up to 120 regular season, out-of-market games a week and are available in addition to those games seen on FOX, the ESPN networks, regional sports networks, and team television station affiliates.

Monsters HD, 200 Jericho Quadrangle, Jericho, NY 11753; *Telephone*: 516-803-6010; *Email*: Contact channel through its web site; *Web site*: http://www.voom.com

Monsters HD is a high definition multiplexed channel from Voom that airs horror, fright, suspense, and monster movies.

Moody Broadcasting Network, 820 North LaSalle Boulevard, Chicago, IL 60610; *Telephone*: 800-621-7031, 312-329-4000; *Launch Date*: May 1982; *Broadcast Day*: 24 hours; *Subscribers*: 30,000; *Email*: mbn@moody.edu; *Web site*: http://mbn.org

Operated by the Moody Bible Institute, the Moody Broadcasting Network provides religious-based programming, consisting of music, dramas, education, and national phone-in programs.

Moore Television Network, 5865 Ridgeway Center Parkway #300, Memphis, TN 38120; *Telephone*: 901-820-4517; *Launch Date*: 2004; *Broadcast Day*: 24 hours; *Email*: Contact the network through its web site; *Web site*: http://www.consumersourcing 550.com

Planned for future operation

MOOV HD, 200 Jericho Quadrangle, Jericho, NY 11753; *Telephone*: 516-803-6010; *Launch Date*: October 2003; *Broadcast Day*: 24 hours; *Email*: Contact channel through its web site; *Web site*: http://www.voom.com, http://www.moovlab.com

MOOV HD is a high definition multiplexed channel from Voom that is the first round-the-clock, commercial-free video art channel.

MOR Music TV (Planned for future operation)

MoreMax, 1100 Avenue of the Americas, New York, NY 10036; *Telephone*: 212-512-1000; *Fax*: 212-512-1182; *Launch Date*: 2001; *Broadcast Day*: 24 hours; *Email*: Contact channel through its web site; *Web site*: http://www.cinemax.com

MoreMax is a multiplexed channel from Cinemax that broadcasts popular and rare movie classics and was initially established to show twice the number of films found on Cinemax. MoreMAX Choice was established to broadcast a different movie each night and MoreMAX Vanguard broadcasts independent films, foreign films, and art house releases.

The Movie Channel, 1100 Avenue of the Americas, New York, NY 10036; 1633 Broadway, New York, NY 10019; *Telephone*: 212-512-1000; *Fax*: 212-512-1182; *Launch Date*: December 1979; *Broadcast Day*: 24 hours; *Subscribers*: 36,000,000; *Email*: Contact channel through its web site; *Web site*: http://www.cinemax.com

A multiplexed channel from Showtime, The Movie Channel airs about 120 movie titles each month and its programming includes *Daily Movie Marathons*, *TMC Overnight*, and *TMC Double Vision Weekends*. Its non-movie broadcasts consist of movie trivia, film facts, celebrity interviews, and behind-the-scenes look at selected movies. TMC has launched two brand channels that air specific movie genres to targeted audiences: TMC HD (broadcasts movies in the highest definition available) and the 24-hour TMC Xtra (airs more than 50 movie titles a month, with no same-day airing of duplicate films).

MoviePlex, 8900 Liberty Circle, Englewood, CO 80112; *Telephone*: 720-852-7700; *Launch Date*: October 1994; *Broadcast Day*: 24 hours; *Subscribers*: 5,300,000; *Email*: Contact channel through its web site; *Web site*: http://www.starz.com

A multiplexed channel from Starz!, MoviePlex provides viewers themed movies by day: Love Stories (Monday), Great Movies of Your Life (Tuesday), Westerns (Wednesday), Action (Thursday), Mystery (Friday), True Stories (Saturday), and WAM! (Sunday). The channel features more than 200 different movies a month, none of them rated R (Restricted).

Movie Ticket *see* **Outstanding Latin Entertainment Channel**

MovieWatch, 3415 University Avenue, Saint Paul, MN 55114; *Telephone*: 651-659-

7000; *Fax*: 651-659-7003; *Launch Date*: August 2003; *Broadcast Day*: 24 hours; *Email*: Contact channel through its web site; *Web site*: http://www.moviewatch.com

MovieWatch broadcasts movies, original programs, documentaries on how movies are made, and interviews with well-known film makers. Original programs include *Moviewatch Dailies* (an updated daily entertainment magazine show); *QuickLook* (a half-hour, in-depth look at current movies in theaters and on cable television); *Reel Lives* (the ultimate spoof on biography shows, this program uncovers the "real lives" of some favorite movie characters); *The Directors* (each episode features the life and work of a renowned director, complete with clips from his or her movies and interviews with the actors who starred in them); and *Day in the Life* (takes viewers onto the movie set and into the lives of those who make movies, such as a gaffer, best boy, and foley artist).

MSNBC, One MSNBC Plaza, Secaucus, NJ 07094; *Telephone*: 201-583-5000; *Launch Date*: July 1996; *Broadcast Day*: 24 hours; *Subscribers*: 82,000,000; *Email*: Contact channel through its web site; *Web site*: http://www.msnbc.com

An all-news network, MSNBC is *a* joint venture between Microsoft and NBC and broadcasts breaking news stories, in-depth analyses of the day's top stories, and original programming. Popular shows include *Abrams Report, Hardball, Countdown with Keith Olbermann, Deborah Norville Tonight, Scarborough Country, Imus on MSNBC,* and *Lester Holt Live.*

Mun2, 2470 West 8th Avenue, Hialeah, FL 33010; *Telephone*: 305-882-8700; *Fax*: 305-889-7203; *Launch Date*: October 2001; *Broadcast Day*: 24 hours; *Subscribers*: 9,000,000; *Email*: Contact channel through its web site; *Web site*: http://www. mun2tv.com

A Telemundo channel (part of the National Broadcasting Corporation), Mun2 targets its programming to the 18-34 year-old U.S.-based Latino market, with shows airing in English and Spanish. Programming includes comedies, music videos, general entertainment, variety, lifestyle, and informational shows.

Programs include *Video Mix*; *Mun2 News*; *La Conexión* (a magazine show that explores how Latinos on the west coast are helping to define urban American culture and lifestyle); *FuZion* (a magazine show that provides viewers local information on their favorite stars, events, and fashion); *Futurama* (an animated cartoon from the creators of *The Simpsons*); *SpeedLogic* (focuses on the racing of cars, motorcycles, and motorboats); *The Roof* (a live and interactive music show that provides viewers the latest and hottest alternative music from hip-hop, reggeton, pop, and dance music hits); *The Report* (a 15-minute news alternative show produced by young newspeople who want to inform their own generation about issues important to them); *Midnite Video Mix* (gives viewers another music block to enjoy their favorite videos by request by logging on to their web site); *No Cover* (a 60-minute weekly show that features all genres of dance music, including house, trans, and techno, from the hottest clubs all over the nation); *mun2 Top Ten* (allows viewers to vote for their favorite videos via email, which are then aired); *Ritmo y Sabor* (airs musical interviews and newly-released videos); *Chat* (the first talk show that provides a forum for young U.S. Latinos); *Toma 1* (monthly 30-minute show that features interviews with Latino artists involved in music, theater, comedy, and Hollywood); *Buena Onda* (presents interviews, music videos, and updated information focusing on regional Mexican music); *Keepin' It Reel* (a weekly half-hour show featuring the reactions of the "average viewer on the street" to movie trailers and films); *Gamer.tv* (a weekly magazine show that focuses on the video game world, including recent releases and industry news); *Adrenalina* (a 30-minute show that gives viewers an inside look into adventurous sports and sporting events from around the world); *Jamz* (provides viewers an inside view of reggeton, a musical form combining hip hop, rap and reggae); *Loco Comedy Jam* (a one-hour stand-up comedy showcase); *NY Underground* (features Latin rap and hip hop music and musicians from the Bronx to Washington Heights, New York); and *Hottest Video Mix* (a late night music block where viewers request their favorite videos).

MunHwa Broadcasting Corporation, 8900 Liberty Circle, Englewood, CO 80122; *Telephone*: 303-712-5400; *Fax*: 303-268-5465; *Launch Date*: 2002; *Broadcast Day*: 24 hours; *Email*: Contact channel through its web site; *Web site*: http://www.mbcamerica.tv

The South Korean MunHwa Broadcasting Corporation, available in the United States through the International Channel, broadcasts news, sports, dramas, cultural shows, and general entertainment programming.

Museum Channel (Planned for future operation)

Music Alley *see* **Outstanding Latin Entertainment Channel**

Music Choice TV, 300 Welsh Road, Horsham, PA 19044; *Telephone*: 215-784-5840; *Fax*: 215-784-5870; *Launch Date*: May 1990; *Broadcast Day*: 24 hours; *Subscribers*: 44,000,000; *Email*: Contact the channel through its web site; *Web site*: http://www.musicchoice.com

Music Choice TV provides uninterrupted music for homes and businesses and also distributes televised concerts and music shows through its *Music Choice Concert Series*. The service offers 54 channels of commercial free, CD-quality music in a wide variety of music genres, including 1970s music, 1980s music, Americana, Alternative Rock, Big Band and Swing, Bluegrass, Blues, Canciones de Amor Internacional, Classical Masterpeices, Classic Country, Classic Disco, Classic R & B, Classic Rock, Contemporary Christian, Contemporary Instrumentals, Dance, Easy Listening, Gospel, Hit List, Jazz, Latin Love Songs, Light Classical, Metal, Mexicana, Musica Latina, New Wave, Party Favorites, Power Rock, Progressive / Adult Alternative, R & B and Hip Hop, Rap, Reggae, Rock, Rock en Espanol, Salsa Y Merenque, Show Tunes, Singers and Standards, Smooth Jazz, Smooth R & B, Soft Album Mix, Soft Rock, Solid Gold Oldies, Soundscapes, Sounds of the Season, Taste of Italy, Tejano, and Today's Country.

Music of Praise Television (The MP Network), 6000 Fairview Road #1200, Charlotte, NC 28210; *Telephone*: 704-552-3585; *Fax*: 704-552-3705; *Email*: network@ thempnetwork.com; *Web site*: http://www.thempnetwork.com

Following broadcast models established by Music Television (MTV), Video Hits 1 (VH1), and Country Music Television (CMT), Music of Praise Television airs original programs, a variety of Christian-related music videos (including Christian rock, inspirational and contemporary gospel), artist profiles and interviews, and industry news to its primary 18-34 year-old age group.

Music Television, 1515 Broadway, 23rd Floor, New York, NY 10036; *Telephone*: 212-258-8000, 212-846-4629; *Fax*: 212-846-1893; *Launch Date*: August 1981; *Broadcast Day*: 24 hours; *Subscribers*: 90,000,000; *Email*: Contact network through its web site; *Web site*: http://www.mtv.com

Owned by Viacom, Music Television was the first 24-hour music video network and revolutionized the music industry and the way musical acts are presented to the public today. The network's first video, *Video Killed the Radio Star*, by The Buggles says it all and set the stage for a radical upheaval in the business. From its upstart beginnings viewed with caution by the music industry, MTV is now a musical icon and sets the trends in the music world. The network can now be seen in more than 400 million homes and 162 countries around the world. Straying from its initial slate of showing only music videos, the network now airs video contests, reality shows, news reports and programs, animation specials, documentaries, awards shows, and music-related events.

MTV began its broadcasting history in a low-key manner with the simple phrase, "Ladies and gentlemen, rock and roll," spoken on camera by John Lack, one of the network's creators. This introduction was immediately followed by the music-video clip *Video Killed the Radio Star*. One of the earliest and greatest cable success stories, MTV was established by Warner Amex Satellite Entertainment Company and the key to its initial success was the availability of low-cost programming in the form of music videos. Originally these were provided to the network without cost by record companies, which thought of them as advertising for their records and performers.

Its broadcasting model guided MTV into presenting a constant flow of videos, a programming structure that differed significantly from other musical fare available at the time on competing networks. Operating like a Top 40 radio station for television (the network even had Video Jockeys), MTV could "make" or "break" musical acts, depending on how often they played the artist's videos. In a very short period of time, MTV usurped the star-making power traditionally held by radio for decades. As the power and impact of MTV has grown, artists have made more complicated and intricate videos to support recently-released songs and albums. While the songs may or may not get much airplay on the radio, the videos will play on MTV and guarantee the artist an audience.

Many of the earliest MTV videos came from Great Britain, where the tradition of making video clips was well-established. One of the earliest indications of MTV's commercial importance was the success of the British band Duran Duran in the American market. The band had not received much radio airplay in 1981, but the presence of MTV, and the network's frequent playing of the band's video, gave the group instant success and stardom. Early in its history, the network proved to be vital in helping the careers of numerous artists, such as Madonna, Michael Jackson, Prince, Peter Gabriel, and U2.

While innovative initially, the network's programming model soon appeared flat and repetitious and its ratings began to slip. To recover its luster and attract new viewers, MTV diversified its musical offering and moved into rap, dance music, and heavy metal, while also introducing programs specifically aimed at various music genres, such as *Yo! MTV Raps*, *Club MTV*, and *Headbangers' Ball*. This programming change away from the network's original model also signaled a move away from an all-video format. And, although still focused on music-related fare, soon MTV became a full-service network and began offering news, sports, sitcoms, documentaries, cartoons, game shows, original programming, and cartoons.

As MTV grew and began to diversify, the network created multiple affiliated channels to broadcast a mix of music genres targeted to specific audiences. The 24-hour MTV2 (http:// www.mtv2.com) was launched in August 1998 and broadcasts a mix of musical genres, concerts, news, album previews, video premiers, weekend stunts, music specials, and interactive programming. MTV Español, launched in August 1998, is a 24-hour music channel that airs Latin pop, rock en español, and Latin alternative music videos aimed at the young Latino audience in the United States. The 24-hour MTV Hits, launched in May 2002, airs an all-hit format aimed at the teenage music audience. MTV Indie airs music and movies by independent artists, musicians, and film makers. MTV Jams, launched in May 2002, is a 24-hour music video channel that plays hip hop, R&B, soul, and urban music genres. MTV Latino airs Latin music by today's top stars. MTV Ritmo provides old-style and new Latin music by stars from the past and today's biggest hits. MTV Rocks airs classic rock-and-roll music by 1960s and 1970s artists.

MTV affiliate channels include the College Television Network (http://www.mtvu.com; airs music and programs from college stations throughout the United States); planned for future operation, LOGO will air programming targeted to the gay and lesbian audience; Nickelodeon, launched in April 1979, broadcasts 24-hours a day and was the first network developed just for kids; Nick2, launched in May 1998, broadcasts 24 hours a day and gives viewers the opportunity to watch their favorite Nickelodeon and Nick at Nite shows at different times of the day; Nick At Night's TV Land (http://www.nick-at-nite.com, http://www.nickatnite.com), launched in April 1996, airs 24 hours a day and is the only network dedicated to showing the best of everything television has from the past 50 years, including classic shows, original specials, and gone-but-never-to-be-forgotten commercials; the 24-hour Nickelodeon GAS (Games and Sports for Kids), launched in March 1999, celebrates the way kids play, from board games to video games to extreme sports; Nicktoons, launched in January 1999, is a 24-hour channel aimed directly at kids; Spike TV (http://www.spiketv.com) is a 24-hour network that bills itself as the "First Network For Men"; VH1 (airs original programs, lite rock, and adult rock videos); VH Uno, launched in November 1999, is a 24-hour music channel aimed at the Latino audience and airs Latin pop and ballads, tropical music, salsa , and urban hip-hop; VH1 Classic (http://www.vh1classic.com), launched in May 2000, celebrates artists from the 1960s, 1970s, and 1980s; VH1 Country, launched in August 1998, features country music videos and country artists who cross over into popular music; VH1 Mega Hits, launched in May 2002, plays chart-topping hits from the 1990s and today; VH1 Smooth provides soft rock, jazz, new age, and adult contemporary music; and VH1 Soul, launched in August 1998, features soul, neo-soul, and R & B hits.

Muslim Television (Planned for future operation)

My Pet Television, 7115 Macapa Drive, Los Angeles, CA 90068; *Telephone*: 310-444-3006; *Launch Date*: September 1996; *Broadcast Day*: 8 hours per day; *Email*: Contact channel through its web site; *Web site*: http://www.pettv.com

In alliance with the Humane Society of the United States, My Pet Television airs original and acquired programming aimed at America's 60 million pet owners, including *Lifestyles of the Rich and Furry*, *Hoof Beats*, *Petsville USA*, and *K9 Kapers*.

Mystery, 8900 Liberty Circle, Englewood, CO 80112; *Telephone*: 720-852-7700; *Launch Date*: Fall 1994; *Broadcast Day*: 24 hours; *Email*: Contact channel through its web site; *Web site*: http://www.starz.com

A multiplexed channel from Starz!, Mystery features commercial-free classic and contemporary mystery movies.

The N *see* **Noggin**

Narrative Television Network, 5840 South Memorial Drive #312, Tulsa, OK 74145; *Telephone*: 800-801-8184, 918-627-1000; *Fax*: 918-627-4101; *Launch Date*: 1988; *Subscribers*: 25,000,000; *Email*: Contact network through its web site; *Web site*: http://www.narrativetv.com

The Narrative Television Network broadcasts programs and movies aimed at America's 13 million blind and visually impaired viewers and their families. The network adds the voice of a narrator to the existing programming sound track without interfering with any of the original audio or video. The network also makes live theater and other special events accessible via a wireless receiver.

For its pioneering work in making the world of television accessible to visually impaired people, NTN has received honors from the American Council of the Blind and the American Foundation for the Blind. The network has narrated thousands of hours of programming, including such popular shows as *Matlock*, *Bonanza*, *The Andy Griffith Show*,

The Streets of San Francisco, as well as hundreds of movies. NTN was selected by the American Foundation for the Blind to narrate its landmark video, *What Do You Do When You See A Blind Person?*, which is recognized as the definitive video in the field of accessibility for the visually impaired.

NASA Television, Mail Code PM-1, Washington, D.C. 20546; *Telephone*: 202-358-3572; *Launch Date*: January 1980 (mission coverage), July 1991 (educational, historical programming); *Broadcast Day*: 24 hours; *Email*: Contact channel through its web site; *Web site*: http://www.nasa.gov/ntv

Sometimes called the Air & Space Network, NASA Television is a government-owned service of the National Aeronautics and Space Administration that broadcasts lift-off-to-landing shuttle mission coverage, press conferences, and public affairs events. News feeds, educational, and informational programming about America's space program are aired during non-mission times.

NASCAR in Car, P.O. Box 2875, Daytona Beach, FL 32120; *Telephone*: 386-253-0611; *Email*: Contact channel through its web site; *Web site*: http://www.nascar.com

NASCAR In Car is a pay-per-view service from NASCAR (National Association for Stock Car Auto Racing) that is available through a variety of cable and satellite television providers. The service provides enhancements that allows the viewer to better enjoy each NASCAR race, including five to seven separate in-car camera feeds (each featuring a different driver), real time statistics and data displayed on virtual dashboards, and in-car team audio.

The Nashville Network *see* **Spike TV**

National Broadcasting Company, 30 Rockefeller Plaza, New York, NY 10112; *Telephone*: 212-664-4444; *Fax*: 212-664-4426; *Launch Date*: 1926; *Broadcast Day*: 24 hours; *Email*: Contact network through its web site; *Web site*: http://www.nbc.com

Starting as a radio network in the 1920s and evolving into a television broadcaster in the 1940s, the National Broadcasting Company was founded in 1926 by General Electric, RCA, and Westinghouse. RCA became the sole owner of the network in 1932 and in 1986, RCA was purchased by General Electric, which today wholly owns and operates NBC.

NBC has grown to become a diverse, international media company. In addition to the NBC Television Network and the NBC Television Stations Division, the company owns Bravo, the Consumer News and Business Channel (CNBC), MSNBC, ShopNBC, and Telemundo. Additionally, NBC owns at least a part of CNBC Europe, CNBC Asia Pacific, the Arts & Entertainment Network, the History Channel, and has a non-voting interest in Paxson Communications Corporation.

Since its inception, NBC has been a network of firsts, including the first permanent broadcasting network in America; conducting the first U.S. coast-to-coast radio broadcast (the 1927 Rose Bowl); being granted the first license for a commercial television station (now WNBC) in 1941; the first to offer an early-morning news program (in 1952); airing the first color telecast (1953); broadcasting the first made-for-television movie (in 1964); the first to broadcast in stereo (in 1984); and the first major television network to launch a full-scale web site (http:///www.nbc.com) in 1995.

NBC produces hundreds of hours of programming a week and reaches viewers in more than 100 countries on six continents. The network owns and operates 14 NBC-affiliated television stations in major U.S. markets, while generating more than $1 billion annually in revenue from advertising sales. The NBC Television Network broadcasts approximately 5,000 hours of television programming each year, transmitting to more than 200 affiliated stations across the United States. These independently-owned affiliates then broadcast the NBC signal to an estimated 99 percent of all homes in the United States with television sets.

The financial and ratings fortunes of NBC have always been closely tied to those of its parent company, the Radio Corporation of America (RCA), and later General Electric. Unlike CBS, which was created as an independent programming enterprise, NBC came into existence as the subsidiary of an electronics manufacturer, RCA, which viewed programming as a form of marketing and as an enticement for customers to purchase radio and television receivers for the home. The power of being a national network helped RCA in its lobbying efforts to see its technology adopted as the industry standard, especially during the early years and in the battle over color television.

RCA was formed after World War I when General Electric signed licensing agreements with Westinghouse, AT&T, and United Fruit. This alliance created RCA specifically to market radio receivers produced by General Electric and Westinghouse. Due to internal competition and government antitrust efforts during the 1920s and 1930s, the alliance disbanded and RCA emerged as an independent company. In November 1926, before becoming a fully independent company, RCA formed NBC as a wholly-owned subsidiary and quickly created another network, then naming them NBC-Red and NBC-Blue.

In the 1930s RCA evolved into a radio manufacturer with two networks, a powerful lineup of radio stations, and a roster of major stars. From this position of strength, RCA began establishing itself as the standard for research into television technology. NBC began experimental broadcasts from New York's Empire State building as early as 1932 and by 1935 was spending millions of dollars annually to fund television research, money that came from the two lucrative NBC radio networks. In 1939 NBC became the first network to introduce regular television broadcasts with its inaugural telecast of the opening day ceremonies at that year's New York World's Fair.

In the late 1930s, RCA's dominance of the broadcast industry led the Federal Communications Commission (FCC) to investigate the legal status of networks, or "chain broadcasting" as it was then called. The FCC's findings led to the 1941 release of its *Report on Chain Broadcasting*, which criticized RCA's control of a majority of the available high-powered stations and called for the separation of NBC's two networks from RCA. After losing its appeal, in 1943 RCA sold NBC-Blue to Edward J. Noble and this network's name would eventually be changed to the American Broadcasting Company (ABC).

After World War II, when CBS tried to stall efforts to establish technological standards in order to promote its own color-television technology, RCA lobbied for the development of television in accordance with existing NTSC technical standards established in 1941. The FCC agreed with RCA and its system was finally selected as the industry standard in 1953. Throughout this period, network television played a minor role at RCA and in the early 1950s NBC accounted for only one-quarter of RCA's corporate profits. RCA's business plan called for using NBC to create an appeal for broadcast television so that more RCA sets could be sold.

Throughout the 1950s and 1960s, NBC routinely finished second in the ratings behind CBS and its prime-time schedule relied heavily on dramas (such as *Philco/Goodyear Playhouse* and *Kraft Television Theater*) and comedy-variety shows (with such stars as Milton Berle, Jimmy Durante, Sid Caesar, Imogene Coca, Dean Martin, Jerry Lewis, Bob Hope, and Perry Como).

During this time, under the leadership of Sylvester "Pat" Weaver, NBC introduced several key innovations to television programming. One early idea was introducing the "magazine concept" of television advertising, in which advertisers no longer sponsored an entire series, but paid to have their ads placed within a program, such as how ads appear in a magazine. This fundamental change shifted the balance of power from advertisers to the networks, which were then able to exert more control over programming. Another major innovation occurred when NBC expanded the network schedule into the "fringe" time periods of early morning and late night by introducing the shows *Today* and *Tonight*. Weaver made another substantial contribution when he became the first network executive to introduce "event" programming that broke the routine of regularly-scheduled shows. These expensive, one-shot broadcasts, which he called "spectaculars" were extremely effective in attracting an audience and profitable. One such program, broadcast live, was the Broadway production of *Peter Pan* that attracted a then-record audience of 65 million viewers.

In 1956, former ABC president Robert Kintner took over programming and supervised the network's expansion of NBC news, the shift to color broadcasting, and the network's diversification beyond television programming. Through RCA, NBC branched out during the 1960s and acquired financial interests in Hertz rental cars, a carpet manufacturer, and real-estate holdings. The network moved into expanding international markets by selling programs overseas, which placed NBC's shows in more than eighty countries. By the mid–1960s NBC had invested in thirteen television stations and one network in eight countries.

Programming under Kintner continued the network's traditional reliance on dramas and comedy-variety shows as the network formed an alliance with the production company MCA-Universal, whose drama series came to dominate the network's schedule into the 1970s. After introducing movies to prime-time with *Saturday Night at the Movies* in 1961, NBC and MCA-Universal developed numerous 90-minute series (such as *The Virginian*), made-for-TV movies (the first one being *Fame Is the Name of the Game* in 1966), and the movie series (*The NBC Mystery Movie*, which initially featured *Columbo*, *McCloud*, and *McMillan and Wife*).

After competing with CBS for audience share since its inception, in the 1970s NBC watched as ABC took control of the ratings race with a schedule focused primarily on sitcoms, and left NBC in third place. In an attempt to reverse its ratings decline, in 1978 NBC hired the legendary Fred Silverman, the man credited with ABC's sudden surge in the ratings. However, for a variety of reasons, Silverman was not able to bring his programming magic to the network and his three-year tenure is considered by many television historians to be the lowest point in the history of NBC. He presided over steadily declining ratings, affiliate desertions, and a string of bad programs.

Constantly mired in third place, in 1981 NBC turned to Grant Tinker and offered him the position of NBC chairman. A co-founder of MTM Enterprises, Tinker had presided over the independent production company that had produced three classic television programs: *The Mary Tyler Moore Show*, *Lou Grant*, and *Hill Street Blues*. Over the next three years Tinker and programming genius Brandon Tartikoff brought the network back to respectability by patiently nurturing talent and by launching several successful programs, such as *Cheers*, *St. Elsewhere*, and *Family Ties*. Their judge of quality and talent combined with an extraordinary level of patience is exemplified by their handling of the show *Cheers*. Finishing its initial year as the lowest rated show on television, Tinker and Tartikoff believed in the show and kept it on the network schedule. The result was that *Cheers* went on to become one of television's greatest shows ever.

While its ratings were already on the rise, the network's turning point came when in 1984 Tartikoff convinced comedian Bill Cosby to return to series television with *The Cosby Show*. The program was an instant success from its first airing and single-handedly completely changed NBC's financial and ratings fortunes. Using the show as an anchor, NBC was able to call its Thursday night line-up "Must See TV." Network profits under Tinker climbed from $48 million in his first year to $333 million by 1985.

With its steady ratings success, by the

mid–1980s NBC was generating 43 percent of RCA's $570 million annual profits, considered to be a hugely disproportionate share for a single division. In the merger-mania era of the 1980s, RCA (and with it NBC) became a prime target for a corporate takeover and was finally purchased by General Electric in 1985 for $6.3 billion. When Tinker left NBC in 1986, General Electric executive Robert Wright was named network chairman. Due to the various shows left behind by Tinker and Tartikoff, NBC dominated the ratings until the late 1980s, when its audience share and profits suddenly collapsed (the network lost $60 million in 1991), leaving its show *Cheers* as its only top-10 program on network television.

Rumors were rampant in the industry that NBC would be sold and when the network began taking steps to stem its annual losses, management was criticized for taking seemingly draconian cost-cutting measures, especially within the news division. General Electric was criticized for its lack of understanding of network television and for not knowing how to run NBC. During this period, the network suffered a series of public relations problems, including a fraudulent news report on the news magazine show *Dateline* and for its inept attempts to name a successor to Johnny Carson as host of its legendary *Tonight Show* when he announced his retirement without notice.

Through all its public and financial woes, General Electric held steady and kept Wright in charge. The strategy proved to be correct and by 1996 the network was once again the undisputed leader of network television with five top-rated shows. Under the programming direction of Warren Littlefield, NBC has solid hits with *Seinfeld*, *E.R.*, *Frasier*, and *Friends*. General Electric also spent money to guarantee NBC the rights to the most valuable televised sporting events, including $4 billion for the rights to broadcast the Olympics well into the twenty-first century.

NBC has diversified during the General Electric era and now owns minor stakes in cable channels Arts and Entertainment, Court TV, American Movie Classics, Bravo, Sports Channel America, and the History Channel. NBC also created a cable network, CNBC, a business-news channel and the highly popular MSNBC, a joint venture with Microsoft.

NBC Entertainment creates and produces programming for the network's prime time, late-night, daytime, and Saturday-morning schedules. Through its NBC Studios subsidiary, the network also provides entertainment programming to domestic and international marketplaces. NBC News started first on radio and brought its division into the television world, and later to the internet. NBC News provides more than 25 hours of weekly programming in the United States, including its daily *Nightly News*, *Today*, and *Meet the Press*. Also under the NBC News umbrella is *MSNBC*, a 24-hour cable news channel and internet service launched in 1996.

NBC Sports provides such programs as the Olympics, NASCAR (including the Winston Cup and the Daytona 500), golf (the U.S. Open, Ryder Cup, The Players Championship, and the President's Cup), tennis (French Open and Wimbledon), thoroughbred racing (such as the Breeders' Cup and Triple Crown coverage), Notre Dame football, and the Arena Football League.

NBC Enterprises is responsible for the global distribution of NBC-owned products, which includes foreign and domestic program syndication, strategic marketing, and ancillary exploitation of owned product in home video, merchandising, licensing, music, and publishing, as well as strategic production and co-production alliances and co-ventures. This programming includes all shows produced by NBC Studios, *NBC News*, *CNBC*, and *MSNBC*.

NBC Cable is responsible for distributing CNBC, CNBC World, Bravo, MSNBC, Telemundo, mun2, and ShopNBC to cable-television systems and satellite-television providers across the country. NBC Cable also maintains interests in the Arts &

Entertainment Network, the History Channel, and National Geographic Channel International.

Brand channels from NBC include Bravo (http://www.bravotv.com), launched in December 1980, the first 24-hour network dedicated to film and the performing arts. Evolving over time, the network now shows arts and entertainment programming, such as original series, independent and mainstream feature films, theater, dance, music, and documentaries; the 24-hour Independent Film Channel (http://www.ifctv.com), launched in September 1994, offers independent films, uncut and commercial-free in addition to original series and live events; a joint venture between NBC and Dow Jones (publisher of the *Wall Street Journal*), the 24-hour Consumer News & Business Channel (CNBC) (http://www.cnbc.com) was launched in April 1989 and provides real-time, international financial market coverage and business information to more than 175 million homes worldwide; CNBC World (http://www.nbccableinfo.com) is a 24-hour network that provides global financial market information in real-time, live, worldwide; MSNBC (http://www.msnbc.com) is a joint venture between Microsoft and NBC, was launched in July 1996, and is a 24-hour, all-news network. The network delivers breaking news and in-depth reporting on the day's top stories to 80 million U.S. households and 20 million users a month on the internet; the 24-hour Mun2 (http:// /www.mun2tv.com) was launched in October 2001 and broadcasts a programming mix to the young Latino market; ShopNBC (http://www.shopnbc. com) was launched in October 1999 and is a home shopping service that offers department-brand name merchandise; Telemundo (http://www.telemundo.com) was launched in January 1987 and is a 24-hour Spanish-language network aimed at the Hispanic viewing audience in America. The network reaches 92 percent of U.S. Hispanic viewers through its 15 owned-and-operated stations, 32 broadcast affiliates, and distribution to nearly 450 cable systems in 118 markets; and Telemundo Internacional (http://www.telemundo intl.com), launched in March 2000, is a 24-hour Spanish-language network with a mix of entertainment, sports, and updated news broadcasts.

National Educational Television— Now defunct, National Educational Television was an educational network that aired from 1952 to 1969 and was the predecessor of the Public Broadcasting System. Founded in 1952 by the Ford Foundation, NET was originally created as a limited service for exchanging and distributing educational programs produced by local television stations. In 1954 the network expanded its schedule and aired five hours of programming per day that included in-depth documentaries and hour-long interviews with people of literary and historical importance.

In 1958 NET became more aggressive in its programming and tried to establish itself as America's fourth network (joining ABC, CBS, and NBC). To broaden its vision, the network began importing programs from the British Broadcasting Corporation. The Corporation for Public Broadcasting (founded in 1967 and partially government funded) initially collaborated with NET but then broke away and started its own broadcasting entity (PBS) in 1969 and took over NET's subsidiaries and functions, which forced NET to disband. The children's educational programs *Sesame Street* and *Mister Rogers' Neighborhood* both first aired on NET before moving on to PBS.

National Geographic Channel, 1145 17th Street Northwest, Washington, D.C. 20036; *Telephone*: 202-912-6500; *Launch Date*: January 2001; *Broadcast Day*: 24 hours; *Subscribers*: 47,000,000; *Email*: Contact channel through its web site; *Web site*: http:// www.nationalgeographic.com/channel

The National Geographic Channel provides viewers with a direct connection to adventures all over the world and unique access to scientists, journalists, and film makers. Building on the National Geographic Society's

38-year history of award-winning documentary production, NGC airs series and specials that cover natural history, world cultures, science, and adventure, as well as more than 350 hours of original programming.

The National Geographic Society was founded in the United States in January 1888 by 33 men with the stated purpose of "organizing a society for the increase and diffusion of geographical knowledge." Gardiner Greene Hubbard became its first president and his son-in-law, Alexander Graham Bell, eventually succeeded him. The NGS sponsors explorations around the world and publishes a monthly magazine, *National Geographic*, which was started nine months after the society began.

National Greek Television, 30-97 Steinway Street, Astoria, NY 11103; *Telephone*: 718-726-0900; *Launch Date*: December 1987; *Broadcast Day*: 24 hours; *Subscribers*: 500,000

National Greek Television is a Greek-language, ethnic channel that broadcasts news, sports, talk shows, dramas, comedies, movies, and documentaries originating from Greece, as well as locally-produced programming aimed at the Greek-American community.

National Iranian Television, 21050 Erwin Street, Woodland Hills, CA 91367; *Telephone*: 818-716-0000, 720-853-2913; *Fax*: 720-853-2901; *Broadcast Day*: 24 hours; *Subscribers*: 500,000; *Email*: Contact channel through its web site; *Web site*: http://www.nitv.tv

National Iranian Television's programming consists of news, current affairs, cultural, educational and entertainment programming, all in Farsi.

National Jewish Television, P.O. Box 480, Wilton, CT 06897; *Telephone*: 203-834-3799; *Launch Date*: May 1981; *Broadcast Day*: 3 hours every Sunday; *Subscribers*: 10,000,000

National Jewish Television provides America's Jewish community family-based programming that focuses on the Jewish way of life, religion, people, documentaries, children's programs, and news magazines.

The National Network (The New TNN) *see* **Spike TV**

Native American Nations Program Network, P.O. Box 38307, 105 Freeport Road, Pittsburgh, PA 15215; *Telephone*: 412-782-2921; *Fax*: 412-782-4242; *Launch Date*: September 2003; *Broadcast Day*: 24 hours

The Native American Nations Program Network airs entertainment, news, sports, business, specials and features, gaming and player-participation programs, talk shows, races, and trading post shopping (featuring Native American collectibles, art, wall hangings, and clothing).

NATtv, 12517 Sherman Way, North Hollywood, CA 91605; *Telephone*: 818-765-1991; *Fax*: 818-765-1159; *Email*: service@nattv.com; *Web site*: http://www.nattv.com

NATtv is the first Thai-language television network in the United States and airs programming aimed at the Thai and Southeast Asian viewing audience.

NBA League Pass (NBA TV), National Basketball Association, 450 Harmon Meadow Boulevard, Secaucus, NJ 07094; *Telephone*: 201-865-1500; *Launch Date*: November 1999; *Broadcast Day*: 24 hours; *Email*: Contact channel through its web site; *Web site*: http://www.nba.com/nba_tv

NBA League Pass is a pay-per-view service from the National Basketball Association that is available through a variety of cable and satellite television providers. The service offers viewers an all-access pass for everything related to basketball. NBA TV is the first such service launched by a professional sports league and provides viewers with nationally-exclusive live regular season and playoff NBA games, behind-the-scenes access, original programming, and an insider's perspective of the league and the game.

New Abilities TV Network, P.O. Box A, White Springs, FL 32096; *Broadcast Day*: 24 hours; *Email*: natv@alltel.net; *Web site*:

http://www.newabilitiestv.org, http://www.forthepeople.org

Operated by the non-profit People's Network, Inc., the New Abilities TV Network aims its programming to the more than 50 million handicapped viewers in the United States, Canada, Mexico, and the Caribbean. Weekday programming is anchored by the *For the People Show*, hosted live by Chuck Harder. The balance of the network's broadcasts consists of uninterrupted classic movies and favorite television shows (such as *Bonanza*, *The Lone Ranger*, *Burns and Allen*, *You Bet Your Life*, *The Andy Griffith Show*, *Red Skelton*, *Beverly Hillbillies*, and *Highway Patrol*).

Weekend programming features informational shows, talk shows, call-in shows, specials, and documentaries aimed directly at the network's handicapped audience. Specific program topics focus on health, nutrition, handicapped issues, travel films for the handicapped, job development for the handicapped, and features on national handicapped organizations.

New England Cable News, 160 Wells Avenue, Newton, MA 02459; *Telephone*: 617-630-5000; *Fax*: 617-630-5057; *Launch Date*: March 1992; *Broadcast Day*: 24 hours; *Subscribers*: 3,000,000; *Email*: Contact the network through its web site; *Web site*: http://www.necn.com, http://www.necnews.com

A partnership between the Hearst Corporation and the Comcast Corporation, New England Cable News is the largest regional news network in the country and provides round-the-clock breaking news, sports, weather, and traffic. The network's original programming includes *NewsNight*, an in-depth news analysis program; *New England Business Day*, a business news program; *New England Dream House*, a home improvement program; *Sports LateNight*, a sports news and daily wrap-up program; and *The Phantom Gourmet*, a restaurant review program. NECN serves a six-state area that includes Massachusetts, Maine, New Hampshire, Vermont, Connecticut and Rhode Island and broadcasts from its studios in Newton, Massachusetts, Manchester, New Hampshire, Hartford, Connecticut, and Burlington, Vermont.

New England Sports Network, 70 Brookline Avenue, Boston, MA 02215; *Telephone*: 617-536-9233; *Fax*: 617-536-7814; *Launch Date*: March 1984; *Broadcast Day*: 24 hours; *Subscribers*: 4,000,000; *Email*: Contact network through its web site; *Web site*: http://www.nesn.com

The New England Sports Network airs Boston Red Sox baseball, Boston Bruins hockey, college sports, and other sports programming to six New England states and satellite owners throughout the United States.

New York 1 News, 75 Ninth Avenue, 6th Floor, New York, NY 10011; *Telephone*: 212-379-3311; *Fax*: 212-379-3570; *Launch Date*: September 1992; *Broadcast Day*: 24 hours; *Subscribers*: 2,000,000; *Email*: Contact channel through its web site; *Web site*: http://www.ny1.com

New York 1 News is a regional news channel devoted to covering events and features in and pertaining to New York City.

Newborn Channel, 9 Old Kings Highway South, Darien, CT 06820; *Telephone*: 203-559-3657; *Launch Date*: 1992; *Broadcast Day*: 24 hours; *Email*: Contact channel through its web site; *Web site*: http://www.newborn.com

Produced by iVillage Parenting Network, the Newborn Channel is the only round-the-clock channel with programming aimed to postpartum hospital patients and their families. Viewers have over 30 programs to choose from, including *Adjusting To Fatherhood*, *Breastfeeding*, *Postpartum Blues*, *Bathing Baby*, *Car Seat Safety*, *Importance of Immunizations*, and *Care of the New Mother*.

Newsworld International, 1230 Avenue of the Americas, New York, NY 10020; *Telephone*: 212-413-5000; *Fax*: 416-205-5912; *Launch Date*: September 1994; *Broadcast*

Day: 24 hours; *Subscribers*: 4,500,000; *Email*: Contact channel through its web site; *Web site*: http://www.nwitv.com

Newsworld International provides news from countries around the world to viewers who seek a global perspective of the day's events. A unique feature of the channel is its presentation of unedited newscasts from major countries around the world, available in both English and the originating language.

NFL Network (NFL Sunday Ticket), National Football League, 280 Park Avenue, New York, NY 10017; *Telephone*: 212-450-2000; *Launch Date*: November 2003; *Broadcast Day*: 24 hours; *Email*: Contact channel through its web site; *Web site*: http://www.nfl.com

NFL Network (NFL Sunday Ticket) (National Football League) is a pay-per-view service from the National Football League that is available through a variety of cable and satellite television providers. This service focuses on the NFL and the sport of football. The service airs features from NFL Films, original programs, pre-season games, coaches' shows, and press conferences.

NHL Center Ice, National Hockey League, 1251 Avenue of the Americas, New York, NY 10020; *Telephone*: 212-789-2000; *Fax*: 212-789-2020; *Launch Date*: November 2003; *Broadcast Day*: 24 hours; *Email*: Contact channel through its web site; *Web site*: http://www.nhl.com

NHL Center Ice is a pay-per-view service from the National Hockey League and is available through a variety of cable and satellite television providers.

Nickelodeon, 1515 Broadway, 23rd Floor, New York, NY 10036; *Telephone*: 212-258-8000, 212-846-4629; *Fax*: 212-846-1893; *Launch Date*: April 1979; *Broadcast Day*: 24 hours; *Subscribers*: 86,000,000; *Email*: Contact network through its web site; *Web site*: http://www.mtv.com

An MTV (Music Television) network and owned by Viacom, Nickelodeon was the first network developed just for kids. The 24-hour Nick2, launched in May 1998, gives viewers the opportunity to watch their favorite Nickelodeon and Nick at Nite shows at different times of the day. Nick At Night's TV Land (http://www.nick-at-nite.com, http://www.nickatnite.com), launched in April 1996, airs 24 hours a day and is the only network dedicated to showing the best of everything television has from the past 50 years, including classic shows, original specials, and gone-but-never-to-be-forgotten commercials. Nickelodeon GAS (Games and Sports for Kids), launched in March 1999, celebrates the way kids play, from board games to video games to extreme sports. It is a 24-hour channel aimed at the 6-11 age group. Nicktoons, launched in May 2002, is a 24-hour channel aimed directly at kids.

NIMA Television, 1828 Euclid Avenue, Berkeley, CA 94702; *Telephone*: 510-540-5652; *Fax*: 510-540-5443; *Launch Date*: 1989; *Email*: info@nimatv.com; *Web site*: http://www.nimatv.com

Nima Television broadcasts Iranian programs to San Francisco, California Bay Area audiences.

Nippon Golden Network, 567 South King Street #110, Honolulu, HI 96813; *Telephone*: 808-538-1966; *Launch Date*: January 1982; *Broadcast Day*: 24 hours; *Subscribers*: 29,800,000

The Nippon Golden Network is a Japanese-language pay service available in Hawaii and southern California. Programming includes news, sports, dramas, and musicals, many with English subtitles.

Noah's World International, 11448 Kanapali Lane, Boynton Beach, FL 33437; *Telephone*: 561-732-2108; *Launch Date*: May 2003; *Broadcast Day*: 24 hours; *Email*: Contact channel through its web site; *Web site*: http://www.noahsworldtv.com

Noah's World International broadcasts programs that visit and explore various countries around the world, including travel, vacations, places of interest, culture, history, business and investments, global interchange, and interviews with politicians and business leaders. Nations highlighted are those friendly to the United States, such as Israel, Norway, Finland, Switzerland, Holland, Sweden, Hungary, and the United Kingdom.

Noggin (The N), 1633 Broadway, New York, NY 10019; *Telephone*: 212-654-3000; *Fax*: 212-846-1767; *Launch Date*: February 1999; *Broadcast Day*: 24 hours; *Subscribers*: 37,000,000; *Email*: Contact channel through its web site; *Web site*: http://www.noggin.com; http://www.the-n.com

Noggin is a 24-hour commercial-free educational channel dedicated to preschoolers and broadcasts such shows as *Sesame Street* and *Blue's Clues*, as well as original programming. The network also airs interactive games on television and on its web site. During the hours of 6:00 P.M. to 5:00 A.M. Noggin becomes a nighttime network for teens.

NorthWest Cable News, 333 North Dexter Avenue, Seattle, WA 98109; *Telephone*: 206-448-3600; *Fax*: 206-448-3690; *Launch Date*: December 1995; *Broadcast Day*: 24 hours; *Subscribers*: 2,100,000; *Email*: nwcn@nwcn.com; *Web site*: http://www.nwcn.com

NorthWest Cable News airs news coverage from the Northwest to viewers in Washington, Oregon, Idaho, Montana, and Alaska.

Nostalgia Network (Nostalgia Television) *see* **GoodLife TV Network**

Novellas Channel, 4424 Simpson Avenue, Valley Village, CA 91607; *Telephone*: 323-460-2051; *Fax*: 818-980-6547; *Broadcast Day*: 24 hours; *Email*: Contact channel through its web site; *Web site*: http://www.novelaschannel.com

The Novellas Channel is the first and only round-the-clock Spanish-language network entirely dedicated to broadcasting soap operas, one of the most popular television genres of the channel's Latino audience.

NTV America, One Executive Drive #190, Fort Lee, NJ 07024; *Telephone*: 201-242-8998; *Launch Date*: October 2002; *Broadcast Day*: 24 hours; *Subscribers*: 30,000; *Email*: Contact channel through its web site; *Web site*: http://www.ntvamerica.com

NTV America is a Russian-language channel that broadcasts original NTV programming from Moscow. NTV America airs nine daily live news broadcasts from Russia, feature films, serials, game shows, and Russian and European soccer.

Oasis TV, Inc., 9887 Santa Monica Boulevard #200, Beverly Hills, CA 90212; *Telephone*: 310-553-4300; *Fax*: 310-553-1159; *Launch Date*: September 1997; *Broadcast Day*: 24 hours; *Subscribers*: 1,650,000; *Email*: Contact channel through its web site; *Web site*: http://www.oasistv.com

Oasis TV is an integrated programming service that provides internet, broadband, cable, satellite, and broadcast television shows that target the holistic body/mind/spirit New Age lifestyle market. The network was the world's first round-the-clock holistic/personal growth cable/satellite programmer and airs more than 3,000 hours of content, including original shows and acquired programs that cover such areas as festivals, current affairs, science and metaphysics conferences, eco-fairs, expos, and concerts.

Odyssey Television (Planned for future operation)

Ohio News Network, 770 Twin Rivers Drive, Columbus, OH 43215; *Telephone*: 614-280-6300; *Launch Date*: May 1997; *Broadcast Day*: 24 hours; *Subscribers*: 1,500,000; *Email*: Contact network through its web site; *Web site*: http://www.onnnews.com

The Ohio News Network is a state-wide round-the-clock news channel that features local news, weather (with the use of Ohio DopplerNet, a forecasting technology that pinpoints the exact timing and location of storms), and sports (including high school football and basketball state championship games).

Omni Broadcasting Network, 8275 South Eastern Avenue #200, Las Vegas, NV 89123; *Telephone*: 702-938-0467; *Fax*: 702-990-8681; *Email*: info@obnholdings.com; *Web site*: http://www.obn-tv.com; http://obn-tv.com

The Omni Broadcasting Network airs its programming on both broadcast television and cable channels. Its content derives from numerous international sources and includes original material produced especially for OMNI either through its sister company, Eclectic Entertainment, or from independent producers and suppliers. While the network generally targets the 25-54 age market, it is beginning to expand its programming content to attract younger viewers.

ORB TV, Omni Resource Business Group, P.O. Box 1308, Culver City, CA 90232; *Telephone*: 310-669-6180; *Broadcast Day*: 18 hours; *Email*: Contact channel through its web site; *Web site*: http://www.orbtv.com

ORB TV broadcasts programs with a global perspective on the latest in scientific, artistic, and cultural events and discoveries. Programming includes documentaries, concerts, interviews with artists and scientists, domestic and international films, videos, animation, and experimental multimedia projects.

Orbit ESPN Sports *see* **Entertainment Sports Television Network**

Outdoor Channel, 43445 Business Park Drive #103, Temecula, CA 92590; *Telephone*: 800-770-5750, 909-699-6991; *Fax*: 909-676-8037, 909-699-6313; *Launch Date*: 1993 (as a part-time service), 1994 (as a full-time channel); *Broadcast Day*: 24 hours; *Subscribers*: 26,000,000; *Email*: info@outdoorchannel.com; *Web site*: http://www. outdoorchannel.com

The Outdoor Channel airs outdoor-related programming for active sportsmen including hunting, fishing, off-road activities, competitive shooting, and motor sports. Its programming is aimed at all viewers, regardless of skill level. The channel is a subsidiary of Global Outdoors, Inc., first began in 1993 as a part-time service, and became a full-service channel in April 1994.

Programs feature fishing (hosted by world-renowned anglers and includes fishing action and practical how-to information for anglers of all skill levels); hunting (all aimed at promoting outdoor hunting activities and improving viewers' skills); and outdoor traditions (various shows, such as *Wednesday Night Horsepower*, that offers viewers the best in motorsports and rodeo).

Original programs include *Inside R/C* (broadcasts from big-time competitions and small-town club events and features radio-controlled monster trucks, race cars, helicopters, airplanes, and robots); *Circle of Honor* (profiles individuals who have lived extraordinary lives while making significant contributions to traditional outdoor sports); *Whistle Stops* (traveling by train, the show visits people, places, and events across the United States, including special hideaways and scenic vistas); *Rodeo Roundup* (covers rodeos at all levels, from high school to professional Championship Bull Riding); *Angler on Tour* (a behind-the-scenes look at the life of a professional angler); *Out in the Country* (a mix of interviews with country music personalities, music videos, and live performances from top country artists); *SpeedZone* (details competition and competitors pushing their machines to the limit and features everything from boat racing to off-roading in the desert to powerboat racing on the open ocean); and *American Rifleman Television* (a show for the firearm enthusiast that features reviews, expert appraisals, and profiles of historically significant firearms).

Outdoor Life Network, Two Stamford

Plaza, 281 Tresser Boulevard, 9th Floor, Stamford, CT 06901; *Telephone*: 203-406-2500; *Fax*: 203-406-2534; *Launch Date*: July 1995; *Broadcast Day*: 24 hours; *Subscribers*: 58,000,000; *Email*: info@great outdoors. com; feedback@ olntv.com; *Web site*: http:// www.olntv.com

From bull riding to cycling, fly-fishing to mountaineering, and recreational sports to competitive events, Outdoor Life Network's programming allows viewers to share and discover outdoor interests and activities. With events such as the Tour de France, Professional Bull Riding, the Gravity Games, AMA Supermoto, and FIS World Cup Skiing, the network provides viewers with nonstop action programming.

Owned by Comcast, the network's prime-time programming is divided into four categories: Outdoor Adventure, Action Sports, Animals and The Outdoors, and Field & Stream. Broadcast events include the Tour de France, Giro d'Italia and Vuelta a Espana cycling competitions, the world's preeminent rodeo event, the Calgary Stampede, boating's ultimate racing series and America's Cup qualifier, the Louis Vuitton Cup, FIS World Cup Skiing and Snowboarding events, the United States Olympic Team Trials, and the oldest and most challenging of all adventure races, the Raid Gauloises.

Other favorite network programs include *Gear Guide* (a gear and equipment testing series); *Adventure Crusoe* (an interactive series that takes viewers around the world and challenges them to guess the mystery location); *Adventure Center* (an interactive news magazine program that covers the latest in adventure news); and *Wild Survival* (recounts stories of human drama in the wilderness through eyewitness accounts and special re-enactments).

OuterMax, 1100 Avenue of the Americas, New York, NY 10036; *Telephone*: 212-512-1000; *Fax*: 212-512-1182; *Launch Date*: May 2001; *Broadcast Day*: 24 hours; *Email*: Contact channel through its web site; *Web site*: http://www.cinemax.com

OuterMax is a multiplexed channel from Cinemax that broadcasts science fiction, horror, and fantasy movies.

Outstanding Latin Entertainment Channel, 2205 Northwest 23rd Avenue, Miami, FL 33142; *Telephone*: 305-661-6532; *Fax*: 305-661-2748; *Email*: info@olecnetwork.com; *Web site*: http://www.olecnetwork.com

Planned for future operation, the Outstanding Latin Entertainment Channel will attempt to be the premier provider of niche Hispanic programming. OLEC has divided its target audience into separate viewer segments and has developed unique channels for each group, including Amigos (a children's educational and entertainment channel (geared to kids 1-13) that will feature wholesome programming in both animated and non-animated forms); the 24-hour Furia (will provide viewers a close look at the intense confrontation and conflict of extreme action sports in which the participants display their fury and desire to compete; the channel's target audience is males over 13 and will showcase such events as boxing, wrestling, martial arts, strongman competitions, and other individual physical sports; the channel will also broadcast fictional series and documentaries); the 24-hour Movie Ticket (will offer action, adventure, suspense, and mystery blockbuster films from Hollywood and foreign producers to viewers in Spanish; its films are targeted to the male audience, 13 and older); Pasión (will broadcast the best Latin soaps and drama series; each day eight different shows will air with contemporary themes: one youth targeted show and two classic dramas, all captivating the attention of the modern woman; the channel's target audience is females, age 13 and older); Alegria (will be the only 24-hour Spanish broadcast channel dedicated exclusively to the world of humor and comedy; the channel's target audience is the entire family); Puro TV (will provide audiences with reality shows and documentaries, including action-life programming, true and amazing events, stories and people, and educational programming; the 24-hour channel targets men and women 18 and older); Music Alley (aimed at the Ñ Generation (males and females 13 and older who demand entertainment that caters to both their Hispanic roots and their very American identities; Music Alley will be an all-in-one music channel that will feature dance, trance, rock, punk, pop, and ballads); and G-Spot (a 24-hour adult channel aimed at males 21 and older that will feature exotic beauties and locales).

OVATION — The Arts Network, 5801 Duke Street, Suite D-112, Alexandria, VA 22304; 201 North Union Street #210, Alexandria, VA 22314; *Telephone*: 800-OVATION, 703-813-6310; *Launch Date*: April 1996; *Broadcast Day*: 20 hours; *Subscribers*: 7,000,000; *Email*: Contact network through its web site; *Web site*: http://www.ovationtv.com

From B.B. King to Bach, Pavarotti to Pop Art, Alvin Ailey to architecture, OVATION brings the arts to viewers, including art news from around the world and children's arts programs. It is the only channel devoted exclusively to the arts and gives the viewer a behind-the-scenes and front-row-center view to all of the arts, from performances to artist profiles. The network's programming includes jazz, pop, classical and world music, performances of opera, dance and drama, up-close and personal looks at the lives of artists and performers, happenings in the arts from across the United States and around the world, and special presentations of the arts for children.

Oxygen Media, Inc., 75 9th Avenue, 7th Floor, New York, NY 10011; *Telephone*: 212-651-2070; *Fax*: 212-651-2030; *Launch Date*: February 2000; *Broadcast Day*: 24 hours; *Subscribers*: 50,000,000; *Email*: feedback@oxygen.com; *Web site*: http://www. oxygen.com

The Oxygen network aims its programming toward women viewers and airs acquired and original shows, such as *Oprah After the Show* (Oprah Winfrey played a role in starting this network); the hidden-camera prank show, *Girls Behaving Badly*; the live call-in show, *Talk Sex with Sue Johanson*; and the hit show from Britain, *Absolutely Fabulous*. A unique feature of this channel is its use of The Stripe, which is displayed at the bottom of the television screen during programs. The Stripe provides information related to what is being aired and complements what the viewer is watching on the screen. Information includes facts about shows, stars, and movies on Oxygen; directions to the channel's Web offerings for the current show; and messages from the channel's advertising partners.

Parent Television (Planned for future operation)

Pars TV Network, 18720 Oxnard Avenue #102, Tarzana, CA 91356; *Telephone*: 818-881-5800; *Fax*: 818-705-5446; *Email*: info@parstvnetwork.com; *Web site*: http://www.parstvnetwork.com

The Pars TV Network broadcasts Persian-language programs.

Pasión *see* **Outstanding Latin Entertainment Channel**

Patient Channel, P.O. Box 414, Mail Code EC-05, Milwaukee, WI 53201; *Telephone*: 800-736-4367; *Fax*: 262-506-2600; *Email*: tip-tv@med.ge.com; *Web site*: http://www.gemedicalsystems.com/educationpatient_channel/

Launched by GE Medical Systems to hospitals in the United States, the Patient Channel provides updated informational, patient-oriented programming covering the most common medical conditions and related topics. Programs feature explanations, case studies, and messages of hope for better understanding of medical conditions. Related topics help patients and family members understand and deal with associated issues.

Sample programs include *Advanced Breast Cancer: New Reasons for Hope*; *Advanced Prostate Cancer*; *BabyTalk: You and Your Baby— The First Few Days*; *Breathe Easy: Asthma & Allergies in Women*; *Cancer Related Fatigue: Three Patients Share Their Stories*; *Cholesterol: Issues and Answers*; *Depression: Beating the Blues*; *Diabetes: Taking Control*; *Hospital Stays: What You Need To Know*; *Living with Cancer*; *Melanoma: From SPF to RX*; *Obesity: Winning the Battle*; *Ovarian Cancer*; *Rhythms of the Heart: Advances in Arrhythmias*; *Stroke: Issues and Answers*; *Taking Medications: A to Z*; and *The Truth About Exercise & Nutrition*.

PAX TV (Paxson Communications), 601 Clearwater Park Road, West Palm Beach, FL 33401; *Telephone*: 800-700-9789, 561-659-4124; *Fax*: 561-655-7246; *Launch Date*: August 1998; *Broadcast Day*: 24 hours; *Subscribers*: 95,000,000; *Email*: Contact channel through its web site; *Web site*: http://www.pax.tv

PAX TV airs family-oriented programming with minimum violence and sexual themes, and no foul language, including dramatic series, movies, sports, and special events. Popular shows on the network include *Bonanza*, *Candid Camera*, *Diagnosis Murder*, *Family Feud*, *Miracle Pets*, and *Shop 'Til You Drop*. PAX TV also shows a variety of sporting events, featuring such teams as the Anaheim Angels, the Florida Marlins, the Kansas City Royals, the New York Yankees, the Tampa Bay Devil Rays, and the Atlanta Hawks.

PBS Kids *see* **Public Broadcasting Service**

Pennsylvania Cable Network, 401 Fallowfield Road, Camp Hill, PA 17011; *Telephone*: 717-730-6000; *Fax*: 717-730-6005; *Launch Date*: September 1979; *Broadcast Day*: 24 hours; *Subscribers*: 3,000,000; *Email*: Contact network through its web site; *Web site*: http://www.pcntv.com

The Pennsylvania Cable Network is the state's public affairs network and provides live and same-day coverage of the Pennsylvania Senate, House, and other governmental activities. PCN also televises state events (such as high school sports championships), tours, museums, and manufacturing facilities.

Pentagon Channel *see* **Armed Forces Radio and Television Service**

People's Network *see* **New Abilities TV Network**

Performance Showcase, P.O. Box 4282, Montebello, CA 90640; *Telephone*: 323-724-1466

Performance Showcase provides an outlet for producers, directors, writers, actors, commentators, reporters, hosts, musicians, and television and film crews to air both old and new, amateur and professional pilot productions.

Persian Entertainment Network, 6431 Independence Avenue, Woodland Hills, CA 91367; *Telephone*: 818-592-0077; *Fax*: 818-475-5410; *Launch Date*: April 2004; *Broadcast Day*: 24 hours; *Email*: info@penonline.tv; *Web site*: http://www.penonline.tv

The multi-language Persian Entertainment Network airs concerts, music videos, Broadway plays, and movies aimed primarily at Persian viewers around the world. The network's music videos are aired in one-hour blocks for specific genres, such as Dance Hour and Pop Hour.

Pet Network (Planned for future operation)

Planet Central Television (http://www.pctvi.com) (Planned for future operation)

Playboy TV Networks (Playboy Television), 2706 Media Center Drive, Los Angeles, CA 90065; *Telephone*: 323-276-4000; *Fax*: 323-276-4500; *Launch Date*: November 1982 (as The Playboy Channel), December 1989 (as a pay-per-view service); *Broadcast*

Day: 24 hours; *Subscribers*: 4,500,000; *Email*: info@playboy.com; *Web site*: http://www.playboytv.com; http://www.playboy.com-/pbtv-tv, http://www.pbtvnetworks.com

Playboy TV airs adult-oriented programming targeted to men and couples. Playboy Enterprises, Inc. is a brand-driven, international multimedia entertainment company that publishes editions of *Playboy* magazine around the world (with more than 15 million international readers), operates Playboy and Spice television networks, distributes programming via home video and DVD globally, licenses the Playboy and Spice trademarks internationally for a range of consumer products, and operates Playboy.com, a men's lifestyle and entertainment web site destination.

Playboy TV and the company's Spice-branded movie channels are available in more than 113 million U.S. cable and direct-to-home satellite households. The company also operates more than 20 international Playboy and Spice networks with partners in more than 50 countries throughout Europe, Latin America, and Asia.

Brand channels from the Playboy TV Networks include the Adam & Eve Channel (http://www.cyberspice.com; programmed to be a companion channel to Spice); The Hot Networks was launched in March 1999 and include Hot Net and Hot Zone; Spice, Spice 1, Spice 2, Spice Pay-Per-View, Spice Platinum, Spice Ultra XXX; Vivid TV;, and the X! Channel.

Playgirl TV (http://playgirltv.com) (Planned for future operation)—Playgirl TV will be the first adult entertainment service produced for and by women. It will include popular segments taken from *Playgirl* magazine.

Pleasure, 7007 Winchester Circle #200, Boulder, CO 80301; *Telephone*: 303-786-8700; *Launch Date*: September 1998; *Broadcast Day*: 24 hours; *Subscribers*: 8,000,000; *Email*: Contact channel through its web site; *Web site*: http://www.noof.com

Available through The Erotic Network, the Pleasure channel is an adult pay-per-view network that uses a soft edit standard and focuses on feature-length premieres from top stars and studios.

Pogo TV *see* **Cartoon Network**

Polvision, 3656 West Belmont Avenue, Chicago, IL 60618; *Telephone*: 773-588-6300; *Fax*: 773-267-4913; *Email*: info@polvision.com; *Web site*: http://www.polvision.com

Polvision airs Polish-language programming.

Popcorn Channel (Planned for future operation)

Praise Television, 28059 U.S. Highway 19 North #300, Clearwater, FL 33761; *Telephone*: 800-921-9692, 727-536-0036; *Fax*: 727-530-0671; *Launch Date*: September 1992; *Broadcast Day*: 24 hours; *Subscribers*: 66,000,000; *Email*: comments@ praisetv.com; *Web site*: http://www.praisetv.com

Praise Television (also called the Worship Network) is a family entertainment network with an emphasis on contemporary Christian music and relaxation through music videos, concert performances, countdown programs, and artist biographies.

Prevue Channel *see* **TV Guide Channel**

Prison Television Network, 18495 U.S. Highway 19 North, Clearwater, FL 33764; *Telephone*: 888-843-5512, 727-210-0187; *Fax*: 727-210-2445; *Email*: info@ptnoutreach.org; *Web site*: http://www.ptnoutreach.org

The Prison Television Network serves to meet the spiritual and educational needs of the growing prison population.

Product Information Network, 9697 East Mineral Avenue, Englewood, CO 80155; *Telephone*: 303-784-8321, 303-792-3111; *Launch Date*: April 1994; *Broadcast Day*: 24 hours; *Subscribers*: 35,000,000; *Email*: Contact network through its web site; *Web site*: http://www.jones.com/pin.html

A joint venture between the Jones Media Networks, Ltd. and Cox Communications, Inc., the Product Information Network is an informational channel created to air round-the-clock short- and long-form advertising. PIN provides viewers with full-length product demonstrations and service information, in addition to serving as a venue for customer inquiries, purchases, and deliveries.

Proto X Television (Planned for future operation)

Public Broadcasting Service, 1320 Braddock Place, Alexandria, VA 22314; *Telephone*: 703-739-5000; *Launch Date*: 1969; *Broadcast Day*: 24 hours; *Subscribers*: 100,000,000; *Email*: Contact network through its web site; *Web site*: http://www pbs.org

The Public Broadcasting Service is a private, non-profit media enterprise owned and operated by the nation's public television stations. Available to 99 percent of American homes with televisions, PBS reaches nearly 100 million people each week. The service oversees program acquisition, distribution, and promotion; education services; new media ventures; fund raising support; engineering and technology development; and video marketing for member stations. Popular programs include *American Masters, Antiques Roadshow, Austin City Limits, BBC World News, Charlie Rose, Evening at Pops, Frontline, Great Performances, McLaughlin Group, Mister Rogers' Neighborhood, The NewsHour with Jim Lehrer, NOVA, P.O.V., Sesame Street*, and *This Old House*.

PBS programming features children's shows, cultural, educational, history, nature, news, public affairs, science, and skills programs. Broadcast fare is obtained from PBS stations, independent producers, and sources around the world. PBS does not produce programs on its own. The majority of PBS funding originates from The federal government (23.5 percent); state governments (18.3 percent); Corporation for Public Broadcasting and federal grants/contracts (16.4 percent); businesses (16.1 percent); state colleges and universities (6.5 percent); and foundations (5.5 percent).

PBS Ready To Learn helps increase school readiness for America's children with a line-up of educational and entertaining children's programming each weekday, coupled with short video segments. PBS Ready To Learn includes workshops, free children's books, a magazine, and other learning resources to help parents, teachers, and child-care providers prepare young children to enter school ready to learn. The PBS Adult Learning Service, a partnership involving local PBS stations and colleges, provides college credit television courses to nearly 500,000 students each academic year.

PBS Kids (http://www.pbskids.org) provides entertainment and learning-based programs to children with the goals of stimulating their curiosity, encouraging interaction, and fostering their imagination. Programs on PBS KIDS are designed to help children in each of the four key areas of childhood development: cognitive, social, emotional, and physical. Popular PBS Kids programs include *Dragon Tales, Arthur, Sesame Street, Clifford the Big Red Dog*, and *Barney*.

Puma TV, 2029 Southwest 105th Court, Miami, FL 33165; *Telephone*: 305-554-1876, 305-321-6737; *Launch Date*: 1997; *Broadcast Day*: 24 hours; *Subscribers*: 2,300,000; *Email*: Contact channel through its web site; *Web site*: http://www.condista.com

Puma TV is a music channel aimed at the Hispanic market and its programming is formatted to appeal to different segments of the population, various musical tastes, and age groups. The channel also airs a variety of informative programs on fashion, modeling, and entertainment.

The Puppy Channel, 2529-D Laurelwood Drive, Clearwater, FL 33763; *Telephone*: 727-712-0740; *Broadcast Day*: 24 hours; *Email*:

Contact channel through its web site; *Web site*: http://www.thepuppychannel.com

Part of Channemals, a family of cable, satellite, and internet networks under development and planned for future operation, the Puppy Channel's programming will consist of puppy-related videos, accompanied by relaxing instrumental music, with no talk, and very few people.

Puro TV *see* **Outstanding Latin Entertainment Channel**

Q Television Network, 303 North Indian Canyon Boulevard, 3rd Floor, Palm Springs, CA 92262; *Telephone*: 760-323-4455; *Launch Date*: September 2004; *Broadcast Day*: 24 hours; *Email*: info@qtelevision.com; *Web site*: http://www.qtelevision.com

The Q Television Network is the nation's first round-the-clock all gay and lesbian channel. QTN programs include *Yestergay with Melinda* (dedicated to social, political, and civil rights and focuses on events, parties, parades, politicians, entertainers and human interest stories); *Wow! Women on Women* (a lesbian talk show dedicated to issues of concern to all women; guests include authors, entertainers, politicians, and homemakers and topics discussed include child care, healthcare, the latest fashions, travel tips, lesbian and gay adoption, and reproductive rights); *Qews Break* (five-minute snapshots of issues concerning the gay and lesbian community on a local, state, national, and international level); *Q On The Move* (shot entirely on location throughout the county, this show focuses on gay and lesbian events, human interest stories, and fun happenings); and *Q the Music* (airs the latest, most popular music videos).

QVC (Quality, Value, Convenience) Shopping Channel, Studio Park, 1365 Enterprise Drive, West Chester, PA 19380; 1200 Wilson Drive, West Chester, PA 19380; *Telephone*: 484-701-1000, 215-430-1051; *Fax*: 484-710-1350; *Launch Date*: November 1986; *Broadcast Day*: 24 hours; *Subscribers*: 86,400,000; *Email*: Contact channel through its web site; *Web site*: http://www.qvc.com

QVC, Inc., a $5 billion company, markets a wide variety of brand name products in such categories as home furnishing, licensed products, fashion, beauty, electronics, and fine jewelry. Affiliate subsidiaries include QVC.com, Q Direct, Q Records and Video, QVC@, QVC Local, Q2, QVC Fashion Channel, and QVC ProductWorks.

QVC is the world's largest electronic retailer and, while it did not invent the home-shopping business, the network has taken the concept to a new, and very profitable high. Hourly segments feature knowledgeable hosts and interesting, sometimes famous, guests, and each product is given a thorough presentation.

QVC, Inc. was created by Joseph Segel, founder of The Franklin Mint, and established a new record in American business history for first full-fiscal-year sales by a new public company, with revenues of over $112 million. By 1993, QVC had become the number one televised shopping service in sales and profits, and was available in more than 80 percent of all U.S. cable homes. Its domestic and international sales have increased steadily since then, with over 150 million units shipped each year and $5 billion in sales.

Important dates in the channel's time line include November 24, 1986 (first live broadcast from studios in West Chester, Pennsylvania); January 1, 1987 (programming expands to 24 hours a day, 7 days a week); September 1, 1987 (the channel's 100,000-square-foot Lancaster, Pennsylvania distribution center opens); October 31, 1989 (QVC buys the CVN Shopping Channel); November 26, 1989 (first $10 million day, 125,000 phone orders); January 30, 1994 (immediately after the 1994 Superbowl, QVC sells over 6,000 Dallas Cowboys Superbowl Champs T-shirts in a matter of minutes); September 25, 1994 (the channel sells 155,000 copies of *In the Kitchen with Bob* cookbook, the most copies of a single title ever sold by one retailer in a single day); February 1, 1995

(QVC's sister channel, Q2, expands to seven days a week, 18 hours a day); February 10, 1995 (Comcast Corporation and Tele-Communications, Inc. acquire QVC); March 15, 1995 (QVC ships its 200 millionth package, equivalent to one package for every adult in America); January 28, 1997 (QVC goes live from Super Bowl XXXI and Green Bay Packer fans order 30,000 championship locker room caps in 20 minutes); June 29, 2000 (QVC unveils its Studio Tour that provides visitors with a behind-the-scenes look at QVC's operations); September 2000 (QVC becomes the Official U.S. Olympic Team Shopping Channel and is the only electronic retailer permitted to broadcast from Sydney and present Olympic programming featuring USOC-licensed apparel, pins, and collectibles); December 19, 2000 (QVC reaches the $1 billion mark in net sales for the fourth quarter and becomes the first company of its kind to reach that mark); and August 8, 2001 (the 2,500-square-foot QVC@ THE MALL flagship store opens at the Mall of America).

Racetrack Television Network *see* **HorseRacing TV**

RadioTV Network, 5670 Wilshire Boulevard #1300, Los Angeles, CA 90036; *Telephone*: 323-634-0070; *Fax*: 323-965-5411; *Launch Date*: 1998; *Broadcast Day*: 24 hours; *Email*: Contact network through its web site; *Web site*: http://www.rtvnet.com

The RadioTV Network televises some of the most well-known radio personalities and top radio programs in the United States. The network takes viewers directly into the booths, behind the scenes, to the concerts, and up close and personal with celebrity guests. Personalities and programs on the air include Mancow Muller (Chicago), Kidd Kraddick (Dallas-Fort Worth), and Rick Dees (Los Angeles).

RAI International, 9502 East Littleton, Knoxville, TN 37922; *Telephone*: 865-291-2863; *Launch Date*: 1999 (in the United States); *Broadcast Day*: 24 hours; *Email*: Contact network through its web site; *Web site*: http://www.international.rai.it

RAI International, and its American-based channel RAI USA, broadcast on the International Channel and provide a link between Italian-Americans and their homeland. The channels promote the culture of Italy through a programming mix of festivals, soccer games, concerts, movies, cooking shows, game shows, documentaries, and news.

Rang-A-Rang TV, 2221 Chain Bridge Road, Vienna, VA 22182; *Telephone*: 703-356-1795, 703-255-9500, 720-853-2913; *Fax*: 703-255-2032, 703-991-2184, 720-853-2901; *Launch Date*: 1989 / 2003; *Broadcast Day*: 24 hours; *Email*: info@rang-a-rang,com; *Web site*: http://www.rang-a-rang.com, http://www.rangarangtv.com

Rang-A-Rang airs programming for Farsi-speaking and Iranian viewers in the United States that includes current affairs shows, music programs, and movies.

Rave HD, 200 Jericho Quadrangle, Jericho, NY 11753; *Telephone*: 516-803-6010; *Launch Date*: October 2003; *Email*: Contact channel through its web site; *Web site*: http://www.voom.com

Rave HD is a high definition multiplexed channel from Voom that shows music videos, concerts, and artist interviews.

RDS *see* **Entertainment Sports Programming Network**

Real Estate Channel, 1000 Universal Studios Plaza, Building 22-A, Orlando, FL 32819; *Telephone*: 407-224-6830; *Launch Date*: December 2003; *Broadcast Day*: 24 hours; *Email*: Contact channel through its web site; *Web site*: http://www.realestatechannel.com

A wholly-owned subsidiary of Multi-Channel Ventures, LLC, the Real Estate Channel airs educational, information, and direct selling programming for the real estate and home improvement industry through the Home Improvement Channel (http://www.homeimprovementchannel.com), which provides viewers with demonstrations and information on how to improve the value of their homes.

Real Hip-Hop Network, 1101 Pennsylvania Avenue Northwest, 7th Floor, Washington, D.C. 20004; *Telephone*: 888-260-4776; *Launch Date*: September 2004; *Broadcast Day*: 24 hours; *Email*: Contact network through its web site; *Web site*: http://www.ssm-media.com, http://www.rhn.tv

The Real Hip Hop Network airs music videos and programs that focus on the essence of the hip hop genre and culture. In addition to music videos, the network also airs live concerts, fashion shows, break dancing contests and demonstrations, news rap battles, and DJ competitions.

Reality Central (The Reality Television Cable Channel) (Reality 24-7), 1520 Second Street, 2nd Floor, Santa Monica, CA 90401; *Telephone*: 310-395-0551; *Launch Date*: November 2004; *Broadcast Day*: 24 hours; *Email*: contactus@realitycentral.com; *Web site*: http://www.realitycentral.com

Reality Central celebrates the "reality television" genre and its programming includes original news, information, gossip, biography about reality series and stars, premiers of popular international reality series, talk shows, call-in programs, enhanced versions of popular American series, and a reality series about the making of Reality Central. Programs on the network include *Reality 24-7 News* (daily series that focuses on all aspects of reality television including developments on current series, new series in production, casting reports, and gossip and personality features); *The Real Deal* (daily talk show focusing on the reality television industry); *Back To Reality* (features interviews with reality show contestants and allows them to share their personal experiences, unedited and uninhibited); and *Meet the Makers* (follows the Reality 24-7 staff as they work to make the network a reality and to produce further shows).

Reality TV USA, 240 Center Street, El Segundo, CA 90266; *Telephone*: 310-356-4843; *Fax*: 310-356-4843; *Broadcast Day*: 24 hours; *Email*: Contact channel through its web site; *Web site*: http://www.realitytvusa.com

Reality TV USA broadcasts only reality-based programs, including: *America's Most Wanted: Final Justice* (hosted by John Walsh and reviews unique cases and examines how they were resolved); *Animal Rescue* (tracks the stories of animals in danger and shows the amazing rescue attempts that save them from death); *Arrest and Trial* (from the creators of *Law & Order*, this show recounts sensational, true crimes by combining actual footage and interviews with dramatic reenactments); *Crime Strike* (follows the efforts of crime victims who take the law into their own hands to defend themselves against violent crime); *Emergency Call* (follows the work of emergency response teams); *Girl Cops* (follows the lives of female cops on the beat); *Global Cops* (takes a world-wide look at policing techniques, trouble spots, and crime fighting in major cities around the globe with actual footage of policemen putting their lives on the line); *Hospital* (a candid and intimate look behind the scenes at a big hospital); *In the Line of Duty* (follows the work of firefighters, paramedics, police, and rescue workers as they risk their lives to save others); *L.A.P.D.* (follows the men and women of the Los Angeles Police Department); *On Thin Ice* (exposes the behind-the-scenes secrets of the professional skating world); *Power of Attorney* (offers ordinary people the opportunity to be represented by the nation's most talented and prestigious lawyers); *Rescue 911* (stories of professional rescuers and ordinary people performing extraordinary acts of bravery in life-or-death situations); and *Taking It Off* (chronicles the hardships and triumphs of people trying to win the battle of the bulge).

Reformation Channel, Jesus is Lord Ministries, P.O. Box 115, Cashtown, PA 17301; *Telephone*: 717-337-1607; *Fax*: 717-337-1983; *Email*: Contact channel through its web site;

Web site: http://www.worldbroadcast.org/TRC/TRC%20Home%20Page.htm, http://www.world broadcast.org

The Reformation Channel is an outreach ministry of the Word Broadcasting Network and airs a variety of pastors from across the country who preach the word of God and the Good News of Christ.

ResearchChannel, 240 Gerberding Hall, Box 351208, Seattle, WA 98195; *Telephone*: 877-616-7265; *Fax*: 206-543-4641; *Email*: info@researchchannel.org; *Web site*: http://www.researchchannel.org

The ResearchChannel is a consortium of research universities and corporate research divisions dedicated to broadening the access to, and appreciation of, individual and collective activities, ideas, and opportunities in basic and applied research. Calling itself the "C-SPAN of scientific and medical research," one of the major goals of the ResearchChannel is to use modern technology to ensure that its information is available to, and can be accessed by, anyone, anywhere in the world at any time.

Resort Sports Network, 7 Custom House Street, Fifth Floor, Portland, ME 04101; P.O. Box 7528, Portland, ME 04112; *Telephone*: 207-772-5000; *Fax*: 207-775-3658; *Launch Date*: 1986; *Email*: Contact network through its web site; *Web site*: http://www.rsn.com

The Resort Sports Network broadcasts programming to vacation resorts and provides content targeted to both residents and visitors in specific viewing areas. The network's media base includes the RSN Television Network (29 affiliates broadcasting to 80 prime destination-area markets in North America); its web site, which features the RSN Resort Cam(r) network (a collection of daily updated images from North America's top destination areas); and RSN Outdoor Updates, which can be seen three days a week nationwide on The Weather Channel, and daily in select urban markets on CNN Headline News and other cable outlets.

RFD-TV (Rural Farm TV), 3201 Dickerson Pike, Nashville, TN 37207; *Telephone and Fax*: 615-227-9292; *Launch Date*: December 2000; *Broadcast Day*: 24 hours; *Subscribers*: 32,000,000; *Email*: info@rfdtv.com; *Web site*: http://www.rfdtv.com

RFD-TV is the first round-the-clock television network directed at serving the needs and interests of rural America by providing news and information programming to rural homes and businesses. Programming includes equine (on-scene shows from the nation's top horse clinicians, horse expos, and breed associations for the large audience of horse owners and horse lovers); agricultural (daily information to full and part-time farmers and ranchers, including news, weather, and special features); rural lifestyle (features living in rural America for the small acreage owner, small town, and those interested in the rural lifestyle with travels and documentaries from the backroads of America); and music and entertainment (traditional country music is showcased from the Willie Nelson library of programming, along with original productions for bluegrass, gospel, and polka music).

Ritmoson Latino, 5999 Center Drive, Los Angeles, CA 90045; *Telephone*: 310-348-3370; *Fax*: 310-348-3643; *Broadcast Day*: 24 hours; *Subscribers*: 750,000; *Email*: ritmosonlatino@televisanetworks.com; *Web site*: http://www.tutv.tv, http://www.ritmoson.com

A brand channel from TuTV, Ritmoson Latino is a music and lifestyle channel that features Latin music programming. The channel features Spanish music videos from top Latin stars such as Ricky Martin, Gloria Estefan and Chayanne, along with fresh, daily original entertainment news and lifestyle programs including *Tu y Yo*, *Fama*, *Así Suena*, *Toda la Música*, and *Latin Top*. Ritmoson Latino is distributed to Mexico, Latin America, the United States, and Europe.

Romance Classics *see* **Women's Entertainment**

Ruckus Network, 12901 Worldgate Drive, 7th Floor, Herndon, VA 20170; *Telephone*: 703-481-0040; *Fax*: 703-437-6403; *Launch Date*: January 1997 (as the College Entertainment Network); *Broadcast Day*: 18 hours per week; *Subscribers*: 10,000,000; *Email*: info@ruckusnetwork.com; *Web site*: http://www.ruckusnetwork.com

Formerly called the College Entertainment Network, the Ruckus Network is the world's first student entertainment access channel. The network provides segments from the nation's college television stations together on one network and features scheduled blocks of programs from extreme sports to entertainment.

Rush HD, 200 Jericho Quadrangle, Jericho, NY 11753; *Telephone*: 516-803-6010; *Launch Date*: October 2003; *Broadcast Day*: 24 hours; *Email*: Contact channel through its web site; *Web site*: http://www.voom.com

Rush HD is a high definition multiplexed channel from Voom that airs high adrenaline extreme action sports.

Russian Television Network, 1 Bridge Plaza, Fort Lee, NJ 07024; *Telephone*: 310-441-2110; *Fax*: 310-414-2101; *Broadcast Day*: 24 hours; *Email*: ininfo@i-channel.com; *Web site*: http://www.i-channel.com

The Russian Television Network and the Russian Television Network of America broadcast American television in the Russian language. A joint venture of Asia Entertainment, Inc. and International Channel Networks, the two channels air on the International Channel.

S | Networks, Rockefeller Center, 1230 Avenue of the Americas, New York, NY 10020; *Telephone*: 212-726-2000; *Launch Date*: May 2002 (24 hours a day in 2003); *Broadcast Day*: 24 hours; *Email*: info@snetworks.tv, info@sovereign newmedia.com; *Web site*: http://www.snetworks.tv; http://www.SovereignNewMedia.com

The S | Networks (the "S" stands for Sovereign) is a digital media channel that delivers programming aimed at young adult viewers in urban population centers. The network's brand channels include S | Arts (celebrates artists of color and features profiles on actors, musicians, painters, writers, poets, and film makers; programs include theatrical performances, artist biographies, concerts, documentary films, and specials); S | Caribbeanet (focuses on Caribbean and Pan-African-oriented programming, including music videos, carnival coverage, regional news, and Caribbean-oriented sports); S | Comedy (ethnic comedic and variety programming, including stand-up classic routines and comedy concerts); S | Glory (inspirational and motivational programming from diverse faith-based organizations as well as renowned religious personalities and motivational speakers; programs include inspirational music videos, movies, conventions, and children's programming); S | Music (features urban and contemporary music artists and its programs include music videos, artist biographies, performance footage, and concert clips); S | Sports (focuses on semi-pro, professional, extreme, and international sports and its programs include street sports, amateur boxing matches, competition from various athletic leagues, sports movies, documentaries, game shows, talk shows, celebrity fitness challenges, and charity memorabilia auctions); and S | Worldcast (focuses on international customs, news, and issues; programming includes syndicated international programs, foreign films and interviews with news makers).

SafeTV Channel (Safe Television for All Ages), 3556 Liberty Avenue, Springdale, AR 72762; *Telephone*: 888-777-9392, 476-361-2900; *Fax*: 479-361-2323; *Email*: ksbntv@safetv.org; *Web site*: http://www.safetv.org

The SafeTV Channel broadcasts on Sky Angel (http://www.skyangel.com) and airs family-oriented, worship-based programs. Content includes international news, breaking news reports, outdoor and sports programs (such as *Sportsline Live*), educational shows (such as *Classic Arts* and *Cutting Edge*

Medical Report), and home and garden shows (such as *Lifestyle Magazine* and *P. Allen Smith Gardens*).

Saigon Broadcasting Television Network, 10501 Garden Grove Boulevard, Garden Grove, CA 92843; *Telephone*: 310-441-2110; *Fax*: 310-414-2101; *Broadcast Day*: 24 hours; *Email*: ininfo@i-channel.com; *Web site*: http:// www.i-channel.com

The Saigon Broadcasting Television Network airs on the International Channel and its programming originates mainly in the United States and targets the Vietnamese-American audience. The network airs news, talk shows, children's programs, cultural, history, and general entertainment.

Science Channel, One Discovery Place, Silver Spring, MD 20910; *Telephone*: 240-662-2000; *Launch Date*: October 1996; *Broadcast Day*: 24 hours; *Subscribers*: 30,000,000; *Email*: Contact channel through its web site; *Web site*: http://www.discovery.com

A brand entity of the Discovery Channel, the Science Channel strives to uncover the clues to the questions that have eluded mankind for centuries and reveals life's greatest mysteries and smallest wonders.

Science Television (Science Channel), P.O. Box 598, Fort George Station, New York, NY 10040; *Telephone*: 917-593-2537; *Email*: Contact channel through its web site; *Web site*: http://www.scitv.com

Science Television produces and distributes videos for the professional and educational use of the scientific community.

Sci-Fi Channel, 1230 Avenue of the Americas, New York, NY 10020; *Telephone*: 212-413-5000; *Launch Date*: September 1992; *Broadcast Day*: 24 hours; *Subscribers*: 80,000,000; *Email*: Contact channel through its web site; *Web site*: http://www.scifi.com

Owned and operated by NBC Universal, the Sci-Fi Channel airs science fiction-related movies, new and original series, special events, and classic sci-fi fantasy, horror, and paranormal programming. Popular shows on the channel include *Amazing Stories, The Outer Limits, Quantum Leap, Roswell, Scare Tactics, Sliders, Stargate SG-1, Star Trek, Timecop*, and *The Twilight Zone*.

SCOLA, 21557 270th Street, McClelland, IA 51548, P.O. Box 1846, Council Bluffs, IA 51502; *Telephone*: 712-566-2202; *Fax*: 712-566-2502; *Launch Date*: August 1987; *Broadcast Day*: 24 hours; *Subscribers*: 4,500,000; *Email*: scola@scola.org; *Web site*: http:// www.scola.org

SCOLA is an educational channel that airs re-transmitted news broadcasts from 40 countries to more than 8,000 schools, colleges, and universities. The channel also airs international audio programming from Radio France International, the World Radio Network, Vatican Radio, a foreign news channel, a foreign variety programming channel, and a channel devoted exclusively to Chinese. SCOLA's primary mission is to help the people of the world learn about one another; their cultures, their languages, and their ideologies. Its brand channels include Channel One (news), Channel Two (documentaries and entertainment), and Channel Three (Chinese programming). Channels One and Two include programs from nearly seventy countries and all shows are shown unedited and in the original language.

Scream Channel, 10 East 40th Street, 48th Floor, New York, NY 10016; *Telephone*: 201-794-1234; *Launch Date*: October 2004; *Broadcast Day*: 24 hours; *Email*: Contact channel through its web site; *Web site*: http:// www.screamchannel.com

The Scream Channel broadcasts horror, suspense, and thriller-oriented entertainment aimed at the 18-49 year-old male audience.

Screen Gems Network, Sony Pictures Television, 10202 West Washington Boulevard, Culver City, CA 90232; *Telephone*: 310-244-4000; *Fax*: 310-244-2626; *Launch Date*:

September 1999; *Email*: Contact network through its web site; *Web site*: http:// screen gemsnetwork.com, http://www.sonypictures.com

The Screen Gems Network is the first broadcast-based service for classic television programming and offers viewers more than 350 classic television shows and over 5,000 vintage movies from the past. The network offers behind-the-scenes insights to favorite shows; the ability for the viewer to purchase show-theme products; trivia games about past and present shows; and inside information about individual programs and episodes. A sample of the classic shown aired on the network include *Charlie's Angels*, *The Partridge Family*, *I Dream of Jeannie*, *Bewitched*, and *Starsky & Hutch*.

Scripps Networks, 312 Walnut Street, 2800 Scripps Center, Cincinnati, OH 45202; *Telephone*: 866-366-4010, 513-977-3000; *Fax*: 513-977-3721; *Email*: Contact network through its web site; *Web site*: http://www.scrippsnetworks.com

In 1878, Edward W. Scripps borrowed $10,000 from his brothers and launched *The Penny Press* newspaper in Cleveland, Ohio. From this start, he launched newspapers in other cities and built the first national newspaper chain. In 1907, he challenged the entrenched Associated Press, which at the time struck exclusive agreements with only one newspaper in each market, which discouraged the launch of competing newspapers. Scripps challenged the AP by creating the United Press International, which would be a service available to all who wanted it, and became a leading force in worldwide journalism for years. He also created a syndicated features service, which still exists toady as United Media. Taking advantage of emerging technologies, in the 1930s Scripps launched two radio stations and in the 1940s he owned some of the earliest local television stations in the United States. Two of his earliest stations still exist to this day, WEWS (whose call letters matched his initials) in Cleveland, Ohio and WCPO in Cincinnati, Ohio (named for its affiliation with *The Cincinnati Post*).

In 1950, the Scripps newspaper chain launched the comic strip *Peanuts*, written by Charles Schulz. From this beginning, the strip expanded quickly, and eventually worked its way into more than 2,000 newspapers around the world. From the 1950s into the 1980s, the Scripps chain solidified its position as a national newspaper publisher and expanded its media reach by owning and operating several local television stations. In the early 1980s Scripps entered the cable television industry and eventually became one of America's 15 largest cable operators.

With emerging technologies came opportunities for Scripps. In the 1990s the company began to invest in information and entertainment content and in 1994 announced plans to launch Home & Garden Television. Realizing the trend toward consolidation within the cable system industry and a changing market, Scripps sold its cable television systems in 1996 and began focusing its broadcast focus on niche channels, such as the Do-It-Yourself Network, the Fine Living Network, The Food Network, Home & Garden Television, and the Shop at Home Network.

Seminar TV (The Seminar TV Network), P.O. Box 6140, Oceanside, CA 92052; *Telephone*: 760-639-6020; *Launch Date*: Fall 2003; *Broadcast Day*: 1 hour a day; *Email*: Contact channel through its web site; *Web site*: http://www.seminartv.com

Seminar TV broadcasts personal development and business training programming.

Senior Citizens Network, 8306 Wilshire Boulevard, Building 181, Beverly Hills, CA 90211; *Telephone and Fax*: 805-484-6903; *Launch Date*: 2002; *Broadcast Day*: 24 hours; *Email*: info@ scntv.com; *Web site*: http://www.scntv.com

Using the tag line "Lifestyle for the 50+," the Senior Citizens Network provides programming aimed at viewers 50 years of age or older and focuses on all aspects of the senior citizens life, including lifestyle, romance, entertainment, exercise, health, finance, performing arts, travel, and crafts. SCN TV airs all original programming, edited for violence and offensive content. SCN also operates the Senior Citizens Internet Television (http://www.seniortelevision.com); *Senior Citizens Magazine* (*Lifestyle Magazine for the 50+*) (http://www.seniorcitizensmagazine.com); Senior Citizens Hosting (Internet ISP Business-to-Business Provider, http://www.seniorcitizenswebhosting.com); and Senior Citizens Films (Cinema for the 50+) (http://www.senior citizensfilms.com).

Setanta Sport USA, 501 2nd Street #360, San Francisco, CA 94107; *Telephone*: 415-546-1022; *Fax*: 415-546-1033; *Email*: setanta.us@setanta.com; *Web site*: http://www.setanta.com

Setanta is comprised of four separate operating divisions: Setanta Sport, Setanta Media, Setanta Screens, and Setanta Television. Setanta Sport broadcasts major sporting events from around the world while Setanta Television provides production services to Setanta Sport and third-party broadcasters. Setanta Media provides mobile phone content to network operators and maintains the company's web site. Setanta Screens supplies large LED screens to the sports and entertainment industries.

Sewing & Needle Art Network (Planned for future operation)

Shalom TV, P.O. Box 678, Harmony, PA 16037; *Telephone*: 724-816-7301; *Broadcast Day*: 24 hours; *Email*: Contact channel through its web site; *Web site*: http://www.shalomtv.com, http://www.shalomtv.org

Shalom TV is a digital cable television network that celebrates Jewish culture and provides educational and entertaining English-language telecasts that focus on issues of interest to the Jewish community. The channel covers Jewish-oriented public affairs events, including lectures, forums, and observances, along with televising long-format temple tours and interviews with prominent Jewish figures.

The Shepherd's Chapel Network, P.O. Box 416, Gravette, AR 72736; *Telephone*: 800-643-4645, 479-787-6026; *Email*: Contact network through its web site; *Web site*: http://www.shepherdschapel.com

The Shepherd's Chapel Network broadcasts the teachings of Pastor Arnold Murray as he reads from, and interprets, the Holy Bible. The network's main focus is its daily, one-hour Bible study class, which originates from its chapel in Gravette.

Shoma TV, 16661 Ventura Boulevard #405, Encino, CA 91436; *Telephone*: 818-784-2511; *Fax*: 818-784-9113; *Email*: info@appadana.com; *Web site*: http://www. jaamejam.com

Planned for future operation.

Shop at Home Network, 5388 Hickory Hollow Parkway, Nashville, TN 37013; P.O. Box 305249, Nashville, TN 37932; *Telephone*: 800-224-9739, 615-263-8000; *Fax*: 615-263-8084; *Launch Date*: June 1986; *Broadcast Day*: 24 hours; *Subscribers*: 48,000,000; *Email*: customerservice@shopat home.com; *Web site*: http://www.shopathometv.com

Part of the Scripps Networks, the Shop at Home Network sells a variety of merchandise, including jewelry, housewares, fitness, sports memorabilia, electronics, cookware, and health and beauty through its television broadcasts and web site.

ShopNBC, 6740 Shady Oak Road, Eden Prairie, MN 55344; *Telephone*: 952-943-6000; *Fax*: 952-943-6566; *Launch Date*: October 1991; *Broadcast Day*: 24 hours; *Subscribers*: 56,000,000; *Email*: Contact channel through its web site; *Web site*: http://www.shopnbc.com

An NBC brand channel, ShopNBC is a home shopping television channel that sells jewelry, watches, home computers, electronics, beauty and products, apparel, fitness, leisure, and gifts.

Short TV, 251 53rd Street, Brooklyn, NY 11220; *Telephone*: 212-226-6258; *Fax*: 212-925-5802; *Launch Date*: January 1999; *Broadcast Day*: 24 hours; *Subscribers*: 2,500,000; *Email*: info@shorttv.com; *Web site*: http://www.shorttv.com

Short TV is the first and only cable network solely dedicated to airing the short film genre produced and directed by emerging film makers.

Showtime, 1633 Broadway, New York, NY 10019; *Telephone*: 212-708-1600; *Fax*: 212-708-1212; *Launch Date*: July 1976; *Broadcast Day*: 24 hours; *Subscribers*: 36,000,000; *Email*: Contact channel through its web site; *Web site*: http://showtimeonline.com; http:///www.sho.com

Showtime is a premium service that airs more than 200 movie titles a month, award-winning original pictures, original and acquired series, and Championship Boxing. Showtime has launched several brand channels that broadcast specific programming aimed at target markets. The 24-hour Showtime Beyond was launched in September 1999 and broadcasts about 50 movies a month, including science fiction, horror, and fantasy, as well as original series. Showtime Event Television (http://www.showtimeevents.net) was launched in 1979 and is the production and distribution arm of Viacom, Inc. (the owner of Showtime). The channel is a pay-per-view service with heavy emphasis on sporting events. SET has produced and distributed seven of the top ten pay-per-view events of all time, including the top four boxing events: Holyfield vs. Tyson II, Lewis vs. Tyson, Tyson vs. Holyfield I, and Tyson vs. McNeeley. In addition to its main fare of sporting events, SET also airs music concerts (including The Last Kiss, Spice Girls in Concert—Wild!, The Backstreet Boys, Tina Turner, the Rolling Stones, Prince's Trust-Party in the Park, Pink Floyd, Phil Collins, Music For Montserrat: An All-Star Charity Concern featuring Paul McCartney, Elton John and Eric Clapton, and the Moscow Music Peace Festival).

The 24-hour Showtime Extreme was launched in 1998 and airs only action movies, with more than 60 titles a month. The programming mix includes first-run and classic action titles, martial arts movies, and Japanese animation. The 24-hour Showtime Family Zone was launched in March 2001, shows about 50 movie titles a month, and targets its programming to the entire family, with no R-rated movies ever shown. Showtime Next (http://shownext.com) was launched in March 2001 and is Showtime's 24-hour interactive channel that targets the so-called Gen Y viewers (age 18-24). The channel shows about 50 titles a month, including first-run and original pictures, short films, and animation. In combination with its web site, the channel features content that interacts between broadcast television and the internet.

Showtime Pay Per View was launched in 1979 and is the pay-per-view production and distribution arm of Viacom, Inc and is managed by Showtime Networks, Inc. Showtime Pay Per View focuses on sports and event distribution, and has produced and distributed seven of the top ten pay-per-view events of all time. The 24-hour Showtime Showcase (initially called Showtime 3) was launched in July 2001 and airs Showtime originals seven days a week, with a dedicated prime-time (8:00 P.M.—11:00 P.M.) movie block. ShowTime Too (initially called Showtime 2) was launched in Spring 2001 and is a 24-hour multi-feed channel that features an average of 75 titles a month, including theatrical, original pictures, and series. The channel airs no same-day duplication with Showtime. ShowTime Women was launched in March 2001 and airs movies that highlight women, in front of, and behind, the camera. The 24-hour channel airs about 50 movies a month and original series.

Other brand channels from Showtime include Flix (launched in August 1992 and is a 24-hour service that features movies from the 1970s, 1980s, and 1990s; the channel airs about 55 titles per month, none of which are duplicated on other Showtime Networks);

The Movie Channel (launched in December 1979 and airs about 120 movie titles each month; programming includes *Daily Movie Marathons*, *TMC Overnight*, and *TMC Double Vision Weekends*; the 24-hour channel also features movie trivia, film facts, celebrity interviews, and behind-the-scenes look at selected movies); and TMC Xtra (a 24-hour movie channel that airs 50 movies a month, mainly blockbusters, with no same-day duplication with The Movie Channel).

Sí TV, 3030 Andrita Street, Building D, Los Angeles, CA 90065; *Telephone*: 323-256-8900; *Launch Date*: 1997 (as a production company), February 2004; *Broadcast Day*: 24 hours; *Subscribers*: 10,000,000; *Email*: Contact channel through its web site; *Web site*: http://www.sitv.com

Sí TV is the first English-language, Latino-themed cable network and features original and acquired programming including comedies, lifestyle, variety shows, talk shows, music and dance shows, short films, feature films, animated sitcoms, stand-up comedy routines, children's programming, and sporting events. The channel is aimed at the 18-34 year-old general market and the bi-cultural Latino audience.

Sign City Television, 3060 Sutherland Springs, Seguin, TX 78155; *Telephone*: 830-303-3220; *Subscribers*: 28,000,000; *Email*: Contact channel through its web site; *Web site*: http://www.davideo.tv

Operated by Davideo Productions, Sign City Television broadcasts programs to deaf and hearing-impaired viewers throughout America. All of the channel's shows are presented in sign language (the third-most used language in the United States after English and Spanish) and/or captions with a complete sound track broadcast simultaneously. The channel's programming can also be enjoyed by hearing audiences as well.

The channel was established in association with the parents of deaf or hearing-impaired children, professionals who work with the deaf, educators of the deaf, and other individuals dedicated to helping make television a meaningful part of a deaf or hearing-impaired person's life. Closed captioned broadcast programs, mandated by the Telecommunications Act of 1996, only provide access to conventional television programming, while SCTV provides the deaf community with its own platform for producing programs in their own language. The channel also provides the deaf community access to health and technological information specifically targeted to hard of hearing people to help viewers improve the quality of their lives.

Silent Network *see* **America's Disability Network**

Sky Angel (The Sky Angel Family of Networks), Dominion Sky Angel, P.O. Box 7609, Naples, FL 34101; *Telephone*: 888-759-2643; *Broadcast Day*: 24 hours; *Email*: Contact network through its web site; *Web site*: http://www.skyangel.com

The Sky Angel satellite system is a unique direct-to-home television service that offers a variety of channels, all focused on delivering a Christ-centered and family-friendly choice of broadcast programs. Its channels include AngelOne, AngelTwo, Christian Television Network Detroit, Cornerstone Television Network, Daystar Television Network, Faith TV, Familyland Television, FE TV (Spanish language), Golden Eagle Broadcasting, Gospel Music Television Network, Guardian Television Network, The Inspirational Network, KTV—Kids and Teens Television, Liberty Channel, Safe TV, Spirit Television, Superchannel TBN, Three Angels Broadcasting Network, TVU (music videos and programming), World Harvest Television Network, and The Worship Channel.

The Sky Angel networks focus on teaching and ministry; help programs (addressing issues important to everyday life); special events (live broadcasts of national Christian events such as Promise Keepers, women's conferences, Christian concerts, and parenting seminars); news from a Christian perspective (*The 700 Club*, *Listen America*, and Marlin Maddoux's *Point of View*); movies (films with a Christian message); sitcoms and dramas (classic television favorites and wholesome prime-time dramas); Christian music (videos and concerts 24 hours a day); home life; talk and health; sports and outdoors; educational programs and documentaries (creation science and nature from a biblical perspective, documentaries that explore the life of great Christian leaders and historical figures), and kids and teens programming (the exclusive 24-hour children's channel, KTV-Kids and Teens Television, with cartoons, puppet shows, dramas, and sing-alongs).

Skyview World Media, Two Executive Drive #6000, Fort Lee, NJ 07024; *Telephone*: 201-242-3000; *Fax*: 201-944-5961; *Launch Date*: 1992; *Subscribers*: 100,000; *Email*: Contact channel through its web site; *Web site*: http://www.skyviewmedia.com

Skyview World Media is North America's leading provider of foreign language ethnic programming, made available in Russian, Arabic, Italian, Filipino, Greek, Chinese, Asian (sub-continent), Vietnamese and Ukrainian.

SNEHA TV, P.O. Box 8442, Reston, VA 20195, 1851 Alexander Bell Drive, Reston, VA 20171; *Telephone*: 877-763-4288, 703-391-1048; *Fax*: 703-391-1060; *Launch Date*: April 2004; *Broadcast Day*: 24 hours; *Subscribers*: 1,000; *Email*: info@snehatv.com; *Web site*: http://www.snehatv.com

SNEHA TV airs programs aimed at the Telugu-speaking audience. This channel is the first America-based broadcast entity to air news and entertainment to an American audience from the popular news channel TV9 in India.

SOAPnet (The Soap Network), 3800 West Alameda Avenue, Burbank, CA 91505; *Telephone*: 818-569-7500; *Launch Date*: January 24, 2000; *Broadcast Day*: 24 hours; *Subscribers*: 36,000,000; *Email*: Contact network through its web site; *Web site*: http://www.soapnet.com

SOAPnet is the first and only round-the-clock network devoted to daytime dramas (soaps) and soap opera fans. SOAPnet offers same-day episodes of popular soaps at night; classic soaps; and news and information from the world of soaps. The channel also airs its original series *Soap Talk*, a one-hour soap fueled talk show, and *Soap Center*, an entertainment magazine show.

¡Sorpresa!, 6125 Airport Freeway #200, Fort Worth, TX 76117; *Telephone*: 817-222-1234; *Launch Date*: March 2003; *Broadcast Day*: 24 hours; *Subscribers*: 20,000,000; *Email*: Contact channel through its web site; *Web site*: http://www.htvn.net, http://www.sorpresatv.com

¡Sorpresa! airs programming aimed at the Hispanic audience and broadcasts family-oriented content, including nightly news from Mexico City, Mexican cinema, sitcoms, and specials that reflect the culture and values of the traditional Mexican family in the United States.

Soundtrack Channel, 1335 Fourth Street #400, Santa Monica, CA 90401; *Telephone*: 310-899-1315; *Fax*: 310-587-3387; *Launch Date*: March 2002; *Broadcast Day*: 24 hours; *Subscribers*: 15,000,000; *Email*: contactstc@stcchannel.com; *Web site*: http://www.stcchannel.com

The Soundtrack Channel features music videos from movies and television programs, including original movie music videos specially produced for the channel. STC also airs entertainment, news, interviews, behind-the-scenes insights, and information about new releases coming to television, theaters, DVD/Home video, and Pay-Per-View. Programs include *STC Countdown* (details best and most-anticipated movies of the season), *Out Now* (highlights the latest movies being released on video and DVD), *STC Previews* (give viewers a behind-the-scenes look at upcoming films and the stars in them, and

Sound Check (a behind-the-scenes look at the making of a specific music video).

Southern Entertainment Television (The SET), P.O. Box 1303, Nokomis, FL 34274; *Telephone*: 941-485-5500; *Launch Date*: September 2004; *Broadcast Day*: 24 hours; *Email*: info@theset.net; *Web site*: http://www.theset.net

Southern Entertainment Television develops, markets, and supports music video programming services and offers three music genre channels: Southern Gospel, Bluegrass, and Traditional Black Gospel. SET 1 airs round-the-clock Southern Gospel music performances from legendary artists, today's popular stars, local-area performers, and Gospel greats. SET 2 is the first-ever all-Bluegrass music channel and features top musicians as well as backyard pickers and singers. SET 3 airs original Black Gospel music; great Gospel artists perform all day, every day.

Space Television Network (http://www.-space-tv.com) (Planned for future operation)

Spanish International Network *see* **Univision**

Speed Channel (Speedvision Network), 9711 Southern Pine Boulevard, Charlotte, NC 28273; *Telephone*: 704-731-2222; *Launch Date*: January 1996; *Broadcast Day*: 24 hours; *Subscribers*: 65,000,000; *Email*: Contact channel through its web site; *Web site*: http://www.speedtv.com

Owned by the Fox Cable Networks Group, the Speed Channel is the first and only round-the-clock cable network devoted exclusively to motor sports and the human fascination for speed. In addition to original NASCAR programming, the channel airs the world's most well-known racing events, including CART, F1, Classic Cars, LeMans, the American LeMans Series, World Rally, and car shows from around the world.

Spice, 2706 Media Center Drive, Los Angeles, CA 90065; *Telephone*: 323-276-4000; *Fax*: 323-276-4500; *Broadcast Day*: 24 hours; *Email*: info@playboy.com; *Web site*: http://www.spice.com, http://www.playboytv.com

Part of the Playboy TV Networks, Spice TV is an adult-oriented pay-per-view channel that airs more than 50 different movies each month with featured movie premieres each weekend. The network has a variety of brand channels that broadcast specific genres and programming aimed at targeted audiences, including Spice 1, Spice 2, Spice Pay-Per-View, Spice Platinum, Spice TV, and Spice Ultra XX. Other adult-themed, pay-per-view brand channels from Spice include Adam & Eve Channel (http://www.cyberspice.com), The Hot Networks (includes Hot Net and Hot Zone), Vivid TV, and the X! Channel.

Spike TV, 1515 Broadway, 23rd Floor, New York, NY 10036; *Telephone*: 212-258-8000, 212-846-4629; *Fax*: 212-846-1893; *Launch Date*: August 2003; *Broadcast Day*: 18 hours; *Subscribers*: 90,000,000; *Email*: Contact network through its web site; *Web site*: http://www.spiketv.com

Spike TV is an MTV (Music Television) channel that uses the tag line "First Network For Men" and airs programs aimed at the male 18-49 viewing audience. Popular programs include *Blind Date*, *Car and Driver Television*, *Highlander*, *Horsepower TV*, *Paintball 2Xtremes*, *Real TV*, *Star Trek: Deep Space 9*, *Star Trek: The Next Generation*, *Tough Truckin,' Trucks!*, *World's Wildest Police Chases*, and *World Wrestling Entertainment*. In one of the more bizarre episodes of modern television, actor and director Spike Lee sued the network to change its name (since HE was the original Spike)—- he lost.

Formerly called The Nashville Network (TNN), with country programming such as *The Dukes of Hazzard*, the network changed its name to The National Network (or The New TNN) after being acquired by Viacom in the late 1990s. Programming changed sig nificantly and evolved into today's Spike TV.

Spirit Television, P.O. Box 1887, Westerville, OH 43086; *Telephone*: 877-474-8700, 614-890-9977; *Fax*: 614-839-1329; *Launch Date*: March 2004; *Broadcast Day*: 24 hours; *Email*: spirit@spirit-television.com; *Web site*: http://www.spirit-television.com

Spirit Television broadcasts on Sky Angel (http://www.skyangel.com) and airs adult-contemporary Christian music videos, on-air personalities, and music news and programming.

Sporting Channel (Planned for future operation)

Sports-i ESPN (Japan) *see* **Entertainment Sports Television Network**

The Sportsman Channel, W236 S7050 Big Bend Drive #6, Muskegon, WI 53103; *Telephone*: 262-971-1600, 206-662-3800; *Fax*: 262-679-8316; *Launch Date*: April 2003; *Broadcast Day*: 24 hours; *Subscribers*: 11,000,000; *Email*: Contact channel through its web site; *Web site*: http://www.thesportsmanchannel.com

The Sportsman Channel provides entertaining and informative hunting and fishing programming from around the world, including wildlife management, dog training, cooking, and outdoor survival techniques.

Stand Up Comedy Television, 77 West Warner Drive, Chicago, IL 60601; *Telephone*: 312-442-9000; *Fax*: 312-442-9010; *Broadcast Day*: 24 hours; *Email*: info@standuptv.com; *Web site*: http://www.standuptv.com, http://www.standupcomedytelevision.com

Planned for future operation, Stand-Up Comedy Television will broadcast four hours per week of live commercial-free stand-up performances originating from its Studio Stages. The network will also offer original and syndicated comedy programming, including classic comedians in both sitcoms and full- length movies.

Star Sports Asia *see* **Entertainment Sports Television Network**

Star Sports India *see* **Entertainment Sports Television Network**

Star Sports South East Asia *see* **Entertainment Sports Television Network**

Starz! (Starz! / Encore), 8900 Liberty Circle, Englewood, CO 80112; *Telephone*: 720-852-7700; *Fax*: 720-852-4098; *Launch Date*: March 1994; *Broadcast Day*: 24 hours; *Subscribers*: 13,500,000; *Email*: Contact channel through its web site; *Web site*: http://www.starz.com

Starz! (Starz! / Encore) is a premium movie channel that shows about 800 features a month, uncut and commercial-free. The network has launched several 24-hour brand channels that air specific movie genres aimed at targeted audiences, including Black Starz! (the only movie channel dedicated to showcasing the work of Black actors, producers, and directors and features exclusive first-run theatrical releases, recent popular titles, classic movies, independent films, Pan African films (films from Africa and by persons of African descent around the world), and original productions); Encore (launched in April 1991, and re-launched in May 1999, airs first-run and contemporary movies, uncut and commercial free; the channel features hosted movie segments, interviews, movie trivia between films, and Encore Originals, such as The Directors documentary series geared toward movie lovers; Encore focuses on movies that had box office success or critical acclaim and include notable stars and/or directors); Starz! Action Channel (martial arts movies, action-hero and war films, crime stories, and animated action short subjects); Starz! Family (launched in May 1999, is the first and only channel that shows only family-oriented movies); Starz! Kids (launched in March 1994, is the only all-movie premium channel featuring films for kids ages two to eight); Starz! Love Stories (launched in Fall 1994, broadcasts movies that focus on dramatic love stories, relationships, and passion); Starz! MoviePlex (launched in October 1994, airs movies with a different theme each day:

Love Stories—Monday, Great Movies of Your Life—Tuesday, Westerns—Wednesday, Action—Thursday, Mystery—Friday, True Stories—Saturday, and WAM! (America's Kidz Network)—Sunday; the channel never shows R-rated programming and features more than 200 different movies per month); Starz! Mystery (launched in fall 1994, features commercial-free mystery movies, 24 hours a day); Starz! True Stories (launched in fall 1994, presents real-life drama and showcases events ripped from the headlines and biographical dramas on celebrated figures, entertainment, sports, politics, and history); Starz! WAM! (launched in fall 1994, is a commercial-free children's channel that airs kid-friendly programming for children ages eight to 16; the channel also airs 60 hours a week of subject-specific educational programs); and Starz! Westerns (launched in fall 1994, presents classic and current commercial-free western movies).

Style Network, 5750 Wilshire Boulevard, Los Angeles, CA 90036; *Telephone*: 323-954-2400; *Fax*: 323-954-2662; *Launch Date*: October 1998; *Broadcast Day*: 24 hours; *Subscribers*: 34,000,000; *Email*: Contact network through its web site; *Web site*: http://www.stylenetwork.com

An E! Entertainment channel, the Style Network is the only cable service devoted exclusively to style, beauty, fashion, and home design. Some of the network's most popular shows include *Fashion Emergency*, *Guess Who's Coming To Decorate*, *How Do I Look?*, *Martha Stewart Living*, and *Style Court*.

Success Channel (Planned for future operation)

Sun TV (Sun Network), 2245 Godby Road, Atlanta, GA 30349; *Telephone*: 404-766-9197; *Broadcast Day*: 6:30 A.M.—12:00 A.M. (EST) (Saturday and Sunday); *Subscribers*: 700,000; *Email*: Contact network through its web site; *Web site*: http:// www.sunnt.com

Sun TV broadcasts original programming from the Caribbean, Central, and South America, including news, sports, entertainment, sitcoms, soaps, talk shows, and tourism-related features.

Sundance Channel, 1633 Broadway, 8th Floor, New York, NY 10019; *Telephone*: 212-708-1600, 212-654-1500; *Launch Date*: February 1996; *Broadcast Day*: 24 hours; *Subscribers*: 17,000,000; *Email*: Contact channel through its web site; *Web site*: http://www.sundancechannel.com

Under the guidance of actor/director Robert Redford, the Sundance Channel brings television viewers feature films, shorts, documentaries, world cinema, and animation, all shown uncut and commercial-free. Through its original programs, the channel connects viewers with film makers, the creative process, and the world of independent film. The channel is a venture between Robert Redford, Showtime Networks, Inc., and Universal Studios. While the channel operates independently of the non-profit Sundance Institute and the Sundance Film Festival, it shares the overall Sundance mission of supporting independent artists and providing them with wider opportunities to present their work to audiences. The 24-hour Sundance Documentary Channel airs international, independent, non-fiction films, both shorts and features.

Sunshine Network, 1000 Legion Place #1600, Orlando, FL 32801; *Telephone*: 407-648-1150; *Fax*: 407-245-2571; *Launch Date*: March 1988; *Broadcast Day*: 24 hours; *Subscribers*: 6,300,000; *Email*: Contact network through its web site; *Web site*: http://www.sunshinenetwork.com

The Sunshine Network broadcasts exclusive statewide coverage of the NBA Orlando Magic; NBA Miami Heat; NHL Tampa Bay Lightning; pre-season football; coaches and magazine shows for the NFL; Miami Dolphins; Jacksonville Jaguars; Florida State University; University of Florida; University of Central Florida; year-round action from the SEC, ACC, MAC, Atlantic Sun, and Sunshine State conferences; Florida high school championships; and original studio-based programs such as *Tailgate Saturday* (live post-game coverage after all FSU and UF football games), *SportsTalk Live* (a live media discussion show and live Saturday college football morning preview and evening review shows), *Florida Fishing Report* (a one-hour live show featuring expert anglers); *Under the Lights* (provides viewers a behind-the-scenes look at some of Florida's top sports stories and sports news makers); local and regional golf, tennis, boxing, and the Special Olympics.

Super Value Channel, 1930 West Holt Avenue, Pomona, CA 91768; *Telephone*: 866-782-7467, 909-623-5940; *Fax*: 909-494-4199; *Launch Date*: 2001; *Broadcast Day*: 24 hours; *Email*: sales@svcshops.com; *Web site*: http://www.svcshops.com

The Super Value Channel is an ethnic home-shopping service that produces shopping programs in the languages viewers use at home. Aimed to audiences in the Continental United States, Hawaii, Alaska, Canada, and Mexico, the channel broadcasts to viewers in Chinese, Korean, Japanese, Iranian, and Spanish. The channel offers a wide variety of products, including health and fitness, skin care, cosmetics, electronics, cookware, home appliance, designer jewelry, watches, apparel, and automobiles.

Superchannel TBN, 4520 Parkbreeze Court, Orlando, FL 32808, P.O. Box 608040, Orlando, FL 32860; *Telephone*: 407-297-0155, 407-298-5555; *Email*: superchannel@ wacxtv.com; *Web site*: http://www.wacxtv.com

Owned by the non-profit Associated Christian Television System, Inc., SuperChannel TBN broadcasts on Sky Angel (http://www.skyangel.com) and features a mix of Trinity Broadcast Network programs, including *Praise the Lord*, *International Intelligence Briefing*, and *Billy Graham Classic Crusades*. SuperChannel WACX-TV is a commercial broadcast station dedicated to providing the best in Christian television to an ever expanding audience around the world.

Sur, 2029 SW 105th Court, Miami, FL 33165; *Telephone*: 305-554-1876, 305-530-3561; *Fax*: 305-554-6776; *Launch Date*: August 1991; *Broadcast Day*: 24 hours; *Subscribers*: 2,800,000; *Email*: Contact network through its web site: *Web site*: http://www.condista.com

Sur is a Latin-American cable network that re-transmits live daily newscasts, sportscasts, and the most popular shows from Argentina, Chile, Bolivia, Brazil, Peru, Ecuador, Colombia, Venezuela, Panama, the Dominican Republic, El Salvador, and Mexico.

Tamasha TV, 22817 Ventura Boulevard #777, Woodland Hills, CA 91364; *Telephone*: 818-347-9411; *Fax*: 818-347-9418; *Broadcast Day*: 24 hours; *Email*: tamashatv@ tamashatv.com; *Web site*: http://www.tamashatv.com

Tamasha TV broadcasts Persian-language programs.

Tapesh Television Network, 6301 DeSoto Avenue, Suite E, Woodland Hills, CA 91367; *Telephone*: 818-593-4094; *Fax*: 818-593-4062; *Launch Date*: 1989; *Email*: info@tapeshtv.com; *Web site*: http://www.tapeshtv.com

Operated by the Persian Broadcasting Company, the Tapesh Television Network airs Persian-language programming to viewers around the world.

TechTV, 650 Townsend Street, 3rd Floor, San Francisco, CA 94103; *Telephone*: 415-355-4000; *Fax*: 415-355-4392; *Launch Date*: May 1998; *Broadcast Day*: 24 hours; *Subscribers*: 44,000,000; *Email*: Contact channel through its web site; *Web site*: http://www.techtv.com

TechTV (sometimes referred to as the Interactive Channel) showcases all facets of modern technology, including both hardware and software.

TeleFutura Network, 605 Third Avenue, 12th Floor, New York, NY 10158. 9405 Northwest 41st Street, Miami, FL 33178; *Telephone*: 212-455-5200 (New York), 305-471-3900 (Florida); *Fax*: 212-986-4731 (New York),

305-471-4065 (Florida); *Launch Date*: January 2002; *Broadcast Day*: 24 hours; *Subscribers*: 7,200,000; *Email*: Contact channel through its web site; *Web site*: http://www.univisionnetworks.com

TeleFutura is a round-the-clock, general-interest Spanish-language broadcasting network that targets its programming to America's Hispanic households and airs Spanish-language series, movies, original talk shows, game shows, first-run novellas, sports programming, and news.

Telehit, 5999 Center Drive, Los Angeles, CA 90045; *Telephone*: 310-348-3370; *Fax*: 310-348-3643; *Broadcast Day*: 24 hours; *Subscribers*: 750,000; *Email*: telehit@ televisanetworks.com; *Web site*: http://www.tutv.tv

A TuTV brand channel, TeleHit targets the Latin youth market and broadcasts live original programming, including top-of-the-charts music videos, celebrity interviews, live concerts and entertainment news. The channel airs today's favorite performers, such as Maná, Alejandra Guzmán and Shakira and popular shows, including *Fresco*, *Black & White*, *Zona Publica*, and *Válvula de Escape*.

Telemundo, 2470 West 8th Avenue, Hialeah, FL 33010; *Telephone*: 305-884-8200, 305-889-3300); *Launch Date*: January 1987; *Broadcast Day*: 24 hours; *Subscribers*: 35,000,000; *Email*: Contact channel through its web site; *Web site*: http://www. univisionnetworks.com, http://www.telemundo.com

A National Broadcasting Company (NBC) brand channel, the Spanish-language Telemundo is the primary source for entertainment, news, and sports for most Hispanic viewers in the United States. Programming includes novelas, sports, talk shows, original sitcoms, news, children's programming, blockbuster movies, reality shows, general entertainment, music specials, the Olympics, the Golden Globe Awards, the National Basketball Association, the Women's National Basketball Association, and the Latin Billboard Awards. The 24-hour Telemundo Internacional (http://www.telemundointl.com), launched in March 2000, is a Spanish-language television channel that broadcasts general entertainment, sports, and up-to-the-minute news reports.

Created in December 1986, the Telemundo Group, Inc. was formed with the specific intent of creating programming aimed at the Hispanic market and in 1987 launched the Hispanic American Broadcasting Company in Miami, Florida. Ever growing, between 1988 and 1991 Telemundo expanded its station affiliates and it programming reached 78 percent of the Hispanic households in the United States. Additionally, U.S.-produced programming also expanded to include *Noticiero Telemundo/CNN* (a joint venture with CNN to produce a nightly national news program), *Cocina Crisco* (the first Spanish-language cooking show produced in the United States), *Angelica Mi Vida* (the first Spanish-language soap opera produced in America and based on the lives of Hispanic Americans), *Cara a Cara* (a talk show), and *Ocurrio Asi* (a tabloid news program).

In 1992 Joaquin Blaya, former president and chief executive officer of Univision Holdings, joined Telemundo as president and chief executive officer and continued the network's expansion. New programs were created that targeted younger audiences and second generation Hispanics such as *Ritmo Internacional* and *Padrisimo*. He also created the first nation-wide ratings service focused on the Hispanic community's viewing habits and in another joint venture with Reuters and British Broadcasting Corporation World Television, the network established a 24-hour Spanish-language television news service called *Telenoticias*.

This expansion created a financial strain on the network and by 1993 Telemundo was forced to file for bankruptcy. Through restructuring, Apollo Advisors became the major shareholder in 1994 and in March 1995 the company named Roland Hernandez president and chief executive officer of the network. One of his early moves was to open Telemundo's first west coast production facility in

Hollywood in an attempt to attract Spanish-speaking talent on both the east and west coasts. By 1995, Telemundo owned and operated six television stations in Los Angeles, New York, Miami, San Francisco/San Jose, San Antonio, and Houston/Galveston and was producing 50 percent of its own programming.

Telenovela International Television Network, *Telephone*: 877-212-1567; *Launch Date*: 2004; *Broadcast Day*: 24 hours; *Email*: info@telenovelatv.com; *Web site*: http://www.telenovelatv.com

A division of Bacteria Entertainment, the Telenovela International Television Network is the first Hispanic channel that focuses entirely on the popular novella genre (soap operas) of programming. The network airs 38 shows a day, all with no commercials.

The Tennis Channel, 2850 Ocean Park Boulevard #150, Santa Monica, CA 90405; *Telephone*: 310-656-9400, 310-314-9400; *Fax*: 310-656-9433; *Launch Date*: May 2003; *Broadcast Day*: 24 hours; *Subscribers*: 3,000,000; *Email*: Contact channel through its web site; *Web site*: http://www.thetennischannel.tv, http://www.thetennischannel.com

The Tennis Channel is a round-the-clock network devoted to tennis and other bacquet sports, and provides coverage of the game, its elite championships (the ATP, the WTA, the WTT, and the Champions), and its athletes. The channel also broadcasts instruction from the finest teachers, legendary matches, college and international tournaments, in-depth profiles of the greatest players, analysis and news, and the latest on equipment and tennis getaways.

Texas Cable News, 570 Young Street, Dallas, TX 75202; *Telephone*: 214-977-4500; *Fax*: 214-977-4501; *Launch Date*: January 1999; *Broadcast Day*: 24 hours; *Subscribers*: 1,500,000; *Email*: Contact channel through its web site; *Web site*: http://www.txcn.com

The Texas Cable News channel airs round-the-clock regional news headlines every 15 minutes and weather updates every 10 minutes.

The Theatre Channel, P.O. Box 2676, Venice, CA 90294; *Telephone*: 310-823-6508; *Broadcast Day*: 24 hours; *Email*: info@theatrechannel.com; *Web site*: http://www. theatrechannel.com

The Theatre Channel airs performances from national and international theatres in a variety of genres, including mainstream, alternative/avant-garde, ethnic, and children. The channel also shows live backstage interviews, insights to life in the theatre, theatre reviews, workshops, and festivals.

Three Angels Broadcasting Network, 3391 Charlie Good Road, P.O. Box 220, West Frankfort, IL 62896; *Telephone*: 618-627-4651; *Fax*: 618-627-2726; *Launch Date*: November 1986; *Broadcast Day*: 24 hours; *Email*: mail@3abn.org; *Web site*: http:// www.3abn.org

Using the tag line "Mending Broken People Network," the Three Angels Broadcasting Network airs on Sky Angel (http://www.skyangel.com) and is a round-the-clock Christian television and radio network. The network produces 85 percent of its own programming, all aimed to soothe the soul, and includes sermons, musical programs, talk shows, teen and children's fare, cooking programs, natural home remedies, stop-smoking and weight-loss clinics, addiction rehabilitation programs, gospel music programs, and health lectures. Special events include weekly live broadcasts and interviews, on-location evangelistic series, holiday specials, and live prophecy seminars.

Initially started as a small, local channel, the network has grown into an international media group that provides Christian lifestyle programming to every continent in the world. The network includes studios in North America and Europe, television stations in the Philippines and Papua New Guinea, a music label, a radio network, full-time English and Spanish television networks, and full global satellite coverage. The network also produces 3ABN Latino (a full-time Spanish/Portuguese television network that began broadcasting in 2003), 3ABN Radio (a round-the-clock Christian radio network), and religious-related music videos.

ThrillerMax, 1100 Avenue of the Americas, New York, NY 10036; *Telephone*: 212-512-5948; *Launch Date*: June 1998; *Broadcast Day*: 24 hours; *Email*: Contact channel through its web site; *Web site*: http://www.cinemax.com

A multiplexed channel from Cinemax, ThrillerMax broadcasts mystery, suspense, and thriller movies, including recent box office Hollywood hits and independent films.

Tickets on Demand, 1540 Logan Street #11, Denver, CO 80203; *Telephone*: 720-434-0157; *Launch Date*: July 2004; *Broadcast Day*: 24 hours; *Email*: Contact channel through its web site; *Web site*: http://www.ticketsondemand.tv

Tickets On Demand is a digital ticketing channel for live performance events and screenings. Viewers can search events, based on location and category, and find out the availability to purchase tickets for concerts, movies, and sporting and theatrical events while watching an informative audio/video caption.

Toon Disney, 3800 West Alameda Avenue, Burbank, CA 91505; *Telephone*: 818-569-7500; *Launch Date*: April 1998; *Broadcast Day*: 24 hours; *Subscribers*: 44,000,000; *Email*: Contact channel through its web site; *Web site*: http://www.toondisney.com

A brand spin-off from the Disney Channel, the all-cartoon Toon Disney airs Disney animation (cartoons either created or distributed by Disney) and is aimed at children ages 2 to 11.

Total Christian Television, P.O. Box 1010, Marion, IL 62959; *Telephone*: 618-997-9333; *Launch Date*: May 1977; *Email*: Contact channel through its web site; *Web site*: http://www.tct-net.org

The non-profit Total Christian Television channel airs family-oriented religious programs aimed at bringing the gospel of Jesus Christ into its viewers homes. The channel can be seen in more than 100 million homes in the United States, Canada, and in 160 countries throughout the world.

Total Living Network, 2880 Vision Court, Aurora, IL 60506; *Telephone*: 630-801-3838; *Fax*: 630-801-3839; *Email*: Contact network through its web site; *Web site*: http:// www.tln.com

The Total Living Network airs religious-based programs aimed at empowering its viewers and to introduce them to the word of Jesus Christ.

Totally Broadway TV, 2255 Glades Road #221A, Boca Raton, FL 33431; *Telephone*: 561-998-8000; *Launch Date*: June 2002; *Broadcast Day*: 24 hours; *Email*: Contact channel through its web site; *Web site*: http://www.broadway.com

Totally Broadway TV provides on-demand access to Broadway show excerpts, behind-the-scenes videos, interviews with actors, reviews, and insight. Combining the best features of television and the internet, the channel allows customers to search for show times and information for touring shows in their own city.

Totally Hollywood TV, 2255 Glades Road #221A, Boca Raton, FL 33431; *Telephone*: 561-998-8000; *Launch Date*: June 2002; *Broadcast Day*: 24 hours; *Email*: Contact channel through its web site; *Web site*: http://www.hollywood.com

Operated by Hollywood Media Corporation, Totally Hollywood TV provides on-demand video relating to the newest movies, features the most recent theatrical movie trailers, movie premiere coverage, and celebrity interviews.

Travel Channel, One Discovery Place, Silver Spring, MD 20910; *Telephone*: 240-662-2000; *Launch Date*: February 1987; *Broadcast*

Day: 24 hours; *Email*: Contact channel through its web site; *Web site*: http://www.travelchannel.com

A Discovery Channel broadcast entity, the Travel Channel is devoted exclusively to travel entertainment, taking viewers to the world's most popular destinations.

Triangle Television Network, 810 North Farrell Drive, Palm Springs, CA 92262, 1000 East Tahquitz Cny Way, Palm Springs, CA 92262; *Telephone*: 760-416-5356; *Fax*: 760-332-2245; *Broadcast Day*: 24 hours; *Email*: info@ttntv.com; *Web site*: http://www. triangletelevisionnetwork.com

The Triangle Television Network is the nation's first round-the-clock gay, lesbian, bisexual, and transgender television network.

Trinity Broadcasting Network, 2823 West Irving Boulevard, Irving, TX 75061; P.O. Box A, Santa Ana, CA 92711; *Telephone*: 800-735-5542, 972-313-9500; *Fax*: 972-313-1010; *Launch Date*: May 1973; *Broadcast Day*: 24 hours; *Subscribers*: 108,000,000; *Email*: comments@tbn.org; *Web site*: http://www.tbn.org; http://www.tbnnetworks.com

The Trinity Broadcasting Network is a round-the-clock religious channel offering commercial-free inspirational programming that appeals to viewers of a wide variety of religious leanings. Programs include gospel music concerts from Nashville, talk shows, contemporary Christian music videos, positive children's shows, health and fitness shows, and uplifting worship services from America's premier churches. TBN's programs are translated into numerous foreign languages at its facilities in Irving, Texas and produces more original Christian programs than any other religious network and is also a recognized leader in the production of major Christian movies. The 24-hour Trinity Broadcasting Network Enlace USA, launched in May 2002, is a multi-faith Hispanic channel from TBN that features 70 percent Hispanic-produced programs from Latin America and 30 percent Spanish-language programs from the United States.

TBN Networks includes The Church Channel ([http://www.churchchannel.tv], a 24-hour multi-denominational religious network that features church service programs from around the country) and JCTV (which calls itself "America's premier Christian youth music network" and features faith-based programming aimed at the 13-to-25 age group, including music videos, reality shows, game shows, comedies, extreme sports, and specials).

TR!O (Popular Arts TV), 1230 Avenue of the Americas, New York, NY 10020; *Telephone*: 212-413-5000; *Fax*: 212-413-6507; *Launch Date*: September 1994; *Broadcast Day*: 24 hours; *Subscribers*: 20,000,000; *Email*: Contact channel through its web site; *Web site*: http://www.triotv.com

TR!O airs programming that reflects pop culture, television, film, music, fashion, television, and stage. The channel is a subsidiary of Universal Television Group, a division of Vivendi Universal Entertainment (see http://www.universalstudios.com), the U.S.-based film, television, and recreation entity of Vivendi Universal, a global media and communications company.

Tri-State Media News, 2215 DuPont Parkway, New Castle, DE 19770; *Telephone*: 877-876-6397; *Launch Date*: April 1999; *Broadcast Day*: 12 hours; *Subscribers*: 1,000,000; *Email*: Contact channel through its web site; *Web site*: http://www.tsmnews.com

Tri-State Media News delivers 12 hours per day of local news five days per week to subscribers in southeastern and central Pennsylvania, southern New Jersey, and northern Delaware. In the midst of this 12-hour news block, the channel airs its interactive talk show, *CHAT 24*.

TSN *see* **Entertainment Sports Television Network**

Turner Broadcasting System Superstation, 1050 NW Techwood Drive, Atlanta, GA 30318; *Telephone*: 404-827-1700; *Fax*:

404-885-4326; *Launch Date*: December 1976; *Broadcast Day*: 24 hours; *Subscribers*: 87,200,000; *Email*: tbs.superstation@turner.com; *Web site*: http://www. turner.com; http://www.tbssuperstation.com

The Turner Broadcasting System Superstation is Ted Turner's flagship entertainment network and was one of the nation's very first national cable networks. The general entertainment network airs comedies, reality series, original programs, movies, hosted movie showcases, and sports from the world of Major League Baseball (highlighting the Atlanta Braves), and college football. Since its inception, the Turner Broadcasting System has grown from a regional outdoor advertising firm into one of the world's largest and most successful media conglomerates. Beginning in the late 1960s, Ted Turner changed his father's company, Turner Advertising, first into Turner Communications Company and then into Turner Broadcasting System. Each name change represented a stage in the building of an empire that would come to encompass broadcast television and radio, cable program services, movie and television production companies, home video, and sports teams.

TBS began with Ted Turner's purchase of a failing Atlanta UHF station, WJRJ, in 1968, and immediately changing its name to WTCG (for Turner Communications Group). The channel's initial programming consisted of old movies and syndicated television series, many of which he purchased outright with a view toward unrestricted future showings. He used the channel's schedule to counter-program the network affiliates, going after children viewers and those who did not watch network news. By the early 1970s, WTCG began broadcasting local sports programming, including professional wrestling, Atlanta Braves baseball, Atlanta Hawks basketball, and Atlanta Flames hockey. In 1976, Ted Turner purchased Major League Baseball's Atlanta Braves outright.

TBS enjoyed almost instant success with its program combination of movies, television programs, and sports coverage. By 1972 WTCG garnered a 15 percent share of the Atlanta audience and the station's signal had begun to be carried by microwave to cable systems in the Atlanta region. Taking his cue from the innovative success of Home Box Office, Turner quickly used the same satellite technology to extend his station's signal across the United States. He established a separate company, Southern Satellite Systems, to uplink WTCG's signal to an RCA communications satellite. In 1976, the channel became the second satellite-delivered cable program service (after HBO) and the first satellite superstation. The superstation was renamed WTBS in the late 1970s and over the following decades, Turner used WTBS as his base to launch multiple channels, including the Cable News Network.

Turner Classic Movies (http://www.turnerclassicmovies.com), launched in April 1994, airs nothing but movies, 24 hours a day and features more than 300 different titles each month, all commercial-free and without interruption. Turner Network Television, launched in October 1988, uses the tag line "We Know Drama" and is cable's only network combining award-winning original films, broadcast premieres, one-hour off-network dramas (such as *Law & Order* and *NYPD Blue*), original series; and championship sports coverage, including NASCAR, the PGA, the British Open, and the NBA. TNT Latin America (http://www.tntla.turner.com) is a separate specific-language channel that broadcasts in Spanish, Portuguese, and English. The 24-hour Turner South (http://www.turnersouth.com), launched in October 1999, presents a mix of original programming, movies, regional news, and sports (the Atlanta Braves, the Atlanta Hawks, and the NHL's Atlanta Thrashers) to affiliates in Alabama, Georgia, Mississippi, South Carolina, Tennessee, and regions of North Carolina.

TuTV, 5999 Center Drive, Los Angeles, CA 90045; *Telephone*: 310-348-3370, 310-216-

3434; *Fax*: 310-348-3643, 310-348-3698; *Launch Date*: 2002; *Email*: info_at_tutv@univision.net; *Web site*: http://www.tutv.tv

TuTV, a joint venture between Univision and Televisa, was created in 2002 and delivers five popular Spanish-language channels: Bandamax, De Película, De Película Clásico, Ritmoson Latino, and TeleHit. Grupo Televisa, S.A. (http://www.televisa.com) is the largest media company in the Spanish-speaking world and a major player in the international entertainment business. It has interests in television production and broadcasting, programming for pay television, international distribution of television programming, direct-to-home satellite services, publishing and publishing distribution, cable television, radio production and broadcasting, professional sports and show business promotions, paging services, feature film production and distribution, dubbing, and the operation of a an internet portal. Grupo Televisa also has an equity stake in Univision, the leading Spanish-language television company in the United States.

Univision Communications, Inc. (http://www.univision.net) is the premier Spanish-language media company in the United States. Its operations include Univision Network (the most-watched Spanish-language broadcast television network in the U.S. reaching 97 percent of U.S. Hispanic households); the TeleFutura Network (a general-interest Spanish-language broadcast television network reaching 80 percent of U.S. Hispanic households); Univision Television Group (which owns and operates 23 Univision Network television stations and one non-Univision television station); TeleFutura Television Group (which owns and operates 29 TeleFutura Network television stations); Galavisión (the country's leading Spanish-language cable network); Univision Radio (the leading Spanish-language radio group which owns and/or operates 65 radio stations in 17 of the top 25 U.S. Hispanic markets and four stations in Puerto Rico); Univision Music Group (which includes the Univision Records, Fonovisa Records, and a 50 percent interest in Mexico-based Disa Records labels as well as Fonomusic and America Musical Publishing companies); and Univision Online (the premier Spanish-language internet destination in the United States).

Bandamax features Spanish-language country music videos from top Hispanic artists in the Grupero, Norteño, Banda, Tex-Mex, and Mariachi genres. In addition to music videos, the channel also airs the popular magazine show *Furia Musical*. De Película features the best films drawn from the world's largest library of Spanish language films. Its programming includes contemporary and classic movies from all eras, presented without commercial interruption. De Película Clásico is a classic movie channel featuring the best films from the period during the 1930's, 1940s, and 1950s, known as Mexico's "Golden Era" of film making. The channel segments its programming day for its audience by genre, featuring films with particular appeal to women and families during the day, titles for the whole household during the afternoon, and in prime-time movies targeted more to the male audience, such as westerns, wrestling and action-oriented films. Ritmoson Latino (http:www.ritmosonlatino.com) is a music and lifestyle channel that focuses on the rhythms, dance, and passions of the Latin culture. The channel features Spanish-language music videos from top Latin stars such as Ricky Martin, Gloria Estefan and Chayanne. TeleHit (http://www.telehit) focuses its programming to Latino youth with music videos, celebrity interviews, live concerts, and entertainment news.

TV5, 8900 Liberty Circle, Englewood, CO 80122; *Telephone*: 720-853-2933; *Broadcast Day*: 24 hours; *Email*: Contact channel through its web site; *Web site*: http://www.tv5.org/usa, http://www.i-channel.com

TV5, which broadcasts on the International Channel, is a round-the-clock international French-language broadcaster with more than 500 million worldwide viewers.

The channel airs programming originating in France, Switzerland, Belgium, Canada, Quebec, and French-speaking Africa. Airing in the United States, the channel promotes the diversity of the French-speaking world and airs news, movies, documentaries, and entertainment programs.

TV Asia, 76 National Road, Edison, NJ 08817; *Telephone*: 732-650-1100; *Broadcast Day*: 24 hours; *Email*: Contact channel through its web site; *Web site*: http://www.tvasiausa.com, http://www.i-channel.com

TV Asia, which airs on the International Channel, provides programming produced for South Asian Americans who want to maintain ties with their cultural heritage and way of life. Its viewers include Asian Indians, Pakistanis, Bangladeshis, Sir Lankans, and Indo-Caribbeans living in the United States.

TV Bulgaria USA, 3711 South Industrial #4, Las Vegas, NV 89109; *Telephone*: 866-882-4638, 702-737-7667; *Fax*: 702-737-0646; *Launch Date*: 1999; *Broadcast Day*: 24 hours; *Email*: office@tvbulgaria/net; *Web site*: http://www.tvbulgaria.net

TV Bulgaria is the satellite channel of Bulgarian National Television and features news, current events, popular series, game shows, talk shows, live sporting events, music videos, live concerts, and Bulgarian-made movies.

TVE Internacionale, 1100 Ponce de Leon Boulevard, Coral Gables, FL 33134; *Telephone*: 305-444-4402; *Fax*: 305-554-6776; *Launch Date*: 1989; *Broadcast Day*: 24 hours; *Email*: Contact channel through its web site; *Web site*: http://www.rtve.es

TVE Internacionale airs Spanish-language films, international news, children's programming, comedies, novellas, variety shows, cultural programs, documentaries, and interview programs.

TVG — The Interactive Horse Racing Network, 19545 Northwest Von Neumann Drive #210, Beaverton, OR 97006; *Telephone*: 888-752-9884; *Email*: comments@tvg.com; *Web site*: http://www.tvg.com

Owned by Gemstar — TV Guide International, Inc., TVG — The Interactive Horse Racing Network combines live, televised coverage from over 60 of America's premier race tracks (including Churchill Downs, Beulah Park, Aqueduct, Calder, Louisiana Downs, Hawthorne, Sunland Park, Hollywood Park, and Saratoga Harness) with the convenience of wagering from home online, by telephone, or by a set-up remote control device. TVG broadcasts up to eight live horse races per hour and highlights another four to six races during the hour. In addition to live horse races, the network also airs expert commentary; behind-the-scenes features on the horses and celebrities of racing; programs with racing or equine themes appealing to both the experienced player and the novice fan; handicapping tips; feature stories on the superstars of horse racing (the horses, personalities, and legends of racing); and original programming.

TV Games Network, 12421 West Olympic Boulevard, Los Angeles, CA 90064, 6701 West Center Drive, Los Angeles, CA 90045; *Telephone*: 310-689-2500, 310-242-9500; *Launch Date*: July 1994; *Broadcast Day*: 24 hours; *Subscribers*: 12,000,000; *Email*: Contact network through its web site; *Web site*: http://www.tvgnetwork.com

Owned by TV Guide, Inc., the TV Games Network is the leading interactive horse racing network and combines the exciting sport of live horse racing with the convenience of in-home wagering (via telephone and the internet). The network's in-studio and on-location crew of anchors, analysts, and correspondents brings viewers all the headlines and behind-the-scenes stories from the world of horse racing.

TV Guide Channel, 7140 South Lewis Avenue, Tulsa, OK 74136, 6922 Hollywood Boulevard, Los Angeles, CA 90028; *Telephone*: 800-477-7388, 323-817-4600; *Launch Date*: January 1988; *Broadcast Day*: 24 hours;

Subscribers: 70,000,000; *Email*: Contact channel through its web site; *Web site*: http://www.tvguide.com

Originally called the Prevue Channel, the TV Guide Channel is the premier entertainment guidance network for television viewers seeking recommendations and information on the best programs, hottest stars, and latest trends on local television. The channel airs celebrity interviews, music and entertainment news, and behind-the-scenes close ups on the hottest shows and sporting events. During its continuous, up-to-the-minute streaming broadcast, pay-per-view information (titles and start times) appears on the top half of the screen while local program listings (titles and start times) are displayed on the bottom half of the screen. The 24-hour TV Guide Interactive, launched in October 1996, is a comprehensive source of on-screen television program guidance for digital cable subscribers. Designed to be easy to use and conveniently accessible, TVGI enables viewers to interact with and control program listings (set viewing times, for example) to navigate effortlessly through the vast array of television programming choices and provides integrated access to emerging enhanced digital and interactive television services.

TV Japan *see* **Japan Network Group**

TVK 24, 4525 Wilshire Boulevard #204, Los Angeles, CA 90010; *Telephone*: 323-692-2192; *Broadcast Day*: 24 hours; *Email*: Contact channel through its web site; *Web site*: http://www.tvk24.com

Planned for future operation, TVK 24 will be a Korean-language channel aimed at the Korean-American television audience and will broadcast news, dramas, movies, sports, business, children's, and educational shows.

TV Land, 1515 Broadway, New York, NY 10036; *Telephone*: 212-258-8000; *Launch Date*: April 1996; *Broadcast Day*: 24 hours; *Subscribers*: 80,000,000; *Email*: Contact channel through its web site; *Web site*: http://www.mtv.com

A Music Television channel, TV Land is the only network dedicated to broadcasting the "best of everything" shown on television from the past 50 years, including classic shows such as *The Andy Griffith Show*, *Sanford & Son*, *I Dream of Jeannie*, and *Gunsmoke*, original specials, and classic commercials.

TV One (TV 1), 5900 Princess Garden Parkway, Lanham, MD 20706; *Telephone*: 301-429-3248; *Launch Date*: January 2004; *Broadcast Day*: 24 hours; *Email*: Contact channel through its web site; *Web site*: http://www.tv-one.tv

A joint venture between Radio One, Inc. and Comcast Corporation, TV One programming is aimed primarily at African-American adults; focuses on African-American themes, issues, culture, and politics; and airs entertainment and issue-oriented original programs, classic series, movies, reality and game shows, entertainment news, documentaries, lifestyle and public affairs, and music variety programs.

TV Orient, 25835 Southfield Road #200, Southfield, MI 48075; *Telephone*: 248-569-2020; *Fax*: 248-569-2111; *Launch Date*: 1986; *Broadcast Day*: 24 hours; *Email*: Contact channel through its web site; *Web site*: http://www.radio_tvorient.com

TV Orient is a national Middle Eastern-American television network that broadcasts family-oriented programming to viewers in the United States, Canada, and Mexico. The network airs daily news and commentary on Middle East activities, in English, Aramaic, and Arabic. Programming fare consists of movies, soap operas, documentaries, sporting events, music concerts, music videos, talk shows, health topics, sporting events, educational series, arts and culture, local and international news, and children's shows.

TV Polonia, 8900 Liberty Circle, Englewood, CO 80122; *Telephone*: 720-853-2933;

Broadcast Day: 24 hours; *Email*: Contact channel through its web site; *Web site*: http://www.tvpolonia.com, http://www.i-channel.com

TV Polonia airs on the International Channel and broadcasts Polish-language television programming.

TVU (Music Television), P.O. Box 1887, Westerville, OH 43086; *Telephone*: 614-890-9977; *Fax*: 614-839-1329; *Launch Date*: 2001; *Broadcast Day*: 24 hours; *Email*: tvu@tvulive.com; *Web site*: http://www.tvulive.com

Owned by Sprint Communications and using the tag line, "Where Music is Going," TVU broadcasts on Sky Angel (http://www.skyangel.com) and airs more music videos than any other network in the world (viewers can request music videos via a toll-free request line), in a variety of genres, including pop, rock, and hip hop. The channel also airs originally-produced programs, such as *Ten Most Wanted*, *Planet Hip Hop*, and *The Obadiah Show*.

TVW, P.O. Box 25, Olympia, WA 98507, 1063 South Capitol Way #16, Olympia, WA 98501; *Telephone*: 360-586-5555; *Fax*: 360-586-5678; *Email*: tvw@tvw.org; *Web site*: http://www.tvw.org

TVW, Washington state's public affairs network, is a non-profit broadcast entity that provides unedited coverage of state government legislative sessions and public policy events.

Ultra HD, 200 Jericho Quadrangle, Jericho, NY 11753; *Telephone*: 516-803-6010; *Broadcast Day*: 24 hours; *Email*: Contact channel through its web site; *Web site*: http://www.voom.com

Ultra HD is a high definition multiplexed channel from Voom and is the first channel devoted exclusively to covering the world of fashion, beauty, and style.

United Paramount Network, 11800 Wilshire Boulevard, P.O. Box 251735, Los Angeles, CA 90025; *Telephone*: 310-575-7000; *Fax*: 310-575-7220; *Launch Date*: January 1995; *Broadcast Day*: 24 hours; *Email*: Contact network through its web site; *Web site*: http://www.upn.com

Owned by Viacom, Inc, the United Paramount Network is one of the big six national broadcast entities (along with ABC, CBS, NBC, Fox, and WB) and its programming is geared primarily to the young African-American audience. The Paramount Studio had earlier attempted its own television network with the Paramount Television Service. Planned to launch in 1978, its one-night-only programming would have basically consisted of 30 Movies of the Week. The network's plans called for a Saturday night lineup to be added, mainly the showing of *Star Trek: Phase Two*. However, the network failed to sell enough advertising and acquire enough affiliates to make the network viable.

Paramount succeeded in creating a national network in 1995 when it launched UPN as the United Paramount Network, a joint venture with Chris-Craft Industries' United Television Group. Both companies owned independent stations in several large cities in the United States and each controlled 50 percent of UPN. In 2000, Paramount's parent company, Viacom, bought out Chris-Craft to gain 100 percent control of the United-Paramount venture. Shortly afterward, Viacom changed the network's name to UPN.

Initially, the network relied heavily on movies and several Star Trek series, such as *Star Trek: Voyager* and *Star Trek: Enterprise*. The network expanded its programming by buying the rights to *Buffy the Vampire Slayer* (from the Warner Brothers network) and airing *WWE Smackdown*. Once established, the network expanded its programming fare to include sitcoms and dramas.

United States Military Television Network, 2973 Harbor Boulevard #276, Costa Mesa, CA 92626; *Telephone*: 949-929-4381, 949-305-0020; *Launch Date*: August 2004; *Broadcast Day*: 24 hours; *Email*: info@usmilitary.tv; *Web site*: http://www.usmilitary.tv

The United States Military Television Network presents a side of the military that is generally not seen in the media, their lives through their own eyes. The all-original programming includes news magazine shows; live newscasts with satellite feed from battlefield locations; children's programs and cartoons; music videos; documentaries; military intramural sporting events; and talent search shows appealing to Generation X. The USMTV is the public's primary source for military information.

Lauren Kelly founded the U.S. Military Television Network after observing the treatment of military personnel and their families in a town in which she was living. In 1985, she formed a USO-type military entertainment troupe to entertain the military personnel and raise morale. Her troupe, News From Home, comprised mostly of former Dallas Cowboy Cheerleaders, performed at air shows, enlisted clubs, and officers clubs. She moved to San Diego, California in August of 1990 to produce and air programming through a local cable TV provider to Southern California military installations, which eventually evolved into the United States Military Television Network.

Universityhouse, P.O. Box 5676, Flagstaff, AZ 86011; *Telephone*: 877-867-1824; *Fax*: 520-523-9988; *Launch Date*: January 2000; *Broadcast Day*: 24 hours; *Email*: Contact channel through its web site; *Web site*: http://www.universityhouse.nau.edu

The Universityhouse channel provides educational programming directly to home viewers, from K-12 to accredited college courses. The channel airs both regularly-scheduled courses each semester and a wide selection of non-credit programs offered at different times and dates during the year. The channel's programming is aimed at parent's home-schooling their children, students interested in college courses, and adults interested in furthering their education.

Univision, 605 Third Avenue, 12th Floor, New York, NY 10158; *Telephone*: 212-455-5200; *Fax*: 212-986-4731; *Launch Date*: September 1976; *Broadcast Day*: 24 hours; *Subscribers*: 35,000,000; *Email*: Contact network through its web site; *Web site*: http://www.univision.net; http://www.univisionnetworks.com

Starting from a very small audience base, the Univision Network has grown to become the most watched television entity (in English or Spanish) among the nation's Hispanic population. Programming consists of novellas, national and local newscasts, variety shows, children's programming, musical specials, movies, sporting events, and public affairs programming.

Univision began its history as the Spanish International Network (SIN), the first Spanish-language television network in the United States. SIN was the U.S. subsidiary of Televisa, the Mexican entertainment conglomerate, which today is the world's largest producer of Spanish- language television programming. In the 1960s, it was a widely-held view that the U.S. Spanish- speaking population was so small and poor that it was not considered a viable advertising market and, thus, was basically ignored by the television industry. From a U.S. market perspective, this view was probably correct; however, from the perspective of a Latin American entrepreneur, the existing U.S. Latino audience was one of the wealthiest Spanish-language markets in the world.

SIN was founded by Emilio Azcarraga, the so-called "William Paley of Mexican broadcasting," who owned theaters and recording companies. Throughout his career, he had built a radio, then a television, empire in Mexico, before expanding his operations north of the border. SIN began in the United States with two television stations (KMEX in Los Angels and KWEX in San Antonio) and from this modest start began to expand across the United States. To broadcast its signal, SIN used five basic communications technologies: the UHF band, cable television, microwave, satellite systems, and repeater stations. The use of these systems through the 1960s and 1970s allowed SIN to grow steadily and by 1982, the network reached 90 percent of the Spanish-speaking households in the United States with its 16 owned and operated UHF stations, 100 repeater stations, and 200 cable outlets.

In the early 1980s SIN began using satellites to broadcast its signal and started producing programs in the United States, the first of which was a nightly national newscast, *Noticiero Univisión*. Additionally, the network began providing coverage of U.S. national events, such as the Tournament of Roses Parade and the Fourth of July celebrations and larger SIN-owned stations began airing two hours a day of locally-produced news and public affairs programming. This successful mix of programming convinced SIN that the U.S. and Mexican television audiences had different needs and interests that were not being addressed by the so-called "mainstream" networks. More importantly, the expanding of programming options was an attempt by the network to alter its audience profile from foreign or ethnic groups interested only in Mexican programming, to that of a more American community participating in the same national rituals as the mainstream consumer market. This was an important early step in raising the profile of Hispanic audiences and in making them a viable viewing force within the American television industry.

Azcárraga's marketing skills and vision were matched by his legal skills in maneuvering around U.S. law. The Communications Act of 1934 explicitly barred "any alien or representative of any alien ... or any corporation directly or indirectly controlled by ... aliens" from owning U.S. broadcast station licenses. While the law seemed fairly clear and definitive, the SIN network focused more on what the law did not say. The Act did not prohibit the importation or distribution of foreign broadcast signals or programming. Legally, on paper, and in filings with the Federal Communications Commission, none of the SIN stations or affiliates was owned by Emilio Azcárraga or Televisa. Thus, the foreign ownership prohibition was avoided by means of a time-honored business strategy known, in Spanish, as the "presta nombre," which literally means "lending a name," or in colloquial English, a "front." On paper, SIN stations and affiliates were owned by U.S. citizens with long professional and personal ties to Azcárraga and Televisa, with Azcárraga retaining a 25 percent interest (the limit permitted by law) in the network.

The foreign control of SIN was not successfully challenged until the mid–1980s and in 1986, the FCC forced the sale of SIN. The network was bought for $300 million by Hallmark, Inc., which changed the network's name to Univision, but pledged to continue broadcasting in Spanish. The network has since grown to become the largest Spanish-language television network in the United States and has more than 600 affiliates. Under Hallmark ownership, about half of Univision programming consisted of re-broadcasts of Televisa-produced shows, with the other half being produced in the United States. Hallmark, which had purchased the network with the use of junk bonds, was never able to recoup its $300 million investment and in 1992 sold Univision to the Perenchino Group, of which Televisa was a investor. One of the first moves made was to fire almost one-third of the network's Miami-based staff, which resulted in the cancellation of most U.S.-produced programs, and gave programming control back to Televisa.

Urban America Television Network, 2707 South Cooper #119, Arlington, TX 76015; *Telephone*: 817-303-7449; *Fax*: 817-459-2942; *Email*: info@urban-america-tv.com; *Web site*: http://www.urbanamericatv.com

The Urban America Television Network serves urban viewers in America with programming that includes talk shows, movies with well-known African-American actors, and reality television shows.

Urban Broadcasting Company, 2388 Adam Clayton Powell Boulevard, New York,

NY 10030; *Telephone*: 212-283-7477; *Fax*: 212-283-7157; *Launch Date*: April 2003; *Broadcast Day*: 24 hours; *Email*: info@urbanbroadcasting.tv; *Web site*: http://www.urbanbroadcasting.tv

The Urban Broadcasting Company airs programs aimed at multi-cultural audiences with original programming, music videos, and special events.

Urban Religious Channel *see* **The Word Network**

USA Network, 1230 Avenue of the Americas, New York, NY 10020; *Telephone*: 212-408-9100, 212-413-5000; *Fax*: 212-413-6128; *Launch Date*: 1977 (as the Madison Square Garden Network), April 1980 (as USA Network); *Broadcast Day*: 24 hours; *Subscribers*: 90,000,000; *Email*: Contact network through its web site; *Web site*: http://www.usanetwork.com

Owned and operated by NBC Universal, the USA Network is a general-entertainment network airing original and acquired series (such as *The Dead Zone*, *JAG*, *Law & Order: Special Victims Unit*, *Monk*, *Silk Stockings*, and *Walker, Texas Ranger*), original and acquired movies, specials, and sporting events (including the *U.S. Open Tennis Championships* and the *Westminster Kennel Club Dog Show*). The network also broadcasts is programming fare to South America through its affiliate, USA América Latina (http://www.usalatinamerica.com).

Originally started as the Madison Square Garden Network (not to be confused with the current New York City regional sports network of the same name), it became one of the first national television channels when it chose to use satellite delivery as opposed to traditional television broadcasting. In 1980 the channel changed its name to USA Network to reflect its national broadcast coverage. In 1992 the network launched the Sci-Fi Channel and in 1997 both channels were sold to the Home Shopping Network and renamed itself USA Networks, Inc.

In 1999, USA Networks buys October Films and Gramercy Pictures, renaming them USA Films, and PolyGram Video, renaming it USA Home Video. In 2000, USA Networks buys Canada's North American Television, Inc. which owned Tr!o and News World International. In 2001, USA Networks sells its non-shopping television and film assets (including the USA Network, the Sci Fi Channel, the Trio channel, USA Films (which is renamed Focus Features), and Studios USA) to Vivendi Universal, which all join Vivendi's Universal Television Group. In 2003 NBC buys the Universal Television Group and in 2004 NBC Universal takes over as owner of the USA Network and all affiliate channels, except for News World International, which is bought by an investment group led by former vice president Al Gore and Joel Hyatt.

Varsity Television, 6500 River Place Boulevard, Building 2, Austin, TX 78730; *Telephone*: 877-916-9888, 512-527-2500; *Fax*: 512-527-2599; *Broadcast Day*: 24 hours; *Email*: info@ myvtv.com; *Web site*: http://www.myvtv.com

Varsity Television is the world's first and only teen network that airs programs and movies created exclusively for teens and, in some cases, created solely by teens throughout America. VTV is the only online, on-air, and on-demand network exclusively dedicated to teen life. VTV (America's High School Network — an alliance of high schools throughout the country) delivers animation, avant-garde films, championship games, and student-produced music videos.

Verve TV (info@vervetv.com, http://www.vervetv.com) (Planned for future operation)

Video Hits 1, 1515 Broadway, 23rd Floor, New York, NY 10036; *Telephone*: 212-258-8000, 212-846-4629; *Fax*: 212-846-1893; *Launch Date*: 1985; *Broadcast Day*: 24 hours; *Subscribers*: 90,000,000; *Email*: Contact network through its web site; *Web site*: http://www.vh1.com

An MTV (Music Television) network,

VH1 plays so-called soft rock and adult music genres that were forced off the MTV play list due to the network's expansion of its programming fare. Originally dubbed "video Valium for yuppies" by some music lovers, in actuality VH1's programming format is basically indistinguishable from MTV. Since its launch, VH1 has expanded its programming and, in addition to music videos, it also airs news, documentaries, music awards, reality programs, movies, "Best Of" and "Top 10" shows, and music-related specials. Following MTV's example, as VH1 matured it created affiliated channels to broadcast specific music genres to targeted audiences, including VH Uno (launched in November 1999, is a 24-hour music channel aimed at the Latino audience and airs Latin pop and ballads, tropical music, salsa, and urban hip-hop); VH1 Classic ([http://www.vh1classic.com], launched in May 2000, celebrates the great artists from the 1960s, 1970s, and 1980s); VH1 Country (launched in August 1998, features new country music videos with an urban feel, and country artists crossing over into popular music); VH1 Mega Hits (launched in May 2002, plays chart-topping hits from the 1990s and today); VH1 Smooth (provides soft rock, jazz, new age, and adult contemporary music); and VH1 Soul (launched in August 1998, features soul, neo-soul, and R&B hits).

As an offshoot of MTV, VH1 made a conscious effort to play a different mix of music videos, focusing on the lighter, softer side of popular music. In 1994, VH1 adopted the tag line "New VH1: Music First," altered its play list from adult contemporary to adult top 40, and began playing more rock-oriented artists. Two years later, following the pattern set by MTV, VH1 again revamped its programming schedule and focusing more on music-related shows than on actual videos. This shift in programming philosophy did not go over well with its audience and the channel's ratings and profits began to fall. VH1's financial and ratings fortunes changed relatively quickly in the fall of 1996 with its introduction of *Pop-Up Video*, a very innovative and popular show that offered tidbits of information about the artist and video as music videos were being played. The "Pop Up" concept quickly spread to other shows and is now considered a programming staple.

In September 1997, the channel had another hit with an original show, *Behind the Music*, which features interviews and biographies of popular music's biggest stars (the first episode featured the group Milli Vanilli). The show was an instant hit and is still in production today. VH1 followed this success with another series, *Legends*, which profiles artists who have made significant and lasting contributions to music history. Success continued when the channel aired its first annual *VH1 Divas* concert, the original featuring Céline Dion, Shania Twain, Mariah Carey, Gloria Estefan, Aretha Franklin, and Carole King. Other popular original programs on VH1 include *Movies That Rock* (showcases rock-and-roll and rock-and-roll related movies); *Top 20 Countdown*; and *I Love the....* ([70s, 80, and 90s], which features various comedians and social commentators giving their opinions on popular culture of a specific era).

Video Rola, 10360 USA Today Way, Miramar, FL 33025; *Telephone*: 954-430-7800; *Fax*: 954-430-8400; *Launch Date*: January 2001; *Broadcast Day*: 24 hours; *Subscribers*: 95,000; *Email*: Contact channel through its web site; *Web site*: http:// www.videorola.com

Video Rola broadcasts regional Mexican music and culture-based shows produced in Guadalajara, Mexico. Programs include music videos, top 10 countdown, live concerts, interviews, and cultural programs.

Vivid TV, 2706 Media Center Drive, Los Angeles, CA 90065; *Telephone*: 323-276-4000; *Fax*: 323-276-4500; *Email*: Contact channel through its web site; *Web site*: http://www. playboytv. com

Available through the Playboy TV Networks, Vivid TV is a pay-per-view service that offers adult-oriented programming.

Voom, 200 Jericho Quadrangle, Jericho, NY 11753; *Telephone*: 516-803-6010; *Launch Date*: July 2003; *Email*: Contact channel through its web site; *Web site*: http://www.voom.com

Owned and operated by Rainbow Media Holdings, Voom is a service that brings High Definition Television to more than 39 channels, each targeted to specific programming genres. Multiplexed high definition channels from Voom include Animania HD, Auction HD, Classics HD, Divine HD, Epics HD, Equator HD, Gallery HD (the Art & Museum Channel), Gunslingers HD, HD Cinema (1,3,4,5,6), HD News, HD World Cinema (international films), Monsters HD (monster and horror movie channel), MOOV HD (showcases original video art created by a diverse mix of artists and designers), Rave HD, Rush HD, Ultra HD, and WorldSport HD.

VOY Network, 1800 Century Park East, 6th Floor, Los Angeles, CA 90067; *Telephone*: 888-777-8617, 310-205-0300; *Fax*: 310-362-8669; *Launch Date*: July 2004; *Broadcast Day*: 24 hours; *Email*: contact@voygroup.com; *Web site*: http://www.voy.tv

The VOY Network targets its programming to the English-speaking, 18-49 year-old Hispanic audience and features Latino artists and viewpoints that celebrate the U.S. Hispanic experience and the American way of life. Network programming consists of talk shows, reality, travel, culinary, pop culture and celebrity, history, documentaries, and politics that entertain, energize, and inspire both Latino and mainstream audiences.

WAM! (Starz! WAM!), 8900 Liberty Circle, Englewood, CO 80112; *Telephone*: 720-852-7700; *Launch Date*: 1994; *Broadcast Day*: 24 hours; *Email*: Contact channel through its web site; *Web site*: http://www.starz.com

A brand channel from Starz!, WAM! is the only commercial-free children's channel dedicated to providing kid-friendly, round-the-clock socially-responsible programming for 8-16 year-olds. The channel provides 60 hours a week of subject-specific education, in addition to such popular segments as WAM! After School OH! Zone, Weekend Entertainment Zone, and WAM! At the Movies.

WE: Women's Entertainment, 200 Jericho Quadrangle, Jericho, NY 11753, 150 Crossways Park West, Woodbury, NY 11797; *Telephone*: 516-803-4400, 516-396-3000; *Fax*: 516-803-4398, 516-364-5948; *Launch Date*: January 1997; *Broadcast Day*: 24 hours; *Subscribers*: 51,400,000; *Email*: Contact channel through its web site; *Web site*: http://www.we-womensentertainment.com

A service of AMC Networks, the WE channel is devoted entirely to romance, primarily from a woman's point of view. The programming mix includes romantic films, popular miniseries, original lifestyle programs focusing on the issues that are most important to women, what's hot in the world of romance, and topical specials. A brand channel, Romance Classics (http://www. romanceclassics. com) features romance movies and specials.

The WB (Warner Brothers) Television Network, 4000 Warner Boulevard, Building #34R, Burbank, CA 91522; *Telephone*: 818-977-5000; *Fax*: 818-977-6771; *Launch Date*: 1995; *Email*: Contact network through its web site; *Web site*: http://www. thewb.com

Owned by Time Warner, the relatively-small WB Network is one of the big six national networks (along with ABC, CBS, NBC, Fox, and UPN) and its programming is geared primarily to a younger audience. Available to 92 percent of the nation's households, The WB airs prime time programming Sunday through Friday and its *KidsWB!* airs weekday afternoons and Saturday mornings. Warner Bros. (abbreviated version of Warner Brothers) Entertainment is one of the world's largest producers of film and television entertainment and consists of Warner Brothers Studios, Warner Brothers Pictures, Warner Brothers Television, Warner Home Video, Warner Music Australia, Castle Rock Entertainment, Turner

Entertainment, and Hanna-Barbera Productions.

In its early days, The WB aimed its programming directly at the so-called Generation Y with the airing of such programs as *Charmed* and *Smallville*. While there was some success with this early strategy, the network realized it needed to attract an older audience to remain a viable entity within the television industry. In addition to airing programs aimed at an older audience, The WB is also producing original movies for its prime time schedule.

WealthTV, 4757 Morena Boulevard, San Diego, CA 92117; *Telephone*: 858-270-6900; *Fax*: 858-270-6901; *Launch Date*: June 2004; *Email*: info@herringbroadcasting.com; *Web site*: http://www.wealthtv.net

Operated by Herring Broadcasting, Inc. and housed within a 40,000-square-foot facility, WealthTV is a high-definition lifestyle and entertainment network that provides viewers with a behind the scenes look into how the wealthy achieve, live, and enjoy their success. Programs include *Wealth on Health* (explores how stem cell research may hold the key to curing some of today's most serious illnesses), *World of Wealth* (explores the issues and influences that shape business from a global perspective), *What to Wear* (the hottest fashions from top international designers), *Great Cars* (explores the history of today's most unique and sought-after cars), *WOW* (visits the world's most unique and high-living cities), *WealthTV's International News* (news from around the world), *On the Water* (explores the best of everything water-related, including super-yachts and international races), *Doing Well* (profiles of the world's most successful business leaders and entertainment celebrities), *World Sports* (features original series and powerboat races), *The Ray Lucia Show* (the nationally renowned expert in financial and business management answers questions and discusses the latest issues affecting viewers' financial future), *Karma Trekkers* (visits off-beat locations throughout the world), *The Best of Everything* (journeys to luxurious and exotic destinations around the world), *Private Jets* (shows viewers what it is like to fly better then first class), *Envy* (a magazine format show that focuses on celebrities, cars, bars, destinations, and fast living), and *Well Spent* (focuses on incredible experiences by ordinary people).

Weather Channel, 300 Interstate North Parkway, Atlanta, GA 30339; *Telephone*: 770-226-0000; *Fax*: 770-226-2950; *Launch Date*: May 1982; *Broadcast Day*: 24 hours; *Subscribers*: 85,300,000; *Email*: Contact channel through its web site; *Web site*: http://www.weather.com

The Weather Channel has more than 100 meteorologists and state-of-the-art technology to provide round-the-clock coverage of local/regional/national/international weather, travel and 10-day forecasts, severe weather coverage, on-location updates, and a schedule of education productions and original series. Weatherscan, launched in October 1999, is a 24-hour, all-local weather information network that provides local conditions, observations for surrounding communities, local radar, regional radar, satellite images, 36-hour forecasts, extended forecasts, watches, and warnings. Additionally, cable affiliates have the option of presenting tailored lifestyle information relating to local sporting events, outdoor activities, and other subjects of interest such as golf, skiing, boat and beach, health, and aviation.

WGN Superstation, 2501 West Bradley Place, Chicago, IL 60618; *Telephone*: 773-528-2311; *Fax*: 773-528-6857; *Email*: Contact network through its web site; *Web site*: http://www.superstationwgn.com; http://wwwsuperstation.com

The WGN Superstation broadcasts nationwide to homes, bars, hotels, and motels with a mix of general entertainment programming (recent and classic movies, action-adventure series, kid's and pre-teen favorites, specials, original shows, educational programs, news) and local professional sports, including the Chicago Bulls, Chicago Cubs, and the Chicago White Sox.

Wheels TV, 289 Great Road, Acton, MA 01720; *Telephone*: 978-264-4333; *Fax*: 978-264-9547; *Broadcast Day*: 24 hours; *Subscribers*: 75,000,000; *Email*: Contact channel through its web site; *Web site*: http://www.wheelstv.net

Operated by Automotive Networks, LLC and planned for future operation, Wheels TV will be the first-ever, general-interest automotive network and will focus exclusively on automobiles, motorcycles, and trucks. The network will air original and acquired programming that explores the fascination with motor vehicles and will include magazine and lifestyle shows, new vehicle profiles, documentaries, how-to shows, travel, safety and recall alerts, event coverage, news, movies, and television action and comedy series.

The channel's creation, indirectly, can be traced to the late 1980s when the popular *Wild About Wheels* program aired on the Discovery Channel. This first-ever, general-interest automotive entertainment show aired in prime-time for three years on the channel and garnered some of the network's highest ratings. The hit series went on to air in over 100 countries worldwide.

Wine Network, 88 Kearny Street #2100, San Francisco, CA 94108; *Telephone*: 415-772-3601; *Fax*: 415-288-1371; *Launch Date*: September 2004; *Broadcast Day*: 24 hours; *Email*: Contact network through its web site; *Web site*: http://www.winenetwork.tv

The Wine Network airs programming aimed at both the novice and the experienced wine gourmet, including how-to programs on wine basics, travel programs that focus on international wineries, ratings and reviews of new vintages, and related programs on fine dining and culture. Additional programming fare covers related subjects, such as beer and spirits, cigars, food, travel, fashion, health, art and culture, and entertainment.

Wisdom Television, 2481 John Nash Boulevard, P.O. Box 1546, Bluefield, WV 24701; *Telephone*: 304-323-8000; *Fax*: 304-323-2975; *Launch Date*: July 1997; *Broadcast Day*: 24 hours; *Subscribers*: 6,500,000; *Email*: Contact channel through its web site; *Web site*: http://www.wisdommedia.com

Wisdom Television provides information and entertainment to a worldwide audience interested in personal and professional growth, health and wellness, global issues, and a variety of spiritual and intellectual viewpoints. Channel programming includes *Parenting Life* (childcare advice and useful information); *Wisdom at Work* (communication, community, and spirituality in business); *FoodWise* (guide to healthy cooking); and *Wisdom Workshops* (features authors, teachers, and visionaries).

WMax, 1100 Avenue of the Americas, New York, NY 10036; *Telephone*: 212-512-5948; *Fax*: 212-512-1182; *Launch Date*: May 2001; *Broadcast Day*: 24 hours; *Email*: Contact channel through its web site; *Web site*: http://www.cinemax.com

WMax is a multiplexed channel from Cinemax that broadcasts movies aimed at female audiences age 18 to 49, including dramas, romances, and mysteries. WMax Choice airs a specific-genre movie targeted to women each night.

Women's Sports Network (http://www.wsnsports.com) (Planned for future operation)

The Word Network, 20733 West Ten Mile Road, Southfield, MI 48075; *Telephone*: 248-357-4566; *Fax*: 248-350-3422; *Launch Date*: February 2000; *Broadcast Day*: 24 hours; *Subscribers*: 108,000,000; *Email*: Contact network through its web site; *Web site*: http://www.thewordnetwork.org

Sometimes referred to as the Urban Religious Channel, the Word Network broadcasts family-friendly programming throughout the world, including urban ministries, gospel music, interview shows, movies, biographies, religious conventions, and special events. The network broadcasts family-friendly programming aimed at African-Americans audiences across the country and to U.S. Armed Forces viewers around the world.

WorldAsia Television (http://www.worldasia.com) (Planned for future operation)—WorldAsia Television will be America's first English-language, Asian-themed network and will feature fashion, music and music videos, yoga, Feng Shui, holistic health, martial arts, Japanese anime, sports, video games, and lifestyle programs.

World Championship Sports Network (Planned for future operation)

World Cinema, 1111 Stewart Avenue, Bethpage, NY 11714; *Telephone*: 516-803-2300; *Broadcast Day*: 24 hours; *Email*: Contact channel through its web site; *Web site*: http://www.wcinema.com

World Cinema airs new and classic foreign film and television programs, all uncut and commercial-free.

World Colours Television Network (http://worldcolourstv.com) (Planned for future operation)

World Harvest Television Network *see* **Lesea Broadcasting Network**

World Health Digital Network *see* **Health TV Channel, Inc.**

WorldSport HD, 200 Jericho Quadrangle, Jericho, NY 11753; *Telephone*: 516-803-6010; *Launch Date*: July 2003; *Email*: Contact channel through its web site; *Web site*: http://www.voom.com

WorldSport HD is a high definition multiplexed channel from Voom that broadcasts a mix of international sporting events and competitions.

Worship Channel, P.O. Box 428, Safety Harbor, FL 34695; *Telephone*: 877-296-7744; *Email*: Contact channel through its web site; *Web site*: http://www.worship.net

The Worship Channel broadcasts on Sky Angel (http://www.skyangel.com) and creates an atmosphere for personal devotions and worship in the viewer's home. The channel uses scenic videos coupled with traditional hymns and choruses, all overlaid with scripture from God's Holy Word. The videos are incorporated into a program lineup that facilitates Christian growth through Bible study, prayer, and teaching. Special programming includes a daily examination of a select passage of scripture and a weekly sing-along kids' show.

Worship Network *see* **Praise Television**

WTSN *see* **Entertainment Sports Television Network**

X! Channel, 2706 Media Center Drive, Los Angeles, CA 90065; *Telephone*: 323-276-4000; *Fax*: 323-276-4500; *Email*: Contact channel through its web site; *Web site*: http://www.playboy tv.com, http://www.sxtv.com

Available through the Playboy TV Networks, the X! channel (a Spice Entertainment Company) is a pay-per-view service that offers adult-oriented programming.

Yankee Entertainment and Sports Network, The Chrysler Building, 405 Lexington Avenue, 36th Floor, New York, NY 10174; *Telephone*: 646-487-3600; *Fax*: 646-487-3612; *Launch Date*: March 2002; *Broadcast Day*: 24 hours; *Email*: info@yes networktv.com; *Web site*: http://www. yesnetwork.com/index.cfm, http://www.yes networktv.com

The Yankee Entertainment and Sports Network airs New York Yankees baseball, New Jersey Nets basketball, Manchester United soccer, sports news and information, entertainment programming, local events coverage, and college sports to viewers in New York, Connecticut, Pennsylvania, and New Jersey.

Your TV International *see* **Shoma TV**

Youth Sports Broadcasting Channel, P.O. Box 4282, Montebello, CA 90640; *Telephone*: 323-724-1466; *Broadcast Day*: 24 hours

The Youth Sports Broadcasting Channel focuses on all youth sports, age 18 and under. Broadcasts include live and prerecorded sports activities from schools, leagues, parks, playgrounds, and dirt lots from neighborhoods around the country.

Zee TV and **Zee TV USA**, 1615 West Abram Street #200, Arlington, TX 76013; *Telephone*: 817-274-2933; *Broadcast Day*: 24 hours; *Email*: Contact channel through its web site; *Web site*: http://www.i-channel.com

Zee TV and Zee TV USA air on the International Channel and are the most popular satellite channels in India. Both channels are aimed at serving the needs of South Asians living abroad and both channels broadcast news, movies, dramas, children's programs, and talk shows.

Zhong Tian Channel, 1255 Corporate Center Driver #212, Monterey Park, CA 91754; *Telephone*: 323-415-0068; *Launch Date*: 1995; *Broadcast Day*: 24 hours; *Email*: Contact channel through its web site; *Web site*: http://www.i-channel.com

The Zhong Tian Channel airs programming derived from Chinese Television International's Zhong Tian news entertainment and information channel. Located in Taiwan, ZTC is designed to provide the world's 1.2 billion Chinese viewers with the latest news, sports, dramas, variety shows, and general-entertainment programming. ZTC broadcasts to Chinese communities in Hong Kong, Taiwanm Japan, the Philippines, Singapore, Malaysia, Australia, North America, South America, and a large part of the Asia Pacific region.

Canadian Networks

Aboriginal People's Television Network, 339 Portage Avenue, 2nd Floor, Winnipeg, Manitoba R3B 2C3, Canada; *Telephone*: 888-278-8862, 204-947-9331; *Fax*: 204-947-9307; *Launch Date*: September 1999 (as APTN); *Subscribers*: 9,000,000; *Email*: info@aptn.ca; *Web site*: http://www.aptn.ca

The launch of the Aboriginal Peoples Television Network represented a significant milestone for Aboriginal Canada; for the first time in broadcast history, First Nations, Inuit, and Metis people had the opportunity to share their stories with the rest of the world on a national television network dedicated to Aboriginal programming. With documentaries, news, news magazines, dramas, entertainment specials, movies, children's series, cooking shows, public affairs and education programs, APTN offers Canadians a look into the diverse world of Indigenous peoples in Canada.

The CRTC-licensed APTN evolved from Television Northern Canada (TVNC), an Aboriginal television network that was established in 1992 to broadcast Northern and Aboriginal programming from the Yukon to northern Labrador. The service also operates APTN Latin America and APTN USA. Seventy percent of APTN programming originates in Canada, with 60 percent of the programs broadcast in English, 15 percent in French, and 25 percent in a variety of Aboriginal languages. The channel actually consists of two separate feeds, which carry much of the same programs. The Southern feed of APTN is a cable-only specialty service and all cable systems in Canada are required by the CRTC to carry this channel as part of their basic cable package. However, since most cable systems consider APTN to be an unprofitable service with very few viewers, they usually carry the signal in the high region of their frequency spectrum, normally above channel 60. This placement of APTN has rendered the service unavailable on many older television sets where the channels do not reach as high and ignored by many "channel surfers," whose television sets usually return to channel 2 once they reach allocated pay-TV blocks of programming. APTN's Northern feed has its own over-the-air transmitters, and carries most of the same programs as are shown on the Southern feed.

About God (Planned for future operation)—About God will be an English-language service aimed at young Canadian television viewers with shows focusing on spirituality.

Academy Television (Planned for future operation)—Academy Television will be an English-language service that will broadcast formal credit course lectures and documentary style course-related programs, provided in association with Canadian and international colleges and universities.

Access TV (The Education Station), Access Media Group, 3720-76 Avenue, Edmonton, Alberta T6B 2N9, Canada; *Telephone*: 780-440-7777; *Email*: Contact channel through its web site; *Web site*: http://www. accesstv.ca, http://www. accesslearning.con, http://www.chum limited.com

A specialty channel from CHUM Limited, Access TV combines entertainment and education and airs children's programming, first-run movies, dramatic series, quiz shows, documentaries, and talk shows. The channel, in partnership with Alberta Learning, educational institutions and educators, brings multimedia learning opportunities into the home for viewers of all ages. Many of the programs, including all the dramas, are connected to formal courses of study offered by the province's post-secondary institutions and to the formal objectives of Alberta Learning.

Action Channel (Planned for future operation)—the Action Channel will be a 24-hour English-language service focusing on action-oriented programming of all types and targeted to male audiences 18-49.

Adrenaline Drive, 5324 Calgary Trail #200, Edmonton, Alberta T6H 4J8, Canada; *Telephone*: 780-430-2800; *Email*: Contact channel through its web site: *Web site*: http://moviecentral.ca

Adrenaline Drive is part of Movie Central, a specialty channel from Corus Entertainment, that airs action and adventure programs.

Adult Alternative Music Channel (Planned for future operation)—the Adult Alternative Music Channel will be a 24-hour English-language service dedicated to adult alternative music videos and related programming.

Adventure One (Planned for future operation)—Adventure One will be an English-language service devoted entirely to documentaries and human-interest programming that pushes the boundaries of exploration and adventure.

ALL TV (Doragi Television Network) (Planned for future operation)—ALL TV will be an all-Korean channel that will air news and general-entertainment programming.

Alliance Atlantis Broadcasting, Inc., 121 Bloor Street East #1500, Toronto, Ontario M4W 3M5, Canada; *Telephone*: 416-967-1174; *Fax*: 416-960-0971; *Email*: Contact network through its web site; *Web site*: http://www.allianceatlantis.com

Alliance Atlantis Broadcasting is a Canadian broadcaster, creator, and international distributor of filmed entertainment content with significant ownership interests in 18 Canadian specialty channels, including BBC Canada, BBC Kids, Discovery Health Channel, Food Network Canada, HGTV Canada, Historia, History Television, Independent Film Channel Canada, Life Network, National Geographic Channel, One: the Body, Mind and Spirit Channel, Pride Vision, The Score, Scream, Series+, Showcase, Showcase Action, and Showcase Diva.

Alpha Punjabi (Punjabi Channel), 107-12827 76th Avenue, Surrey, British Columbia V3W 2V3, Canada; *Telephone*: 604-590-3510; *Fax*: 604-648-8381; *Email*: Contact channel through its web site; *Web site*: http://www.alphapunjabi.com, http://www. apnatv.net

Alpha Punjabi broadcasts all Punjabi-language programming, including news, arts and entertainment, and public affairs. Its most-watched program is the channel's daily *Punjabi Television News*, the first Punjabi news broadcast in North America.

ANA Canada (Planned for future operation)—ANA Canada will air programming targeted to Arabic-speaking audiences (at least 85 percent of its shows will be in Arabic) and its broadcast fare will be derived primarily from the existing international service of the ANA Television Network.

Animal Planet Canada, P.O. Box 1200, Agincourt, Ontario M1S 5R6, Canada; *Telephone*: 800-370-2332; *Fax*: 416-332-4230; *Launch Date*: September 2001 (in Canada); *Email*: comments@animalplanet.ca; *Web site*: http://www.animalplanet.ca

Jointly owned and operated by Bell Globemedia and the Discovery Networks, Animal Planet Canada is a Canadian Television

Network (CTV) channel that is dedicated to providing entertaining and informative programming that acknowledges the bond between humans and animals. Programming includes original series, documentaries, funny animal videos, search and rescue adventures, high-energy safaris, and general entertainment. Although much of its programming is shared with the American-based Discovery Channel, the Canadian channel produces some of its own programming, including a daily science news program, *Daily Planet.*

Animal World (Planned for future operation)—Animal World will be an English-language service dedicated to animals and their environments. Programming will examine the effect of man's increasing impact on the environment and the ecosystems in which animals live.

Arabic Television Network (Planned for future operation)—the 24-hour Arabic Television Network will air general-interest programming targeting Arab-speaking audiences, with at least 75 percent of its broadcast fare being in Arabic and no more than 10 percent being in English.

Arabic TV (Planned for future operation)—Arabic TV will air general-interest programming with no less than 90 percent of its broadcast fare being in Arabic.

Armed Forces Network (Planned for future operation)—the Armed Forces Network will offer programming that will focus on the armed forces as a central theme. Topics will include world-wide conflicts; the manufacture of weapons; inside the army, navy and air force; history of wars; the men and women behind war; world leaders; religious conflicts; combating terrorism; underground movements; world peace; political warfare; hot beds of war; and the future of war.

Art Channel (Planned for future operation)—the Art Channel will be an English-language service devoted solely to visual art and artists and their impact on and relationship to culture and society. The Art Channel will present entertaining, informational, and instructive programming focusing on the visual arts, including profiles of Canadian artists along with their works and influences; instructional programming relating to learning and access to the visual arts; related talk shows; and coverage of visual arts events.

Arts & Loisirs (the French-language version of America's Arts & Entertainment Network)

arTV, 1400, Boul. Rene—Lévesque Est, Bureau A 53-1, Montreal, Quebec H2L 2M2, Canada; *Telephone*: 514-597-3636; *Fax*: 514-597-3633; *Launch Date*: September 2001; *Email*: Contact channel through its web site; *Web site*: http://www.artv.ca

arTV, originally licensed as La Télé des Arts, is the French-language counterpart of Bravo! and is an arts and culture channel.

Asian Television Network, 130 Pony Drive, Newmarket, Ontario L3Y 7B6, Canada; *Telephone*: 905-836-6460; *Fax*: 905-853-5212; *Broadcast Day*: 24 hours; *Email*: atn@asiantelevision.com; *Web site*: http://www.asiantelevision.com

The Asian Television Network airs programming aimed at the South Asian population in Canada. ATN owns and operates the only CRTC-licensed channel that provides programming in several south Asian languages and in English. Additionally, the network owns and operates three digital specialty language services, two regional language channels, and one Hindi movie channel. Programming includes serials, magazine format shows, movies, entertainment shows, beauty contests, music videos, and a daily news program broadcast in Hindi, Punjabi, Gujarati, Urdu, and other South Asian languages. Brand channels include: ATN Alpha Punjabi (a Punjabi-language channel that features serials, dramas, movies, and news); ATN—ARY

(24-hour Urdu language channel that provides family entertainment, news, sporting events, comedies, game shows, fashion, music videos, serials, and dramas); ATN B4U Hindi Movie Channel (a 24-hour movie channel); ATN — Kairali (a 24-hour Malayalam channel); ATN — Sony (a partnership that airs Sony Television programs); the ATN Tamil Channel (Tamil programming from South Asia, including movies, serials, religious programs, Tamil news, music and variety shows, Canadian community events, sporting events, and talent shows); ATN Urdu Channel; and ATN ZEE TV.

Astral Media Communications, BCE Place, 181 Bay Street #100, P.O. Box 787, Toronto, Ontario M5J 2T3, Canada; 2100, rue Sainte-Catherine Ouest, Bureau 1000, Montréal, Québec H3H 2T3, Canada; *Telephone*: 514-939-5000; *Fax*: 514-939-1515; *Launch Date*: 1993 (as The Movie Network); *Broadcast Day*: 24 hours; *Email*: Contact through web site; *Web site*: http://www.astral.com, http://www.astralmedia.com

Astral Media Communications is Canada's largest operator of English- and French-language specialty, pay, and pay-per-view television services and currently owns, or co-owns, 19 channels. The company is the largest private sector supporter of Canadian feature films and owns 24 radio stations, including 16 French-language FM stations in Québec and six FM and two AM English-language stations in the Atlantic Provinces. Specialty channels include Canal D, Canal Indigo, Canal Vie, Family Channel Canada, Historia, The Movie Network, MoviePix, MusiMax, MusiquePlus, Series+, Super Écran, TéléToon, Viewer's Choice Canada, VRAK Television, and Ztele (or TeleZ).

Atlantic Satellite Network, P.O. Box 1653, 2885 Robie Street, Halifax, Nova Scotia B3J 2Z4, Canada; *Telephone*: 902-453-4000; *Fax*: 902-454-3302; *Email*: programming@ctv.ca, atvnews@ctv.ca; *Web site*: http://www.asn.ca

The Atlantic Satellite Network is the Atlantic Television System's sister satellite station covering Atlantic Canada. Through cable and satellite distribution, ASN is broadcast around the Maritime region and throughout the country, reaching many Atlantic Canadians living outside the region. ASN's most popular program is *Breakfast Television*, a 90-minute show that features interviews, entertainment segments, and news. The show focuses on local artists and hosts daily musical performances from emerging and established Maritime musicians. ASN also broadcasts more than 25 hours per week of educational programming from universities, community colleges, high schools, and other learning institutions. The network also shows popular American programs, such as *Relic Hunter*, *Roswell*, the *Star Trek* series, *Whose Line is it Anyway*, *Buffy the Vampire Slayer*, and *7th Heaven*, as well as movies.

Atlantic Television System, P.O. Box 1653, Halifax B3J 2Z4, Canada; *Telephone*: 902-453-4000; *Fax*: 902-454-3202; *Email*: Contact channel through its web site; *Web site*: http://www.atv.ca

A wholly-owned Canadian Television Network affiliate, the Atlantic Television System broadcasts news and local information programming throughout the Maritime region. Each week, ATV produces 27 hours of local programming, including *Live at Five*, the *ATV Evening News*, and *Breakfast Television*. With three stations throughout the region, ATV reaches viewers across Nova Scotia, New Brunswick, and Prince Edward Island. ATV also broadcasts many of Canada's favorite shows, including *CSI: Miami*, *The Osbournes*, *Law & Order*, and *Third Watch*.

Auction Channel (Planned for future operation) — the Auction Channel will be an English-language service featuring live auctions intended to provide Canadians access to the world of collectibles and aims to become the channel for serious collectors. The channel will unite live television and internet auctions, and its programming will include real-time and delayed auctions, fixed-priced dealer e-commerce, business-to-business dealer e-commerce, as well as news and community information.

Auto Channel (Planned for future operation)—the Auto Channel's programming will focus on all things dealing with cars and will feature experts who will inform, sell, trade, repair, compare, build, rebuild, and provide consumer alert information on all cars.

Automobile Channel (Planned for future operation)—the 24-hour Automobile Channel will be an English-language service dedicated to those Canadians devoted to their cars and trucks. Programming will feature informative material on repairs, transportation safety, highway advisories, current news, the latest auto design, antique cars, and consumer trends.

Aviation TV (Planned for future operation)—Aviation TV will be an English-language service dedicated to all aspects of flight and aviation including airplanes and flyers.

BBC Canada, 121 Bloor Street East #200, Toronto, Ontario M4W 3M5, Canada; *Telephone*: 866-813-3222, 416-967-3249; *Fax*: 416-967-0044; *Launch Date*: September 2001; *Email*: Contact channel through its web site; *Web site*: http://www.bbccanada.com

A partnership between BBC Worldwide Ltd. and Alliance Atlantis Broadcasting, BBC Canada airs British comedy and dramatic programs from the British Broadcasting Corporation. The service also offers BBC World and BBC Kids (http://www.bbckids.ca), which airs children's educational and entertainment programs.

Bell Globemedia, Inc., 9 Channel Nine Court, Scarborough, Ontario M1S 4B5, Canada; *Telephone*: 416-332-5700; *Fax*: 416-332-5022; *Email*: Contact company through web site; *Web site*: http://www.bellglobemedia.ca

Bell Globemedia is a multi-media company, comprised of CTV Inc. (Canada's premier private broadcaster) and *The Globe and Mail* (the leading daily national newspaper). The brand channels it owns (wholly or in part) include Animal Planet Canada, CTV Newsnet, CTV Travel, Discovery Channel, Discovery Civilization, ESPN Classic Canada, NHL Network, Outdoor Life Network, RDS, Report on Business Television, Talk TV, The Comedy Network, TSN, and Viewer's Choice Canada.

Big Pop TV (Planned for future operation)—Big Pop TV will be an English-language service dedicated to the pop music format and will focus on Top 40 pop music videos.

Biography Channel Canada, 545 Lake Shore Boulevard West, Toronto, Ontario M5V 1A3, Canada; *Telephone*: 866-260-0033; *Launch Date*: September 2001; *Broadcast Day*: 24 hours; *Email*: info@thebiographychannel.ca; *Web site*: http://www.the biographychannel.ca

A venture between Rogers Cable, Shaw Cable, and the A&E Networks, the Biography Channel Canada is similar to America's Biography Channel with the exception that it focuses on Canadian content. Each evening is devoted to a different theme, with daytime programming consisting of documentaries and movies. American biographic themes originate from A&E while Canadian biographies originate from CHUM Limited and the Canadian Broadcasting Corporation.

Book Television: The Channel, 299 Queen Street, Toronto, Ontario M5V 2Z5, Canada; *Telephone*: 416-591-7400; *Fax*: 416-591-0080; *Email*: Contact channel through its web site; *Web site*: http:// www.booktelevision.com, http://www.chum limited.com

Owned and operated by CHUM Limited, Book Television: The Channel focuses on words and how they affect our lives through novels, comics, movies, erotica, the media, advertising, street slang, and music lyrics. Popular segments on the channel include *Word News* (which airs every hour) and *The Word This Week* (which airs weekly).

BPM TV (Beats Per Minute) (Dance Channel), 115 Gordon Baker Road, 8th Floor, Toronto, Ontario M2H 3R6, Canada; *Telephone*: 416-756-2404; *Fax*: 416-756-5526; *Email*: Contact channel through its web site; *Web site*: http://www.bpmtv.com

Owned and operated by Stornoway Communications Limited, BPM TV broadcasts programs that feature the worldwide popularity of dance in all its forms and various genres. It is the only channel focusing exclusively on the culture of movement (language, activity, fashion, dance), dance music (a previously untapped genre of music), and music videos.

Bravo! Canada, 299 Queen Street West, Toronto, Ontario M5V 2Z5, Canada; *Telephone*: 416-591-5757; *Fax*: 416-591-7482; *Launch Date*: January 1995; *Email*: Contact channel through its web site; *Web site*: http://www.bravo.ca

Bravo! Canada is a CHUM Limited specialty channel that focuses on all aspects of the arts, including music, theater, ballet, literature, drama, visual arts, modern dance, opera, architecture, and artist profiles. Similar to America's Bravo channel, Bravo! Canada differentiates itself by focusing not only on the arts, but by airing movies and popular television shows, such as *Sex and the City* and *Beggars and Choosers*.

Bridges TV (Planned for future operation)

Business Channel (Planned for future operation)—the Business Channel will be an English-language service dedicated to live and taped coverage of annual general meetings and other corporate events that pertain to the conduct of business of public and private corporations, with a focus on Canadian businesses. The channel will also provide a limited amount of French-language programming.

Cable Public Affairs Channel, P.O. Box 81099, Ottawa, Ontario K1P 1B1, Canada; 1750-45 O'Connor Street, Ottawa, Ontario ON K1P 1A4, Canada; *Telephone*: 877-287-2722, 613-364-1160; *Fax*: 613-567-2749; *Launch Date*: 1992 (as the Cable Parliamentary Channel); *Broadcast Day*: 24 hours; *Subscribers*: 10,000,000; *Email*: comments@cpac.ca; *Web site*: http://www.cpac.ca

Following the format of America's C-SPAN, the Cable Public Affairs Channel provides comprehensive coverage of national politics and current affairs, including specials, documentary reports, and unedited, unfiltered coverage of Parliamentary proceedings, Supreme Court hearings, and political events. The channel broadcasts from every province and airs elections, political conventions, conferences, speeches, and public affairs events. The channel is available in English and French and is streamed online through its web site. CPAC is Canada's only national, non-commercial, bilingual network specializing in long-form, public affairs programming. The channel is funded primarily by Canada's cable companies, receives no government funding, and is not affiliated with any government department or agency.

CPAC was created by the cable industry in the fall of 1992 as the Cable Parliamentary Channel and was an experimental service whose primary mandate was to carry House of Commons proceedings. In 1995 the channel was licensed by the CRTC as a national programming entity and in 1996 it relaunched as the Cable Public Affairs Channel, to reflect an expanded schedule of public affairs programming.

The CPAC time line includes: 1977 (Canada becomes the first country in the world to televise live Parliamentary debates, beginning with the Speech from the Throne by Queen Elizabeth II); 1986 (the Canadian cable television industry proposes enhancing the Parliamentary Channel to include public affairs programming); 1988 (the CBC and the cable industry join forces to form the Canadian Parliamentary Channel, which replaced the current Parliamentary Channel);

1991 (due to budget constraints, the CBC stops funding the channel and the House of Commons begins paying for satellite transmission of its proceedings, at an annual cost to the taxpayers of $2 million); 1992 (a group of 30 Canadian cable companies forms to distribute the service (by now known as the Cable Parliamentary Channel) and in October takes over operation of the channel); 1995 (the channel is granted a seven-year renewal of its broadcasting license, distributes live coverage of House of Commons proceedings daily, and fills the rest of its schedule with conferences, speeches, and proceedings from provincial legislatures); 1996 (the channel relaunches as the Cable Public Affairs Channel, to reflect its increased coverage of public affairs programming); and 2002 (the CRTC renews CPAC's broadcasting license for a seven-year period, making it a mandatory channel for most cable and satellite providers in both official languages).

CablePulse24, 299 Queen Street West, Toronto, Ontario M5V 2Z5, Canada; *Telephone*: 416-591-7849; *Fax*: 416-593-6397; *Launch Date*: January 1998; *Broadcast Day*: 24 hours; *Email*: news@pulse24.com; *Web site*: http://www.pulse24.com

CablePulse24 is a CHUM Limited specialty channel and is Canada's first regional round-the-clock English-language news and information channel, including time, date, weather, traffic, headline news, sports scores, and updated stock market quotations. CP24, like CTV Newsnet, makes use of an enhanced screen, showing market data, weather information, and live shots from Ontario Ministry of Transportation cameras.

Canadian Broadcasting Corporation, 181 Queen Street, Ottawa, Ontario K1P 1K9, Canada, P.O. Box 500 Station A, Toronto, Ontario M5W 1E6, Canada; *Telephone*: 866-306-4636, 416-205-3700 (Toronto), 613-288-6000 (Ottawa); *Fax*: 613-724-5074 (Ottawa); *Broadcast Day*: 24 hours; *Email*: Contact network through its web site; *Web site*: http://www.cbc.ca

Before the existence of television, the Canadian Broadcasting Corporation was initially created as the Crown Corporation in 1936 by an Act of Parliament, which had acted as the result of the findings of a Royal Commission that was concerned about the growing American influence in radio. Today the CBC operates much like the British Broadcasting Corporation and offers viewers and listeners Canadian-grown programs. The publicly-financed CBC operates four radio networks (CBC Radio One and CBC Radio Two in English, La Chaîne Culturelle FM and La Radio de Radio-Canada in French) and two television networks (one in each language) covering Canadian news, information, and entertainment. In addition, the CBC operates cable television channels, satellite channels, and a digital pay audio service (Galaxie) with 45 music channels. Public funds provide the majority of the CBC's operating budget, while it also generates revenue through advertising and subscription fees. The CBC is subject to the regulations of the Canadian Radio-Television and Telecommunications Commission (CRTC) and is accountable to the Parliament of Canada through the Minister of Canadian Heritage.

CBC's television services include: English and French Television networks; television services for Canada's North, in English, French and eight aboriginal languages; two specialty cable television channels, CBC Newsworld in English and Le Réseau de l'information in French; and three specialty-cable services in partnership with other Canadian broadcasters and producers, Télé des arts, Land and Sea, and The Canadian Documentary Channel. CBC's radio services include four commercial-free national radio networks, CBC Radio One and CBC Radio Two in English, and La Première Chaîne and La Chaîne culturelle in French; radio services for Canada's North, in English, French and eight Aboriginal languages; a pay-audio service, Galaxie, with 45 channels of continuous music; and an international short-wave radio service, Radio-Canada International. CBC

Newsworld (http://www.newsworld.cbc.ca) is Canada's English-language, 24-hour, all-news channel and followed America's Cable News Network as the second such network in the world when it went on the air in August 1989. CBC Newsworld's financing is entirely separate from that of CBC and its revenues derive from advertising and cable fees. CBC Newsworld relies heavily on international sources for its broadcasting content, including local CBC reporters, CBC national news, and internationally-packaged programming from the BBC, ITN, and CNN.

The Canadian Broadcasting Corporation time line includes: 1901 (first transatlantic wireless signal is broadcasts from Cornwall to Newfoundland); 1922 (first licensing of private commercial stations); 1927 (first national broadcast: July 1, Diamond Jubilee of Confederation); 1930 (Canadian Radio League is formed, first Canadian television experiments are conducted); 1932 (the Canadian Broadcasting Act creates the Canadian Radio Broadcasting Commission [CRBC]); 1936 (the Canadian Broadcasting Act replaces the CRBC with the CBC); 1938 (farm broadcasts begin on the French radio network); 1939 (farm broadcasts begin on the English radio network); 1941 (formal opening of the CBC News Service and one of its first special broadcasts include a Winston Churchill speech from the House of Commons in Ottawa); 1945 (official opening of CBC International Service, which is renamed Radio Canada International in 1972); 1946 (opening of the first CBC FM stations in Toronto and Montreal); 1952 (opening of the Canadian TV service: CBFT Montreal (bilingual) and CBLT Toronto (English); CBC supplies radio programs to Canadian troops in Korea; first Canadian urban cable TV is launched in London, Ontario; 1955 (first telecast of the opening of Parliament); 1958 (the new Broadcasting Act establishes the Board of Broadcast Governors (BBG) to regulate all Canadian broadcasting; first coast-to-coast live TV broadcast with completion of the microwave network from Nova Scotia to British Columbia; CBC Northern Radio Service is established); 1961 (CTV Network opens); the CBC issues proposals for satellite use in Canada); 1965 (the first regular CBC stereo broadcasts from a single station in Winnipeg); 1966 (color television introduced in Canada); 1967 (first taped television in the North); 1968 (first televised national debate among Canadian political party leaders); 1969 (Radio-Québec is established; CBC discontinues tobacco advertising); 1970 (CRTC introduces a mandate that broadcasting content must be 60 percent for public and private television; TV Ontario is established; the CRTC issues the CBC is first network license); 1971 (the first French-language private television network (TVA) begins operations); 1972 (the Anik satellite is launched and the CBC rents three channels for radio and television network distribution; CBC's International Service is renamed Radio Canada International); 1973 (the first live television signal is broadcast to the North, via the Anik satellite; official opening of La Maison de Radio-Canada in Montreal; Access Alberta is established); 1974 (the French FM stereo network begins broadcasting; the CBC discontinues most radio commercials); 1975 (the English FM stereo network opens); 1976 (the CRTC is renamed the Canadian Radio-Television and Telecommunications Commission; the CBC is host broadcaster for the Summer Olympics in Montreal); 1978 (the first television production facilities are established in the North at Yellowknife); 1979 (live television coverage of the House of Commons begins via satellite and cable: 1980 (the B.C. Knowledge Network is established); 1981 (the CBC introduces closed captioning on Canadian television programs); 1983 (the first general-channel pay-television operation begins); 1984 (the first specialty-channel pay television operation begins); 1986 (the second private French television channel (Quatre Saisons) begins operations in Montreal; a commemorative postage stamp is issued for the CBC's 50th anniversary); 1987 (the CRTC licenses 10 new specialty channels (CBC All-News Channel, VisionTV, YTV, MeteoMedia: Weather Now, TV5, Le Canal

Famille, Musique Plus, Le Réseau des sports, MétéoMedia: Mété-Instant, and The Family Channel Canada; the CRTC also authorizes distribution of The Sports Network and MuchMusic on basic cable); 1988 (the international French-language channel TV5 starts broadcasting in Canada); 1989 (the CBC English all-news channel, Newsworld, is launched; the French private channel, Le Réseau des Sports, begins broadcasting); 1994 (the CBC, in partnership with Power Broadcasting Inc., launches two new specialty channels to the United States: Trio and Newsworld International); 1995 (CBC's French language all-news channel is launched; the CBC is granted a license to operate a new audio music service called Galaxie); 1997 (Galaxie, the first pay audio service delivered, around-the-clock, via direct-to-home satellite and cable, is launched; the CBC files applications for six new specialty services: Le Réseau des Arts (arts, performance, and cultural programming), Le Réseau de l'économie (Canadian and international economic activity), Le Réseau de l'histoire (Canadian and world history), Land & Sea (serving the needs and interest of Canadians living in rural areas), Télé classique (the best of Canadian and international television over the years), and The People Channel (focus on historical figures and contemporary characters); and 1998 (the International Olympic Committee awards CBC, in partnership with NetStar, the broadcast rights to the next five Olympic Games; the CRTC approves Canada-wide broadcasting to the French-language network, TVA).

Canadian Consumer Channel (Planned for future operation)—the Canadian Consumer Channel will be an English-language service dedicated to providing Canadians with timely, useful information about the goods and services they consume on a daily basis. The channel will air unbiased buying advice on major products in all categories; ratings on brands in all categories; information on product repair history and recalls as well as environmental concerns; and in-depth investigative reports on financial services, employment services, travel packages, and other services of interest to Canadian consumers.

Canadian Distance Education Network *see* **Knowledge Network**

Canadian Forces Radio and Television, 245 Cooper Street, Ottawa, Ontario K2P 0G2, Canada; *Telephone*: 613-996-6826; *Fax*: 613-992-2362; *Broadcast Day*: 24 hours; *Email*: Contact channel through its web site; *Web site*: http://www.cfpsa.com/

Owned by the Canadian Forces Personnel Support Agency, Canadian Forces Radio and Television is Canada's counterpart to America's AFRTS, and distributes English and French television services via satellite round-the-clock to Canadian Forces units serving overseas. The programs available on CFRT originate from all major domestic television services in Canada, and include newscasts, entertainment programs, and sporting events. CFRT's schedule is determined mainly by requests and needs from the personnel who receive its service and is not available within Canada.

Canadian Home Shopping Network *see* **The Shopping Channel**

Canadian Learning Television, 3720-76 Avenue, Edmonton, Alberta T6B 2N9, Canada; *Telephone*: 780-440-7777; *Fax*: 780-440-1656; *Launch Date*: September 1999; *Email*: Contact channel through its web site: *Web site*: http://www.clt.ca

Owned and operated by CHUM Limited, Canadian Learning Television is Canada's only national educational television specialty service and offers a mix of educational and entertainment programs. CLT is a national version of Access Alberta and its programming is shared with provincial educational broadcasters. In addition to programs aimed at educating its viewers, the channel also shows movies, game shows, and infomercials.

Canadian Science Channel (Planned for future operation)—the Canadian Science Channel will be operated by Canadian Television Network, Inc. and will focus on science and science-related topics.

Canadian Television Network, P.O. Box 9, Station O, Scarborough, Ontario M4A 2M9, Canada; 9 Channel Nine Court, Scarborough, Ontario M1S 4B5, Canada; *Telephone*: 416-332-5000; *Fax*: 416-332-4230; *Launch Date*: 1961; *Email*: Contact network through its web site; *Web site*: http://www.ctv.ca

Owned by Bell Globemedia, the Canadian Television Network is a Canadian broadcast communications company with conventional television and specialty-channel operations across Canada, reaching 99 percent of English-speaking Canadian households. Through its specialty channels, CTV offers a wide range of news, sports, information, and entertainment programming. CTV Inc. also owns the Atlantic Satellite Network, a satellite television service in the Maritimes and Newfoundland and Labrador. One of its early highlights occurred in 1972 when CTV launched *Canada AM*, which became the prototype for ABC's *Good Morning America*.

CTV's specialty channels include CTV Newsnet (Canada's 24-hour headline news channel); Report on Business Television (Canada's all-business news network); TalkTV (an all-talk specialty channel); The Comedy Network (Canada's first 24-hour network dedicated to comedy); TSN (The Sports Network, the highest-rated Canadian specialty channel); RDS (Canada's first 24-hour French-language all-sports channel); the award-winning Discovery Channel; and the Outdoor Life Network (Canada's adventure destination for outdoor enthusiasts). CTV owns a minority interest in Viewer's Choice Canada, CTV Travel (a round-the-clock travel channel, equivalent to America's Travel Channel), Animal Planet Canada, Discovery Civilization, ESPN Classic Canada, and the NHL Network.

The Canadian Television Network Ltd. was incorporated in 1961 as Canada's first private television network. Unlike other North American networks, CTV has no owned and operated stations and controls no production facilities. Instead, the network consists of major independent stations located in cities throughout Canada. Although CTV has grown to become one of the most popular Canadian networks (with over 20 percent of the English-speaking audience), it has been accused of getting high ratings by airing American imports in prime time and relegating its few inexpensive Canadian productions to off-peak hours.

CTV's network structure evolved in three distinct phases. From 1961 to 1965, the network was controlled by its founder, Spencer Caldwell, who initially planned to supply affiliates with 10 hours of programming per week. Gradually he had hoped to increase the weekly broadcast hours until CTV would rival the Canadian Broadcasting Corporation. His expansion plans failed for three primary reasons: he underestimated start-up costs and was forced to borrow from affiliate stations; his agreements with the affiliates hindered network growth since CTV was required to compensate the affiliates if it could not sell all its air time; and since CTV could only supply 10 hours of programming per week, the affiliates were forced to seek other outlets to fill their air time.

In 1965 and on the verge of bankruptcy, Caldwell sold out to the affiliates. Until 1993 CTV operated as a cooperative, with each affiliate being a shareholder in the network. By this time, the network was providing over 39 hours of programming per week and affiliates could no longer demand compensation for unsold air time. While workable initially, this structure introduced new problems with broadcast operations: each affiliate served varied markets and held different views of programming needs based on their viewer demands; as major local independents, the affiliates derived as much profit from local market dominance as from network affiliation and they focused more on their own profitability rather than the network's; although larger affiliates attracted a larger share of the audience and contributed proportionally more to network profits, they had only one vote and could be overruled on programming decisions by smaller affiliates; some shareholders acquired more than one affiliate but were restricted to a single vote, and some shareholders owned stations unaffiliated with CTV and sometime competed directly with CTV for program acquisition and network share. These forces worked together to stop CTV's growth as a network, which hindered its ability to produce Canadian content, as dictated under the Broadcasting Act.

The network's third corporate structure began in January 1993. CTV currently operates under the Canadian Business Corporations Act and consists of seven shareholders who have each invested $2 million into the network. The network provides 42 hours of programming per week and purchases air time from affiliates for a fixed annual sum. This structure brings CTV closer to the American network model, although CTV still has no owned and operated stations.

Affiliate channels include CTV NewsNet (http://news.ctv.ca), CTV SportNet (http://www. ctvsportsnet.ca), and CTV Travel (the English-language counterpart to Canal Évasion), which segments its programming by day: *Mystery Mondays* (takes viewers to some of the world's most mysterious and unusual places); *Casino Crazy* (airs on Tuesdays and shows viewers the glitz and glamour of the world's greatest casinos); *Far Out* (airs on Wednesdays and takes viewers around the world to find the weirdest and wackiest people, places, and cultural practices); *Travel Goes Hollywood* (airs on Thursdays and shows documentaries about moviemaking and favorite movies); *Culture Shock* (airs on Fridays and takes viewers around the world in search of the most remote and unique cultures); Saturday night programming focuses on male viewers and airs programs of interest to them, such as poker, golf, fishing, big buildings, and super fast motorcycles); and Sunday night programming focuses on the entire family.

Canal D (Documentary Channel), 2100 rue Sainte-Catherine Ouest, Bureau 800, Montréal, Québec H3H 2T3, Canada; *Telephone*: 514-939-3150; *Fax*: 514-939-3151; *Launch Date*: January 1995; *Email*: Contact channel through its web site; *Web site*: http://www.canald.com

Canal D, an Astral Media Communications specialty channel, is the French-Canadian counterpart to A&E and airs French-language documentaries that focus on the latest discoveries, in addition to comedies, dramas, and movies.

Canal Évasion (Escape Channel), 1205 Avenue Papineau #350, Montreal, Quebec H2K 4R2, Canada; *Telephone*: 514-590-0050; *Fax*: 514-590-0146; *Launch Date*: January 2000; *Email*: info@canalevasion.com; *Web site*: http://www.canalevasion.com

Owned by Serdy Communication Inc., Canal Évasion is a French-language travel channel (its English-language counterpart is CTV Travel).

Canal Indigo, 2100 rue Sainte-Catherine Ouest, Bureau 1000, Montréal, Québec H3H 2T3, Canada; *Telephone*: 514-939-5090; *Fax*: 514-939-5098; *Broadcast Day*: 24 hours; *Email*: Contact channel through its web site; *Web site*: http://www.canalindigo.com

Canal Indigo, an Astral Media Communications channel, broadcasts French-language pay-per-view movies, specials, and sporting events, all commercial-free. Viewer's Choice owns 40 percent of the channel and is the largest shareholder and managing partner of Canal Indigo.

Le Canal Nouvelles, 1600, boul. de Maisonneuve Est, Montreal, Quebec H2L 4P2, Canada; *Telephone*: 514-790-6688; *Fax*: 514-526-4857; *Launch Date*: 1997; *Broadcast Day*: 24 hours; *Email*: Contact channel through its web site; *Web site*: http://reseau.tva.ca/cgi-bin/tva.cgi?08- lcn_info.shtml

Owned by Groupe TVA, Inc., Le Canal Nouvelles (more commonly known as LCN) is a private French-language news service and is a counterpart to CTV Newsnet. LCN's broadcast format is to air four 15-minute news segments per hour with updated headlines being shown at the bottom of the screen.

Canal Plaisir (http://www.10network.com-/canal-plaisir/) (Planned for future operation)—owned by Ten Broadcasting Inc., the 24-hour Canal Plaisir will be a French-language specialty channel that focuses on adult entertainment programming, including movies, a live call-in show, talk shows, educational programming, and other sex-related topics.

Canal Savoir (Knowledge Channel), 4750 Avenue Henri-Julien, Bureau 100, (Local 0058), Montreal, Quebec H2T 3E4, Canada; *Telephone*: 888-640-2626, 514-841-2626; *Fax*: 514-284-9363; *Email*: info@canal.qc.ca; *Web site*: http://www.canal.qc.ca

Canal Savoir is a non-profit organization that owns and operates an educational television channel that provides remote telelearning services to its viewers. The channel incorporates various educational institutions and universities, all in an effort to deliver quality distance learning programs that allow viewers to earn college-level credits.

Canal Vie (Le Canal Vie) (Life Channel), 2100 Rue Sainte-Catherine Ouest, Bureau 700, Montreal, Quebec H3H 2T3, Canada; *Telephone*: 514-939-3150; *Fax*: 514-939-3151; *Launch Date*: September 1997; *Email*: Contact channel through its web site; *Web site*: http://www.canalvie.com

Canal Vie is a French-language Astral Media Communications specialty channel that airs programs aimed primarily at the female audience and is the joint counterpart of the Life Network, Food Network Canada, and the digital service Discovery Health, showing programs similar to those found on those three services.

Canal Z, 1717 boul. René Lévesque Est, Montréal, Quebec H2L 4E8, Canada; *Telephone*: 514-529-3233; *Fax*: 514-529-3236; *Launch Date*: January 2000; *Broadcast Day*: 24 hours; *Email*: ztele@ztele.com; *Web site*: http://www.ztele.com

Owned by Astral Media Communications, Canal Z is a French-language specialty channel aimed at the male 18-49 audience that features programs on science and technology, space exploration, the paranormal, science fiction, computer science, and more.

CanWest Global System, 3100 CanWest Global Place, 201 Portage Avenue, Winnipeg, Manitoba R3B 3L7, Canada; *Telephone*: 204-956-2025; *Fax*: 204-947-9841; *Email*: Contact company through its web site; *Web site*: http://www.canwestglobal.com, http://www.canadacom/globaltv/

Owned by CanWest Global Communications Corporation, the CanWest Global System is a third service within the Canadian Broadcasting System and is Canada's largest private sector broadcaster. Each owned and operated station is licensed as an independent entity and its five stations reach 16 of the largest English-language markets in Canada, a potential audience of 13 million viewers. CGS has achieved ratings and financial success by targeting its programming to the 18-49 market with such shows as *Survivor*, *Friends*, *The Simpsons*, *Will & Grace*, the reality series *Popstars*, and *Train 48*.

CanWest Global owns and operates CH Hamilton (http://www.canada.com/ hamilton/chtv), CH Vancouver Island (http://www.canada.com/victoria/chtv), and the multi-lingual CH Montreal (http://www.canada.com/montreal/chtv), independent stations with a strong presence in the local markets they serve and with distinct program schedules, separate from the Global Television Network. CanWest also owns CHBC Kelowna (http://www.chbc.com) in British Columbia and CKRD Red Deer (http:// www.canada.com/reddeer/rdtv) in Alberta, both of which are operated as CBC affiliates.

Specialty channels operated by CanWest include: Cool TV (focuses on the world of jazz); DejaView (airs popular television shows from the 1960s, 1970s, and 1980s); Fox Sports World Canada (covers the entire international sporting scene, including cricket, Premier League soccer, and Aussie Rules football); Lonestar (airs classic westerns of the past, such as *Bonanza*, *Rawhide*, and the *Big Valley*); Men TV (broadcasts programming related to men's health, lifestyle and fashion, casino life, cooking show, and leisure series); Mystery (initially planned to be called *13th Street*) airs thrillers, suspense, horrors, and police dramas; Prime TV (a 24-hour national channel that targets an adult audience looking for quality entertainment and information programming, with shows like *M*A*S*H**, *Murder She Wrote*, *All in the Family*, and *The Cosby Show*); and Xtreme Sports (airs high-voltage xtreme sporting events from around the world).

Caribbean & African Network (Planned for future operation)—the 24-hour Caribbean & African Network will broadcasts 90 percent of its Caribbean-themed programs in English

Celebration: Vision Inspired Music (Planned for future operation)—Celebration: Vision Inspired Music will be an English-language service dedicated to religious, spiritual, and inspirational themes.

Celtic Country (Planned for future operation)—the 24-hour Celtic Country channel will be an English-language music video service dedicated to country, Celtic, and popular Maritime (Nova Scotia, New Brunswick, Prince Edward Island, Newfoundland and the Gaspé region of Quebec) music and music-related programming.

Challenge TV (Planned for future operation)—Challenge TV will be an English-language service that will broadcast old and new game shows.

Christian Channel (Planned for future operation)—the Christian Channel will be an English-language service that will provide religious programming from a variety of Christian perspectives dealing with a mix of spiritual, religious, and humanitarian topics.

CHUM Limited, 299 Queen Street West, Toronto, Ontario M5V 2Z5, Canada; *Telephone*: 416-591-5757; *Fax*: 416-591-7465; *Broadcast Day*: 24 hours; *Email*: Contact company through its web site; *Web site*: http://www.chumlimited.com

Available in over 120 countries worldwide, CHUM Limited is one of Canada's leading media companies and content providers, owns and operates 30 radio stations, eight local television stations, and 18 specialty channels, as well as an environmental music distribution division. CHUM's local television stations include Citytv (Toronto), Citytv (Vancouver), The New VR (Barrie), The New RO (Ottawa and the National Capital Region), The New PL (London), The New NX (Wingham), The New WI (Windsor) and The New VI (Victoria and Vancouver Island).

The CHUM Limited historical time line includes: 1954 (under its original name, York Broadcasters Limited, CHUM buys Toronto radio station CHUM-AM; in 1957 the station is reformatted and becomes Canada's first Top Forty 24-hour rock station; this purchase marks the start of the creation of the CHUM broadcasting empire); 1969 (CHUM becomes a Muzak franchise holder with the purchase of The Associated Broadcasting Corporation, now known as CHUM Satellite Services; CHUM becomes the majority stockholder of CKVR-TV, the largest privately owned CBC affiliate in Canada); 1978 (CHUM acquires Toronto television station Citytv, Canada's first commercial UHF station); 1984 (CHUM launches MuchMusic, Canada's first 24-hour, 7-day-a-week music station, which is now considered a national force in the growth and support of Canadian music); 1986 (CHUM launches

MusiquePlus, its French counterpart to MuchMusic); 1993 (CHUM becomes the first Canadian broadcaster in Canada to own more than one AM and FM station in a market); 1994 (CHUM Radio Network becomes the first news/talk network supplying programs to CHUM owned and non-CHUM stations alike); 1995 (CHUM launches Bravo! Canada; CHUM re-launches ACCESS — The Education Station); 1997 (CHUM launches MusiMax, Canada's French-language adult contemporary music station; SPACE: The Imagination Station, Canada's English-language science fiction, science fact, speculation, and fantasy channel launches); 1998 (CablePulse24 launches, Canada's first regional 24-hour-a-day English-language news and information channel; MuchMoreMusic launches, bringing music fans adult contemporary music videos, international music specials, documentaries, movies, and original programming); 1999 (CHUM launches Canadian Learning Television and Star! The Entertainment Information Channel, Canada's first specialty television service dedicated to the world of showbiz news and information); 2001 (CHUM launches FashionTelevisionChannel, BookTelevision: The Channel, CourtTV Canada, Drive-In Classics, SexTV: The Channel, MuchVibe, and MuchLoud); and 2004 (CHUM agrees to buy Craig Media).

CHUM Limited specialty channels include: ACCESS TV (The Education Station) (60 percent), Book Television: The Channel (60 percent), Bravo! Canada, CablePulse24 (70 percent), Canadian Learning Television (CLT) (60 percent), Court TV Canada (60 percent), Drive-In Classics, FashionTelevisionChannel Canada, MuchLoud, MuchMoreMusic, MuchMoreRetro, MuchMusic, MuchVibe, MusiMax (50 percent), MusiquePlus (50 percent), SexTV: The Channel, SPACE: The Imagination Station, and Star! The Entertainment Information Channel.

Classical Channel (Planned for future operation) — the 24-hour Classical Channel will be an English-language music video service dedicated to classical music videos and related programming.

Classics TV (Planned for future operation) — Classics TV will be an English-language service devoted to broadcasting timeless and classic popular television and film programming from Canada and around the world.

Collectors Network (Planned for future operation) — the Collectors Network will be an English-language service devoted to programming focusing exclusively on the world of collecting, collections, auctions, and the preservation and exhibition of collections.

The Comedy Network Canada, 9 Channel Nine Court, Scarborough, Ontario M1S 4B5, Canada, P.O. Box 9, Station O, Toronto, Ontario M4A 2M9, Canada; *Telephone*: 416-332-5300 (Scarborough), 416-299-2626 (Toronto); *Fax*: 416-332-5301 (Scarborough), 416-299-2653 (Toronto); *Launch Date*: October 1997; *Email*: mail@thecomedynetwork.ca; *Web site*: http://www. .thecomedynetwork.com

Owned by Bell Globemedia, The Comedy Network Canada is the country's counterpart to America's Comedy Central and airs many of Comedy Central's programs to Canadian viewers, along with its own original programming. Popular shows on the network include *The Simpsons*, *King of the Hill*, *Just for Laughs*, *The Man Show*, *Chapelle's Show*, *100 Greatest Standups*, *Comedy Club 54*, *The Daily Show*, *Absolutely Fabulous*, *Crank Yankers*, *Puppets Who Kill*, *Win Ben Steins Money*, *I'm with Busey*, *Kids in the Hall*, *SCTV*, *Canadian Comedy Shorts*, *Halifax Comedy Festival*, *In Living Color*, *Reno 911*, and *South Park*.

Comic Strip, 5324 Calgary Trail #200, Edmonton, Alberta T6H 4J8, Canada; *Telephone*: 780-430-2800; *Email*: Contact channel through its web site: *Web site*: http://moviecentral.ca

Comic Strip is part of Movie Central, a

Corus Entertainment specialty channel, and airs nothing but comedy-related concerts and movies.

Cool TV, 201 Portage Avenue, 30th Floor, Winnipeg, Manitoba R3B 3K6, Canada; *Telephone*: 204-926-4812; *Fax*: 204-926-1674; *Email*: info@globaltv.ca; *Web site*: http://www.canwest mediasales.com/television/specialty/cooltv/description.html

Owned and operated by CanWest Global Communications Corp., Cool TV is a specialty channel devoted exclusively to jazz music, jazz lovers, and all things jazz related, including music videos, movies, concerts, specials, and shows. The channel features today's best artists in concert; allows viewers the opportunity to learn about the culture that made jazz what it is; airs concerts such as the Montreal Jazz Festival to Blue Note Specials; and every night shows a classic jazz-related movie.

Corus Entertainment, 64 Jefferson Avenue, Unit 18, Toronto, Ontario M6K 3H4, Canada; 5324 Calgary Trail #200, Edmonton, Alberta T6H 4J8, Canada, 170 Queen Street, Kingson, Ontario K7K 1B2, Canada; *Telephone*: 780-430-2800, 613-544-2340; *Fax*: 780-437-3188, 613-544-5508; *Launch Date*: September 1999; *Email*: Contact network through its web site; *Web site*: http://www.corusent.com

Corus Entertainment is one of Canada's largest integrated media and entertainment companies. Built from the media assets originally owned by Shaw Communications Inc., and spun off as a separate, publicly-traded company in 1999, Corus has experienced quick growth and has acquired numerous broadcast entities and specialty channels. Its television services include Country Music Television (CMT), Discovery Kids, The Documentary Channel, Scream TV, TeleLatino Network, TéléToon, Treehouse TV, the W Network, Youth Television (YTV), pay-TV movie service on six thematic channels under the Movie Central brand, three local over-the-air television stations, Digital ADventure advertising services for television, and Max Trax, a residential subscription digital music service.

Specialty channels include Country Canada (Land and Sea) (http://www.cbc countrycountry.ca) celebrates all things Canada, including its land and its people; Country Music Television (CMT) Canada (http://www.cmtcanada.com, launched in 1995, the channel is Canada's source for 24-hour country music videos and music-based programming; CMT also airs drama series, awards shows [*Canadian Country Music Awards*], artist interviews, sitcoms [*Reba*, starring Reba McEntire], movies, and specials [the talent search show *Nashville Star*]); Discovery Kids (http://www.discoverykids.ca) (offers children of all ages informative and entertaining programming with an emphasis on action, adventure, and the environment); the Documentary Channel (http://www.documentarychannel.ca) (provides a mix of documentaries on all subjects from film makers around the world); the multi-themed Movie Central (includes MovieMax) (http://www.moviecentral.ca) is a 24-hour premium service that broadcasts Hollywood blockbusters and independent films, uncut, 24/7, and commercial-free; Movie Central was the first channel for HBO programming in Canada; Genre channels from Movie Central include Adrenaline Drive (action and adventure), Comic Strip (comedies), Encore Avenue (re-play of popular movies and classic movies), Heartland Road (romance), and Shadow Lane (suspense and mysteries); Scream TV ([http://www.screamtelevision.ca] the only 24-hour specialty television service in Canada dedicated to thriller, suspense, and horror programming); TeleLatino ([http:// www.tlntv.com] is Canada's premier specialty service channel providing programming in Italian, Spanish, English, and French; programming includes news reports from Italy and Latin America, international sports, music and fashion coverage, international soaps, variety shows, and feature films); launched in 1997, Teletoon ([http://www.teletoon.com] provides a mix of classic cartoons and brand new animation from Canada and around the world, in both English and French, 24 hours-a-day); launched in 1997, Treehouse TV ([http:// www.treehousetv.com] is the first and only specialty network in North America dedicated to providing programming for preschoolers, age six and younger); the W Network ([http://www.wnetwork.com] is the leading Canadian specialty channel among female viewers and airs popular dramas, blockbuster movies, reality series, and inspirational lifestyle programs); and Youth Television (YTV) ([http://www.ytv.com], Canada's leading youth network that is seen in over 8.2 million Canadian households, and is aimed at audiences aged 2-17 and their families; this channel airs 17 of the top 20 children's shows in Canada; the channel's broadcast day is divided into several programming blocks, including (1) preschool [30 hours of commercial-free programming per week]; (2) The Zone (Canada's highest-rated after-school block), (3) Vortex [a Saturday morning animation-fest for young kids), and (4) evenings (dedicated to teens and family viewing]).

Country Canada (Land and Sea), P.O. Box 500, Station A, 250 Front Street West, Toronto, Ontario M5W 1E6, Canada; *Telephone*: 866-362-3378; *Launch Date*: September 2001; *Email*: Contact channel through its web site; *Web site*: http:// cbccountrycanada.ca/

A Corus Entertainment specialty channel, Country Canada focuses its programming on all things Canadian, including its people and history, and targets its shows to rural viewers. Programs include a news program known as *CBC News CountryWide*, which is broadcast from St. John's in the day and Winnipeg at night, and all regional editions of *Canada Now*, except for the British Columbia edition. CBC programs are aired throughout the day, including an English-subtitled version of Radio-Canada's acclaimed program *La Semaine Verte*.

Country Music Television Canada, P.O. Box 20010, Calgary Place, Calgary, Alberta T2P 4J2, Canada; *Telephone*: 403-468-1230; *Fax*: 403-466-4544; *Launch Date*: December 1994; *Email*: Contact channel through its web site; *Web site*: http://www. cmt.ca; http:// www.cmtcanada.com

A Corus Entertainment specialty channel, Country Music Television Canada (which started initially as the New Country Network) is primarily a music video service, similar to its American counterpart, only with much more Canadian-based content. CMT in the United States was allowed to buy part of the service and its name was changed to CMT Canada. In recent years, the service has moved its programming away from only videos and now shows concerts, biographies, specials, and television programs, such as *Little House on the Prairie* and *Reba*.

Court TV Canada, 3720-76 Avenue, Edmonton, Alberta T6B 2N9, Canada; *Telephone*: 780-440-8871; *Email*: Contact network through its web site; *Web site*: http:// www. courttvcanada.ca

A counterpart to the U.S. channel, Court TV Canada is a CHUM Limited specialty channel that provides legal coverage and analysis of ongoing trials by day and crime- and justice-oriented programming by night, including movies, dramas, documentaries, and original series.

Craft TV (Planned for future operation)

Craig Media, 535 7th Avenue Southwest, Calgary, Alberta T2P 0Y4, Canada; *Telephone*: 403-508-2222; *Fax*: 403-508-2224; *Email*: Contact company through its web site; *Web site*: http://www.craigmedia.com

Craig Media is a privately-held television broadcaster that has interests in five television stations (A-Channel Calgary, A-Channel Edmonton, A-Channel Manitoba, CKX-TV Brandon, and Toronto1) and operates several digital cable networks. Specialty channels operated by Craig Media include: Music Television (MTV) Canada (launched in October 2001 and is Canada's version of the popular MTV music service from the United States); MTV2 (a follow-up channel to MTV that broadens the channel's musical offerings; MTV2 focuses more on music vides now that MTV has broadened its broadcasting fare to include reality programs and soap operas); and TV Land Canada (http://www.tvlandcanada.com). The company announced in 2004 that CHUM Limited had agreed to buy Craig Media and all its assets.

Crime Channel (Planned for future operation)—the Crime Channel will air programming focusing on crime and criminals, the roots of crime, the pursuit and punishment of criminals, criminal justice, and society's attempts to control crime.

Crossroads Television System, 1295 North Service Road, P.O. Box 5321, Burlington, Ontario L7R 4X5, Canada; *Telephone*: 905-331-7333; *Fax*: 905-331-7222; *Email*: cts@ctstv.com; *Web site*: http://www.ctstv.com

The Crossroads Television System provides family-oriented entertainment, including Christian ministries and entertainment programming for safe family viewing portraying Judeo-Christian values. The channel's shows air no gratuitous coarse language, gratuitous violence, or explicit sexual scenes. Popular shows include *James Robison—Life Today*, *Charles in Charge*, *Dr. Quinn, Medicine Woman*, *Full House*, *Growing Pains*, *Happy Days*, *The Hughleys*, *The Muppet Show*, *Touched by an Angel*, *Faith Journal*, *Good News Sports*, *Coach*, *Eye To Eye*, *Insights Into Sikhism*, *Islam Today*, *Muslim Chronicle*, *Jesus Calls*, and *The 700 Club*.

DejaView (Pop TV), 3100 CanWest Global Place, 201 Portage Avenue, Winnipeg, Manitoba R3B 3L7, Canada; *Telephone*: 204-956-2025; *Fax*: 204-947-9841; *Email*: Contact channel through its web site; *Web site*: http://www.canwestglobal.com, http://www.canada.com/globaltv/, http://www.canwestmediasales.com/television/specialty/dejaview/description.html

Owned and operated by CanWest Global Communications Corp., DejaView broadcasts popular shows from the 1960s, 1970s and 1980s, including *I Dream of Jeannie*, *The Dick Van Dyke Show*, *Gilligan's Island*, *Dragnet*, *Adam-12*, *The Rockford Files*, *The A-Team*, *Magnum, P.I.*, *Simon & Simon*, *Knight Rider*, *The Incredible Hulk*, and *Three's Company*.

Discovery Channel Canada, 9 Channel Nine Court, Scarborough, Ontario M1S 4B5, Canada; *Telephone*: 416-332-5000; *Fax*: 416-332-4230; *Launch Date*: December 1994; *Broadcast Day*: 24 hours; *Email*: comments@discovery.ca; *Web site*: http://www. discovery.ca, http://www.discoverychannel.ca

Owned and operated by Bell Globemedia, Discovery Channel Canada is a Canadian Television Network specialty channel that is the Canadian counterpart of the American service and broadcasts science and nature-based programs. The channel's flagship program is *Daily Planet*, formerly known as *@discovery.ca*. In August 2003, Discovery Channel Canada followed the lead of its American counterpart and launched its high-definition television service. Discovery Civilization Channel Canada is also a Canadian Television Network specialty channel and caters to viewers interested in culture and world events. Popular programs include *Flashback*, *Treasures*, *Lost Worlds*, *On the Edge*, and *Civilization Rocks* and the channel's programming focuses on politics, race, sex, religion, education, pop culture, and people and places.

Discovery Civilization Channel Canada, 9 Channel Nine Court, Scarborough, Ontario M1S 4B5, Canada; *Telephone*: 416-332-5000; *Fax*: 416-332-4230; *Broadcast Day*: 24 hours; *Email*: comments@discoverycivilization.ca; *Web site*: http://www.discovery civilization.ca

Discovery Civilization Channel Canada is a Bell Globemedia specialty channel that takes viewers around the world to discover other lands, peoples, and history.

Discovery Health Channel Canada, 121 Bloor Street East #200, Toronto, Ontario M4W 3M5, Canada; *Telephone*: 866-967-3248, 416-967-3246; *Email*: Contact channel through its web site: *Web site*: http://www.discoveryhealth.ca

Owned and operated by Alliance Atlantis Broadcasting, the Discovery Health Network Canada is a Canadian Television Network specialty channel that is devoted exclusively to useful, practical, reliable, and entertaining programming related to health, wellness, and medicine. The service replaced the Health Network in Canada, which was subsequently taken over by Discovery Networks.

Discovery Kids Canada, 64 Jefferson Avenue, Unit 18, Toronto, Ontario M6K 3H4, Canada; 5324 Calgary Trail #200, Edmonton, Alberta T6H 4J8, Canada, 170 Queen Street, Kingson, Ontario K7K 1B2, Canada; *Telephone*: 780-430-2800, 613-544-2340; *Fax*: 780-437-3188, 613-544-5508; *Email*: Contact channel through its web site; *Web site*: http://www.corusent.com, http://www.discoverykids.ca

Discovery Kids Canada is a Corus Entertainment specialty channel that explores real life adventures on the planet and targets its programming to younger viewers. Popular segments on the channel include *Strange But True*, *Brain Teasers*, *Real-Life Adventures*, and *Science & Nature*.

Discovery Wings Canada, P.O. Box 9, Station O, Scarborough, Ontario M4A 2M9, Canada; 9 Channel Nine Court, Scarborough, Ontario M1S 4B5, Canada; *Telephone*: 416-332-5000; *Fax*: 416-332-4230; *Email*: Contact channel through its web site; *Web site*: http://www.ctv.ca

Discovery Wings Canada is a specialty channel from the Canadian Television Network that focuses on aviation, aviation history, and modern aviation technology.

Documentary Channel, 64 Jefferson Avenue #18, Toronto, Ontario M6K 3H4, Canada; *Telephone*: 416-534-1191; *Launch Date*: September 2001; *Email*: Contact channel through its web site; *Web site*: http://www.docschannel.ca/

The Documentary Channel is a Corus Entertainment specialty channel that airs nothing but documentaries, including *Masterworks*, *Director's Cut*, and *Festival*.

Drive-In Classics, 299 Queen Street West, Toronto, Ontario M5V 2Z5, Canada; *Telephone*: 416-591-7400; *Broadcast Day*: 24 hours; *Email*: driveinclassics@ driveinclassics.ca; *Web site*: http://www.driveinclassics.ca

Drive-In Classics is an English-language CHUM Limited specialty channel that offers classic "drive-in" movie genres, such as blaxploitation, spaghetti westerns, car chase movies, creature features, and gangster flicks of the 1950s, 1960s, and 1970s.

Encore Avenue, 5324 Calgary Trail #200, Edmonton, Alberta T6H 4J8, Canada; *Telephone*: 780-430-2800; *Email*: Contact channel through its web site: *Web site*: http://moviecentral.ca

Encore Avenue is part of Movie Central, a Corus Entertainment specialty channel, that shows popular and classic movies.

ESPN Canada *see* **The Sports Network**

ESPN Classic Canada, 9 Channel Nine Court, Scarborough, Ontario M1S 4B5, Canada; *Telephone*: 416-332-5000; *Fax*: 416-332-7657; *Email*: Contact channel through its web site; *Web site*: http://tsn.ca/classic

A joint venture between the Canadian Television Network and Bell Globemedia, ESPN Classic Canada is operated through The Sports Network (TSN) and broadcasts classic moments, highlights, biographies, and contests from the world of sports.

Exploration Network (Planned for future operation) — the 24-hour Exploration Network will be an English-language service dedicated exclusively to the exploration of geography, people, places, and cultures in Canada and around the world.

Fairchild Television, B8—525 West Broadway, Vancouver, British Columbia V5Z 4K5, Canada, 35 East Beaver Creek Road #8, Richmond Hill, Ontario L4B 1B3, Canada; *Telephone*: 604-708-1313. 905-889-8090; *Fax*: 604-708-1300, 905-882-7140; *Launch Date*: 1983; *Email*: Contact channel through its web site; *Web site*: http://www. fairchildtv. com

Owned by the Fairchild Media Group, Fairchild TV is an ethnic premium cable television network, broadcasting in Cantonese. Its sister Vancouver cable station, TalentVision, broadcasts in Mandarin. Fairchild TV and TalentVision together reach 75 percent of the Chinese population in Vancouver. The Fairchild Body and Soul Channel (planned for future operation) will provide an Eastern-inspired combination of programming focused on physical and spiritual well-being, including wellness, feng shui, tai chi, martial arts, fitness, and yoga. All programming will be broadcast in Mandarin, Cantonese, Japanese, Vietnamese, and other East Asian languages. The Fairchild Children's Channel (planned for future operation) will broadcast programs aimed at families and children. All programming will be in Mandarin, Cantonese, Japanese, Vietnamese, and other East Asian languages. The Fairchild Food Channel (planned for future operation) will focus its programming on food, cooking, food cultivation and preparation, restaurant reviews, and nutrition. All shows will be in Mandarin, Cantonese, Japanese, Vietnamese, and other East Asian languages. The Fairchild Movie Channel (planned for future operation) will feature films, made-for-television movies, and long-form documentaries. All programming will be broadcast in Mandarin, Cantonese, Japanese, Vietnamese, and other East Asian languages. The Fairchild Music Channel (planned for future operation) will air music videos, concerts, performances, and artist interviews. At least 70 percent of the channel's programs will be broadcast in Mandarin, Cantonese, Japanese, Vietnamese, and other East Asian languages. The Fairchild News Channel (planned for future operation) will feature news, information, public affairs, and financial programming. All shows will be broadcast in Mandarin, Cantonese, Japanese, Vietnamese, and other East Asian languages. The Fairchild Spiritual Channel (planned for future operation) will present a mix of religious programming representing a diversity of religious faiths in Canada. No less than 70 percent of all programming will be in Mandarin, Cantonese, Japanese, Vietnamese, and other East Asian languages while no more than 30 percent will be in English. The Fairchild Technology Channel (planned for future operation) will focus on technology, computers, technological advances, new media, and the internet. All programming will be broadcast in Mandarin, Cantonese, Japanese, Vietnamese, and other East Asian languages.

Family Channel Canada, BCE Place, 181 Bay Street, Box 787, Suite 200, Toronto, Ontario M5J 2T3, Canada; *Telephone*: 416-956-2030; *Fax*: 416-956-2035; *Email*: info@familychannel.ca; *Web site*: http://www.familychannel.ca, http://www.famuily.ca

A specialty channel from Astral Media Communications, Family Channel Canada is a premium, commercial-free network that airs family-focused shows to more than 4.5 million homes across Canada. Programming includes a mix of series, movies and specials, and a large portion of Disney-produced shows.

FashionTelevisionChannel Canada, 299 Queen Street West, Toronto, Ontario M5V 2Z5, Canada; *Telephone*: 416-591-7400; *Fax*: 416-591-0080; *Launch Date*: September 2001; *Broadcast Day*: 24 hours; *Email*: Contact channel through its web site; *Web site*: http://www.ftchannel.com

FashionTelevisionChannel Canada is an English-language CHUM Limited specialty channel and Canada's first and only fashion channel dedicated to the world of architecture, photography, style, art, beauty, and design. Popular shows include *America's Next Top Model* (super-model Tyra Banks hosts this reality show that challenges its contestants in a variety of skills and narrows the field each week until a winner is selected and given a modeling contract); *Hair Wars* (a reality show where contestants compete to create a new hair style); *The History of Urban Fashion* (the latest Hip-Hop fashion collections are modeled on the runway as some of Canada's top urban acts perform their hit songs); *FashionTelevision* (a style program that takes viewers around the world in a search for the creations of today's news makers in fashion, art, architecture, and photography); *This Week in Fashion* (focuses on the worlds of interior and industrial design, designer profiles, and fashion trends); *Fashion Night in Canada* (features Canadian and European designer collections, live from the FashionTelevision Channel Runway); and *Naked in the House* (takes viewers behind the cameras for a look at a group of photographers as they take one roll of film each of the same nude model and then compare the results).

Festival Channel (Planned for future operation)—the Festival Channel will be an English-language service that will focus on the numerous festivals happening across Canada and around the world.

Festival Portuguese Television (Planned for future operation)—the 24-hour Festival Portuguese Television will air programming targeted to the Canadian Portuguese community. No less than 90 percent all programming will be in Portuguese.

Fine Living, 121 Bloor Street East #200, Toronto, Ontario M4W 3M5, Canada; *Telephone*: 800-555-5684; *Email*: Contact channel through its web site: *Web site*: http://www.fineliving.ca

Fine Living is an Alliance Atlantis Broadcasting specialty channel that is dedicated to the art of living and shows viewers how to live the good life. Program topics include restoring vintage cars, discovering ways to simplify life, planning a family road trip, uncovering new wineries, making a career change, hosting an elegant event, techniques to enhance a living space, and recharging the body and soul. The channel's schedule covers five main areas: adventure, favorite things, every day activities, personal space, and transportation. Popular programs include *Radical Sabbatical* (focuses on extraordinary stories of people who have risked it all to pursue their passions), *Sheila Bridges: Designer Living* (helps viewers to design their lives), *Fantasy Camp* (profiles camps for adults that provide the ultimate in wish fulfillment), *Simply Wine* (a series that demystifies the world of wine), *Life in the Fast Lane* (examines how to make great choices for mobile lifestyles, regardless of budget), and *The Perfect Party* (looks at ways to create memorable experiences for partygoers and house guests).

Food Network Canada, 121 Bloor Street East #200, Toronto, Ontario M4W 3M5, Canada; *Telephone*: 800-555-5684; *Launch Date*: October 2000 (as a Canadian-only channel); *Email*: Contact channel through its web site; *Web site*: http://www.foodtv.ca

Food Network Canada is an Alliance Atlantis Broadcasting specialty channel that airs programming solely dedicated to food and is the Canadian counterpart of the Food Network in the United States. The U.S. channel was brought into Canada in1997 and in 2000, the Canadian version of the channel displaced the U.S. version, and it took almost all the cooking shows away from the Life Network, one of its sister channels. Favorite programs include *Martin Yan—Quick and Easy*, *Jamie's Kitchen*, *30-Minute Meals*, *Boy Meets Grill*, *Calorie Commando*, *Emeril Live!*, *Food 911*, and *Recipe for Success*.

Fox Sports World Canada, 3100 CanWest Global Place, 201 Portage Avenue, Winnipeg,

Manitoba R3B 3L7, Canada; *Telephone*: 204-956-2025; *Fax*: 204-947-9841; *Broadcast Day*: 24 hours; *Email*: Contact channel through its web site; *Web site*: http://www. canwest-global.com, http://www.canada.com/globaltv/, http://www.canwestmediasales.com/television/specialty/ foxsports/description.html

Owned and operated by CanWest Global Communications Corp., Fox Sports World Canada is the first and only round-the-clock, English-language, all international sports network in Canada and offers a distinct line-up of programming that positions the network as the leading televised broadcaster of international sporting events. FSWC provides international sporting news and events to Canadian viewers and features a mix of sports not generally shown on mainstream television, such as cricket, Premier League soccer, Aussie Rules football, and rugby. FSWC also keeps fans updated on the latest Canadian-related sports news through *FOX Sports World Report* and *Sky Sports News*.

Front Row (Planned for future operation)—Front Row will be an English-language service broadcasting a mix of documentaries, mini-series, music specials and shows, and feature films.

G4TechTV Canada, 545 Lake Shore Boulevard West, Toronto, Ontario M5V 1A3, Canada; *Telephone*: 866-260-0055; *Launch Date*: September 2001; *Email*: info@ g4tech tv.ca; *Web site*: http://www.g4techtv.ca

Owned by Rogers Cable and Shaw Cable and based on its American counterpart channel, programming on G4techTV Canada is aimed at viewers interested about all things related to technology. G4techTV is the lifestyle network that showcases how the latest trends, products, and events enhance viewers' lives.

Gameshow Network (Planned for future operation)—the Gameshow Network will be an English-language service dedicated solely to the broadcast of game shows, including interactive game programs featuring games of skill and chance.

Gaming Channel (Planned for future operation)—the 24-hour Gaming Channel will be an English-language service providing live-event interactive programming about gaming or involving gaming. The service's programs will include shorts and Canadian original programs about gaming that will be knowledge-based and entertaining, with a focus on providing unique insights into daily events of the gaming world and its participants. The service will also allow viewers to play along with Bingo Games and will provide experimental, interactive and informational programming on gaming odds, lotteries, and the gaming experience in general.

Golden Age TV (Planned for future operation)—Golden Age TV will be an English-language music video service targeted at the 50+ age group and will feature big band, jazz, soft instrumental, and other musical genres.

The Green Channel, 342 MacLaren Street, Ottawa, Ontario K2P 0M6, Canada; *Telephone*: 888-238-4580, 613-238-5642; *Email*: Contact channel through its web site; *Web site*: http://www.thegreenchannel.ca, http://www.expressvu.com

The Green Channel is a Bell ExpressVu specialty channel that focuses on the environment and environment-related issues.

Heartland Road, 5324 Calgary Trail #200, Edmonton, Alberta T6H 4J8, Canada; *Telephone*: 780-430-2800; *Email*: Contact channel through its web site: *Web site*: http://moviecentral.ca

Heartland Road is part of Movie Central, a Corus Entertainment specialty channel, and shows romance-related movies, mainly aimed at the female viewing audience.

High School Television Network (HSTN) (Planned for future operation)

Historia TV, 2100 Ste-Catherine West, Bureau 800, Montreal, Quebec H3H 2T3, Canada; *Telephone*: 800-361-5194, 514-939-3150; *Fax*: 514-939-3151; *Launch Date*: January 2000; *Email*: info@historiatv.com; *Web site*: http://www.historiatv.com

Owned by Astral Media Communications, Historia TV combines the pleasure of learning with the thrill of discovering the past and tells the stories of people, places, institutions, holidays, and traditions by presenting the latest in original productions. Historia is essentially the French-language version of History Television, and is one of the seven French specialty services now carried in Western Canada on Shaw Digital Cable.

History Television Canada, 121 Bloor Street East #1500, Toronto, Ontario M4W 3M5, Canada; *Telephone*: 416-967-1174; *Fax*: 416-960-0971; *Launch Date*: October 1997; *Email*: Contact channel through its web site; *Web site*: http://www.historytelevision.ca, http://www.allianceatlantis.com

An Alliance Atlantis Broadcasting specialty channel, History Television Canada (similar to its counterpart in the United States) airs 250 hours a year of original historical programming, including documentaries, drams, biographies, and specials. Additionally, the channel broadcasts popular series, such as *Crime Stories*, *Tactical to Practical*, *JAG*, *For King and Country*, and *Turning Points of History*.

HobbyTV (Planned for future operation)—the 24-hour HobbyTV channel will be an English-language service dedicated to hobbyists and their activities.

Home & Garden Television, 121 Bloor Street East #200, Toronto, Ontario M4W 3M5, Canada; *Telephone*: 416-444-9494; *Fax*: 416-444-0018; *Launch Date*: October 1997, relaunched in November 2001; *Email*: Contact channel through its web site; *Web site*: http://www.hgtv.ca

An Alliance Atlantis Broadcasting specialty channel that was re-launched in November 2001, Home & Garden Television (similar to its American counterpart) shows viewers how to better enjoy their homes and gardens. Popular programs include *Antiques Roadshow*, *Bob Vila's Home Again*, *Collector Inspector*, *Design for Living*, *Designer Guys*, *House and Home*, *Kitchens and Bathrooms*, *Room Service*, and *This Old House*.

Horror Channel/The Creep Show (Planned for future operation)—the Horror Channel will be an English-language service dedicated to broadcasting horror and thriller movies.

Hustler Channel (http://www.10network.com)—Previously known as TEN Channel 1, planned for future operation, and owned by Ten Broadcasting, Inc., the Hustler Channel will feature pay-per-view adult content from *Hustler* magazine.

iChannel (Issues Channel), 115 Gordon Baker Road, 8th Floor, Toronto, Ontario M2H 3R6, Canada; *Telephone*: 416-756-2404; *Fax*: 416-756-5526; *Launch Date*: September 2001; *Email*: Contact channel through its web site; *Web site*: http://www.ichanneltv.com

Owned by Stornoway Communications Limited, iChannel is a Canadian public affairs channel that provides insightful, thought provoking, entertaining, and quality programming from around the world in an attempt to increase the diversity and viewing opportunities available to Canadian audiences. Various geopolitical, social, public policy, and health issues are presented and analyzed with the depth and context not found on any other channel.

Independent Film Channel Canada, 1668 Barrington Street #500, Halifax, Nova Scotia B3J 2A2, Canada; *Telephone*: 902-420-1577, 902-423-2662; *Fax*: 902-420-0521, 902-423-7862; *Launch Date*: August 2001; *Email*: Contact channel through its web site; *Web site*: http://www. ifctv.ca

Owned by Alliance Atlantis Broadcasting, the Independent Film Channel Canada is Canada's first English-language specialty television service dedicated to independent film, the film making process, and the world of film makers. The channel features non-Hollywood feature films, shorts, documentaries, experimental works, and international festivals.

Inner Peace Television Network *see* **Salt and Light Television**

ITBC Television Canada, 1085 Bellamy Road North #15, Toronto, Ontario M1H 3C7, Canada; *Telephone*: 877-886-5787, 416-850-3391; *Fax*: 416-850-3392; *Email*: info@itbc-net.net; *Web site*: http://itbcnet.net, http://www.tamiltv.ca

Owned by Medianet Canada Ltd. and planned for future operation, ITBC Television Canada will broadcast Tamil-language programming.

Jazz & Blues TV (Planned for future operation)—the 24-hour Jazz & Blues TV channel will be an English-language music video service dedicated to jazz and blues music and related programming.

Jewish Television Network (Planned for future operation)—the 24-hour Jewish Television Network will be an English-language service broadcasting magazine shows and documentaries aimed at the Canadian Jewish community. The service will broadcast predominately in English, with some Hebrew, French, and Yiddish programming.

Kennel Club Network (Planned for future operation)—the Kennel Club Network will offer a mix of programming exploring the world of dogs.

Knowledge Network, 4355 Mathissi Place, Burnaby, British Columbia V5G 4S8, Canada; *Telephone*: 800-663-1678, 604-431-3000; *Fax*: 604-431-3387; *Email*: Contact network through its web site; *Web site*: http://www.knowtv.com

The Knowledge Network (Canadian Distance Education Network) is the educational television network of the province of British Columbia and is a part of the Province's larger effort to make post-secondary education available to all parts of the province using various delivery systems. In 1978, the Province established the Open Learning Institute (OLI) with the task of developing and delivering educational programming using distance education methods. These methods included correspondence courses, audio, film, teleconferencing, videodiscs, and strategies for reaching outside the conventional classroom. In 1980, in order to further the goals of distance education, the Province created the Knowledge Network as part of OLI, which now reaches over 90 percent of all households in British Columbia. However, its mandate has led the network to pursue two different types of audiences: those that need general public education programs which might also interest casual viewers and formal instruction, which would only interest registered students. This dual focus has led to a diversification in the types of programs offered.

In 1988, OLI was re-organized, renamed the Open Learning Agency (OLA), and refocused to serve three distinct audiences: the Open University (offers courses in the arts, sciences, and administrative studies); the Open College (responsible for adult basic education and vocational courses); and the Knowledge Network (responsible for the delivery of general education courses and educational programming). The Knowledge Network devotes roughly half of its 6,000 annual broadcast hours to traditional educational material, such as credit and non-credit courses, college and university lectures, and K-12 content. The network devotes the other half of its broadcasting hours to content of a more general and entertaining nature, including programs devoted to film (international, Hollywood, and Canadian), documentaries, how-to programs, music programs, and children's shows.

The Learning Channel Canada, 9 Channel Nine Court, Scarborough, Ontario M1S 4B5, Canada; *Telephone*: 416-332-5000; *Fax*: 416-332-4230; *Broadcast Day*: 24 hours; *Email*: comments@discovery.ca; *Web site*: http://www.discovery.ca, http://www. discoverychannel.ca

The Learning Channel Canada is a Discovery Channel Canada specialty channel that, like its American counterpart, focuses on educational and general-entertainment programming.

Legal Television Network (Planed for future operation)

Life Network, 121 Bloor Street East #200, Toronto, Ontario M4W 3M5, Canada; *Telephone*: 416-444-9494; *Fax*: 416-444-0018; *Launch Date*: December 1994, re-launched in 2002; *Email*: info@lifenetwork.ca; *Web site*: http://www.lifenetwork.ca

An Alliance Atlantis Broadcasting specialty channel, the Life Network offers lifestyle and real-life situations programming. Initially, the channel was theme driven by day: health on Monday, habitat on Tuesday, Food Plus on Wednesday, explorations on Thursday, relationships on Friday, and a Best of Life schedule on the weekends. Life Network now focuses mainly on reality programming and has moved its habitat shows to Home & Garden Television (a sister network) and its Food Plus shows to Food Network Canada (another sister network). Popular shows include *Adoption Stories*, *America's Next Top Model*, *Animal Miracles*, *Campus Vets*, *Candid Camera*, *Crash Test Mommy*, *Dogs with Jobs*, *Exchanging Vows*, *Extraordinary Lives*, *Fashion File*, *Hollywood Confidential*, *Life's Birth Stories*, *Life's Weird Homes*, *Love Is Not Enough*, *Magnificent Obsessions*, *Say Yes and Marry Me!*, *Spectacular Spas*, *Surviving in the Wild*, *The Surreal Gourmet*, *Trading Places*, *Weird Weddings*, and *Zoo Diaries*.

Live Horse Racing Channel *see* **The Racing Network Canada**

Lonestar, 3100 CanWest Global Place, 201 Portage Avenue, Winnipeg, Manitoba R3B 3L7, Canada; *Telephone*: 866-729-7140, 204-956-2025; *Fax*: 204-947-9841; *Broadcast Day*: 24 hours; *Email*: Contact channel through its web site; *Web site*: http://www. canwestglobal.com, http://www.canada.com/globaltv/, http://www.canwestmediasales. com/television/specialty/lonestars/description.html

Owned and operated by CanWest Global Communications Corp., Lonestar shows western programs and movies, including *The Lone Ranger*, *Bonanza*, *Dr. Quinn, Medicine Woman*, *Wells Fargo*, *Big Valley*, *Gunsmoke*, *Zorro*, *Wanted: Dead or Alive*, and Canadian rodeos.

Luso! Television (Planned for future operation)—the 24-hour Luso! Television channel will broadcast programs aimed at the Portuguese-speaking community, no less than 90 percent of which will be in Portuguese.

Martial Arts Channel (Planned for future operation)—the 24-hour Martial Arts Channel will be an English-language service dedicated to the martial arts and will feature judo, karate, aikido, kick-boxing, and tae kwon-do.

Men TV, 81 Barber Greene Road, Don Mills, Ontario M3C 2A2, Canada; *Telephone*: 416-446-5311; *Fax*: 416-443-6070; *Launch Date*: September 2001; *Email*: info@mentv.ca; *Web site*: http://www.mentv.ca, http://www.canwestmediasales.com/ television/specialty/mentv/description.html

Owned by Groupe TVA, Inc. and CanWest Global Communications Corp., Men TV broadcasts lifestyle programming that focuses on male-oriented topics, such as classic cars, casinos, fashion, fitness, and sex. Programs include *COPS*, *World's Wildest Police Videos*, *Hollywood's Greatest Stunts*, *Cheers*, *MAD TV*, and *Benny Hill*. The channel also airs how-to programs (*Red Hot & Ready* (barbecue), *That's Boating*, and *Let's*

Talk Sex), wine, beer, *M-Style, Taste!*, and *Jazz Then and Now*. Reality shows include *Wild & Crazy, Most Amazing Videos, Impact TV, Out of Bounds*, and *Men of Music*.

MEscape, BCE Place, 181 Bay Street #100, Toronto, Ontario M5J 2T3, Canada; *Telephone*: 800-565-6684, 416-956-2010; *Fax*: 416-956-2018; *Broadcast Day*: 24 hours; *Email*: Contact channel through its web site; *Web site*: http://www.tmn.ca/ mescape

Mescape is part of The Movie Network that features escapist stories and adventures.

Météo Média, 1755 René-Lévesque Boulevard, Montreal, Quebec H4A 4P2, Canada, 1 Robert Speck Parkway #1600, Mississauga, Ontario L4Z 4B3, Canada; *Telephone*: 800-463-9463, 514-597-1591; *Launch Date*: September 1988; *Email*: Contact channel through its web site; *Web site*: http://www.meteomedia.com

Owned by Pelmorex, Inc., Météo Média is the French-language feed of The Weather Network, which consists of a national feed and a local feed for the Greater Montreal Area.

MExcess, BCE Place, 181 Bay Street #100, Toronto, Ontario M5J 2T3, Canada; *Telephone*: 800-565-6684, 416-956-2010; *Fax*: 416-956-2018; *Broadcast Day*: 24 hours; *Email*: Contact channel through its web site; *Web site*: http://www.tmn.ca/ mexcess

Mexcess is part of The Movie Network and focuses on action-packed adventure movies.

MFest, BCE Place, 181 Bay Street #100, Toronto, Ontario M5J 2T3, Canada; *Telephone*: 800-565-6684, 416-956-2010; *Fax*: 416-956-2018; *Broadcast Day*: 24 hours; *Email*: Contact channel through its web site; *Web site*: http://www.tmn.ca/mfest

Mfest is part of The Movie Network and features independent films, mostly from international film festivals.

MFun, BCE Place, 181 Bay Street #100, Toronto, Ontario M5J 2T3, Canada; *Telephone*: 800-565-6684, 416-956-2010; *Fax*: 416-956-2018; *Broadcast Day*: 24 hours; *Email*: Contact channel through its web site; *Web site*: http://www.tmn.ca/mfun

Mfun is part of The Movie Network and focuses on animation, comedies, and lighthearted adventures.

Miracle Channel, 450 — 31 Street North, Lethbridge, Alberta T1H 3Z3, Canada; *Telephone*: 403-380-3399; *Fax*: 403-380-3322; *Launch Date*: April 1995; *Broadcast Day*: 24 hours; *Email*: mail@miraclechannel.ca; *Web site*: http://www.miraclechannel.ca

The Miracle Channel is an interdenominational ministry founded by Dr. Dick Dewert and operated by The Miracle Channel Association, a non-profit, charitable organization run by an elected board. The Miracle Channel is Canada's first and only 100 percent Christian television station and provides a mix of Christian programming, including children's programming, talk shows, Christian music videos, *Lessons for Leaders* (a leadership training show), *Behind the Scenes* (gives viewers a behind-the-scenes look at how the station operates), and *Life-Line* (the station's flagship program which offers guest interviews and spiritual ministry).

Model Network (Planned for future operation)—the Model Network will be an English-language service devoted to models, including model trains, model villages, model worlds, model people, model underwater worlds, and model universes.

Movie Central, 5324 Calgary Trail #200, Edmonton, Alberta T6H 4J8, Canada; *Telephone*: 780-430-2800; *Launch Date*: April 2001; *Email*: Contact network through its web site: *Web site*: http://moviecentral.ca

A Corus Entertainment specialty channel, Movie Central is a pay-movie television service formed from the merger of Superchannel (launched in January 1983) and MovieMax! (launched in December 1994).

Movie Central is comprised of six channels, each with a different theme: Blockbusters (Movie Central), Action (Adrenaline Drive), Dramas (Heartland Road), Suspense (Shadow Lane), Vintage (Encore Avenue), and Comedy (Comic Strip). The service also airs Home Box Office specials and series, such as *The Sopranos*.

The Movie Network, BCE Place, 181 Bay Street #100, Toronto, Ontario M5J 2T3, Canada; *Telephone*: 800-565-6684, 416-956-2010; *Fax*: 416-956-2018; *Launch Date*: February 1983; *Broadcast Day*: 24 hours; *Email*: tmnpix@tmn.ca; *Web site*: http:// www.tmn.ca, http://www. themovienetwork.ca

Owned by Astral Media Communications, The Movie Network provides premier entertainment (over 150 movies and original programs each month) through five channels (M, MFun, MExcess, MEscape, and MFest), each of which operate 24 hours a day and offers a mix of movie genres targeted to specific audiences. Originally called First Choice, The Movie Network is an English-language pay-television specialty channel modeled after America's Home Box Office and Cinemax. M is the main channel (showing new-release movies and special events), MFun airs comedic movies, MExcess focuses on action movies, MEscape shows films with a much calmer ambience, and MFest shows independent films. TMN has a supplementary service known as MoviePix (http:// www.moviepix.ca), which is made up of two channels: MPix (http://www. mpix.ca) airs older films while MPix Two airs a time-shifted duplicate of the MPix schedule.

Movieola (The Short Film Channel), P.O. Box 6143, Station A, Toronto, Ontario M5W 1P6, Canada; *Telephone*: 416-492-1595; *Fax*: 416-492-9539; *Launch Date*: September 2001; *Broadcast Day*: 24 hours; *Email*: info@movieola.ca; *Web site*: http://www. movieola.ca

Movieola shows short films, including festival winners, cult favorites, dramas, comedies, cartoons, animation, and documentaries, all are 30 seconds to 40 minutes in length.

Mpix and Mpix Too, BCE Place, 181 Bay Street #100, Toronto, Ontario M5J 2T3, Canada; *Telephone*: 800-565-6684, 416-956-2010; *Fax*: 416-956-2018; *Broadcast Day*: 24 hours; *Email*: Contact channels through their web sites; *Web site*: http://www.tmn. ca/ mpix, http://www.tmn.ca/mpixtoo

Mpix and Mpix Too are part of The Movie Network that focus on older, classic movies. Mpix Too basically shows repeats of Mpix features, but at later times.

MSNBC Canada, 545 Lakeshore Boulevard West, Toronto, Ontario M5V 1A3, Canada; *Telephone*: 416-260-0070; *Fax*: 416-260-3621; *Launch Date*: September 2001; *Broadcast Day*: 24 hours; Email: info@msnbccanada.ca; *Web site*: http://www. msnbccanada.ca

Operated by MSNBC, Rogers Broadcasting Limited, and Shaw Cable, MSNBC Canada (a joint venture between Microsoft and the National Broadcasting Company) provides viewers round-the-clock breaking news, talk shows, news analysis, and special documentaries. Like its American counterpart, the network's prime time programming includes live panel discussions, investigative documentaries, talk shows, and informative news features that take an in-depth look at current and breaking stories.

MuchLoud, 299 Queen Street West, Toronto, Ontario M5V 2Z5, Canada; *Telephone*: 416-591-7400; *Fax*: 416-591-0080; *Email*: Contact channel through its web site: *Web site*: http://www.muchloud.com

MuchLoud is a CHUM Limited specialty channel that provides alternative, metal, and punk music and features artist interviews, specials, classic archival material, music videos, and updated concert information.

MuchMoreMusic, 299 Queen Street West, Toronto, Ontario M5V 2Z5, Canada; *Telephone*: 416-925-6666; *Fax*: 416-926-4042;

Launch Date: October 1998; *Email*: Contact channel through its web site: *Web site*: http://www.muchmoremusic.com

MuchMoreMusic is a CHUM Limited specialty channel that airs music videos, specials, movies, and documentaries. The majority of the videos aired on this channel are old videos or those from the Adult Contemporary music genre. Segments on this channel include *The Loop* (an hourly news update), *Pop-Up Video, Rock 'n' Roll Jeopardy*, and *Retro Boogie Dance Party*. MuchMoreMusic is the English-language counterpart to MusiMax.

MuchMoreRetro, 299 Queen Street West, Toronto, Ontario M5V 2Z5, Canada; *Telephone*: 416-591-5757; *Broadcast Day*: 24 hours; *Email*: info@muchmoreretro.com: *Web site*: http://muchmoremusic.com

MuchMoreRetro is a CHUM Limited specialty channel that broadcasts music videos from the 1980s and 1990s.

MuchMusic, 299 Queen Street West, Toronto, Ontario M5V 2Z5, Canada; *Telephone*: 800-265-6824, 416-340-7207; *Fax*: 416-591-6824; *Launch Date*: August 1984; *Broadcast Day*: 24 hours; *Email*: Contact channel through its web site; *Web site*: http://www.muchmusic.com

MuchMusic is a CHUM Limited specialty channel similar in style and structure to America's Music Television (MTV) and has been instrumental in setting the national Canadian music trend. While the channel's main focus is on mainstream rock and pop music videos, other music genres are also aired. MuchMusic also produces its own compilation albums targeted as specific music genres. MuchMusic is the English-language counterpart to MusiquePlus.

MuchPop, 299 Queen Street West, Toronto, Ontario M5V 2Z5, Canada; *Telephone*: 800-265-6824, 416-340-7207; *Fax*: 416-591-6824; *Broadcast Day*: 24 hours; *Email*: Contact channel through its web site; *Web site*: http://www.chumlimited.com

MuchPop is a CHUM Limited English-language specialty channel that airs music videos focusing on pop music.

MuchVibe, 299 Queen Street West, Toronto, Ontario M5V 2Z5, Canada; *Telephone*: 800-265-6824, 416-340-7207; *Fax*: 416-591-6824; *Broadcast Day*: 24 hours; *Email*: muchvibe@muchmusic.com: *Web site*: http://www.muchvibe. ca

MuchVibe is a CHUM Limited specialty channel and is Canada's only all-urban music source, providing a mix of old school and today's hottest hits.

Music Television Canada and Music Television 2 Canada, 535 Southwest 7th Avenue, Calgary, Alberta T2P 0Y4, Canada; *Telephone*: 888-688-2899, 604-609-2336; *Launch Date*: October 2001; *Email*: Contact channel through its web site; *Web site*: http://www.mtvcanada.com

Music Television Canada (MTV Canada) and Music Television 2 Canada (MTV2 Canada) are both Craig Media specialty channels that, like their American counterparts, offer viewers the best choices in music videos, reality programs, concerts, award programs, and music-related specials.

MusiMax, 355 rue Sainte-Catherine Ouest, Montréal, Quebec H3B 1A5, Canada; *Telephone*: 514-284-7587; *Fax*: 514-284-1889; *Launch Date*: September 1997; *Broadcast Day*: 24 hours; *Email*: Contact channel through its web site; *Web site*: http://www.musimax.com

MusiMax is a CHUM Limited and Astral Media Communications specialty channel that provides French-language adult music and features contemporary, oldies, rock, soul, and R&B. The channel is the French-language counterpart of MuchMoreMusic and airs concerts, documentaries, artist interviews, and music-related specials.

MusiquePlus, 355 rue Sainte-Catherine Ouest, Montréal, Quebec H3B 1A5, Canada; *Telephone*: 514-284-7587; *Fax*: 514-284-1889;

Launch Date: 1986; *Broadcast Day*: 24 hours; *Email*: Contact channel through its web site; *Web site*: http://www.musique plus.ca

MusiquePlus is a CHUM Limited and Astral Media Communications specialty channel and was the world's first French-language, round-the-clock channel that featured hip-hop, punk, R&B, electronica, impromptu performances by renowned artists, music videos, interviews, news, and information. The service is the French-language counterpart of MuchMusic.

Mystery, 81 Barber Greene Road, Don Mills, Ontario M3C 2A2, Canada; *Telephone*: 416-446-5311; *Fax*: 416-443-6070; *Launch Date*: September 2001; *Email*: Contact channel through its web site; *Web site*: http://www.canada.com/entertainment/ tvchannels/mystery/, http://www.canwestmediasales.com/television/specialty/mystery/description.html

Owned by Groupe TVA Inc. and CanWest Global Communications Corp., the Mystery channel (which was initially planned to be called *13th Street*) airs programs and movies in the mystery, suspense, and thriller genres, including police dramas and reality shows. Popular programs include *Andromeda*, *Medical Detectives*, *Peter Gunn*, *Unsolved Mysteries*, *RIP: Cemeteries of the World*, *L.A. Dragnet*, *The Shield*, *24*, and *Without a Trace*.

National Geographic Channel Canada, 121 Bloor Street East #200, Toronto, Ontario M4W 3M5, Canada; *Telephone*: 866-967-3251, 416-967-3251; *Email*: Contact channel through its web site; *Web site*: http://www.nationalgeographic.ca

The National Geographic Channel Canada is an Alliance Atlantis Broadcasting specialty channel that allows viewers access to the world's most adventurous scientists, explorers, adventurers, writers, film makers, and photographers as they scour the globe for stories and images unseen by most viewers. Programs take viewers into uncharted territory with compelling stories and stunning visuals from around the world.

National Hockey League Network, 9 Channel Nine Court, Scarborough, Ontario M1S 4B5, Canada; *Telephone*: 416-332-5000; *Fax*: 416-332-4675; *Email*: Contact network through its web site; *Web site*: http://www.tsn.ca/nhl_network/

Owned by Bell Globemedia, the National Hockey League Network is a Canadian Television Network specialty channel that is broadcast through The Sports Network (TSN) and broadcasts a slate of weekly National Hockey League games.

Nature TV (Planned for future operation)—Nature TV will be an English-language service with programming focusing on the entertaining and informative aspects of nature and wildlife and will feature plants, animals, marine life, geography, and people who explore the natural world.

Nautical Channel (Planned for future operation)—the 24-hour Nautical Channel will be an English-language service that will appeal to the hobbyist and the student of nautical life. The channel will inform viewers interested in the role played by maritime shipping and travel in our present day economy.

Nostalgia TV (Planned for future operation)—Nostalgia TV will be an English-language service dedicated to classic television series, sitcoms, and feature films. The service will also include occasional magazine style shows focusing on this genre.

Ocean Life TV (Planned for future operation)—Ocean Life TV will be an English-language service devoted to information and entertainment with the theme of water and life in, on and around oceans, including television series with water themes, underwater adventures and exploration, water and beach sports, and tours of ocean and ocean-front locations.

Odyssey Television Network (OTN1 and OTN2), 437 Danforth Avenue #300,

Toronto, Ontario M4K 1P1, Canada; *Telephone*: 416-462-1200; *Fax*: 416-465-1818; *Launch Date*: 1997 (Odyssey One), 2001 (Odyssey Two); *Email*: Contact channel through its web site; *Web site*: http://www.odysseytv.ca

Odyssey Television is the main Greek-language television service in Canada and consists of two distinct channels: Odyssey One is carried mostly on digital cable services across Canada and features programs from Antenna (the second-largest television service in Greece), while Odyssey Two features programs primarily from Greece's Mega television service.

OMNI 1 and OMNI 2, 545 Lake Shore Boulevard West, Toronto, Ontario M5V 1A3, Canada; *Telephone*: 888-260-0047, 416-260-0047 (OMNI 1), 416-260-0060 (OMNI 2); *Fax*: 416-260-3621; *Launch Date*: 1979 (OMNI 1), 2002 (OMNI 2); *Email*: info@omni.tv, info@omni1.ca, info@omni2.ca; *Web site*: http://www.omnitv.ca

OMNI 1 is Canada's first free, over-the-air multi-lingual and multi-cultural television channel and broadcasts 60 percent of its programming in 15 languages to viewers representing more than 18 cultures. The channel airs more than 22 hours of original programming each week, including a one-hour Italian-language newscast each week night and a Portuguese-language newscast each week day. Forty percent of the channel's programming is in English and includes talk shows and comedies. Building on this success, OMNI 2 significantly expanded the variety of languages, number of hours, and choice of programming being offered to multi-cultural viewers. OMNI 2 broadcasts in 20 additional languages targeting 22 more multi-cultural viewer segments.

On Trial: The Court Channel (Planned for future operation)—On Trial: The Court Channel will be a 24-hour English-language service devoted to courtroom situations and legal issues. Programming will include information and educational programming, drama, and reality television, all related to legal issues.

One: Body, Mind and Spirit Channel, 80 Bond Street, Toronto, Ontario M5B 1X2, Canada; *Telephone*: 416-595-6465; *Fax*: 416-595-1340; *Launch Date*: September 2001; *Email*: info@onebodymindspirit.com; *Web site*: http://www.onebodymindspirit.com

Owned by Alliance Atlantis Broadcasting and VisionTV, One: Body, Mind & Spirit channel focuses on topics that will improve all aspects of viewers' lives and airs programs from Canada and around the world.

Ontario Legislature, Broadcast and Recording Service, Legislative Building, Queen's Park, Toronto, Ontario M7A 1A2, Canada; *Telephone*: 416-325-7900; *Fax*: 416-325-7916; *Email*: Contact channel through its web site; *Web site*: http://www. ontla.on.ca

The Ontario Legislature, Broadcast and Recording Service broadcasts legislative proceedings, hearings, and other government-related activities.

Outdoor Life Network Canada, 9 Channel Nine Court, Scarborough, Ontario M1S 4B5, Canada; *Telephone*: 416-332-5640; *Fax*: 416-332-5624; *Launch Date*: October 1997; *Email*: Contact network through its web site; *Web site*: http://www.facethe elements.ca

Owned by Bell Globemedia, Outdoor Life Network Canada is a Canadian Television Network specialty channel (operated through The Sports Network [TSN]) that is a counterpart of the American channel of the same name.

Pacific Food Channel (Planned for future operation)—Owned by Sextant Entertainment Group, Inc., the 24-hour Pacific Food Channel is an English-language specialty channel that airs programs with a focus on Pacific Rim-area food. Programming will include cooking shows, health, nutrition, how to shop for unusual ingredients, wine, and food history.

Paris Première, 115 Scarsdale Road, Toronto, Ontario M3B 2RC, Canada; *Telephone*: 416-383-6600; *Email*: Contact channel through its web site; *Web site*: http://www.expressvu.com

Paris Première is a Bell ExpressVU French-language specialty channel that shows viewers French culture, fashion, cinema, and the Parisian lifestyle.

Passion Television (Planned for future operation)—the 24-hour Passion Television channel will be an English-language service devoted to human sexuality. All programming will emphasize a positive, healthy view of sexuality, and will be informative, entertaining and educational. Daytime programming will focus on the biological, educational, and theoretical aspects of human sexuality.

PAWS: The Pet Channel (Planned for future operation)—the 24-hour PAWS: The Pet Channel will be an English-language service devoted exclusively to informative, instructional, and entertaining programs about pets and their owners.

Pets and Animals TV (Planned for future operation)—the 24-hour Pets and Animals TV channel will be an English-language service devoted to programming about pets and animals. All movies broadcast on the service will have pets or animals as the central theme.

Poetry Channel (Planned for future operation)—the Poetry Channel will be an English-language service that will present programming where viewers meet poets, learn about new poets, and explore the rich language, culture and history of this form.

PrideVision Television, 370 King Street West #308, P.O. Box 56, Toronto, Ontario M5V 1J9, Canada; *Telephone*: 877-774-3388; *Fax*: 416-977-8128; *Launch Date*: September 2001; *Broadcast Day*: 24 hours; *Email*: inquiries@pridevisiontv.com; *Web site*: http://www.pridevisiontv.com

Owned and operated by the Headline Media Group, PrideVision Television is the world's first gay, lesbian, bisexual, and transgender (GLBT) network. The network airs news, information programs, and entertainment shows that focus on issues of interest to the GLBT community, including current affairs, documentaries, health and fitness, comedies, lifestyle, the arts, finance, biographies, relationships, music, cooking, and travel from Canada and around the world.

Prime TV, 81 Barber Greene Road, Don Mills, Ontario M3C 2A2, Canada; *Telephone*: 416-446-5311; *Fax*: 416-443-6070; *Launch Date*: October 1997; *Broadcast Day*: 24 hours; *Email*: Contact channel through its web site; *Web site*: http://www.canada.com/ entertainment/tvchannels/prime/, http://www.canwestmediasales.com/television/ specialty/prime/description.html

Owned by CanWest Global Communications Corp., Prime TV is a national service targeting an adult audience looking for entertainment and information programming. While the service was started initially as a channel devoted to showcasing the lifestyle of senior citizens, Prime TV quickly discarded that genre and focused on becoming one of the top-ranked Canadian specialty channels with a line-up of dramas, lifestyle and current affairs programming, documentaries, news, and movies, all aimed at Canada's largest and most affluent demographic, those 50 years plus. Broadcast fare includes *All in the Family*, *The Cosby Show*, *The Golden Girls*, *M*A*S*H*, *The Price is Right*, *Diva on a Dime* (how to get the latest fashion clothes for less), *Great Taste, No Money* (low-budget house renovating tips), *Antique Hunter* (allows viewers to discover collectibles from across North America), *Room to Grow* (gardening tips), *Open Homes* (shows viewers how to increase the value of their homes), *The Apprentice* (the very popular show featuring Donald Trump), *The Insider* (based on the insider segment from the popular news magazine show, *Entertainment Tonight*), *Unsolved Mysteries* (hosted by

Robert Stack), *Extreme Makeover*, and *Taste! The Beverage Show* (focuses on the world of wine, beer and, spirits).

The Racing Network Canada, 555 Rexdale Boulevard, Toronto, Ontario M9W 5L2, Canada; *Telephone*: 888-675-7223, 416-675-7223; *Email*: info@trncanada.com; *Web site*: http://www.trncanada.com

The Racing Network Canada provides viewers live thoroughbred and standardbred racing from racetracks all over North America and Australia. TRN's multiplexed channels include the Live Horse Racing Channel (a 24-hour service featuring racing from tracks all over North America); the Live Canadian Odds Channel (displays live Canadian Pool Odds from all tracks carried on TRN Canada); Full Card Favourites 1 (provides live daily full card racing primarily from Woodbine and Mohawk Racetracks); Full Card Favourites 2 (provides live daily full card racing from Meadowlands, and the NYRA [Belmont Park, Aqueduct and Saratoga]); and TRN West (provides coverage of full card racing from Hastings Racecourse and Faser Downs, as well as other Canadian racetracks).

The Racing Network is not a wagering service, but a programming and distribution network offering racing products to customers in their own homes. The affiliate wagering service is HorsePlayer Interactive, also owned and operated by Woodbine Entertainment Group (WEG), which is one of the oldest and largest racing organizations in North America. WEG owns and operates two racetracks in Ontario— Woodbine and Mohawk. Woodbine is host to thoroughbred and harness racing while Mohawk is host to harness racing. WEG accounts for approximately 50 percent of the total $1.6 billion wagered on horse racing in Canada, and 70 percent of all wagering in Ontario.

Real Estate Channel (Planned for future operation)— the Real Estate Channel will be an English-language service offering real estate and real estate-related programming.

Reality Zone (Planned for future operation)— the 24-hour Reality Zone will be an English-language service dedicated to reality television and will feature programs about real people in dramatic situations. The service will feature programs detailing the daily lives of trained professionals such as police officers, rescue workers, firefighters, and paramedics and will deal with revelations, confessions, acts of physical bravery and courage as well as with the zany, the ridiculous and the outrageous.

Report on Business Television, 720 King Street West, 10th Floor, Toronto, Ontario M5V 2T3, Canada; *Telephone*: 416-957-8100; *Fax*: 416-957-8181; *Launch Date*: 1999; *Email*: info@robtv.com; *Web site*: http://www.robtv.com

Owned by Bell Globemedia, Report on Business Television is a Canadian Television Network specialty channel that is the Canadian counterpart of CNNfn. It has a partnership with CNNfn to broadcast some of that channel's programming.

Reseau de l'information, 1400 René-Lévesque Boulevard East, Montreal, Quebec H2L 2M2, Canada; *Telephone*: 514-597-7734; *Fax*: 514-597-5977; *Launch Date*: January 1995; *Email*: rdi@montreal.src.ca; *Web site*: http://www.radio-canada.ca/rdi/distribution/, http://radio-canada.ca/nouvelles/

Owned by La Société Radio-Canada, Reseau de l'information (more commonly known as RDI), is the French-language counterpart of CBC Newsworld, broadcasting out of Maison de Radio-Canada in Montreal.

Réseau des Sports, 1755 Boul. René-Lévesque Est, Bureau 300, Montréal, Quebec H2K 4P6, Canada; *Telephone*: 514-599-2244; *Fax*: 514-599-2299; *Launch Date*: September 1989; *Email*: info@rds.ca; *Web site*: http://www.rds.ca

Owned by Bell Globemedia, Réseau des Sports (RDS) is the French-language counterpart of The Sports Network (TSN).

Rogers Sportsnet, 250 Yonge Street #1800, Toronto, Ontario M5B 2N8, Canada; *Telephone*: 800-628-7780, 416-595-4463; *Fax*: 416-595-0917; *Launch Date*: October 1998; *Email*: Contact channel through its web site; *Web site*: http://www.sportsnet.ca/

Owned by Rogers Sportsnet Inc. and News Corp., Rogers Sportsnet is the Canadian version of FOX Sports Net. Formerly CTV Sportsnet, it is a regional sports service, broadcasting on four separate feeds, each with the same basic schedule but broadcasting at different times of the day: Rogers SportsNet East, Rogers SportNet Ontario, Rogers SportsNet Pacific, and Rogers SportsNet West.

Salt and Light Television, 114 Richmond Street East, Toronto, Ontario M5C 1P1, Canada; *Telephone*: 888-302-7181, 416-971-5353; *Broadcast Day*: 24 hours; *Email*: info@saltandlighttv.org; *Web site*: http://www.saltandlighttv.org

Operated by the Inner Peace Television Network (launched in July 2002), Salt and Light Television is Canada's Catholic television network and is available to all Canadian viewers. In addition to religious-based broadcasts, the channel airs movies, a cooking show, prayer and devotions, and programs from the Vatican, with shows being aired in English, French, Spanish, Italian, Polish, and German.

Saskatchewan Communications Network, 2440 Broad Street, North Block, Regina, Saskatchewan S4P 3V7, Canada; *Telephone*: 306-787-0490; *Fax*: 306-787-0496; *Launch Date*: 1989; *Email*: info@scn.ca; *Web site*: http://www.scn.sk.ca

The Saskatchewan Communications Network was created by an act of the Legislature to provide increased access to information for the people of the province. Through its interrelated networks, SCN provides viewers educational, informational, cultural, and training programs. Affiliated networks include the SCN Broadcast Network (launched in 1991, delivers informational programming that highlights the culture and heritage of the region), the E-Learning Network (broadcasts post-secondary and high school classes to over 180 classrooms in more than 150 communities), and SCN Technology Services (uses satellite digital video compression (DVC) technology to provide video/audio channels and data transmission capability to deliver E-Learning and Broadcast Network programs).

Saskatchewan Legislative Network, Legislative Building, Room 123, Regina, Saskatchewan S4S 0B3, Canada; *Telephone*: 306-787-2181; *Fax*: 306-787-1558; *Email*: info@legassembly.sk.ca; *Web site*: http://www.legassembly.sk.ca

The Saskatchewan Legislative Network broadcasts legislative proceedings, hearings, and other government-related activities.

Satellite Bingo Network, *Telephone*: 888-772-4646; *Launch Date*: 1996; *Email*: Contact network through its web site; *Web site*: http://www.satellitebingo.com

The Satellite Bingo Network uses technology to broadcast a big money bingo game nightly to more than 100 bingo halls throughout the region. The 15-minute game, hosted nightly by a satellite bingo caller, is played live from a bingo hall and the signal is sent via a satellite uplink to all the halls on the system. When "Bingo!" is called, the information is transmitted to the studio where winning cards are verified.

The Score (Headline Sports), 370 King Street West #304, P.O. Box 10, Toronto, Ontario M5V 1J9, Canada; *Telephone*: 416-977-6787; *Fax*: 416-977-0238; *Launch Date*: October 1997; *Broadcast Day*: 24 hours; *Subscribers*: 5,500,000; *Email*: feedback@headlinesports.com; *Web site*: http://www.thescore.ca

Owned and operated by Headline Media Group, Inc., The Score airs sports news and highlights in a 15-minute wheel format and is the counterpart to America's ESPNEWS. The Score began as a sports wire service called Sportscope and then went national as Headline Sports, before adopting its current name. The channel shows a continuous sports update ticker at the bottom of the screen and sports highlights throughout the day. Since 2000, The Score added to its broadcast by televising live sporting events, such as wrestling and simulcast horse racing.

Scream TV (HorrorVision), 64 Jefferson Avenue, Unit 18, Toronto, Ontario M6K 3H4, Canada; 5324 Calgary Trail #200, Edmonton, Alberta T6H 4J8, Canada, 170 Queen Street, Kingson, Ontario K7K 1B2, Canada; *Telephone*: 780-430-2800, 613-544-2340; *Fax*: 780-437-3188, 613-544-5508; *Launch Date*: 2001; *Email*: scream@corusent.com; *Web site*: http://www.screamtelevision.ca

Scream TV is a joint venture between Corus Entertainment and Alliance Atlantis Broadcasting and is Canada's only specialty television service dedicated to modern thrillers, suspense, legendary classics, and horror genres.

Séries+, 2100 Ste-Catherine Ouest #800, Montreal, Quebec H3H 2T3, Canada; *Telephone*: 800-361-5194, 514-939-3150; *Fax*: 514-939-3151; *Launch Date*: January 2000; *Broadcast Day*: 24 hours; *Email*: Contact channel through its web site; *Web site*: http://www.seriesplus.com

Originally licensed as Canal Fiction (the Fiction Channel) and owned by Astral Media Communications and Alliance Atlantis Broadcasting, Séries+ is a specialty channel that airs French-language dramas and movies.

SexTV: The Channel, 299 Queen Street West, Toronto, Ontario M5V 2Z5, Canada; *Telephone*: 416-591-5757; *Fax*: 416-591-7465; *Broadcast Day*: 24 hours; *Email*: Contact channel through its web site; *Web site*: http://www.chumlimited.com, http:// www.sextvthechannel.com

SexTV: The Channel is a CHUM Limited channel and is Canada's first and only round-the-clock English-language specialty service devoted entirely to sex, and all sex-related topics.

Shadow Lane, 5324 Calgary Trail #200, Edmonton, Alberta T6H 4J8, Canada; *Telephone*: 780-430-2800; *Email*: Contact channel through its web site: *Web site*: http://moviecentral.ca

Shadow Lane is part of Movie Central, a Corus Entertainment specialty channel, and shows mysteries and suspense films.

Shop TV Canada, One Yonge Street, 9th Floor, Toronto, Ontario M5E 1E6, Canada; *Telephone*: 416-869-4700; *Fax*: 416-869-4566; *Launch Date*: May 1998 (as Toronto Star TV), April 2003 (as ShopTV Canada); *Broadcast Day*: 24 hours; *Subscribers*: 1,500,000; *Email*: info@tmgtv.ca; *Web site*: http://www.shoptvcanada.com

Owned by Torstar Media Group, Shop TV Canada (formerly known as Toronto Star TV) is a home-shopping network that airs both short- and long- form infomercials, ranging from 30 seconds to 30 minutes in length. Initially a local channel only, with its name change ShopTV Canada plans to expand its broadcasts across Canada.

The Shopping Channel, 59 Ambassador Drive, Mississauga, Ontario L5T 2P9, Canada, P.O. Box 1000, Mississauga, Ontario L4T 4C2, Canada; *Telephone*: 888-202-0888, 905-565-3500; *Fax*: 905-565-2642; *Launch Date*: January 1987; *Broadcast Day*: 24 hours; *Email*: customer service@theshoppingchannel.com; *Web site*: http://www. theshoppingchannel.com, http://www.tsc.ca

Owned by Rogers Communications, Inc., The Shopping Channel (which operates similar to America's QVC) is a home-shopping service (originally called the Canadian Home Shopping Network) that sells fashion, jewelry, cosmetics, and household appliances.

Short Film Channel (Planned for future operation) — the Short Film Channel will be an English-language service dedicated exclusively to short films, the film makers, the subjects, the festivals, and the technical aspects of their film making.

Showcase Television, 121 Bloor Street East #200, Toronto, Ontario M4W 3M5, Canada; *Telephone*: 416-967-2473; *Fax*: 416-967-0044; *Launch Date*: December 1994; *Email*: Contact channel through its web site; *Web site*: http://www.showcase.ca/action, http://www.showcase.ca/ diva/

Owned by Alliance Atlantis Broadcasting, Showcase Television is an all-fiction specialty channel that features adrenaline-pumping action and romance movies; shows and movies from the CBC, Home Box Office, and Showtime; and original programming.

Silver Screen Classics, P.O. Box 6143, Station A, Toronto, Ontario M5W 1P6, Canada; *Telephone*: 416-492-1592; *Fax*: 416-492-9539; *Broadcast Day*: 24 hours; *Email*: info@ silverscreenclassics.com; *Web site*: http://www.silverscreenclassics.com

Silver Screen Classics broadcasts movies that have stood the test of time and have inspired and entertained for the past 80 years. Movies include silent classics, 15-chapter serials, film noir, screwball comedies, musical extravaganzas, melodramas, romance, action, critically-acclaimed standards, cult hits, and second-feature gems. All films are shown commercial-free with advertising shown between movies.

The Single's Channel (Planned for future operation)

Soap Opera TV (Planned for future operation)—Soap Opera TV will be an English-language service dedicated exclusively to programs relating to the world of soap operas. The service will include parodies of soap operas as well as a daily magazine show devoted to the genre.

SPACE: The Imagination Station, 299 Queen Street West, Toronto, Ontario M5V 2Z5, Canada; *Telephone*: 416-591-5757; *Launch Date*: October 1997; *Broadcast Day*: 24 hours; *Email*: Contact channel through its web site: *Web site*: http://www.spacecast.com

SPACE: The Imagination Station is an English-language CHUM Limited specialty channel that broadcasts science fiction, science fact, speculation, fantasy, popular series, feature films, documentaries, specials, and daily original productions. This channel is basically the equivalent of America's Sci-Fi Channel.

Speed Channel Canada (Planned for future operation)

Spike TV (formerly The Nashville Network) (Planned for future operation)

SportsNet *see* **Rogers SportNet**

The Sports Network, 9 Channel Nine Court, Scarborough, Ontario M1S 4B5, Canada; *Telephone*: 416-332-5000; *Fax*: 416-332-7658; *Launch Date*: September 1984; *Broadcast Day*: 24 hours; *Email*: audiencerelations@tsn.ca; *Web site*: http://www.tsn.ca

Owned by Bell Globemedia and The Walt Disney Company, The Sports Network was Canada's very first specialty television channel and has grown to be one of the most popular. TSN is an all-sports channel that airs sporting events, news, and headlines and is the counterpart to America's ESPN.

Star! The Entertainment Information Station, 299 Queen Street West, Toronto, Ontario M5V 2Z5, Canada; *Telephone*: 416-591-7400; *Launch Date*: September 1999; *Broadcast Day*: 24 hours; *Email*: Contact channel through its web site; *Web site*: http://www.star-tv.com

Star! The Entertainment Information Station is a CHUM Limited specialty channel that focuses on the world of show business news and information, behind-the-scenes features, interviews with the world's biggest stars, and red-carpet coverage of awards, premieres, and galas from the world of entertainment. The channel is the counterpart of

America's E!. Programs include E!'s *True Hollywood Story*, *Talk Soup*, and *News Daily*; shows from FashionTelevisionChannel and MovieTelevision; encores of popular American late-night talk shows, the day after they air on the American networks; and original programming.

Stornoway Communications Limited, 115 Gordon Baker Road, 8th Floor, Toronto, Ontario M2H 3R6, Canada; *Telephone*: 416-756-2404; *Fax*: 416-756-5526; *Email*: Contact company through its web site; *Web site*: http://www.stornoway.com

Stornoway Communications was founded in 2000 specifically to apply to the Canadian Radio-Television and Telecommunications Commission for digital specialty licenses and interactive web casting. Stornoway Communications owns and operates BPM TV and iChannel, both of which launched in September 2001.

Super Écran, 2100, rue Sainte-Catherine Ouest #800, Montréal, Québec H3H 2T3, Canada; *Telephone*: 514-939-5090; *Fax*: 514-939-5098; *Launch Date*: February 1983, 1992 (as Super Écran); *Email*: Contact channel through its web site; *Web site*: http://www.superecran.com

Super Écran is an Astral Media Communications specialty channel and North America's only French-language pay-television network offering first-run movies, exclusive series, and variety shows, uncut and commercial free. This service is similar to the English-language The Movie Network. Super Écran operates four channels (S1 through S4), all of which operate 24 hours a day, seven days a week.

Sur Sagar Television (Planned for future operation)—Sur Sagar Television will broadcast programming that will focus on Punjabi religious teachings and religion; music and dance videos based on Punjabi culture; and news and information concerning East Indian countries and Punjabi communities in Canada. No less than 50 percent of all programming will be in Punjabi, no more than 25 percent of all programming will be in Hindi, and no more than 25 percent of all programming will be in English.

TalentVision, B8—525 West Broadway, Vancouver, British Columbia V5Z 4K5, Canada, 35 East Beaver Creek Road #8, Richmond Hill, Ontario L4B 1B3, Canada; *Telephone*: 604-708-1313. 905-889-8090; *Fax*: 604-708-1300, 905-882-7140; *Launch Date*: 1998; *Email*: Contact channel through its web site; *Web site*: http://www. talentvision.com

Owned by the Fairchild Media Group, TalentVision broadcasts Mandarin-language programming, including dramas, comedies, news, reality shows, and sports.

Talk TV (T!), 9 Channel Nine Court, Scarborough, Ontario M1S 4B5, Canada, P.O. Box 9, Station O, Toronto, Ontario M4A 2M9, Canada; *Launch Date*: September 2000; *Telephone*: 416-332-6049 (Scarborough), 877-674-2428 (Toronto), 416-332-5030 (Toronto); *Fax*: 416-332-6041 (Scarborough), 416-332-5054 (Toronto); *Email*: comments@talktv.ca; *Web site*: http://www.talktv.ca

Owned by Bell Globemedia, Talk TV is a Canadian specialty channel that is similar in operation to the now-defunct American channel known as America's Talking. The main program on Talk TV is called *The Chatroom*, an unscripted talk show that airs four times every weekday. Talk TV also airs other contemporary talk shows and news magazine programs.

Tech TV Canada *see* **G4TechTV Canada**

Télé-Annonces, 1200 rue Papineau #260, Montréal, Québec H2K 4R5, Canada; *Telephone*: 514-526-1110; *Fax*: 514-526-1354; *Email*: Contact channel through its web site; *Web site*: http://www.teleannonces.com

Télé-Annonces is the only television channel in Quebec to offer an illustrated classified ads service, broadcast simultaneously on the cable network and on the Internet.

TeleLatino Network (TLN Television), 5125 Steeles Avenue West, Toronto, Ontario M9L 1R5, Canada; *Telephone*: 800-551-8401, 416-744-8200; *Fax*: 416-744-0966; *Launch Date*: October 1984; *Broadcast Day*: 24 hours; *Subscribers*: 3,500,000; *Email*: info@tlntv.com; *Web site*: http://www.tlntv.com

Majority owned by Corus Entertainment, the TeleLatino Network is Canada's only national Hispanic and Italian broadcaster and airs about 165 hours per week, equally divided between Italian and Hispanic-directed programming. Programs (including news, sports, dramas, comedies, game shows, kids, and musical variety) air in Italian, Spanish, and English. TLN's Italian programming is provided by various international distributors while its Spanish broadcasts come from Univision, Televisa, Telemundo, CNN en Espanol and others. Additionally, 25 percent of TLN programming is Canadian and provides local access and context.

TéléToon, BCE Place, 181 Bay Street #200, Toronto, Ontario M5J 2T3, Canada, 2100, rue Sainte-Catherine Ouest #1000, Montréal, Québec H3H 2T3, Canada; *Telephone*: 888-884-8666 (Toronto), 416-956-2060 (Toronto), 514-939-5016 (Montreal); *Fax*: 416-956-2070 (Toronto), 514-939-1515 (Montreal); *Launch Date*: 1997; *Broadcast Day*: 24 hours; *Email*: Contact channel through its web site; *Web site*: http://www.teletoon.com

Owned by Teletoon Canada, Inc., Astral Media Communications, Corus Entertainment, and Cinar, TéléToon airs a mix of classic cartoons and new animation from Canada and around the world, in both English and French. The channel is the counterpart to America's Cartoon Network.

Television Northern Canada *see* **Aboriginal People's Television Network**

TEN Channel 1 *see* **Hustler Channel**

TEN Channel 2 *see* **X! Channel**

Theatre Channel (Planned for future operation)—the Theatre Channel will be an English-language service devoted to the world of theatre, plays and related programming, including features, documentaries, shorts and Canadian original programs about the theatre and theatres around Canada.

TrackPower, 580 Granite Court, Pickering, Ontario L1W 3ZA, Canada, 13980 Jane Street, King City, Ontario L7B 1A3, Canada; *Telephone*: 800-550-1777, 905-833-3838 (King City); *Fax*: 905-837-1133 (Pickering), 905-833-6942 (King City); *Email*: info@trackpower.com; *Web site*: http://www.trackpower.com

Planned for future operation, the TrackPower channel will focus on horse racing and racing-related programming.

Treehouse TV, 64 Jefferson Avenue #18, Toronto, Ontario M6K 3H4, Canada; *Telephone*: 416-534-1191; *Fax*: 416-533-0346; *Launch Date*: November 1997; *Broadcast Day*: 24 hours; *Email*: Contact channel through its web site; *Web site*: http://treehousetv.com

Treehouse TV is a Corus Entertainment specialty channel and the Canadian counterpart to the Noggin channel in the United States. The channel's programs are geared mainly toward pre-schoolers. The channel was named after Youth Television's children's program block known as *The Treehouse*, now renamed *YTV Jr.*

Tr!o, North American Television, Inc., 221 Wellington Street West, Toronto, Ontario M5V 3G7, Canada; *Telephone*: 800-890-8746; *Fax*: 416-205-3396; *Email*: mail@triotv.com; *Web site*: http://www.triotv.com

TV5 Québec Canada, 1755 boul. Réné-Lévesque Est, Montréal, Quebec H2K 4P6, Canada; *Telephone*: 514-522-5322; *Launch Date*: September 1988; *Email*: Contact channel through its web site; *Web site*: http://www.tv5.ca/quecan/

Owned by Satellimages/TV5, S.A., TV5 is an international television network, broadcasting French-language programming from the major networks in France, Belgium, Switzerland, and Canada to the rest of the world.

TV Land Canada, 535 7th Avenue Southwest, Calgary, Alberta T2P 0Y4, Canada; *Telephone*: 403-508-2222; *Fax*: 403-508-2224; *Email*: Contact channel through its web site; *Web site*: http://www.craigmedia.com, http://www.tvlandchannel.com

TV Land Canada is a Craig Media specialty channel that broadcasts favorite television programs from the past, mainly those that showed on American television during the 1960s, 1970s, and 1980s, including *Brady Bunch*, *Family Ties*, *The Fugitive*, *Gentle Ben*, *Get Smart*, *Happy Days*, *Hawaii Five-O*, MacGyver, the *Mary Tyler Moore Show*, *Mission Impossible*, *Mork and Mindy*, and *Sanford & Son*.

Viewer's Choice Canada, BCE Place, 181 Bay Street, Box 787, Suite 100, Toronto, Ontario M5J 2T3, Canada; *Telephone*: 416-956-2010; *Fax*: 416-956-2018; *Broadcast Day*: 24 hours; *Email*: Contact channel through its web site; *Web site*: http://www. viewerschoice.ca

Viewer's Choice Canada is a specialty channel operated jointly by Bell Globemedia and Astral Media Communications that offers commercial-free, in-home viewing of hit movies, live championship sporting events, concerts, and other exclusive broadcast events.

VisionTV (Vision Television), 80 Bond Street, Toronto, Ontario M5B 1X2, Canada; 506 Government Street, Victoria, British Columbia V8V 2L7, Canada; 1318 Main Street, Dartmouth, Nova Scotia B2Z 1B2, Canada; *Telephone*: 416-368-3194, 250-360-0848 (Victoria), 902-435-0025 (Dartmouth); *Fax*: 416-368-9774, 250-386-3967 (Victoria), 902-435-2499 (Dartmouth); *Launch Date*: September 1988; *Email*: audience@ visiontv.ca; *Web site*: http://www.visiontv.ca

VisionTV is a multi-faith and multicultural channel that airs original programming promoting understanding among people of different faiths and cultures. One-half of the channel's shows consist of faith programming presented by groups from various denominations, including Catholics, Protestants, Muslims, Sikhs and Hindus. The balance of the schedule features a mix of programs (informercials, series, documentaries, family-friendly shows, comedies, and movies) that explore spirituality, morality, and cultural diversity.

VRAK TV (Canal Famille), 2100 Ste-Catherine Ouest #800, Montreal, Quebec H3H 2T3, Canada; *Telephone*: 514-939-3150; *Fax*: 514-939-3151; *Launch Date*: September 1988; *Email*: Contact channel through its web site; *Web site*: http://www.vrak.tv

Owned by Les Chaînes Télé Astral, Inc., VRAK TV is a specialty television channel for young viewers and families that airs a mix of sitcoms, original productions, dramas, and cartoons. The channel is a joint French-language counterpart of Family and Youth Television. Programs are similar to those found on Family, YTV, and America's WB, but are dubbed into French.

W Network, 64 Jefferson Avenue #18, Toronto, Ontario M6K 3H4, Canada; *Telephone*: 416-534-1191; *Launch Date*: January 1995 (as WTN), April 2002 (as the W Network); *Email*: comments@wnetwork.com; *Web site*: http://www.wnetwork.com/

A Corus Entertainment specialty channel, the W Network, a counterpart of America's Lifetime Television, broadcasts lifestyle programs during the day, and in prime time airs entertainment programming geared towards women viewers. Shows on the network include *Chicago Hope*, *Ally McBeal*, the CBC soap opera *Riverdale*, and *Sunday Night Sex Show*.

WealthNet Television (Planned for future operation)—the 24-hour WealthNet Television channel will be an English-language service for instructional information on all aspects of building personal and small business wealth. It will make use of content experts, case studies and support from Internet-delivered software tools. The value of the channel's programs will be relevant to any Canadian, regardless of where they live or their economic status. The channel aims to better its viewers' total financial health, from choosing the best bank account for their needs, selecting appropriate high-risk reward investments, and exploring the value of entrepreneurship.

The Weather Network Canada, 1 Robert Speck Parkway #1600, Mississauga, Ontario L4Z 4B3, Canada; *Telephone*: 800-463-9463, 905-566-9511; *Launch Date*: September 1988; *Broadcast Day*: 24 hours; *Subscribers*: 8,600,000; *Email*: twnweb@on. pelmorex. com; *Web site*: http://www.theweathernetwork.com, http://www.weather.ca

Owned and operated by Pelmorex, the Weather Network (which was called WeatherNow when it first aired) and its French sister station, MétéoMédia, are Canada's only English and French specialty channels devoted to Canada's weather. Pelmorex's patented Forecast Engine technology allows the channel's meteorologists to issue weather forecasts for the entire country down to a 10 square-kilometer grid, making it one of the most advanced and highest resolution forecasting systems in the world. The channel airs two broadcast feeds: a national feed, and a local feed for the Greater Toronto Area.

Wheels Channel (Planned for future operation)—the Wheels Channel will be an English-language service dedicated to cars, their manufacture, driving and automotive history. The service will schedule documentaries, feature films and drama series as well as magazine style shows focusing on this subject.

Wine Television Network (Planned for future operation)—the 24-hour Wine Television Network will be an English-language service devoted to educational, informative and entertaining programming about wine, including wine tours and travel, wine education, wine law, wine tips, winery tours, and wine reviews.

Women's Sports Network (ceased operations in September 2003)—the Women's Sports network was a specialty channel owned by Bell Globemedia that was the first channel devoted entirely to the sporting lifestyle of women.

Women's Television Network, 1661 Portage Avenue #300, Winnipeg, Manitoba R3J 3T7, Canada; *Telephone*: 800-749-8688, 204-783-5116

Planned for future operation, the Women's Television Network's programming line up will focus on women's issues and women-based entertainment.

World and Roots Music Channel (Planned for future operation)—the World and Roots Music Channel will be an English-language music video service dedicated to World and Roots music videos and related entertaining, informational and instructional programming, exploring indigenous music and roots music traditions in Canada and around the world.

World Cinema Channel (Planned for future operation)—the World Cinema Channel will be an English-language service dedicated to exploring and showcasing the best of contemporary foreign films and classics. The service will also provide film criticism and commentary on international cinema and film festivals.

X! Channel (http://www.10network.com)—Previously known as TEN Channel 2, planned for future operation, and owned by Ten Broadcasting, Inc., the X! Channel will feature adult pay-per-view content derived from *Hustler* magazine.

Xtreme Sports Television, 3100 CanWest Global Place, 201 Portage Avenue, Winnipeg,

Manitoba R3B 3L7, Canada; *Telephone*: 204-956-2025; *Fax*: 204-947-9841; *Broadcast Day*: 24 hours; *Email*: Contact channel through its web site; *Web site*: http://www.canwestglobal.com, http://www.canada.com/globaltv/, *Web site*: http://canada.com/entertainment/tvchannels/xtremesports, http://www.canwestmediasales.com/television.specialty/xtremesports/description.html

Owned and operated by CanWest Global Communications Corp., Xtreme Sports Television airs the most extreme of sports, including survival of the fittest competitions, sportsmania, Thai kick boxing, white water rafting, sky diving, street luge, snowboarding, skateboarding, international surfing, BMX racing, and all ranges of fringe xtreme sports programs and competitions from around the world. Popular programs include *10 Count* (presents the top ten best riders, tricks, spots, videos, and contest performances that define the evolution of the action sports world); *Surge* (covers individual action sports, such as skateboarding, surfing, BMX, snowboarding and MotoX racing); *Ride Guide* (introduces viewers to the wildest of extreme freestyle and professional action from across the continent); *Fear Factor* (the popular reality show from America); *Slamball* (an all-action human video game where two teams defy gravity and hospitalization in their pursuit of victory); and Tony Hawk's SkatePark Tour (takes skateboarding to public skate parks).

Youth Television, 64 Jefferson Avenue #18, Toronto, Ontario M6K 3H4, Canada; *Telephone*: 416-534-1191; *Fax*: 416-533-0346; *Launch Date*: September 1988; *Broadcast Day*: 24 hours; *Email*: Contact channel through its web site; *Web site*: http://www.ytv.com

Owned by Corus Entertainment, Youth Television is a specialty channel children's television service that airs 65 percent Canadian content during its prime time programming schedule. The remaining of the schedule is made up of popular cartoons and children's programming from around the world. YTV airs a MuchMusic-style countdown show called *The Hit List*, which initially focused on urban music, but now plays mostly pop videos.

Zoo Channel (Planned for future operation)—the Zoo Channel will be an English-language service devoted to programming about zoos and their inhabitants, including programming on animals in the wild, their natural environments and manmade habitats, programming of an environmental nature and themes related to human interaction with animals.

Bibliography

Brooks, Tim, and Earle Marsh. *The Complete Directory to Prime Time Network and Cable TV Shows, 1946–Present.* New York: Ballantine Books, 1999.

Brown, Les. *Les Brown's Encyclopedia of Television.* 3rd edition. Detroit: Visible Ink Press, 1992.

Gale Directory of Publications and Broadcast Media. 139th edition. Volume 3. Farmington Hills, MI: Gale, 2004.

Mayer, Martin. *About Television.* New York: Harper & Row, 1972.

McNeil, Alex. *Total Television: The Comprehensive Guide to Programming from 1948 to the Present.* 4th edition. New York: Penguin Books, 1995.

Quigley, Eileen, ed. *International Television & Video Almanac, 2004.* 49th edition. Groton, MA: Quigley, 2004.

In addition to each entry's web site, the following on-line locations also provide comprehensive and in-depth information about television and cable networks in the United States and Canada:

http://newhouse.syr.edu/research/POPTV/. Center for the Study of Popular Television, S.I. Newhouse School of Public Communications, Syracuse University, Syracuse, NY 13244, 315-443-4077.

http://www.broadcastingcable.com. Broadcasting & Cable: The Business of Television, P.O. Box 15157, North Hollywood, CA 91615, 800-554-5729.

http://www.broadcasting-history.ca. History of Canadian Broadcasting, CanadianCommunications Foundation, Canadian Association of Broadcasters, 301-131 Beecroft Road, North York, Ontario M2N 6G9, Canada, 416-221-7965.

http://www.fcc.gov. Federal Communications Commission, Cable Services Bureau, 445 12th Street SW, Washington, D.C. 20554, 888-225-5322.

http://www.hoovers.com. Hoovers, 5800 Airport Boulevard, Austin, TX 78752, 512-374-4500.

http://www.museum.tv. The Museum of Broadcast Communications, 400 North State Street #240, Chicago, IL 60610, 312-245-8200.

http://www.ncta.com. National Cable & Telecommunications Association, 1724 Massachusetts Avenue NW, Washington, D.C. 20036, 202-775-3550.

http://www.tvhistory.tv (a GREAT and comprehensive site that details broadcast history, networks and channels, television set factories, and all things television-related).

http://www.tvradioworld.com. TVRadioWorld (a comprehensive internet broadcastingdirectory and listing of radio and television stations).

http://www.wikipedia.com. Wikipedia (the free on-line encyclopedia), 204 37th Avenue North #330, St. Petersburg, FL 33704, 310-474-3223.

Index